Sondheim's Broadway Musicals

Also of interest:

How Sondheim Found His Sound
by Steve Swayne

Sondheim's Broadway Musicals

Stephen Banfield

Ann Arbor

THE UNIVERSITY OF MICHIGAN PRESS

2006   2005   9 8 7

A CIP catalog record for this book is available from the British Library.

Library of Congress Cataloging-in-Publication Data

Banfield, Stephen, 1951–
    Sondheim's Broadway musicals / Stephen Banfield.
        p.   cm. — (The Michigan American music series)
    Includes bibliographical references and indexes.
    ISBN 0-472-10223-0 (cloth: alk. paper)
    1. Sondheim, Stephen. Musicals. 2. Musicals—New York (N.Y.)—
History and criticism.   I. Title.   II. Series.
ML410.S6872B3   1993
782.1′4′092—dc20   93-12818
                                                          CIP
                                                          MN

ISBN 0-472-08083-0 (pbk. : alk. paper)

To my parents

Acknowledgments

Many people have helped me through this project. First and foremost, heartfelt thanks are due to Stephen Sondheim himself. He was encouraging from the start and willing to open up his creative archive to my unrestricted and repeated scrutiny. He not only waited patiently (if a little nervously) for a long while before being able to see what I was up to but also took considerable time and pains to read and make invaluable comments on the entire manuscript. He answered my frequent queries and speculations, both in the text and outside it, with unfailing promptness and kindness and with an accuracy and detachment at which I can only marvel on the one hand and, on the other, counter with the obvious but important statement that, for all the mistakes, misconceptions, and prejudices that remain, I alone am responsible, no doubt obstinately so in many cases. Over and above this, Stephen Sondheim's personal generosity was considerable, and my total debt to him is enormous. I should also like to thank his staff; they have all become good friends. In particular, Steve Clar bore the burden of my presence and persistence with tact, personableness, and humor, while Louis Vargas not only fed me daily with some of the best food imaginable but on one occasion clothed me as well.

Others have also been generous with their time and correspondence, and I thank Paul Gemignani, Jonathan Tunick, Lonny Price, Irwin Shainman, Jon Alan Conrad, and Marc Katz and Gregg Smith at Music Theatre International, who have all helped me with my research. Paul Salsini's and Sam Brylawski's generosity with their research materials puts them in a special category of assistance, as does Mark Shenton's knowledge of the theater world.

Paul Salsini and Mark Shenton also read and made helpful and encouraging comments on portions of the manuscript. So did Paul Machlin, Roger Marsh, Jonathan Tunick, Alastair Williams, Jeremy Sams, and Richard Crawford. They are all gratefully thanked. So are Jon Alan Conrad, who read the proofs and saved me from sixty-two solecisms, and Adam Collis, who reformatted the manuscript before submission, meticulously eradicating crotchets and quavers.

The book probably owes as much to the company of friends down the years as to anything else, and to them too gratitude and affection are due. John Rutter and David Cannadine first drew my attention to the value of Sondheim's work, and Graham Spicer later fed my interest. Those seeds germinated into a presentation on "Sondheim and the Waltz" at the annual conference of the Sonneck Society for American Music at the University of Colorado in 1986. Richard

Crawford thereupon suggested a small book (and has constantly supported its production), while Steven Ledbetter put me in touch with Paul Lazarus, who put me in touch with Stephen Sondheim. My American sojourns would probably not have been possible and would certainly have been far less stimulating without the generous hospitality and interest of many friends, first and foremost John and Roberta Graziano, then John Hicklin, Raoul, Amy, and Renée Camus, Rufus and Anne Hallmark, Wiley and Janet Hitchcock, Kitty and Bob Keller, Karl and Marie Kroeger; the list could easily go on much longer. Those who offered me publishing and seminar outlets have also played their part. Among the former are James Holmes and Nicholas John, Mel Cooper, Stanley Sadie, and Mark Shenton, and the latter include Wiley Hitchcock, Peter Winkler, John Graziano, Roger Marsh, Susan McClary, David Horn, and Keith Taylor as well as all their students.

Then there are the friends who have accompanied me to productions of Sondheim musicals or listened to tapes, watched videos, read scripts, and bashed and screeched through songs with me at the piano. Their role in the formulation of critical exchange has been a vital one, filled by Stephen Locke, Paul Davies, Graham Spicer, John Cooper, Gordon Toon, Derek and Jackie Hallworth, Tim James, Ian and Kathy May-Miller, Flo Andrews, Andrew Burn, Rufus and Caroline Hallmark, Stephen Newbould, Mark Shenton, Thomas Mann, my friends in the Styche Hall Drama Club, and possibly others to whom I apologize if I have forgotten them. Too numerous to mention, but again to be thanked, are those who have drawn my attention to matters of relevance through correspondence and other friendly contact; and perhaps I should not draw further attention to those who have, on one or two occasions, helped smuggle me into performances of musicals when entry by free trade was unavailing.

Finally, I should like to thank Joyce Harrison at the University of Michigan Press for considerable patience as well as encouragement, and Keele University for various small research grants and a substantial research award. My colleagues in the Music Department there also offered support by showing interest at every stage and by helping me, somewhat at their own inconvenience, to arrange an extended period of study leave for the completion of the book.

Grateful acknowledgment is made to the following authors, publishers, and journals for permission to reprint previously published materials:

BMG Classics, for "Composer's Note" by Stephen Sondheim from the original cast recording of *Merrily We Roll Along,* made available through the courtesy of BMG Classics.

British Film Institute, for excerpts from *The American Film Musical* by Rick Altman (Bloomington: Indiana University Press, and London: British Film Institute, 1987). Copyright © 1987 Charles F. Altman.

Cambridge University Press, for excerpts from *Harold Prince and the American Musical Theatre* by Foster Hirsch (Cambridge: Cambridge University Press, 1989).

Campbell Connelly & Co., for musical and lyric examples from *West Side Story,* music by Leonard Bernstein, words by Stephen Sondheim. Copyright © 1957 (renewed) Leonard Bernstein, Stephen Sondheim. Jalni Publications Inc., USA and Canadian publisher. G. Schirmer Inc., worldwide print rights and publisher rest of the world. Reproduced by permission of Campbell Connelly & Co. Ltd., 8/9 Frith St., London W1V 5TZ. All rights reserved.

Chester Music Ltd., for musical examples from *The Three-Cornered Hat* by Manuel de Falla, copyright © for all countries 1921, renewed in USA 1949 by J. & W. Chester Ltd., London; and for musical examples from *L'histoire du soldat* by Igor Stravinsky, copyright © for all countries 1924 J. & W. Chester/Edition Wilhelm Hansen London Ltd. Reprinted by arrangement with Chester Music Ltd. (London).

Faber and Faber Ltd., for lines from "The Waste Land" from *Collected Poems 1909–1962* by T. S. Eliot. Copyright © 1963 T. S. Eliot. Reprinted by permission of Faber and Faber Ltd.

George Furth, for text from *Company,* copyright © 1970 George Furth, Stephen Sondheim, and Hal Prince. Text used by permission of George Furth. All rights reserved.

Geffen Music, for musical and lyric examples from *Into the Woods,* lyrics and music by Stephen Sondheim. Copyright © 1988 by Rilting Music, Inc. All rights on behalf of Rilting Music, Inc. administered by Geffen Music. All rights reserved. Used by permission.

James Goldman, for text from *Follies,* copyright © 1971 James Goldman and Stephen Sondheim. Text used by permission of James Goldman. All rights reserved.

HarperCollins Publishers, Nick Hern Books, and Elaine Markson Literary Agency, Inc., for excerpts from *Sondheim & Co.* (Second Edition, Updated) by Craig Zadan. Copyright © 1974, 1986, 1987, 1989, 1990 Craig Zadan. Reprinted by permission of HarperCollins Publishers, Nick Hern Books, and Elaine Markson Literary Agency, Inc.

Herald Square Music Inc., for musical and lyric examples from *Company,* lyrics and music by Stephen Sondheim, copyright © 1970 Range Road Music Inc., Quartet Music Inc. and Rilting Music Inc.; for musical and lyric examples from *Follies,* lyrics and music by Stephen Sondheim, copyright © 1971 Range Road Music Inc., Quartet Music Inc., Rilting Music Inc. and Burthen Music Co., Inc.; for musical and lyric examples from *Marry Me a Little,* lyrics and music by Stephen Sondheim, copyright © 1970, 1971 Range Road Music Inc., Quartet Music Inc. and Rilting Music Inc., all rights administered by Herald Square Music, Inc., international copyright secured; and for musical and lyric examples from *Follies 1987,* lyrics and music by Stephen Sondheim, copyright © 1987 Range Road Music Inc., Quartet Music Inc., Rilting Music Inc. and Burthen Music, all rights administered by Herald Square Music, Inc., international copyright secured. Used by permission. All rights reserved.

Jalni Publications Inc., for text from "Tonight," unused text from *West Side Story.* Copyright © 1957 Stephen Sondheim and the Estate of Leonard Bernstein. Copyright renewed 1985 by Stephen Sondheim and the Estate of Leonard Bernstein. Reprinted by permission.

Johns Hopkins University Press, for text from *Into the Woods,* edited by Nina Mankin. Performing Arts Journal Publications, Inc., New York, 1988. Reprinted by permission of The Johns Hopkins University Press.

Arthur Laurents, for text from *Anyone Can Whistle,* copyright © 1965 Arthur Laurents and Stephen Sondheim. Text used by permission of Arthur Laurents. All rights reserved.

Blanche Marvin, for text from *Sweeney Todd: The Demon Barber of Fleet Street,* by C. G. Bond. Copyright © 1974 C. G. Bond. Reprinted by permission of Blanche Marvin on behalf of the author.

Nick Hern Books, for text from *Sunday in the Park with George,* book by James Lapine. Book copyright © 1986 James Lapine. Used by permission of Nick Hern Books.

Penguin Books Ltd., for text from *Praise of Folly* by Erasmus, translated by Betty Radice (Penguin Classics, 1971), 109–10. Translation copyright © Betty Radice, 1971. Used by permission of Penguin Books Ltd.

Jeanine P. Plottel, for text from "Larger than Life" by Stephen Sondheim, *Melodrama,* publication of the New York Literary Forum, 1980.

Stephen Sondheim, for "Theater Lyrics," *Dramatists Guild Quarterly* 8, no. 3 (1971): 6–36; and for "The Musical Theater," *Dramatists Guild Quarterly* 15, no. 3 (1978): 6–29. Reprinted by permission.

Theater Communications Group Inc., for text from *Pacific Overtures,* music and lyrics by Stephen Sondheim, book by John Weidman, additional material by Hugh Wheeler; text copyright © 1976, 1977 by John Weidman, Stephen Sondheim, Harold S. Prince, and Hugh Wheeler; lyrics copyright © 1975 Beautiful Music, Inc./Revelation Music Publishing Corporation. All rights reserved. Revised version copyright © 1986 by John Weidman, Stephen Sondheim, and Hugh Wheeler.

United Music Publishers Ltd., for musical examples from *Nights in the Gardens of Spain* by Manuel de Falla. Reproduced by permission of Editions Max Eschig, Paris/United Music Publishers Ltd.

Tommy Valando Publishing Group, Inc., for musical and lyric examples from *A Little Night Music,* lyrics and music by Stephen Sondheim, copyright © 1973, Revelation Music Publishing Corp. & Rilting Music, Inc.; for musical and lyric examples from *The Frogs,* lyrics and music by Stephen Sondheim, copyright © 1974 Revelation Music Publishing Corp. & Rilting Music, Inc.; for musical and lyric examples from *Pacific Overtures,* lyrics and music by Stephen Sondheim, copyright © 1975, Revelation Music Publishing Corp. & Rilting Music, Inc.; for musical and lyric examples from *Sweeney Todd,* lyrics and music by Stephen Sondheim, copyright © 1978/9 Revelation Music Publishing Corp. & Rilting Music, Inc.; for musical and lyric examples from *Marry Me a Little,* lyrics and music by Stephen Sondheim, copyright © 1973 Revelation Music Publishing Corp. & Rilting Music, Inc., international copyright secured; for musical and lyric examples from *Merrily We Roll Along,* lyrics and music by Stephen Sondheim, copyright © 1981 Revelation Music Publishing Corp. & Rilting Music, Inc.; and for musical and lyric examples from *Sunday in the Park with George,* lyrics and

The musical examples for this book were set by the author using Take Control Music DTP Version 2.0 on an Atari 1040ST computer with Epson LQ–550 24-pin dot matrix printer.

Contents

Introduction

A new full-length study of Stephen Sondheim needs no apology. His work
has long attracted the attention of journalistic and academic critics, and
what he lacks in broad popularity—it is as well to acknowledge at the
outset that for better or worse he does not begin to match Andrew Lloyd
Webber in mass appeal, and probably never will—he makes up for in
special acclaim. It has frequently been contended that he is the best lyricist
Broadway has ever produced, and despite the reservations about his music
that this statement would seem to imply (though it also implies something
about theater criticism, as will be discussed below), there has been no
shortage of assessments such as that of London theater critic Michael
Billington, who saluted him in 1986 as "the greatest living American
composer after Copland" (Billington 1986). Many, like the present author,
would prefer simply to bewail the fact that the language offers no single
word, other than the term *songwriter* with its suggestion of homespun or
hackneyed work or of self-presentation in performance, for an artist who
creates lyrics and music together as an aesthetic entity. And while the
American view of Sondheim as a cultural property to be proud of (or to
resist) is still likely to be matched on the other side of the Atlantic by
ignorance of or indifference to his work, especially outside London, his
British reputation is more than a matter of cult status, as the 1990 Oxford
University Visiting Professorship and the most recent devotion of prime
Christmas television viewing time to *Into the Woods* and *Sunday in the Park
with George* have shown, and it is secured at least to a certain extent by
the fact that, as with the field of commercial popular music in general,
the contemporary musical is an Anglo-American phenomenon whose bar-
riers are set across the Channel rather than the ocean. Moreover, with
ten Broadway musicals and an off-Broadway one to his credit as composer
and lyricist, plus another three as lyricist only, Sondheim has stayed the
course. Although this is a small total compared with the prodigal prewar
outputs of Kern, Gershwin, Rodgers and Hart, and their contemporaries,
one is nonetheless surprised to realize that by now, despite the deliberate
and self-critical nature of his work, he has equalled or outdistanced in

productivity almost all his colleagues working in the commercial musical theater in New York or London since World War II, Rodgers and Hammerstein included. Five hundred or so songs, most of them with music and lyrics by him and most of them for the theater, is not bad going.

But what sort of a study do we need? Broadly speaking, there are three strands of critical writing applicable to the subject: the journalistic, the scholarly, and the theoretical.

Until recently, most writing on the musical theater was journalistic, practiced customarily by critics with a literary rather than a musical background. Theater critics have to write with urbane, immediate, and readable judgment. They do so with astute, often brilliant insight into dramatic problems and perspectives, but within a rigidly evaluative framework: Frank Rich, theater critic of the *New York Times,* like his predecessors, can virtually close a show overnight with a bad review. Once turned historian, a theater critic will tend to measure length of run, production losses, hit numbers, and the like. One way or another, the public is encouraged to respond to the metropolitan commercial theater almost as voters in a democracy or as participants in the multitudinous processes of examination and competition in which most of us are involved on one side or the other throughout life: a musical either succeeds or it fails.

To start unpicking such responses, which many would argue are built in and natural, would be a formidable task. (The art of theater criticism has recently been the subject of two studies, though it has not been possible to consult the one [Anderson 1988] and the other [Wardle 1992] is not yet published at the time of writing; nor have I read Bennett 1990, a theoretical study of theater audiences.) Nevertheless, we may query whether we shall ever have a truly civilized attitude to the theater while we persist in imitating Nero's thumb.

At the same time—and any critic must be acutely aware how deep the paradox runs—the musical theater is above all a celebratory circus, a multidimensional entertainment to be witnessed and enjoyed, carnivallike, rather than judged; if, as one theorist has said of the (film) musical, it is "the most complex art form ever devised" (Altman 1987, ix), another way of seeing "the theater that sings, speaks and dances" is as a "fourth stream" theater with an "aesthetic of opulence" rather than denial (Osolsobě 1981, 2). How can we fix a critical quantification on any product of such a processional amalgam of genres, or even on any one process within it? We do so nonetheless at every moment as members of a theater audience, and the creators of a musical go along with our critical power in their elaborate traditions of response to what "works" in the theater by means of gypsy run-throughs, out-of-town tryouts, previews, and so on. Feedback is paramount.

The evaluative aspect of theater criticism is thus inescapable yet doctrinaire. Criticism's problems tend to be compounded when extended to documentary history. For example, part of a theater critic's job is to deal with performers and performances, yet it is extremely difficult for sustained journalistic criticism to do this without treating the musical theater (or film) with heady anecdotalism. Although circumscribed, this can be a literary art in itself, as one appreciates when it is exercised well, as in Mordden 1976 and 1981. But it suffers from the "insider" mode that bedevils much popular music criticism, especially jazz, when it endlessly compares one name with another, writing "for persons who *feel* elite and knowledgeable of something special" (Holmberg 1984, 28) without the foundation of a cross-generic technical understanding. It is most valuable when most straightforwardly encyclopaedic, as with Bordman (1986).

For a study of the musical theater to get beyond this, it would seem to have to veer off in one of the other two directions mentioned earlier, the scholarly or the theoretical. The first of these emulates the tradition of textual criticism on which classical scholarship was based; the second questions the appropriateness of such procedures, dependent as they are on the notion of textual authority. Modern theory, as is well known, likes to privilege the genre over the author, sometimes the process or the model over the artifact, and in dealing with a collaborative art such as the making of a film or the staging of a musical this begins to seem fair enough. Scholarly criticism must after all be based on the technical detail of source material, and source material for the musical theater is ill-grounded in "authentic" documents. A musical exists in no definitive form, and a performance is created from no single source. The vocal score and the script are separate, the orchestral parts separate again and, as it were, invisible in the absence of an accessible orchestral score (see chap. 2), and the choreography and staging may not be fixed in notation at all. The original cast recording is widely considered a show's most authoritative source, fallaciously in view of the many ways in which it may differ from (let alone foreshorten) what was heard in the theater (see Conrad 1988, 9). Film criticism faces similar difficulties, though at least it can consider the camera's point of view as an uninterrupted and singular authorial directive, and it has the celluloid to go on as definitive artifact (which is presumably why film musical choreography has been dealt with in a scholarly fashion [see Delamater 1981] while it is difficult to envisage the possibility of stage musical choreography presenting any handle for systematic study).

Leaving aside theoretical work on drama in general (of which Elam 1980 and Pfister 1988 are impressive and perhaps seminal examples; Beckerman 1990 and Aston and Savona 1991 are also useful, and more approachable), we can see that film and the film musical in particular have been well served by theoretical studies in the past decade, the film musical notably by Altman 1981 and 1987; Babington and Evans 1985; Britton 1978; and Feuer 1982 (Gorbman 1987, dealing with film music but not film musicals, should also be listed), though according to Babington and Evans in 1985, Britton was still "the only large-scale piece of work on a [single] musical" (1985, 248) and the other items are, for the most part, selective and comparative in their use of detail. Sustained theoretical work on the stage musical has not been forthcoming, or at least is not readily to hand, though the writings of Ivo Osolsobě, piecemeal though they are in English, offer a livelier and more promising perspective on the genre, right back to Offenbach and beyond, than anything else this author has read (see Osolsobě 1974, 1981, 1984, n.d.). Nonetheless, Hawkins (1990) does include musicals (notably *The Phantom of the Opera*) in her discussion of recurrent themes and treatments in high literature and popular modern genres, and her approach might usefully point the way to further discussion.

What none of these books and articles does, however (with the exception of Gorbman), is talk about the music itself, *as* music. This is a familiar complaint where most forms of "nonserious" music are concerned, and it also applies to the mode of scholarly (rather than theoretical) writing, in which the style criticism of van der Merwe (1989) comes as something of a breakthrough (if an eccentric one) for the popular field, followed up as it is by Middleton's magisterial handling of theory as well as style (1990). Even Schuller's commanding work on jazz (1968 and 1989) is still an all-too-rare instance of high scholarship in the sense that it is based throughout on the critical handling of the musical notes themselves as source material (in the form of his own aural transcriptions in the absence of scores). Doubtless it will be a while before we witness the commentator who is equally versed in critical theory, the technicalities of music, and the repertoire of the musical theater; but work is known to be in progress. In the meantime, where do treatments of the music in musicals currently stand?

The answer is somewhere between the pragmatic and the scholarly. Of pragmatic contributions, Lehman Engel's (see Engel 1967 and 1977 for two of them) were empirical taxonomies by a valued practitioner that served their time well enough, while Citron (1985 and 1991) covers some of the same ground from a pedagogically practical standpoint (thus, for instance, he catalogs song types: story songs, descriptive songs, situation songs, list songs, social message songs, birthday songs, and so on [1985, 102–28]). As for scholarly productions, large strides have been taken in recent years. On the one hand, the assault has been bibliographic and documentary. The plurality and obscurity of source material (its recognition boosted by the celebrated Secaucus warehouse discovery of 1982) and the obstacles in the way of establishing an authoritative text, together with momentum transferred from the classical early music movement, have given rise to a burgeoning of "complete editions" of stage musicals in the form of recordings (though not, as yet, in the form of scores and scripts); and encyclopaedic source books of the genre, ever beloved by its aficionados, have not ceased to flow, taking new turns (see Suskin 1986 and 1991; Mandelbaum 1991) and establishing new standards and funds of data (see Krasker and Kimball 1988). On the other hand, Swain (1990) has provided the first sustained critical handling of the music in American musicals.

Swain's contribution is an important one, and I myself started out (and, all said and done, have finished up) with a not dissimilar critical agenda. But I am concerned about three problems where Swain by and large is not. The first is the assimilation of primary source material. The presence and availability of such methodical and comprehensive sketches and drafts may make Sondheim something of a special case in this respect (see chap. 2, on his working methods)—though in truth we cannot be sure of this until similar studies have been made of other composers and lyricists—but special case or no, we must at least say that any study of *Company*, for instance, that took no account of the uncanonical attempts at an ending (see chap. 5) would be an impoverished one. (The difficulty is to balance the original creators' view of a definitive or practicable artifact with posterity's changing interests, and this is yet another issue demanding theoretical investigation.) However, it must be admitted that the very choice of subject in this book biases my approach in one particular direction where sources are concerned, just as my academic milieu (not to mention geographical location) biases it away from oral history, which is nonetheless, quite properly, a flourishing generator of source material for Broadway (see, for example, Guernsey 1985; Sponberg 1991). What different pictures might the perusal of, say, Michael Bennett's notes for *Follies*, if such documents exist, or the systematic interviewing of the entire cast of one of Hal Prince's productions offer?

The second problem is that it is impossible to consider lyrics and music separately in the musical theater. Many have recognized this, including Sondheim (see Sondheim 1974, 64) and Updike ("where no tune comes to mind to fit the words ... lyrics spin themselves a bit vacuously down the page" [Updike 1991, 2]). This recognition renders published collections of lyrics misrepresentative and studies such as Davis 1985; Hischak 1991;

and Furia 1990 of limited insight insofar as they eschew musical notation (see Davis 1985, 226–27, for a tortuous result of this denial). With Sondheim above all, but regardless of whether the same person writes both, tunes and lyrics reflect, counter, and play with each other's structures, and the present book returns repeatedly to instances of this, in the hope that further work may provide a theoretical overview of the phenomenon, perhaps integrating it with a consideration of the function and structure of wit in comparable fields (for attempts at the structural formulation of wit, see Empson 1985, 84–100 [on Pope]; Freud [1905] 1960 [on jokes]).

The third problem follows from this, namely, that to privilege music in the critical discussion of musicals is both necessary, in order to right the balance of its previous neglect, and dangerous, in that music is only one contributor to a multidisciplinary genre. It is inevitable that, given my own background as a classical musician and musicologist, the present book shows a particular bias toward analyzing Sondheim's music, sometimes perhaps at the expense of his lyrics (though it is hoped not too often), more obviously to the exclusion of less authorially coded material such as choreography and vocal performance, about which almost nothing is said. This may be no bad thing in the light of most previous discussion (to which Conrad 1986 is a striking exception), especially when we consider that Sondheim himself has talked about his lyrics in great detail but, even in Oxford, has generally had to stop short of musical technicalities because of the nature of his audience. But to base a critical methodology primarily on musicological precedents, as Swain (1990, ix) does on Kerman (1952), leads all too easily to the premise that all musicals aspire to the condition of opera, a genre in which the composer, at least according to Kerman, *is* the dramatist (for a way out of this view, see Kivy 1988, chap. 11).

Some recent musicals appear to do exactly this, and a comparative study of the crucial split between Sondheim's type of Broadway musical, with spoken dialogue still at a premium, and the all-sung, rock-influenced West End variety exemplified by Lloyd Webber and Boublil and Schönberg (and also found in America in, for instance, William Finn's *Falsetto* trilogy) is yet another urgent need not met by this book (though prepared for to a certain extent by Hirst 1985 and van Leer 1987). Sondheim, however, *Sweeney Todd* notwithstanding (see chap. 9), is not trying to challenge opera on its own territory. In opera, traditionally, the music commands an exclusive viewpoint on the drama, like the authorial film camera referred to earlier; it cannot be resisted or resist itself (which is a way of saying that it is not self-aware and is why it can so rarely cope with wit and irony), though this perception is being increasingly undermined in the age of director's theater and in the light of avant-garde music theater and critical theory. In the musical, however, music—we might do better to call it song, so as to include the lyrics—has traditionally behaved much more self-consciously and *presentationally*, that is, as one mode of representation rather than its governing medium; and indeed we could say the same of dance, comic dialogue, and all the other stage topoi that make up a show. Correspondingly, music is often (though not as pervasively as in the film musical) the *subject* of representation on the stage; it can often not just move in and out of the drama but in and out of itself, and is more dramatically agile, perhaps therefore even more epistemologically aware (thus serving as a model of human self-knowledge), than in most opera. The reflexive and diegetic dimensions of song will be touched upon throughout this study (see especially chap. 6), but yet again they are issues needing further consideration. They receive it in most of the film theory items listed earlier and in Cone 1974, a stimulating little book that has prompted more recent investigations, including further work by Cone himself.

Clearly there is a curve, not a barrier, between all-sung opera and all-spoken drama. But it is important to recognize that the many coordinates along the way, including opera with ballet, opera with spoken dialogue, the book musical, the film musical, the revue, the play with incidental music, and so on, all create their own phenomenology of presentation, and the further we move away from a purely musical genre, the less can scholarly musicology satisfy our critical perceptions and the more we must look toward theory for understanding.

That this has been something of a discovery during the course of writing the present book will be evident from the chapter subheadings, like nothing so much as points on a free agenda for a committee meeting that has not yet been held or at any rate has not yet resulted in motions. Someone else must now take the chair, perhaps adding items such as where the musical stands on the popular-serious spectrum and how this affects our understanding of its parameters; what we can learn about melopoetics, the relationship between music and verbal text (Barricelli [1988], Driver and Christiansen [1989], Scher [1992], and Hartman [1991] all offer insights but omit or fail to develop discussion of vernacular genres); how urgently we require not just a taxonomy but a theory of song (Booth [1981] and Cone [1974] offer obvious starting points); what feminist and gender criticism might tell us about the musical (see Goldstein 1989 and Winer 1989 for a small step in the first direction, Koestenbaum on "the erotics of male literary collaboration" for the second—he does not discuss collaboration in the musical theater or in Hollywood but at least recognizes [1989, 10] that it might fit his theory); and to what extent Sondheim is a representative not of modernism (see below) but of postmodernism, with his playful ambiguities, self-referential structures, and "redraft[ing of] the

contract between writer and reader along lines which many readers . . .
find unfavorable to themselves" (Alexander 1990, 3). Most suggestive of
all, perhaps, is the prospect of locating in the musical a prime model for
Bakhtin's theories of "carnivalization" and of "dialogic" art (see Lodge
1990): *Assassins* is surely an uncannily potent example of both. But this
too is a discussion for next time.

Of course, to the critical theorist the very construction of a subject is
no innocent matter, and the new academic agendas make the choice of a
single author's work as the object of humanistic scholarship seem a quaintly
old-fashioned exercise, perhaps demonstrably untenable when the subject
stands in the collaborative and commercial field of musical theater (after
all, there are two books in existence that cover many of the same objects
as this one but treat Hal Prince as their subject). Yet it might be argued—
and it is really what this book is about—that Sondheim himself has been
aware of the "guilt" of subjectivity and has struggled against it, somehow
determined or destined from the start to make himself the subject of
Broadway by a kind of heroic, almost Schoenbergian defiance of its rules
and demands.

Like any such figure, he calls for disciples, and we can choose not to
respond to the dogma of his epigrammatic teaching. But if we do respond,
the rewards in understanding are great, and we reach the point at which,
instead of judging his musicals, they begin to judge us. Sondheim's artic-
ulations of the ambiguities and dualities of our times quite simply help
us to live, and his insights, tortuous as they often are, surely earn him
a place somewhere in the pantheon of modern humanism. Three examples
from his lyrics may remind us how.

> You're always sorry,
> You're always grateful,
> You're always wondering what might have been.
> Then she walks in.
> And still you're sorry,
> And still you're grateful,
> And still you wonder and still you doubt,
> And she goes out.
> Everything's different,
> Nothing's changed,
> Only maybe slightly
> Rearranged.
> You're sorry-grateful,
> Regretful-happy,
> Why look for answers where none occur?
> You always are what you always were,

Which has nothing to do with,
All to do with her.

Company

The history of the world, my love—
. . . .
—is those below serving those up above.
. . . .
How gratifying for once to know—
. . . .
—that those above will serve those down below!

Sweeney Todd

Must it all be either less or more,
Either plain or grand?
Is it always "or"?
Is it never "and"?
That's what woods are for:
For those moments in the woods . . .
Oh, if life were made of moments,
Even now and then a bad one—!
But if life were only moments,
Then you'd never know you had one . . .
Just remembering you've had an "and,"
When you're back to "or,"
Makes the "or" mean more
Than it did before.
Now I understand—

Into the Woods

All three examples express epiphanies, moments of profound vision about the nature of life. The first sums up the whole mystery of marriage, the paradoxes and contradictions of two-in-one. The second presents in a flash a historic model of society and its revolution in terms of Marxist dialectic. The third, in addition to covering such favorite Sondheim matters as how discrete units become a whole and how choice besets us at every turn, uses the typical romantic image of the forest to explore the romantic concern with transcendental experience and its relation to normal life; Wordsworth never expressed it more succinctly. All three passages utilize concepts of binary polarity and the transformation of opposites into each other (in one case with a play on words, regretful/grateful). This, if you like, is Sondheim's philosophy, and its instinctive relationship to the modernist apprehension of Hegel and Kierkegaard is what, in my view, lends him a quality of greatness.

... [T]he Modernist mind ... seems to want to ... approve [Kierkegaard's] concept of "either/or" in place of the Hegelian "both/and." "Either/or," Kierkegaard claimed, should not be considered as disjunctive conjunctions ... their unique function is to bring life's contraries into the most intimate relationship with each other, whilst at the same time preserving the validity of the contradiction between them. It is then as though the Modernist purpose ought to be defined as the resolution of Hegel with Kierkegaard; committing oneself neither wholly to the notion of "both/and" nor wholly to the notion of "either/or," but (as it were) to both—and to neither. Dauntingly, then, the Modernist formula becomes "both/and and/or either/or." (Bradbury and McFarlane 1976, 88)

Sondheim would enjoy this passage.

Market Drayton, Shropshire
4 January 1992

Chapter 1

Sondheim's Career and Output

The Hammerstein Connection

In the intricate heart of midtown Manhattan, not far from Grand Central Station, it is still possible to escape from the pulse of business and the arteries of commerce. Along Third Avenue, virtually in the shadow of the Chrysler Building and its upstart neighbors, designer skyscrapers one and all, an almost quiet side street, mock Tudor on the one side, brownstone on the other, leads gently downhill as though, instead of the myriad small craft of shops and the great galleon of the United Nations at its foot, we were yet to expect the glittering waters and jostling moorings of Turtle Bay.

Stephen Sondheim has lived and worked here for thirty years, close enough to Broadway to don a crash helmet and cycle to meetings and rehearsals, undeterred by the occasional accident. Perhaps the house, with its friendly dogs and its hospitable kitchen, its balance, light, and harmony of interior design, its meticulously ordered personal archive, its celebrated wealth and wit of games and books and artifacts, has been his crash helmet against the periodic accidents of the theater (though these days long weekends are spent in the country in Connecticut where he does much of his work). Perhaps it has offered him the security that he has never sought, or found, in an established personal relationship.

Sondheim was born in New York City on 22 March 1930 and brought up there; his father was a well-known dress manufacturer and his mother a fashion designer, later interior decorator. In late 1939 or early 1940, he was taken by his father to Kern and Hammerstein's *Very Warm for May* at the Alvin Theatre. Whether or not this was his first or formative experience of a Broadway musical, it is not difficult to imagine the effect of such a visit on a very bright nine-year-old. He seems, however, not to have cemented his own personal ambitions as early as this. Nor perhaps did he know or care that the show was a failure, blamed on Hammerstein; forty-two years later, almost to the day, his own *Merrily We Roll Along* would inaugurate an even shorter and more troubled existence in the same theater, though only after the Alvin had been the scene of two of his triumphs, *A Funny Thing Happened on the Way to the Forum* and *Company*. Was he, moreover, conscious that in the open, away from the cocoon of the auditorium, he would have to face the breakup of his parents' marriage?

This seems to have cast a long shadow over the boy, as well it might, for when his parents divorced in 1940 his mother forbade him to see his father and had him followed to check that he did not. *Into the Woods* enacts what has often been observed, namely, that we begin to come to terms with who our parents were and what they did when we ourselves reach the age or stage of their doings; but for Sondheim, if, as we surely must, we are to view his statements about the reconcilement of generations in this musical and in *Sunday in the Park with George* as more than the mere reflection of the younger James Lapine's preoccupations, the process seems to have taken place later, in his mid-fifties, and was still far from complete as far as his mother was concerned when she died in 1992.

In fact Sondheim's career has shown a peculiar mixture of slowness and precocity, impediment and vector (the very word *career* fascinates him, as we shall see). At the age of four he began playing the piano by ear, with help and encouragement from his father; during his school years he learned piano, organ, and drama sporadically; at fourteen his fascination with words traveled as far as the *New York Times* when he submitted a crossword puzzle (and back again when it was rejected); and his knowledge of Ravel traveled as far as Oscar Hammerstein when, at thirteen, he tried to educate the older man musically by giving him a record of the Piano Trio for his birthday. But when he entered Williams College in 1946 he intended to major in mathematics until an eye-opening freshman music course with Robert Barrow changed his mind. And he never had an early breakthrough on Broadway as a composer, for he was forty before his credentials were thoroughly recognized with *Company*, even if he had found sufficient—though not adulatory—favor as a lyricist from *West Side Story* onward.

The early contact with Hammerstein is the single most important fact in Sondheim's biography. Sondheim's mother, Janet ("Foxy"), had gotten to know Hammerstein's wife, Dorothy, through a mutual friend (see Fordin 1977, 170–71); she went to live in Doylestown, Pennsylvania, after she left Herbert, and Hammerstein, who lived on a large estate nearby, soon became pretty much a surrogate father to the boy. But one wonders exactly when Sondheim's professional aspirations began to turn in Hammerstein's own direction, and what sort of bearing their different multiple talents may have had on the matter (Hammerstein wrote books and lyrics for musicals, but not music; Sondheim attempted all three in some of his early work but has turned out not to be a book writer). Which was the primary impetus: to be a composer, or to work for the stage and screen? Certainly there were artistic epiphanies outside the musical theater for the teenage Sondheim, and it sounds as if a mixed identification with the composer *in* the film *Hangover Square,* which he went to scc twice in 1945, and the composer *of* it was a powerful and indicative one, resurfacing at various later points in his artistic life, primarily in connection with *Sweeney Todd* (see chap. 9) but also in his incomplete novel, *Bequest,* written for a college creative writing course, about a composer of a piano concerto going mad of congenital syphilis, and in his two portrayals, both drawn from plays by George Kaufman, of composers torn between high and low art and the women representing them in *All That Glitters* and *Merrily We Roll Along* (Neil in *All That Glitters* similarly—though only in a dream— murders one of the women and immolates himself).

Even thc *Hangover Square* experience, however, which arose out of a cinemagoing childhood (see Sloman 1988, 40), might be construed as an early intimation of the intrinsic theatricality of music when it is both subject and object; and what is clear is that Sondheim got to know the workings of the musical theater and the growing canon of Rodgers and Hammerstein shows very much from the inside. He was only twelve when he first met Richard Rodgers, thirteen when *Oklahoma!* and *Carmen Jones* opened. Hammerstein took him to an out-of-town preview of *Carousel* on his fifteenth birthday and got him dogsbody work on the preparation of *Allegro* in 1947 during his college vacation.

Sondheim's familiar account of his unique personal apprenticeship under Hammerstein must be given in full.

Oscar Hammerstein gradually got me interested in the theater, and I suppose most of it happened one fateful or memorable afternoon. He had urged me to write a musical for my school (George School, a Friends school in Bucks County). With two classmates I wrote a musical called *By George,* a thinly disguised version of campus life with the teachers' names changed by one vowel or consonant. I thought it was pretty terrific, so I asked Oscar to read it—and I was arrogant enough to say to him, "Will you read it as if it were just a musical that crossed your desk as a producer? Pretend you don't know me." He said "O.K.," and I went home that night with visions of being the first 15-year-old to have a show on Broadway. I knew he was going to love it.

Oscar called me in the next day and said, "Now you really want me to treat this as if it were by somebody I don't know?" and I said, "Yes, please," and he said, "Well, in that case it's the worst thing I ever read in my life." He must have seen my lower lip tremble, and he followed up with, "I didn't say it wasn't talented, I said it was terrible, and if you want to know why it's terrible I'll tell you." He started with the first stage direction and went all the way through the show for a whole afternoon, really treating it seriously. It was a seminar on the piece as though it were *Long Day's Journey Into Night*. Detail by detail, he told me how to structure songs, how to build them with a beginning and a development and an ending, according to his principles. I found out many years later there are other ways to write songs, but he taught me, according to his own principles, how to introduce character, what relates a song to character, etc., etc. It was four hours of the most *packed* information. I dare say, at the risk of hyperbole, that I learned in that afternoon more than most people learn about song writing in a lifetime.

He saw how interested I was in writing shows, so he outlined a kind of course of study for me which I followed over the next six years, right through college. He said, "Write four musicals. For the first one, take a play you admire and turn it into a musical." I admired a play called *Beggar on Horseback* by George S. Kaufman and Marc Connelly, and we actually got permission to do it for three [four] performances at college [as *All That Glitters*]. Next, Oscar told me: "Take a play that you don't think is very good or that you liked but you think can be improved and make a musical out of it." I chose a play called *High Tor* by Maxwell Anderson—I couldn't get permission to put it on in college because Anderson wanted to do a musical of it with Kurt Weill (they never got around to it), but it taught me something about play-writing, about structure, about how to take out fat and how to make points.

Then Oscar said, "For your third effort, take something that is non-dramatic: a novel, a short story." I landed on *Mary Poppins* and spent about a year writing a musical version. That's where I first encountered the real difficulties of playwriting, which is one of the reasons I am not a playwright. It was very hard to structure a group of short stories and make a play out of them, and I wasn't able to accomplish it. Finally Oscar said, "For your fourth, do an original," so right after I got out of college I wrote an original musical [*Climb High*] whose first act was 99 pages long and the second act 60-odd. Oscar had recently given me a copy of *South Pacific* to read and the entire show was 90 pages long, so when I sent him my script I got it back from him with a circle around 99 and just a "Wow!" written on it. (Sondheim 1974, 62–63)

Since we are told that Hammerstein urged the writing of *By George,* one wonders whether his pupil was his conscious creation, fulfilling a deep need and offering a unique opportunity to pass on his art (he had other pupils but Sondheim was the "most special" [Fordin 1977, 242]). All we can say is that, like any great educator, he simply "smelled something" (Fordin 1977, 239, quoting Sondheim) and drew it out. It is also not clear to what extent he continued to tutor Sondheim's writing of the four apprentice shows, though we can read his reaction to *Climb High,* which Sondheim sent him from Hollywood in 1953 (see Fordin 1977, 306–7, for one of Hammerstein's letters of response; another, dated 6 August 1953, is in the Wisconsin archive). What is clear is that Sondheim continued to seek his advice long afterward, when he was faced with difficult career decisions about writing only lyrics, rather than lyrics and music, for both *West Side Story* and *Gypsy,* and that Hammerstein got him his first sizeable job by presenting him as the man for it when, at a Bucks County dinner party in 1953, George Oppenheimer announced that he had been commissioned to supply twenty-nine scripts for the *Topper* television series and needed a co-writer immediately if he was to get them done within six months.

College Activities

By George was started in 1945 and produced at the George School in May 1946; the plot was Sondheim's idea and he wrote the music and some of the lyrics. There was a full complement of numbers, ten in the first act, eight in the second, but the surviving music, three songs entitled "The Reason Why," "I'll Meet You at the 'Donut,'" and "Senior Waltz," is no more than semiliterate juvenilia. The lyrics are not intrinsically witty but give the songs a promising focus of title and refrain. The plot would have been of interest only to those involved.

At George School, Sondheim took the lead in Coward's *Blithe Spirit* and edited the 1946 yearbook (describing himself in the obligatory humor of the photo caption as "an intellectual giant" and "George School's own Rachmaninoff") before moving on to Williams College. Here he became extraordinarily active in the arts and soon "'owned' the theater . . . and to a large degree dominated the humor and literary magazine efforts" (Olesen 1986). In his second semester, he acted in Sophocles' *Antigone* and played Henry in Wilder's *The Skin of Our Teeth* and Garth in Maxwell Anderson's *Winterset;* the following year he played Tiresias in both Yeats's *King Oedipus* and Cocteau's *The Infernal Machine* and starred in Emlyn Williams's murder melodrama *Night Must Fall.* His performances were well reviewed, and later he was especially highly praised in Odets's *Waiting for Lefty.* He was also in Irwin Shaw's *Gentle People* and played Cassius in *Julius Caesar.* Equally well received were his staff columns in the college literary magazine *Purple Cow;* they included "The Brass Goddess" (an apparent and none too flattering portrait of his mother), a detective story by "Hashiell Dammit," and "Utah," an *Oklahoma!* skit complete with contrafacta lyrics. He also wrote "The Rats in the Walls," a play for college radio adapted from H. P. Lovecraft.

At Williams College, the Adams Memorial Theatre, which Sondheim later said was well equipped and gave him ideal conditions (Wilson 1960), was run by David Bryant, a man of practical expertise who clearly offered Sondheim the opportunities he wanted; but the undergraduate drama society, Cap and Bells, had never done a musical. *Phinney's Rainbow* changed that. It was produced in his sophomore year and given four performances in the spring of 1948. Again it was about college life (the topical title—Harburg and Lane's *Finian's Rainbow* had appeared on Broadway the previous year—referred to the Williams president, James Phinney Baxter), but this time it included travesty roles, an opportunity grasped while Williams was still an all-male college, and "The Q-Ladies' Waltz" was a show-stopper. Sondheim and a friend accompanied the performances on two pianos.

Hammerstein came to see *Phinney's Rainbow*. Even before the production, however, and probably without Hammerstein's intervention, BMI, formed in the breach of the ASCAP dispute and at the time searching college campuses for talent (see Salsini n.d.; Suskin 1986, 449–50), had drawn up a royalty contract with Cap and Bells for the publication of three of Sondheim's twenty-odd songs from the show, for which he wrote the music and lyrics, the latter "with help . . . from Joe Horton," co-writer of the book (Klensch 1948, 8). By now the music is technically competent although still stylistically insecure. The title song has a gauche rumba rhythm that hardly helps the lyrics; "Still Got My Heart" suggests that Sondheim was already modeling melodies on Kern, but, like the other songs, it fails to control its harmonic excursions; "How Do I Know?" is tuneful, but only as a homespun waltz. The tunes do not always sit well on the accompaniments, and the lyrics do not sit particularly well on the tunes. Yet some effective internal rhyme is already present ("Just keep up your chin and you'll spy up in the sky / Phinney's Rainbow"), and the conundrums of "How do I know that I know I know, / When I really don't know you?" while intended merely as a take-off of a simpleminded "question" song such as Berlin's "How Deep Is the Ocean?" look forward forty years to Cinderella's "how can you know who you are / Till you know what you want, which you don't?"

Sondheim wrote book, music, and lyrics for *All That Glitters* during the summer of 1948. Again it was produced at Williams, in March 1949, and although as a more serious and ambitious musical (this time with women, from Bennington College) it was less successful with the students, Sondheim said in 1960 "I still think it's pretty good" (Wilson 1960). By 1949 he had had time to think long and hard about it, for it was the first of his apprentice assignments and nearly three years had gone by since the epiphanic afternoon with Hammerstein; in the meantime, *Phinney's Rainbow* cannot have posed real challenges.

The two sides to the dramatic problem were, first, how to mix satire and sentiment, and, second, how to present an artist on the stage (it is about a struggling young composer) or depict a serious composer through a popular medium. It is sobering to note how much of the latter difficulty would resurface not only in *Climb High* but thirty years later in *Merrily We Roll Along,* again to remain unsolved, and as for the former, the rather harsh *Williams Record* reviewer, who at one point drew a parallel with *Allegro,* preferred the satire to the sentiment and complained of too many love scenes and a bad ending (Perrin 1949, 1)—though much of his blame should be directed at the play text, to which Sondheim adhered pretty closely. Certainly Neil's climactic nightmare "Suicide Sequence" and subsequent awakening to find that he can marry the poor girl he really loves must have carried echoes of Joe's homecoming in *Allegro,* but neither in *All That Glitters* nor in *Climb High* was the relationship between integrity and ambition to find a convincing dramatic recipe—again we are reminded of *Merrily*—and Sondheim could certainly not hope to appropriate the effectiveness of Hammerstein's sincerity and simple truths for himself and his generation. On the other hand, the dream sequence plot with its helter-skelter fantasy scenario (Neil's piano remains incongruously on stage throughout), although by no means a new musical theater device, was in some respects still advanced for its period and at several points it prefigured *Anyone Can Whistle* (it was also reminiscent of Weill's *Lady in the Dark*). The play had been published as far back as 1925, and a few years later Kaufman cemented narrative satire in the musical theater in *Of Thee I Sing.* Although his dramatic absurdism was basically a modern equivalent of W. S. Gilbert's, it had a contemporary pacing and setting that also appealed in Sondheim's musical, especially in the scene in the Cady Consolidated Art Factory, where the hero, Neil, married to the industrialist's daughter, is forced to turn out popular songs to formulas (Sondheim wrote "Drink to Zee Moon" in collaboration with Hammerstein's daughter Alice as an example of a "French pathetic" type; this must have been his first use of pastiche for dramatic purposes). The first dream scene was also noteworthy for its "Wedding Sequence" number, a surrealistic marriage service taking place in a railway station and using a technique (taken, along with the actual words, direct from the play) that predated Meredith Willson's *Music Man* opening by a decade: "as Gladys begins the introductions the entire thing turns into a rhythmic chant, both sung and spoken, with accompaniment . . . they all begin to rise and fall on their toes, to the beat of the music." (Such usage was earlier found in film, however—see *George White's 1935 Scandals.*)

The songs, five of which were again published by BMI, held some advances over those from *Phinney's Rainbow* in lyrics and music, but not noticeably in both at once. He was beginning to write melodies with a genuine intimacy of feeling, of which "When I See You" with its haunting flat seventh near the beginning of the chorus is the best, though its modulations are still unconvincingly wayward; the chorus of "I Must Be Dreaming" also has a beautiful opening, easefully parenthetic in melody and harmony, but its development is forced and its climax bungled. The lyric agenda is artfully sharpened in "I Love You, Etcetera" by making it into a negative list song (rather like "Mr. Goldstone," and similarly reflecting the singer's insincerity) that reflexively acknowledges "What more is there to say?" and enumerates clichés after its initial title line (a later line, "I can't put it in rhyme," is followed by the rhyming of "Java" with "have a"). The tune is ungainly, however. The best balance between words and music is probably in "I Need Love," in which lyric wit coincides with cross-rhythm and shifts of phrase structure in the melody; but its opening line, "Ever since I was killed, Daddy," cannot have helped its fortunes upon separate publication. "Let's Not Fall in Love" sets up a memorable title phrase but does so to an awkward, unsustainable pacing of repeated eighth notes rather like the later pitfalls of "A Hero Is Coming" from *Anyone Can Whistle,* and in none of the songs have accompaniment figures yet been individually developed as agents of dramatic tension and character presentation. (At least some of the songs were shown to Cole Porter, who made suggestions when Sondheim visited him at his house near Williamstown in the company of David Bryant [Salsini 1991].)

Sondheim was already talking confidently about his working methods at this early date, explaining to a *Williams Record* reporter (12 March 1949) that "he usually begins with a refrain line, fitting this to a musical motif and then completing the lyrics"; the article also expressed the hope "that Hammerstein and the other half of the team . . . will be able to see the show in Williamstown since they will be in Boston next weekend where their new production 'South Pacific' is trying out." Whether or not they attended, *Variety* did, its reviewer praising the show and seeing in Sondheim "great potential ability as a lyricist-composer" (Salsini n.d.).

Although Sondheim's next two musicals, *High Tor* and *Mary Poppins,* were abandoned, their surviving songs represent something of a break-through in style and approach. The title song of the former is built from a simple melodic motif that sits with ease, grace, and intimacy on an economical yet kinetic vamp; from the very first measure, it thus commands our attention as the central dramatic statement it must have been, and although its extended bridge section is less individual and its ending and overall lyric mode betray the influence of "You'll Never Walk Alone" from *Carousel*, it is the first really personal Sondheim song. It is a pity that Sondheim's adaptation of *High Tor*, a verse play about a haunted beauty spot on the Hudson Palisades, was not completed or is lost, for its highly contrasted groups of characters—the stubborn and romantic backwoodsman, his girlfriend, the crooked pair of realtors, the juvenile thieves, the Dutch settlers and the old Indian—would or must have demanded of the score an objective balance of sympathy and a variety of technique that were to elude him in *Climb High* and even to an extent in *Saturday Night*. "The Sun Is Blue" from *Mary Poppins* is simpler even than "High Tor," a study in wistful heartache disguised as childlike naïveté, achieved as a nursery list song with a French flexibility of rhythm and phrase structure in the melody. "List a While, Lady" from *High Tor*, though less personable, shares some of this song's stylistic features and anticipates the sea-shanty locus of "Pretty Lady" from *Pacific Overtures*. And "No Sad Songs for Me," the single number he wrote in his final semester for the Cap and Bells 1950 revue, *Where To from Here*, while tangential to his later output—it is hardly a popular song in any sense except for the colloquialism of the lyrics—is deeply felt, suggesting a level of emotional identification rarely risked again until *Into the Woods*, for it was written as an affectionate fantasy-tribute to actress Margaret Sullavan, borrowing the title (itself a quotation from Christina Rossetti) of her most recent—and last—film, in which she played a young wife dying of cancer.

How much does this advance owe to his musical training at Williams? He was certainly in good hands there. The chairman of the department, Robert Barrow, probably acting the efficacious role of counsel for the prosecution through his very antipathy to Broadway and its music, sharpened Sondheim's musical technique; he was a Yale graduate and a pupil of Hindemith (whose influence seems apparent at this remove in Sondheim's honors thesis, a three-movement Piano Sonata in C major), had been organist of the National Cathedral in Washington, D.C., and was "one of the best common practice harmony teachers in America" (Salsini 1991, quoting Shainman). Irwin Shainman arrived on the faculty in 1948 (and remained there until 1991); Sondheim was in his very first class, a required general nineteenth-century music course. Shainman was young, a musical theater enthusiast, and had been living, studying, and playing the trumpet in New York where he saw all the Broadway shows; he and Sondheim clearly developed a camaraderie around this shared interest (Shainman 1987; Salsini 1991). But it may be that Joaquín Nin-Culmell, for whom

Sondheim wrote class papers on Ravel's piano concertos and Copland's *Music for the Theatre,* did most to develop his stylistic connoisseurship, at the very least by his presence and pedigree. Like his father, the Cuban Joaquín Nin, he was a composer and a pianist, and had studied composition with Dukas in Paris and de Falla in Granada and piano with Cortot and Viñes, settling in the United States in 1938 and at Williams in 1940 (he left there at the same time as Sondheim, in 1950).

The Franco-Spanish idiom has become a permanent and pervasive element in Sondheim's musical style, as we shall see at various points in this study. The tiny number "Ad" from *Mary Poppins* exhibits it, but it is first fully apparent in the ensemble "Tea." The music of this extended conversation scene (much of whose dialogue is rhythmic speaking) is a neat and effective essay in the French divertissement style of Poulenc or Ibert and owes little to Broadway; while this affinity is less apparent in Sondheim's songs after *Forum,* here it is already remarkably well assimilated and an effective if curious vehicle for drama in its accommodation of romantic ardor and formal pleasantries in the contretemps of etiquette between Bert and Mary. With the waiter involved as well, exchanges come thick and fast and, in their rhythmic placing, offer a striking foretaste of those in "Opening Doors" from *Merrily We Roll Along.* They also submit a very different interpretation of the scene from the one with Dick van Dyke and the penguins.

A Student in New York

Sondheim received his B.A. magna cum laude from Williams in 1950 and left with $3,000 a year for two years to do what he liked with by way of musical study. This was the Hubbard Hutchinson Prize. How high did he want to climb with a composition teacher? Copland, then at the peak of his popularity, with *Appalachian Spring* and the other ballets, the Third Symphony, and the film score to *The Red Pony* recently behind him, might have seemed the obvious choice and, as we have seen, Sondheim had already studied his music as an undergraduate; certainly his stylistic influence has been important throughout Sondheim's career. However, he was not approached. Bernstein, whose astonishing range was already fully recognized through his conducting and his scores for the ballet *Fancy Free* and the musical *On the Town,* was surely another possibility, and again he was to prove influential on Sondheim's music, if one can separate the observation from their later collaboration and friendship.

In wondering whether Sondheim's musical aspirations extended this far, one also has to ask what was his relationship with Richard Rodgers. Rodgers and Hammerstein were good working partners but never quite sure of each other as friends. Rodgers and Sondheim simply never hit it off at all. No doubt they were separated from the start by the generation gap that was precisely what furnished a familial bond between Sondheim and Hammerstein. But it may be that they were musically too far apart as well, for, "High Tor" notwithstanding, Rodgers seems to have cast little influence on Sondheim's music either during his early development or at any later stage until, in *Assassins,* we suddenly notice rather surprising, even shocking similarities of topos. Nor is Rodgers among the acknowledged pastiches in *Follies.* Sondheim has collaborated on various occasions with his daughter Mary, a firm friend whom he first met at Hammerstein's farm when they were both in their early teens, but he only once teamed up with her father, when he wrote lyrics to Rodgers's music for the unsuccessful musical *Do I Hear a Waltz?* in 1965. This was Rodgers's first attempt at working with another lyricist after Hammerstein's death in 1960; Hammerstein himself, understandably enough, seems to have wanted it to happen (see Fordin 1977, 344), and it was surely to be expected that it would prove either binding or alienating. It proved alienating.

In fact, Sondheim went to study privately in New York with Milton Babbitt. Babbitt, who was suggested by Nin-Culmell, seems at first sight to have been an odd choice, for he was and is just about as serious as an avant-garde "serious" composer can be, with formidable mathematical propensities. However, Sondheim's own aptitude for mathematics and analysis was congruent. Indeed, he had purchased *The Schillinger System of Musical Composition,* published complete in 1946, even before he went to college, though he says he never used it as a method. Joseph Schillinger differed from other far-reaching musical theorists of his time, not so much because of his naïve positivism, which has been written off as a pseudo-scientific "key to all mythologies" (though one could argue that he was basically a digital sound engineer waiting for the computer to be invented), but because, alone among them, he applied it to popular and commercial music. In this, like most theorists, he simply put the cart before the horse and made popular syncopation and cross-rhythm respectable by quantifying them post hoc. Gershwin studied with him in the 1930s, though Sondheim was not aware of this when he bought the book (Tommy Dorsey, Vernon Duke, Benny Goodman, Oscar Levant, and Glenn Miller were also Schillinger pupils).

But if Schillinger was the would-be musical scientist, Babbitt was the real one, already working as a laboratory researcher with Vladimir Ussachevsky and Otto Luening on the epoch-making RCA synthesizer at Columbia University in New York (later in the 1950s he became RCA's composer-consultant on the Mark II synthesizer, eventually installed at the Columbia-Princeton Electronic Music Center). Thus Sondheim was present at the birth of American electroacoustic music, going to visit Babbitt once a week and hearing, incredulous at first, about the impending revolution in the manipulation of musical sound.

Neither this nor Babbitt's ever-more integral musical serialism was what he wanted to learn, however. Babbitt, like Schillinger, had a feel for popular music, and had written popular songs, film scores, and an unsuccessful (science-fiction?) musical, *Fabulous Voyage,* in 1946. When Sondheim went to him, Babbitt was working on a show about Helen of Troy that he hoped would become a vehicle for Mary Martin. So in their weekly sessions "we'd spend the first hour analyzing his [popular song] favorites— DeSylva, Brown and Henderson, and Kern—and occasionally Rodgers or Gershwin—and then we'd spend the next three hours on Beethoven, Mozart and others—analyzing them with exactly the same serious tone" (Huber 1986, 39). They also did some species counterpoint.

There can be little doubt that Sondheim's penchant for close motivic working, binding songs and even whole shows with their opening cells of three, four, five, or seven notes, is a legacy from Babbitt and the academic times he represented. They had, after all, as Sondheim recollects, spent half an hour discussing the motivic implications of the first few measures of Mozart's G minor symphony. In this, and in his conscious molding of harmonic line, Sondheim seems to have known what he wanted from Babbitt and got it. His quest, as he has commented, was for structural foundations of theater composition.

> How do you hold something together for three minutes, five minutes, ten minutes . . . forty minutes . . . [and] make it *not* sound like another overture? . . . The reason . . . that I feel I can handle ten and twelve minute musical sequences is because of what Milton taught me. I still reduce everything to long-line sketches . . . but they spring out of the tonal center. (Huber 1986, 39)

This sounds like Schenker, but Sondheim is unacquainted with his work and the "long-line sketches," two of which are examined later in this study (see exs. 6.8b and 9.2), stop short of Schenker's degree of graphic encoding.

Further evidence of Sondheim's study with Babbitt is doubtless to be traced in his analytical sleeve note to Paul Weston's 1957(?) album of Kern songs (Columbia C2L). While not overly cerebral, it does show his concern with the details of Kern's technique at every turn and allows us to judge which of them have rubbed off on his own music. He praises Kern's "melodic rhythm . . . —a direct and simple motif developed through tiny variations into a long and never boring line" and his "maximum development of the minimum of material" ("Milton taught me to make a lot out of a little," Sondheim has said); he notes the "almost symphonic homogeneity of style" from one song to another, "as if all his motifs and melodies had been taken from one enormous melodic line, one endless song," and, conversely, Kern's ability to interpolate "a completely new four-measure phrase" in a recapitulation in a manner "so natural that the listener is not jolted," matters surely apposite to Sondheim's own aims in *Sunday in the Park with George;* and he draws particular attention to the enharmonic retransition in "The Song Is You," a modulation he later used himself at a comparable point of "Too Many Mornings" from *Follies* (mm. 42–45 in the vocal score).

At the bottom of the steps leading up to West College, Sondheim's eighteenth-century dormitory at Williams, is a pair of gatepiers inscribed with the motto "CLIMB HIGH / CLIMB FAR / YOUR GOAL / THE SKY / YOUR AIM / THE STAR." He incorporated this into his fourth and last Hammerstein musical and expanded it as the lyric of its title song. It is a fine number, noble in its economic texture and building of climactic music from the same narrow restraints as the words on the gatepiers, yet rich in the triadic encrustations of its two-note chimes suggesting college bells. But *Climb High* as a whole rings less true. Hammerstein's two letters and his many comments on the script show that he was deeply uneasy about it. He may not have said that its depiction of the charming, talented young man who wants to become a famous actor was self-indulgent, but he made it clear that the biographically based plot device of the broken-off college affair was. Nor did he hesitate to say repeatedly, as he read through the dialogue and the lyrics, that he found the main characters unsympathetic. True, they are supposed to seem so for reasons of dramatic tension, for the opening party scene with its song "Yoo-Hoo!" shows them in their worst light and explains it by presenting the body of the show as a scheme of generic flashbacks with titles on the curtain, such as *Home Is Where the Heart Is: a satirical comedy of manners: Summer* (Act I Scene iii). Yet we have to take too much on trust in sustaining an interest in them at all—above all we have to take David's gifts on trust: we never see him acting—and this suggests that Sondheim was too close to them. What ought to be dramatically engendered sympathy (such as would have been provided by older leads as foils to the young ones or a stay-at-home as foil to David in New York) becomes almost an exercise in self-hatred, for he depicts the repellent aspects of ambition in having to criticize his characters when they should be doing it themselves. They have not yet learned self-mockery as a step to self-knowledge, any more than will Gene, the hero of *Saturday Night* who, in the song "Class," pronounces,

"I don't want to be what I am; / I want to be what I can." We simply do not like these people, and when they are made to emerge as whole numbers at the end of the story the dramatic arithmetic seems faulty. Once again, Franklin Shepard and the *Merrily* conundrum are prefigured.

Yet David is no Pal Joey, and in his best songs, including "Climb High," he is a lovable actor rather than someone putting on a lovable act. In other words, the songs are better than the show. What must have been the third attempt at a final number, "Chris and David II" (replacing its prototype and "Bright Star"), is an emotionally and melodically succinct match for "Climb High." "Where Do I Belong?" similarly attains real intimacy, partly through the purposeful musical motif of three upward steps yoked with infinitive lyric phrases in its verse section: these build it up as a directed structure from the start and are reintroduced as the bridge in the chorus. The end of this song also includes a brief reminiscence of the jingle of the nagging family from "Advice," as though their words still echo in David's ears, and this is one of a number of identifying cross-references beginning to be used by Sondheim to link songs (the opening I-IV progression and melodic steps of the first number, "Yoo-Hoo!" also seem to stalk through other parts of the score, though perhaps only coincidentally, and the representation of New York by a jazz piano vamp appears in a number of songs).

The score's main limitation is a lack of verbal wit and of musical sharpness and diversity to match. The presentational scheme of the flashbacks is not forceful enough for the first of its songs, the modal troubadour ballad "The Lay of a Gay Young Man," to appear more than a stylistic oddity whose reprise as the verse of "A Song For Humming" merely undermines further what is already a verbally awkward song. The New York job-hunting sequence (act 1, scene 4) is dramatically conceived as a "Follies" revue—yet another example of a later idea prefigured—but the musical numbers ("Nice Town, But—," "Pavement Pounding Sequence," "When I Get Famous," "In a Year from Now," "I'm in Love with a Boy," and "I Don't Want to Fall in Love with You") are not to any obvious extent an exploration of referential pastiche. This more or less has to be true of the lyrics, since the songs are not diegetic or "attitude" numbers (see chaps. 4 and 6 for further discussion of this issue), though there is a plan of suitelike differentiation in the music, which presents a jazz piano and jazz waltz formula in the first and third songs respectively and a French *divertissement* promenade in the second. Too many songs in the score, however, including the last three in this sequence, are in quadruple time with a Kernlike grace of texture and melody, in other words vaudeville marches or strolls of one shade or another. The rewards are some good tunes ("I'm in Love with a Boy") and a newfound ease and economy of writing, almost Brittenesque in the accompanying sixteenth-note motifs of "Not for Children" and more conventionally exhibited in the secondary couple's excellent song "In a Year from Now," where the vaudeville ambience is captured in well-poised foxtrot cross-rhythms. This number does contain a Rodgers and Hart pastiche reference to "small hotels" in the lyrics and also includes an early example of Sondheim's mastery of parallel ambiguity in text and music, when the two words "we'll have" are given pivoted meanings—at first the line is "What do you think we'll have?" but then the phrase is reconstrued as "we'll have / To wait and see"; the musical two-note cell to these two words is similarly reinterpreted as an extended unit the second time around.

Long songs are a problem in *Climb High,* and Babbitt's training does not yet seem to have paid dividends in numbers such as "Advice" and "Have You Been Waiting Long?" where either the main melodic and harmonic content is too weak to carry the overall length of the number or the subsidiary material is loose and uninteresting, though it is always tied in or tied up at the end. The best strategies of extension are lyric or dramatic, notably in "I Don't Want to Fall in Love with You," where David's insincere protestations to Teddy are overheard at the next res-taurant table and reinterpreted by Judy to Norman as his real opportun-istic thoughts as he mouths the second stanza.

All things considered, however, the songs in *Climb High* show Sondheim in overall command of a settled and balanced melopoetic technique, one that in most ways is equal to his period and material and is certainly impressive for his age and experience. While the score has not yet relaxed into the concentrated excellence of *Saturday Night,* many of the songs remain worthy of performance; time and again the force of Sondheim's personality is brought home to us by foretastes of phrases, techniques, or preoccu-pations from the later shows. Finally, it is worth considering that, as his only musical of single (in the sense of entirely original) authorship, it holds a unique position in his output, and that, as in a rather different sense with the innocent college conditions surrounding *All That Glitters,* which could simply be authorially created in the summer vacation and presented to a drama society "pretty much ready to go" (Shainman, quoted in Salsini 1991), it belongs to an age of predirectorial theater, one in which "Rodgers and Hammerstein would say, 'Here. We've done this. Stage it'" (Stephen Schwartz, in Sponberg 1991, 131). Might Broadway's recent history have been different had Sondheim chosen to persevere with a role for himself as overall *auteur* rather than go along with the collab-orative model that he has helped to further?

Journeyman Work

Sondheim's first commercial experience occurred during his period of study with Babbitt, but seems not to have amounted to more than the acceptance of a Christmas carol for the play *I Know My Love,* starring the Lunts, in 1951, and the rejection of a charming but inconsequential song, "The Two of You," dated 22 February 1952, sent in for the television show "Kukla, Fran, and Ollie," to be sung by Fran to the two puppets (it eventually surfaced in *Side by Side by Sondheim* in Chicago). If this could be compared with his own hero David having to eat "hummable pie," it at least utilized him as a composer. Most of his other journeyman work was purely literary, and while he doubtless enjoyed it, it must have left him all the more impatient for recognition as a Broadway composer because he had no confidence that such recognition would come naturally, as Hal Prince has testified.

> He [Sondheim] and I had first met in the audience on the opening night of *South Pacific* in April of 1949. He was there with his mentor, Oscar Hammerstein II, and Mary Rodgers introduced us.
>
> It's curious, that. Steve was a composer whose reputation had reached me all the way from Williams College, where he had written book, music, and lyrics for a show called *Climb High* (which was the story of a young man with aspirations to produce on Broadway).
>
> Steve reminds me that soon after we met I reasoned with him over a bacon, lettuce, and tomato sandwich in Walgreen's that we were the natural inheritors of the theatre we were entering. I've always been an optimist, Steve a pessimist. I never doubted the inevitability of his acclaim, but I will persist that his pessimism accounted for some of the delay in getting recognized. (Prince 1974, 29–30)

The chronology here is misleading. Prince is getting confused between *Climb High* and *All That Glitters,* and elsewhere (Zadan 1990, 7) he implies that the drugstore conversation took place after he left the army in 1952. But we need to bear this passage in mind if, as many have done, we find the perception of the young Frank and Charley in *Merrily We Roll Along* that "It's our time . . . coming through" lacking in psychological verisimilitude or guilty of confusing idealism with ambition. Clearly Prince at least, only two years older than Sondheim, felt like them in his early twenties, however "curious" the mixture of confidence and inhibition in Sondheim. With all due allowance for the dangers and complexities of reading self-expression into song, there is much further food for thought in the fact that this first moment of collaboration between Sondheim and

Prince is so suggestively reflected in what, for the time being at least, has been virtually their last, the rooftop scene in *Merrily We Roll Along*.

Thus the breadwinning prose assignments that Sondheim undertook from this period onward must have seemed to him both incumbent and frustrating. At the same time, as a seasoned film buff, he was clearly attracted by genre projects and would continue to be until and beyond 1972, when he and Anthony Perkins wrote the screenplay for the murder mystery *The Last of Sheila* (in 1953, in fact, he spent some time—and all his money—in Italy as unpaid clapper boy for the filming of *Beat the Devil*). Television provided a number of early opportunities. He copyrighted the script for a television spy mystery, "The Man with the Squeaky Shoes," in April 1953, and then moved to Hollywood to write the "Topper" episodes, dated between September and November 1953 (he wrote ten or eleven on his own, Oppenheimer wrote a similar number, and they co-authored the rest). He was not happy there—his mother's presence in California apparently did not help matters (see Zadan 1990, 8)—and returned to set himself up in New York with Flora Roberts as his agent as soon as finances permitted. Early in 1954 he provided more television material, a "Kodak Family Adventure" episode ("Teddy and the Magician") plus two scripts, "Mr. Blandings and the Tree Surgeon" and "The Education of Mr. Blandings," based on *Blandings' Way* by Eric Hodgins; two years later, another television series, "The Last Word," afforded him employment during the six-month lull in *West Side Story* preparations. Also dating from this time is a treatment for a somewhat Conradesque screenplay, *The King of Diamonds,* written in collaboration with Larry Gelbart, and reviews of several films, including *On the Waterfront* and *Guys and Dolls,* published in *Films in Review.* A television play, "In an Early Winter," based on a story by Roger Angell, was produced by Sondheim's college classmate Howard Erskine in 1958, and further undated projects include notes for a play, and the beginning of a script, called *The Forty Million,* an outline for a story called *Struggling Upward* and another for a television play "A Funny Coincidence," a newspaper column entitled "Comments of a Comedian" ghosted for Victor Borge, and a play outline called *The Burglar.*

He kept his hand in with occasional songs, notably "A Star Is Born." Dated 29 March 1954 and written to celebrate the birth of a college friend's first child, it is a real tour de force of a list song, rhyming and scanning no less than sixty-nine film stars. He also worked on what were presumably unsolicited musicals. An undated outline for a stage musical based on *The Madwoman of Chaillot,* a play from 1945 by Jean Giraudoux that was later filmed, survives; and what was probably the first of his collaborations with Mary Rodgers dates from May 1954. This was to be a one-hour musical version for television of Frank Stockton's highly dramatic short story *The Lady or the Tiger?* (which had already been presented as a Broadway musical comedy as early as 1888), but it was never finished. Some songs were sketched: there are lyrics by Sondheim for "I'm Above All That," "Another World," "Lovely Ladies," and "Crime Doesn't Pay," with music, also by him, for "Lovely Ladies," "Opening," "King and Queen Duet," "Fanfare and Arena Sequence," and "Fair Lady," the last four being incomplete sketches. Sondheim has written three other songs in collaboration with Mary Rodgers: "Don't Laugh," the opening number of her short-lived Broadway musical *Hot Spot* about the Peace Corps (1963); "Christmas Island at Christmas Time," a slow calypso (he cannot remember who wrote what in this); and "The Boy From . . . ." This last, the only one to have found its way into his canon, was one of the songs, for all of which (with various lyricists) she wrote the music, in the 1966 revue *The Mad Show*. Sondheim's lyrics seem more knowingly coded than *Mad* magazine would have bargained for, since the answer to all the girl's perplexed questions in the song—"Why are his trousers vermilion?" and so forth—is obvious: the boy is gay (one can only wonder what clientele he hopes to find for his boutique in Llanfair P.G.).

Perhaps *The Lady or the Tiger?* gave way to what must have seemed the ideal opportunity. In early 1954 Sondheim had met Lemuel Ayers when they were both ushers at a wedding. Ayers, who had coproduced *Kiss Me, Kate* and designed its sets as well as those for *Oklahoma!*, was hoping to make a musical out of *Front Porch in Flatbush*, the last play by the Epstein twins (who had written the screenplay for *Casablanca* in 1942). Frank Loesser was approached for the lyrics and music, but he was occupied with other work (presumably the film of *Guys and Dolls* or the writing of *The Most Happy Fella*), and Sondheim got the job after writing three pilot songs.

Saturday Night, which the show became, contains some of Sondheim's most attractive songs and, given how much he must have wanted to prove himself, they are remarkably relaxed. They show two striking and interacting advances over those of *Climb High:* the characterization of musical styles, especially through vamps, and the extent and texture of wit. Both these qualities are assisted by the fact that several of the songs or motifs are placed as dramatic objects (see chap. 6 for a discussion of *diegetic* song). "Isn't It?" is sung and danced to an offstage ball, "A Moment with You" to the gramophone; "Love's a Bond," a clever Al Jolson take-off, is a current hit song (the year is 1929). "Saturday Night" itself is preceded by a representation of Dino's ragtime piano playing, and this sets a casual and sprightly tone for the vamps, which explore a broader and brasher array of jazzy keyboard styles than Sondheim had previously mustered. "One Wonderful Day" and "What More Do I Need?," the latter added as a finale song after the rest of the score was in place, are exhilarating Broadway galops, but more important, in "Class" and especially "Exhibit 'A'" (labeled "In the manner of a softshoe") he has discovered a new poise through the use of stride piano styles in compound time; these enable him to slow down the harmony and spotlight the voice, the lyrics, and the actor during silent beats. Congruently, fills are also more highly developed, "Love's a Bond" being already a close cousin to "Beautiful Girls" from *Follies* in this respect.

Already, too, song as part of the story and song as theatrical convention provide the interaction between pretense and reality, which is what the show is about. Its 1929 setting offers two overriding metaphors for this theme, the stock market (before the crash) and the movies, and Sondheim's lyrics develop these to the fullest. They come together in "A Moment with You," a list song mentioning both Fred Astaire, the corollary to its dance locus, and J. P. Morgan. There are highly amusing references to Valentino and other stars in "In the Movies" ("A Star Is Born" had recently stood Sondheim in good stead here), which is about the difference between the fantasy world of films and the dull reality of Brooklyn. The financial imagery is skillfully placed: for instance, Helen refers to "supply and demand"—rhyming with "band" and exploiting the diphthongs of her fake southern accent to the full on long notes—in "Isn't It?" (she is pretending to have money, and indeed at the end of the show it turns out that she has); and it climaxes with ridiculous overkill in "Love's a Bond," where Jolson's importunate minstrel persona is as aptly captured in the singer's triumphant conviction that "As A. T. and T. will / Go up and up, we will / 'Cause this new love of ours is gilt-edged preferred" as it is in the pat finality of his ragtime melody.

Another exploration of the romance-reality dichotomy comes to the fore in "Class," Gene's motivating statement about himself and therefore the key song for the key character. There is a French cabaret elegance about the Mixolydian cast of the music (is this a stylistic echo of Gershwin?), and it is matched in the overlaying of French words upon the English lyrics. Gene is overt about this facade of fashion in his second-stanza line "When asked, 'Quelle heure?' by Missus Du Pont" (and betrayed by it in his answer: "You say to her, 'Why naturellement, / Ma'mselle!'"), while some of the other references—"chic," "Renoir," "cravat," "peignoir," not to mention his own name, Eugene—veer more toward the subtextual. These are followed up with another crop of French words, badly pronounced, when Bobby, the youngest member of the group, tries to match Gene's poise in "Exhibit 'A'." But the most effective structuring of conflicts about the approach to life comes as a sharpening up of the lyric strategies first used in "I Don't Want to Fall in Love with You" and "In a Year from Now" from *Climb High:* in both "I Remember That" and "One Wonderful Day" we are given opposite viewpoints on love and marriage in successive stanzas. The secondary couple's "I Remember That," the first of Sondheim's "faulty memory" songs, may be indebted to "I Remember It Well" (written by Weill and Lerner for *Love Life* before being refashioned for *Gigi*) and may not be as tight a vignette as "Remember?" in *A Little Night Music* or epistemologically significant like "Someone in a Tree," but it is funny, telling, and touching and set to a lovely Kernlike tune. Hank recalls falling in love (and once again we are aware of the French references).

> I arrived at seven,
> I'd stopped along the way
> To buy a big bouquet
> For you—I remember that.
> In a French-type restaurant,
> Run by a guy named Jake,
> We had a sirloin steak
> For two—I remember that.

Celeste sets the record straight in the second stanza.

> I was dressed at seven,
> But you arrived at eight;
> And you were never late
> Again—I remember that.
> Since you'd bought me flowers,
> You couldn't pay the check;
> You were a nervous wreck
> By then—I remember that.

And so on. In this miniature drama, the character delineation is as sharp as the humor, and both are aided by the differences of syntax in the first four lines of each stanza. "One Wonderful Day" is less subtle—it is a rousing party number for the end of the first act—but just as efficient; and again the syntax cuts across the parallels. This time the girl is romantic, the boy sardonic.

> Wonderful girl meets wonderful boy.
> What a wonderful chance to start a life
> Full of wonder and joy . . .

> You will be married, you will be caught!
> Every day you'll come home and she'll be there—
> What a horrible thought . . .

Sondheim's antinomial genius is already in full spate.

Babbitt appreciated the songs but found the book of *Saturday Night* "filled with all sorts of homespun corn which I find offensive" (Zadan 1990, 9). Certainly we should agree with him today. Gene is rebarbative, and the shallow womanizing of the lads in the story gives rise to some irritatingly shallow music in the title song and "It's That Kind of a Neighborhood" (though the "Fair Brooklyn" section of the latter is a gem). The verse passages of "In the Movies" and the party-song sections of "One Wonderful Day" are also bungled, capitulating to the sophomoric characters they concern rather than portraying them constructively, no doubt because Sondheim has not yet learned to shape a dramatic ensemble or create one of his mimetic interludes (see chap. 8), instead of which he resorts to hand-me-downs in the form of musical quotations. But the score as a whole has a zest that is new and vital, reflecting both its vernacular subject matter (hopeful middle-class youths from Brooklyn) and its period (the late 1920s). With Sondheim's broader range of musical idioms and greater command of wit and verbal structure on offer (the lyrics of "Exhibit 'A'" presage both "Now" in *A Little Night Music* and "Poems" in *Pacific Overtures*), his recourse to a Kern-type ballad for the love duet "All for You" begins to sound decidedly old-fashioned, though one would not want to level the same criticism at the two other love songs, "So Many People" and "What More Do I Need?" which can compete with Gershwin or Warren.

Ayers died suddenly, and *Saturday Night* was never produced. If it had been, would Sondheim have achieved earlier recognition as a composer? In "One Wonderful Day" he wrote a show-stopping tune worthy of Jerry Herman. This would undoubtedly have won him a happy public, as would the confidence, variety, and sheer intelligibility of the score as a whole; but we can hardly imagine that he himself would have been satisfied with *Saturday Night* for long. And the innocence of the material was fast becoming anachronistic: without the foil of age found in, say, *Hello, Dolly!*, youth could no longer hope to hold the stage in such a bourgeois context. A very different set of New York youngsters would demand attention in *West Side Story*.

Sondheim as Lyricist: *West Side Story*

Hitherto in virtually all his work Sondheim had written songs (both words and music), or prose, or both: with the possible exception of *The Lady or the Tiger?* he seems to have had no experience of writing lyrics for or to others' music, it had not occurred to him to do so, and when the prospect arose with *West Side Story* it hardly felt like a step forward, even in the creative company of Leonard Bernstein, Jerome Robbins, and Arthur Laurents. His unease cannot have been helped by the fact that, when they heard *Saturday Night*, both Bernstein and Laurents thought his lyrics better than his music, a judgment by which Bernstein implicitly stood as late as *Company* and which has never quite disappeared (see Zadan 1990, 11–12; Peyser 1987, 393; and Bernstein's diary description of him as "a young lyricist" [Bernstein 1982, 145]). As I have already noted, Hammerstein's advice was sought, given, and followed over both *West Side Story* and *Gypsy:* he urged Sondheim to take the opportunity of working with top-grade professionals on the former when it was offered in November 1955 and when, in the summer of 1958, Ethel Merman's agent refused to take a chance on him as an unknown composer for *Gypsy* and Jule Styne was called in at the last moment for the music, he recommended the experience of writing for a star. Sondheim kept his objectives clear, however, by declining to complete the *Candide* lyrics when Bernstein offered the job to him after John Latouche's death in mid–1956; he was, in any case, in the midst of *The Last Resorts.* And even when he did return to writing only lyrics at a few points later in his career, the circumstances were either relatively unimportant, as with the *Candide* revival, or, coincidentally perhaps, unsuccessful, as with *Do I Hear a Waltz?* and Bernstein's Brecht project.

The genesis of *West Side Story* is complicated and has been fully discussed elsewhere (see Prince 1974, 29–43; Guernsey 1985, 40–54; Peyser 1987, 227–43; Zadan 1990, 11–31; Ilson 1989, 33–43). Here, a few factual and critical observations must suffice. Bernstein had intended writing the lyrics himself, as he had for *Peter Pan,* parts of *On the Town,* and his opera *Trouble in Tahiti,* and when time constraints led to Sondheim being brought in it was, in contractual terms, as colyricist. Eventually, disappointed at his lack of recognition in the out-of-town reviews, Sondheim was given sole credit by Bernstein in the billing and on the vocal score: Bernstein felt "that he had done so much of the lyric writing, certainly more than I had done, and some whole songs were all his" and commented further that "collaboration is this great mysterious thing that gets to the point that you don't really know who wrote what" (Zadan 1990, 25). Sondheim says, rather more categorically, "I ended up writing all the lyrics" (Peyser 1987, 241) and explained to Peyser what "Opening Doors" in *Merrily We Roll Along* graphically illustrates, namely, the adoption of simultaneous creative sessions, whereby

> they would compose in separate rooms in Bernstein's apartment and then, after an hour or so, get together to see what each had done . . .

Bernstein would fight him "on every word. I would say, 'I just met a girl named Maria,' and Lenny would interrupt with 'I just saw a girl. . . .' It was that way from beginning to end. It is true Lenny put in a lot of time on the lyrics but when I sat down to write, it was I who wrote them." (Peyser 1987, 234)

The lyric sheets and sketches in Sondheim's hand in the Wisconsin archive include the "Jet Song," "Something's Coming," "America" (along with a typescript memo from Jerome Robbins attempting to simplify its points of view by cutting out the comments of the negative third character, Rosalia; in the event it was the guarded Bernardo they omitted, though in the film the ritual insults—to new lyrics—are between Bernardo and Anita), "Cool," "One Hand, One Heart," "Tonight," "I Feel Pretty" (with some happily discarded sections such as "Cinderella / Dressed in yella / With an elegant fella to see"), "Somewhere," "Gee, Officer Krupke" (with a "Fuck you!" last line as well as an alternative stretto ending), and "A Boy Like That" / "I Have a Love." In other words, only "Maria" is missing.

A glance at "Maria" in the score somewhat dampens the question of lyric ownership. Bernstein says, "I had a song called 'Maria,' for which I had the title and some kind of lyric that I'd written which was there when Steve came in" (Zadan 1990, 21). He had not quite finished the tune, but the form of the lyric was already fixed, because of the repetitions of the title and its musical motif (twenty-nine of them in the final product) and the need to lead into them verbally. Sondheim's job was therefore to find acceptable rhyming phrases for the interstices between them.

In the case of "Tonight," a dummy lyric by Bernstein, in his hand, survives on the back of Sondheim's sketch sheets for the "Balcony Scene."

Hello my love,
I'd know you anywhere
I've seen you all my life in my mind.

I know my love,
Those arms, that face, that hair—You're the one; there's just
    one of a kind.

Goodbye

ugh. { To dreaming and to waiting,
To loneliness and seeking
The one I wanted so;

Don't go, don't go.
You're here at last, and welcome, my love,
Hello.

Sondheim points out that this would have been a case in which he and Bernstein produced lyrics separately and then came together to fuse the two. He also states that "Tonight" was written first in its "Quintet" guise and then lifted for the "Balcony Scene," which makes it odd that Bernstein is apparently going off at this lyric tangent in the "Balcony Scene." But whatever the process of composition (and there is a radically different version of the "Balcony Scene" musical material among the Bernstein autographs in the Library of Congress), Sondheim's canonic lyric offered a conceit far superior to Bernstein's banal "Hello"/"Goodbye" ploy, one in which he could develop, a little self-consciously perhaps, but very beautifully and very much in tune with the musical *Affekt,* the nocturnal imagery of the "morning star" and "suns and moons all over the place," of a whole universe at Tony and Maria's feet (one even senses a hint of *Tristan* in Tony's supplication for "endless night"). The word *tonight* is, of course, also the final one in "Something's Coming," though the song was a much later addition to the score.

The "Tonight" quintet was already present as a concept and in title, though not yet with a lyric, in the first play script of January 1956. The successive versions of the script in the Wisconsin archive help us to plot the growth of the score, though there is some confusion nonetheless. "One Hand, One Heart" was added to the script fairly early on, in February or March 1956, perhaps when it was cut from *Candide* (see below), and it appeared in the balcony scene. The script in question suggests that it was to be reprised for the mock wedding, but this seems at variance with Laurents's assertion (Guernsey 1985, 49) that "One Hand, One Heart" and "Tonight" simply swapped places. Peyser (1987, 239) confuses the issue further by saying, contrary to the evidence in the scripts, that "Tonight" replaced "Somewhere" in the balcony scene, where it came before "One Hand, One Heart," as a response to criticism by Hammerstein, whereas Fordin (1977, 330) makes it clear (and Sondheim confirms this) that Hammerstein's criticism (that the scene needed a more soaring song) actually concerned "Tonight" and hence went unanswered. Sondheim's recollection further simplifies all this: Bernstein wanted to use two preexistent tunes, "Somewhere" followed by "One Hand, One Heart," in the "Balcony Scene," but Sondheim, Laurents, and Robbins found them too solemn and churchy, so "Somewhere" was kept out of the scripts altogether until late on, "One Hand, One Heart" was eventually allowed only its later reprise, and the "Tonight" "preprise" was fashioned, eventually furnishing the "Balcony Scene" with its only song.

Other details are clearer. "I Feel Pretty" was already mentioned as such in the first script, and Sondheim has said that the tune came first (see chap. 3). "One Hand, One Heart" was originally called "One"; the passage now played instrumentally (p. 106 in the vocal score, mm. 4–10) was vocal, leading up to the title word ("What can they do? / I'm part of you, / And we are one"), and the chorus itself, with dotted half notes where there are now quarter notes, ran as follows.

> One hand, one heart:
> Your hand, my heart.
> Your eyes make me see:
> You're the breath and life of me.

Sondheim was unhappy with this, "stifled" as he was by one-syllable words (see Zadan 1990, 23); but what he does not point out when he describes how he persuaded Bernstein to add the quarter notes is that, in accordance with the repositioning of the song, he transformed the whole voice of the lyric into something imperative and much more specific—a précis of the marriage liturgy, in fact—though the original formula still intrudes at the climax.

"America," "Cool," and the "Tonight" quintet had been written by spring 1956, the music for "Cool" coming before the words and its opening two lines of lyrics coming with it from Bernstein (see Peyser 1987, 234). "Something's Coming," on the other hand, was a very late addition and a song in which, as we shall see in chapter 2, Sondheim created a lyric straight out of Laurents's dialogue (see also Zadan 1990, 21). Earlier he had done the same with "A Boy Like That" (Zadan 1990, 21), and fashioned a complete lyric to which Bernstein then simply added the music (it was the only instance of this "dry" process—see Peyser 1987, 240); both music and words, however, seem to have been adjusted later in the number when a section called "Once in Your Life" was recast as "I Have a Love." "Gee, Officer Krupke," whose music came first, was another late addition, cued into the script of 1 June 1957; "Somewhere," its music written a decade or so earlier (see Peyser 1987, 239), was a later one still, not yet present by 19 July.

Bernstein was nothing if not utilitarian with his music, and the "Officer Krupke" tune appeared on Sondheim's desk because it had been cut from *Candide,* on which Bernstein was working at the same time and whose premiere (and closing) took place between the 1956 and 1957 periods of work on *West Side Story.* "One Hand, One Heart" also came from *Candide,* as we have seen, while "O Happy We" went in the other direction, having been written for the point in the bridal shop scene where Laurents, in his first script of January 1956, called for "a song where Tonio [*sic*] and Maria, acting as their parents, introduce a wish-idea of their families to each other. It should be light and gay." Sondheim drafted a lyric for this episode that yet again uncannily presages something he would write nearly thirty years later, namely, "Children and Art" in *Sunday in the Park with George,* where even a rhyme is the same.

> Papa, you will like him—
> I know you will like him.
> He is brave, he is bright.
> Mama, you will like him—
> I know you will like him—
> He is gentle and polite. . . .

Less well known than the exchanges with *Candide* is the fact that a rejected first-scene number for the Jets, "Mix!" reappeared nine years later as the "Lamah rag'shu goyim" section of the slow movement of *Chichester Psalms.* Few choristers singing this work can have been aware that the "heathen" were originally raging to Sondheim's words.

> Mix!
> Make a mess of 'em!
> Pay the Puerto Ricans back,
> Make a mess of 'em!
> If you let us take a crack,
> There'll be less of 'em,
> There'll be less of 'em.

Another number that came and went, this time in rehearsal in Washington (it is dated 23 August 1957), was the trio "Like Everybody Else" (referred to as "Kids Ain't" in Zadan 1990, 24), with its "moderate rock" tempo and other rock and roll indicators (though Sondheim sees it more as a soft-shoe number). Was this ever reused elsewhere?

"Mix!" was not the only first-scene casualty. There was an eight-minute number in which what is now the instrumental "Prologue" was sung, followed by the canonic "Jet Song" with different lyrics as "My Greatest Day" (including lines such as "How 'bout the day when we made all that mess / With the mice we let loose / In the Bronx Park Express?" for Diesel); a later replacement song, "This Turf Is Ours," was also tried but abandoned (Zadan 1990, 24). Earlier still, Laurents had envisaged a "Rumble Song" in this scene that would be used again for the rumble scene itself. Another musical slot that eventually became instrumental and balletic, having been envisaged as song, occurred in "The Dance at the Gym," where there was another rock and roll number, "Atom Bomb Baby" ("I got a A[tom] B[omb] B[aby] well she gives me a bang. / She rocks me from her underpinnings to her overhang"). These lyrics fitted a modification of the "rocky" tune in the "Blues" section (vocal score, 36–37), already used vocally in a part of the "Jet Song" that was also cut (though it remained in the score—see 20–21).

The presence of these songs in *West Side Story* reminds us what an extraordinarily wide range the music embraces. The verse of the "Balcony Scene" could almost be by Gounod, and the number is as old-fashioned and operettalike as the span and vocal stance of the "A Boy Like That" scena are grandly operatic. The "Cool" twelve-note fugue seems as indebted to Beethoven's *Grosse Fuge* as does "Somewhere"'s melodic contour to his "Emperor" Concerto and its sparse counterpoint to his late quartets, but at the same time the fugue's and the "Prologue"'s assimilation of modern jazz is astonishing and seems to anticipate third stream. The opening of the "Tonight" quintet is pure Stravinsky, highly reminiscent of "Laudate dominum" in the *Symphony of Psalms*. The sheer verve and (especially in "Something's Coming") complexity of Bernstein's Latin American rhythms can be as breathtaking as his film-music sentimentality in "Maria." Everywhere his eclecticism risks all, as he treads what he sees as "the fine line between opera and Broadway" in "my baby, my tragic musical-comedy, whatever that is" (Peyser 1987, 236, 242).

The mixture of genres in the show as a whole is equally striking. Dance had never played such a vital role in a musical; this and the urban setting with its groups of characters ever on the move gave Bernstein scope for what was generically both a modern ballet score and a film score as well as a stage musical, and his experience with his previous "urban" scores, *On the Town, Fancy Free,* and *On the Waterfront,* led naturally into his fusing the three genres symphonically. The book, too, pithy as it is, had a crucial role to play: melodramatic scenes such as the bedroom interrogation and the drugstore episode with its chillingly inarticulate verismo dialogue at the end hold the stage as nonmusical drama through the exploitation of gangster film traditions and the like; whatever fears Laurents may have had that it would turn into a "goddamned Bernstein opera" (Zadan 1990, 14), one of *West Side Story*'s greatest strengths is that it did not, and the generic conventions of ballet, film, stage play, musical comedy, and opera intercut while remaining separate. That is why Maria's final speech works perfectly well as dialogue despite being intended as a dummy lyric for music, and perhaps why the show has so triumphantly survived the embarrassments and weaknesses that time has forced upon its individual generic components.

Sondheim, lacking both the older composer's orchestral experience and extroverted personality, could not at the time have matched the range of Bernstein's music; nor, indeed, has he tried to subsequently (though neither has he been prey to the gross unevenness of Bernstein's later works).

Happy for the most part for orchestration to remain a closed book to him, his only exercise in it was when he wrote some instrumental music for Laurents's Broadway play *Invitation to a March* in 1960 and scored its fugato "Prelude" (on a fanfare motif not unlike the "Grass is green" figure [in *Anyone Can Whistle*], which later becomes a military signal) and later barcarolle and waltz incidentals for trumpet, horn, clarinet, flute, and harp; he was correspondingly happy on this occasion to take it bit by bit to Bernstein for advice. Bernstein for his part felt that he had received "a great education" (Zadan 1990, 25) about lyric writing from Sondheim on *West Side Story* and found the collaboration "a joy" because "he was also a composer and I could explain musical problems to him and he'd understand immediately" (Zadan 1990, 15–16).

Yet the musical scope of *West Side Story* first opened Sondheim's eyes to many of the possibilities he *has* explored—not so noticeably in *Forum*, perhaps, but certainly in the larger-than-life circus music of act 1 of *Anyone Can Whistle* (which may also owe something to *Candide*), its burgeoning generic pastiches across all three acts, and its motivic unity, for which a precedent can be found in *West Side Story*'s use of the $\hat{5}$–$\hat{1}$–$^\sharp\hat{4}$ or $\hat{1}$–$^\sharp\hat{4}$–$\hat{5}$ motif and continual emphasis on the Lydian fourth. More important still, the show broadened the range of his lyrics extraordinarily, their incidental weaknesses (on which he has often harped) notwithstanding. It has become such a classic that we take their technique, plenitude, and durability for granted, but at the time they lifted him completely out of himself and out of too close an identification with his aspiring bourgeois milieu, which had been such a problem in *Climb High* and *Saturday Night,* and verbal power seemed to blossom in direct proportion to his degree of distance from his characters. He too pastiched rock, and revelled virtuosically in city slang (most of it made up by Laurents so that it would not become dated), heavily accented and faulty English, and whole areas of gangster language (for example, "Someone gets in our way, / Someone don't feel so well") with which he would have been amply familiar through films but had not hitherto thought of incorporating into song. He had indeed "grown up" (Fordin 1977, 330), though not perhaps in the way Dorothy Hammerstein meant when she first heard "Maria."

A Decade of Uncertainty

West Side Story was an extraordinary planetary conjunction. Seen by some as the end of an era in musicals, by others as a new dawn, it was undoubtedly the single greatest turning point in Bernstein's career, when he blatantly signed off from Broadway with it and took the New York Philharmonic directorship, confident that he had shown the way for "dozens of kids who would take the next step . . . to some form of American opera" (Zadan 1990, 28–29). At the same time it is easy to forget that it was Laurents's first book for a musical (Ilson 1989, 34); it was also the first show in which Prince used amplification (Prince 1974, 165). Robbins was, in many ways, the pivotal figure, creating his most famous work as choreographer and acting as a link in the venerable chain of Broadway directors between his predecessor George Abbott and his successor Hal Prince, who was here working (as producer) for the first time with Sondheim. The show remains infinitely better known than anything else of Sondheim's, especially in Britain, where its constituency seems virtually boundless and where its initial London production still holds the record for the longest Sondheim run anywhere. The film soundtrack stereo disk similarly remains the longest ever number 1 on *Billboard*'s album charts. And, statistics apart, it is difficult to imagine anything better than its finest moments, such as "I Have a Love," from the pen of either Sondheim or Bernstein.

Thus it still tends to loom behind Sondheim's other achievements as an éminence grise. Nevertheless, the shelving of *Saturday Night* (which was to be resuscitated in 1959, to the extent of an announcement in the *New York Times* on 1 June, but again abandoned when Sondheim felt disinclined to go back over old work) had not left him entirely destitute of musical exposure. In 1955 he wrote a song, "Rag Me That Mendelssohn March," for George Oppenheimer and Arthur Kober's play *A Mighty Man Is He,* and the following year he contributed incidental music to another play, *Girls of Summer,* by N. Richard Nash, that opened on Broadway on 19 November, and fashioned an attractively bluesy title song out of it for promotional purposes with Lena Horne in mind (see Sondheim and Lucas 1981). But none of his projects for musicals got very far at this stage. *The Lady or the Tiger?* was never completed. Plans for a musical about the roguish Mizner brothers (Addison and Wilson) had been discussed with Hammerstein as early as 1953, the year the book *The Legendary Mizners* by Alva Johnston appeared, and seem to have remained alive until some time after 1956, when David Merrick, for purposes of comparison, sent Sondheim a script by Sam Behrman of Irving Berlin's unproduced musical *Sentimental Guy,* similarly based on Johnston's book. Sondheim produced a detailed scheme of scenes and numbers, which included the use of the Runyonesque Wilson as a guitar balladeer (which he had been in his youth), a *Verfremdungseffekt* eventually followed through thirty-five years later in *Assassins;* there are also a few short music sketches, and a charming song, doubtless intended to be the first, depicting Mrs. Mizner's genteel tea, "Afternoon in Benicia," whose draft breaks off after fifty-two measures. The project proceeded no farther than this.

The Last Resorts ran similarly aground. It borrowed or rather bought a title from Cleveland Amory and was "the story of a wry, laconic Hoosier journalist observing the foibles of the Floridian well-to-do as they entertain the Duke and Duchess of Windsor" (Sondheim and Lucas 1981). An outline, presumably Sondheim's, is dated 15 November 1955. Prince was set to produce it in 1956 and Jean Kerr wrote the book, but Sondheim's material was at odds with this and was rejected. Again one song survives, the golfing satire "Pour le sport," which was later performed in a Julius Monk revue (and in *Marry Me a Little*); one other, "High Life," was also completed. The following year, Prince, Sondheim, and Laurents planned to do a romantic musical comedy, doubtless as a relief from *West Side Story*. They fixed upon Anouilh's *Ring Round the Moon,* and Sondheim wrote a waltz for it (see ex. 7.3c), but Anouilh failed to cooperate. There were yet more abandoned projects in the shape of two television musicals. One, with a script by Elaine Carrington dated 15 August 1956 and called *I Believe in You,* was about a summer stock drama coach who finds himself in a "mental institution of a theater" and gave rise to one song, a characteristically intimate but not particularly distinctive title number eventually published in 1990 as "They Ask Me Why I Believe in You." The other, *Happily Ever After,* to a book by Joseph Stein and somewhat similar to Samuel Barber's opera *A Hand of Bridge* in being about two married couples and the fantasies and tensions that accompany their mutual visits, was planned in 1959 but proceeded only as far as one, rather good, number ("I Wouldn't Change a Thing"), and Sondheim recalls no collaboration with Stein. Finally, there was *The Jet-Propelled Couch,* a television play by Stanley Roberts based on a supposedly genuine psychiatric case study in a book by Robert Lindner about a nuclear scientist under the spell of a personal interplanetary fantasy. This had been broadcast as a "Playhouse 90" production on 14 November 1957, and Sondheim planned to expand it into a two-act stage musical in 1958. He completed two songs: one, "Yes," was reused as "Salon at the Claridge #1" in *Stavisky;* the other, "Nobody Reads Books," is lost. One lyric, "Doctor," is extant.

It must have been all the more frustrating to Sondheim that his auditioning for the music as well as the lyrics of *Gypsy* was successful, making him, in a sense, third only to Berlin and Porter as Robbins's choice of composer (see Zadan 1990, 38), only to be thwarted by Merman. Yet once he agreed to be merely lyricist, there was nothing frustrating about the collaboration with Jule Styne, and if some, including Sondheim himself, have seen *Gypsy* as a nearly perfect example—perhaps the last—of an "integrated" musical (see Zadan 1990, 59) and others have even intimated that it contains Sondheim's best work (see Steyn 1987), this means simply that it gave him his one and only opportunity to perfect his elective affinity with the golden age of Broadway stylistics without the challenges and inhibitions that its deconstruction would necessitate once his times had turned their uneasy corner into the 1960s. In other words, linked with Styne, who was a generation older, he could for once be a classic songwriter rather than, as in the pastiches of *Anyone Can Whistle, Company, Follies,* and *Dick Tracy,* a troubled modern songwriter with a classic pedigree. This was all the more true because *Gypsy,* although in some ways one of the last of the classic backstage musicals, owes its lifeblood not to the children's acts, which are musically peripheral and in any case have to be shown to be dead ends, but to the realm of "diegetic fantasy" explored in "All I Need Is the Girl" and "Rose's Turn" and still more to the nondiegetic character songs, especially Rose's.

Thus the tunes and their lyrics, "raising vaudevillian song forms to undreamt of heights" (Steyn 1987, 12), are uniformly excellent while remaining mostly on one level, as straightforwardly satisfying in these terms as are the plot, characterization, star focus, humor, and dramatic realism. Layers of stylistic meaning do have to be negotiated with some songs, of course. The diegetically protean "Let Me Entertain You" is the main, *Show Boat*-like exception to the overall concreteness of idiom, while for purposes of characterization "You Gotta Get a Gimmick" transfers the brassy burlesque sound of the strippers' acts to their conversation, as one might expect. "Mother's Day I" is as telling a recreation of a pre–World War I waltz song as is its alternative ("Tomorrow's Mother's Day") of a vaudeville two-step, and these two pastiches reach so far back in time that they might have begun to raise specters of deconstructive intent had they not been cut. But, for the most part, what Sondheim achieved was a simple concomitant of Styne's effortless mastery of rhythmic and melodic conventions that we can still regard as those of his own period: both men knew their Broadway stock-in-trade, the idiom forged around 1930 and current throughout the 1940s and 1950s, and enjoyed putting it to use. In particular, Styne, who wrote some of the melodies first, made Sondheim's job easier by his frequent use of the foxtrot signifier with its cross-rhythmic triple-time skip (see chap. 4, exs. 4.8c–d and 4.10, and chap. 7, ex. 7.8b, for further discussion). No less than six of the fourteen essential numbers are based on this ("Some People," "You'll Never Get Away from Me," "Broadway," "All I Need Is the Girl," "Everything's Coming Up Roses," and "Together Wherever We Go"), while "Baby June and Her Newsboys" utilizes its faster ragtime or quickstep version and "Nice She Ain't," which was cut, uses a further soft-shoe variant.

The efficacy of this idiom is easily illustrated, since three different sets of lyrics by three different writers take advantage of it in different ways in "You'll Never Get Away from Me" (for explanations of how they arose, see Zadan 1990, 45; Guernsey 1985, 65). The foxtrot skip comes as a kind of *Luftpause* (see chap. 7) after two measures of common-time oompah, and Sammy Cahn's original title line "Why Did You Have to Wait So Long?" uses its long notes (half note–quarter note–half note on the last three words) to illustrate the "wait" and the "long." In Leo Robin's "I'm in Pursuit of Happiness" it is as though the singer is skipping for joy (and the *Luftpause* separates the double *p*). Sondheim's lyric, as Mark Steyn has pointed out, when heard in conjunction with the contour of the tune as well as its rhythm, shows the melody trying unsuccessfully to get "away" from its moorings.

Other marks of craftsmanship that Mark Steyn has pinpointed also involve the foxtrot skip (important rhyme words such as *butts* and *guts* in "Some People," helping to fix Rose's character, use it as their springboard). Reflections of further types of musical structure by Styne occur with equal aptness elsewhere. In "Small World," Rose's scheming mind is fitted out with various melodic gambits that, although conventional enough as music, nicely illustrate her mental improvisations when highlighted by Sondheim's verbal parallels. For the initial two-measure melodic phrase, whose consequent builds on the second measure as a kind of utilitarian extension, the word *come* is used at its first occurrence as the additive link (". . . a stranger who's come here, / Come from another town"), and when Styne repeats his second measure sequentially in the next four-measure phrase the congruence is reflected in the rhetorical repetition of *stranger* ("I'm a stranger myself here"). Later in the song, when Styne combines these processes of extension and sequence, Sondheim matches them with a rhyme that is not only internalized because of the added syllable on the end of the second word ("common . . . [phe]nomenon") but ties the structure up tightly and wittily with the continuity of vowel sound. The whole idea of the artful mental extension, the nub of what Rose is trying to achieve in the song, is then revealed as she sings in the next phrase, "We could pool our resources / By joining forces," adding, as an extended extension, "from now on" (and again the hollow vowel sounds keep everything compact).

The "from now on" is a tiny but classic example of reflexivity in Sondheim's lyrics—the words describing what the music is doing—and, as we shall see in chapter 3, he built fully on such capability when finally given the opportunity to write his own music as well as lyrics in *A Funny Thing Happened on the Way to the Forum. Gypsy* also shows some of the more obvious (though no less effective) types of verbal tricks in which one can revel in *Forum,* such as the spelling-out of letters as the baseline for rhymes and puns or refrains (a looser attempt at this had been made in "Exhibit

'A'" in *Saturday Night*), and the playing around with the simplest two-syllable subject-predicate propositions in tandem with a two-note motif; the virtuosic "I-O-U" passage in "Together Wherever We Go" is an instance of both procedures, comparable with their use in "Free" and "Love, I Hear" in *Forum*.

In fact, at least three of the songs for *Forum* (most likely, "Free," "Pretty Little Picture," and "Impossible") predate *Gypsy*, and it is as well to remember that *Forum*, Sondheim's Broadway project with Burt Shevelove, a colleague whom Sondheim had first met in 1950 or 1951, was instigated as early as 1957, after *West Side Story* settled into its run. Thus, however much *Gypsy* may have interrupted its gestation and however many other abandoned projects, as we have seen, lay strewn around it, with something approaching a portfolio of songs for it already to hand *Forum* was from 1958 onward Sondheim's main chance, and the decision not to proceed with *Saturday Night* in 1959 must have amounted (on his part) to a direct judgment between the two shows and their scores. Dramatically the judgment was incontestable, but musically there were riches in *Saturday Night* for which there would be no scope in *Forum*.

Forum was an accomplished debut but not an ideal one for Sondheim the Broadway composer, who must have found the 1960s a difficult decade. He began psychoanalysis in late 1958 or early 1959; Oscar Hammerstein died in 1960 without hearing a Sondheim score on the New York stage (Sondheim dedicated *Forum* to his memory); *Anyone Can Whistle*, initially announced for 1962, was not produced until 1964 and then closed after nine performances; yet another lyrics-only assignment, *Do I Hear a Waltz?* followed, and was a generally unhappy experience for all concerned; and *The Girls Upstairs*, which became *Follies*, was then more than five years in the making, held up partly by yet another abandoned project, *A Pray by Blecht*. In the meantime, Sondheim's father, who in 1955 had been the birthday recipient of a score of *Saturday Night* with the inscription "To Dad on his 60th—Hope I can give you one of these every year for the next 40 years at least," died in 1966. With his Broadway career still such an unsteady affair, Sondheim spent some of his working time in the latter half of the 1960s as a professional puzzle writer, providing forty-one weekly cryptics for *New York* magazine over the period of a year or so until he started work on *Company* in 1969, at which point he handed over the column to fellow lyricist Richard Maltby, Jr. (both Sondheim's and Maltby's *New York* puzzles were published in book form in 1980).

Smaller musical assignments ran alongside these problematic, large-scale concerns, however. A spirited though relatively modest opening number for Ginger Rogers's nightclub act, "The Night Is the Best Time of the Day," was provided in 1959 (another song for it, "Mr. A," seems to have been sketched but not drafted completely). Shevelove and Sondheim contributed a song, "Ten Years Old," to a television variety salute to the 1950s, "The Fabulous Fifties," but it was cut before the CBS broadcast on 31 January 1960 because the program was too long (this was no great loss; Sondheim's music for the satirical number was largely a matter of quotation). Sondheim wrote lyrics and music for a "minimusical" to a short play by Jules Feiffer, *Passionella,* in 1962, amounting only to one song ("Truly Content") and some incidental vamps for the heroine Ella, an industrial chimney sweep who longs to be a film star and then has a dream of becoming one by getting the part of a chimney sweep. The song, attractively French with jazz waltz touches, was eventually published in 1990, having apparently been resurrected for *Marry Me a Little* only to be omitted from it. As for Feiffer's playlet, in the 1962 show (performed in Huntington, N.J.) it was part of a larger production called *The World of Jules Feiffer,* the other items, all by Feiffer, being a one-act play, *Crawling Arnold,* a cartoon film called *Munro,* and a monologue, *George's Moon,* with incidental music by Sondheim. *Passionella* was used again four years later without Sondheim's music for the third in a group of three stories presented as a Broadway musical, *The Apple Tree,* by Jerry Bock and Sheldon Harnick (the second act was yet another musicalization of *The Lady or the Tiger?*).

Do I Hear a Waltz? tends to be overlooked because of its Broadway failure. The plot might be given another chance to resonate with a modern audience, but Richard Rodgers, whether or not lost without Hammerstein, was past his prime and produced music that is generally unmemorable, more than once veering toward the wrong European country, overendowed with sententious parallel thirds rather than freely soaring melody, and almost entirely starved of the compound time gaiety its setting called for (though it *is* atmospheric, and to be fair to Rodgers, the self-denials were strategic—"we weren't going to resort to tarantellas," he later wrote [Rodgers 1975, 318]—for, as the book and lyrics make clear, Leona refuses to accept Venice for what it has to offer; her dream is of Viennese romance). Rodgers's lush chordal chromaticism is a strange companion for Sondheim's lyrics, which sound less personal than almost any he has written. The two men, working together with "no particular modus operandi" but closely enough (Rodgers 1975, 318), seem to have inhibited each other, and few if any of the songs reach a triumphant structural finish with mutually enhancing music and lyrics, the title number included, tuneful and vivid though it is in many respects. (At some stage Sondheim tried his own hand at a title number, tune and all.) One feels that "Two by Two," a Sondheim "number" lyric allied to a Rodgers march, might have developed satisfyingly, but it was cut without the benefit of "routines" having accrued to help it make its impact; furthermore, Rodgers rejected

Sondheim's original lyrics for "We're Gonna Be All Right"—they can be heard in *Side by Side by Sondheim*—and they were replaced by anodyne ones. It is difficult to get much feel for the characters and the dramatic situations from the songs, for Leona's opening number, "Someone Woke Up," perhaps the best, promises us an excitement and an involvement that are not fulfilled, and the score as a whole sounds tired and lackluster rather than, as was intended, "touching and intimate" (Rodgers 1975, 318). The sharpest lyrics are in the list songs, cataloging the national traits of tourists in "This Week, Americans," the horrors of flying in "What Do We Do? We Fly," the minutiae of haggling in "Bargaining," and images of the universal dance in "Do I Hear a Waltz?", this last done with just enough self-mockery in its humor for it to be genuinely exhilarating. But a comparison of "Take the Moment" with "Moments in the Woods" from *Into the Woods* shows how weak *Do I Hear a Waltz?* is in many parts.

Sondheim's heart was elsewhere, not just in *The Girls Upstairs*, which was set aside early in 1966 with five first-act songs and a script in draft, but, to judge from the results, in the project to which he and James Goldman turned for financial reasons at this point, *Evening Primrose*, for which Goldman wrote the book. The one consummated television musical of Sondheim's career, it was based on a macabre short story by John Collier from his 1961 collection, *Presenting Moonshine*, about a group of hermits living out a secret existence in a department store. It was broadcast as part of an ABC "Stage 67" series on 16 November 1966 and starred Anthony Perkins.

There are four songs, all of them good, with an intimate, wistful romanticism often akin to the "symphonic" side of *Anyone Can Whistle* and amounting to the best personal presentation of Sondheim thus far in his canon: uninterrupted close focus on two "neurotic" characters brings out his most characteristic voice. But since a television musical can also afford to be like a film score, there is a lot of incidental and background music as well, and although David Shire wrote the chase sequence, other passages betoken a genre in which Sondheim's musical technique flourishes. Several times the atmospheric effects anticipate *Sweeney Todd*, and what might be termed the "elevator" figure, a cross-rhythmic eighth-note pattern on the piano, is an evocative sound image picked up again in *Stavisky*. There is an entire piece for two unaccompanied clarinets, a sort of waltz study that ought to have been the work of a Boulanger pupil, and Norman Paris's Coplandesque chamber instrumentation, spare as it is more for budgetary than conceptual reasons, nonetheless serves to emphasize a neoclassical containment in the songs: for instance, the unaccompanied four-note motif on the viola that leads straight into Ella's song,

"I Remember," sets up an abstraction of texture that characterizes the whole number. This approach to instrumental detail is at a remove from the Broadway stage, only to find its way fruitfully back there, at the hands of Jonathan Tunick, in *Into the Woods,* the demonic impetus of whose Witch's farewell to the world is to a certain extent anticipated in Charles's "If You Can Find Me, I'm Here," at least in its jazz waltz guise on Mandy Patinkin's recording. "When?" is the least compelling of the *Evening Primrose* songs, though it amply demonstrates what a bad poet Charles is ("Ella, gay as a tarantella . . . / Pure as larks singing a cappella . . . / Let my poem be your umbrella . . . ") and impressed one critic with the way "the bidding becomes relevant to the lyrics" in the game of bridge it accompanies (Salsini 1992). "Take Me to the World," built to carry a culminatory reprise, more than compensates by way of melodic tumescence. Not the kind of love duet to wrap up a whole evening of stage dialectic but as rightful in its inherently artificial place as a television finale (we sense the distancing invocation of credits) as its cousin "Too Many Mornings," written around the same time, is in its, "Take Me to the World" is also grimly suffused with subtextual references to Charles and Ella's doom as embalmed mannequins in the shop window. In this double layer of general and specific meaning, Sondheim passes his own test of a good song: "everything is implicit in it" (Lewine 1977, 12).

For all its limitations of scale and medium, *Evening Primrose* was Sondheim's voice pure and simple. After it he had to settle for yet more unfulfilled work. A splendidly urgent song, "No, Mary Ann," was written for *The Thing of It Is,* an unproduced film with a screenplay by Goldman based on a novel by him. Sondheim's one experience of play doctoring occurred when he wrote a few lyrics out-of-town to Manos Hadjidakis's music for the musical *Ilya Darling,* which starred Merlina Mercouri. She later dropped the only locatable song that arose, "She Needs Me" (see Huber 1986, 45). Then came what must have been a time-consuming abortive effort, *A Pray by Blecht,* which was to have been a musical based on Brecht's play *The Exception and the Rule.* Robbins had persuaded Sondheim to be counted in, and he sketched music and lyrics for two songs, "Don't Give It a Thought" and "The Year of the . . . ," the latter anticipating the cyclic frame of reference of "Chrysanthemum Tea" in *Pacific Overtures* (in it, for instance, we find the lines "The year of the chicken / There's money to spare / Which helps when you're sick in / The year of the bear / You sweat and you swear / That's all you can do in / The year of the bruin"). Unhappy with his involvement, he then suggested that Bernstein should take over the music and the lyrics for the show, but was called back some time later to write more lyrics to Bernstein's music, which he did for a handful of songs. The whole project eventually foundered after being announced in 1968 for a New York run the following year (see Zadan 1990, 115–16). It would have been a considerable waste of effort for Sondheim had the unwilling exposure to Brechtian techniques not rubbed off productively in *Company*, which shortly afterwards arose suddenly as a major undertaking when Hal Prince, to Sondheim's surprise, proposed as the basis for a musical the collection of short plays by George Furth that Sondheim had shown him. *Company* jumped ahead of *The Girls Upstairs* in the queue, and at one go and by this unexpected route all the pieces of Sondheim's professional life at last fell into place. And by some inscrutable access of momentum, his had finally become a name to conjure with, for that same year, 1970, Anthony Shaffer's play *Sleuth* was produced; it was originally to have been called *Who's Afraid of Stephen Sondheim?*

A Career in Full Flight

From *Company* onward, at least until *Assassins* broke the mold as a non-Broadway show, Sondheim's Broadway musicals followed one another with little interruption from other types of project, either by necessity or temptation, and since this canon is what forms the substance of the present book, little further need be said about them here; it simply remains in this chapter to give cursory mention to the other musical or lyric assignments Sondheim has nevertheless somehow found time to undertake. First, however, it is worth considering how the 1970s, which for Sondheim was above all a decade of collaboration with Hal Prince, also saw many other people join the production team for more than one show or, like Paul Gemignani and Jonathan Tunick, become more-or-less permanent working partners in Sondheim's theatrical enterprise. The details are tabulated in ex. 1.1.

The chart strongly suggests three periods in Sondheim's career. As we have seen, the first period, covering *West Side Story, Gypsy, Forum, Anyone Can Whistle,* and *Do I Hear a Waltz?* shows him working predominantly as lyricist with other composers (and, it might be added, preeminent composers) while aiming toward appropriating both roles to himself. Other senior names appear as collaborators and possibly mentors, including Jerome Robbins, George Abbott, David Merrick, and especially Arthur Laurents (the only book writer with whom Sondheim has worked as many as four times). Then, in 1970, when Sondheim is forty, *Company* appears after a five-year period of theatrical hiatus and consolidation, followed closely by *Follies* and *A Little Night Music.* A new generation of collaborators is on hand as Prince provides a powerful infrastructure by moving into directing as well as producing. Ruth Mitchell, Michael Bennett, Boris Aronson, Florence Klotz, Tharon Musser, Patricia Birch, Harold Hastings,

Ex. 1.1. Sondheim's Theatrical Productions

Show	Source	Book	Lyrics	Music	Orchestration	Musical Direction
West Side Story (1957)	Shakespeare/ Jerome Robbins idea	Arthur Laurents	Sondheim (and Bernstein)	Leonard Bernstein	Bernstein; Sid Ramin and Irwin Kostal	Max Goberman
Gypsy (1959)	Memoirs of Gypsy Rose Lee	Laurents	Sondheim	Jule Styne	Ramin and Robert Ginsler	Milton Rosenstock
Forum (1962)	Plautus plays	Burt Shevelove and Larry Gelbart	Sondheim	Sondheim	Kostal and Ramin	Harold Hastings
Whistle (1964)	—	Laurents	Sondheim	Sondheim	Don Walker	Herbert Greene
Waltz (1965)	Laurents play, *The Time of the Cuckoo*	Laurents	Sondheim	Richard Rodgers	Ralph Burns	Frederick Dvonch
Company (1970)	11 one-act plays by George Furth	Furth	Sondheim	Sondheim	Jonathan Tunick	Hastings
Follies (1971)	—	James Goldman	Sondheim	Sondheim	Tunick	Hastings
Night Music (1973)	Bergman film, *Smiles of a Summer Night*	Hugh Wheeler	Sondheim	Sondheim	Tunick	Hastings
Candide (1974)	Voltaire novel	Wheeler	Latouche, Sondheim and Wilbur	Bernstein	Hershy Kay	John Mauceri
Frogs (1974)	Aristophanes	Shevelove	Sondheim	Sondheim	Tunick	Don Jennings
Overtures (1976)	Play by John Weidman	Weidman, with material by Wheeler	Sondheim	Sondheim	Tunick	Paul Gemignani
Todd (1979)	Play by Christopher Bond	Wheeler	Sondheim	Sondheim	Tunick	Gemignani
Merrily (1981)	Play by George Kaufman and Moss Hart	Furth	Sondheim	Sondheim	Tunick	Gemignani
Sunday (1984)	Life and work of Seurat	James Lapine	Sondheim	Sondheim	Michael Starobin	Gemignani
Woods (Broadway 1987)	Fairy tales	Lapine	Sondheim	Sondheim	Tunick	Gemignani
Follies 1987	—	Goldman	Sondheim	Sondheim	Tunick	Martin Koch
Assassins (1991)	Play by Charles Gilbert, Jr.	Weidman	Sondheim	Sondheim	Starobin	Gemignani

Producer	Director	Choreography	Set	Costumes	Lighting
Robert Griffith, Harold Prince	Robbins	Robbins	Oliver Smith	Irene Sharaff	Jean Rosenthal
David Merrick and Leland Hayward	Robbins	Robbins	Jo Mielziner	Raoul Pène du Bois	Jo Mielziner
Prince	George Abbott	Jack Cole	Tony Walton	Tony Walton	Jean Rosenthal
Kermit Bloomgarden and Diana Krasny	Laurents	Herbert Ross	William and Jean Eckart	Theoni Aldredge	Jules Fisher
Rodgers	John Dexter	Ross	Beni Montresor	Boni Montresor	Fisher
Prince and Ruth Mitchell	Prince	Michael Bennett	Boris Aronson	D. D. Ryan	Robert Ornbo
Prince and Mitchell	Prince and Bennett	Bennett	Aronson	Florence Klotz	Tharon Musser
Prince and Mitchell	Prince	Patricia Birch	Aronson	Klotz	Musser
Chelsea Theatre Center of Brooklyn	Prince	Birch	Eugene and Franne Lee	Franne Lee	Musser
Yale Repertory Theater	Shevelove	Carmen de Lavallade	Michael Yeargan	Jeanne Button	Carol Waaser
Prince and Mitchell	Prince	Birch	Aronson	Klotz	Musser
Various, incl. Richard Barr and Charles Woodward	Prince	Larry Fuller	Eugene Lee	Franne Lee	Ken Billington
Various, incl. Prince and Mitchell	Prince	Fuller	Eugene Lee	Judith Dolan	David Hersey
Shubert/ Playwrights Horizons	Lapine	Randolyn Zinn	Tony Straiges	Patricia Zipprodt and Ann Hould-Ward	Richard Nelson
Various	Lapine	Lar Lubovitch	Straiges	Hould-Ward	Nelson
Cameron Mackintosh	Mike Ockrent	Bob Avian	Maria Björnson	Björnson	Mark Henderson
Playwrights Horizons	Jerry Zaks	D. J. Giagni	Loren Sherman	William Ivey Long	Paul Gallo

and Jonathan Tunick are recurrent names, all of them making brilliant contributions to a trio of critical successes. There is a slight subdivision of this period after the temporary involvement with less canonical projects in 1974, and in its latter part further names enter the picture: Eugene and Franne Lee, Paul Gemignani (who took over the musical direction of *A Little Night Music* during its Broadway run), and Larry Fuller. Hugh Wheeler is also a particularly staunch colleague at this time, and might well have been called upon more than any other book writer had he not died in 1987.

What is also noticeable about the second subperiod, however, is that with *Sweeney Todd* and *Merrily* it appears that Broadway production has become too gargantuan a mechanism to be made airborne by one or two individuals; similarly, the hoary tradition of immediately preceding a Broadway run with several weeks of performances out of town lapses as far as Sondheim is concerned after *Pacific Overtures,* and its loss (being no longer considered practicable) is felt in retrospect to have disadvantaged *Merrily.* Whatever it is that best accounts for the failure of *Merrily* in 1981— it could be suggested that Sondheim and Prince's luck had run out, that their partnership had overstayed its welcome with the public (Prince's always distinctive imprint occasionally gave rise to overportentous or hollow pacing and staging), or that they had simply been drifting apart— the third period begins with a break in their collaboration (though, it must be stressed, this is only one perspective on what is happening: Prince has always worked with others besides Sondheim). Instead, Sondheim works with James Lapine on a workshop basis, where material for a musical can be built up and tried out in various circumstances before the huge commitment to Broadway. Not only that, but eventually, with *Assassins,* he writes a musical whose ninety-minute length seems to signal an acceptance that it is not destined for Broadway at all. There is a workshop basis to the English National Opera's 1987 production of *Pacific Overtures,* too, though it and other opera productions and revivals have not been included in the chart because they contain no critical mass of new material, whereas the 1987 West End production of *Follies* has a rewritten book and five new musical numbers. Perhaps significantly, it is musical continuity that is retained most obviously in this latest period with the collaboration of Gemignani and Tunick (to which Starobin may prove a long-term addition).

There is not a great deal else in the interstices between these musicals. However, it is important to be aware that, once into the 1970s, increasing amounts of Sondheim's time must have been taken up with personal exposure in public and in print. For instance, he gave the first and most important of his talks and panel sessions about the musical theater, the lecture on "Theatre Lyrics" (see Sondheim 1974), at the Dramatists Guild in 1971 some time after *Follies* opened, while in March 1973, two weeks after the opening of *A Little Night Music,* came the first of several recorded celebrity evenings in his honor, *Sondheim: A Musical Tribute,* which began to afford opportunities for his theater songs, including uncanonical ones, to be heard on stage, performed by singing actors but at the same time heard on their own merits rather than governed by the drama. Both these events astutely aided Sondheim's reputation, the former by confirming the consciously intellectual substance of his art to a degree probably beyond what even his most observant admirers had anticipated, the latter by preparing the way for the 1976 revue *Side by Side by Sondheim* that in its turn, by combining excellent performances of excellent songs with a crafty title, has probably done more for his name than any other single event in his career. Articles and interviews also began to appear in the early 1970s, significant among them the *Newsweek* article by Charles Michener, with its period piece of a cover picture and its predictable but desultory attempt to penetrate his private life, in the issue of 23 April 1973 (the week the cast album of *A Little Night Music* was released). Also in 1973 Sondheim became president of the Dramatists Guild. The same year, Frank Sinatra included "Send In the Clowns" on his album *Ol' Blue Eyes Is Back,* though the song's greatest popularity occurred when Judy Collins's cover version entered the charts in 1975 and again in 1977, winning the Grammy Award for Song of the Year in 1977, one of only three Broadway songs ever to have done this. The first edition of Zadan's book, *Sondheim & Co.,* based on a painstakingly comprehensive view of Sondheim at least insofar as interviews could suffice as source material, appeared in 1974.

Meanwhile "Hollywood and Vine," a rare instance of a song with music by Sondheim and lyrics by someone else, George Furth, from the latter's play *Twigs,* was composed in 1971. Two more substantial works, the incidental music for Laurents's play *The Enclave* and the soundtrack for the Alain Resnais film *Stavisky,* followed in 1973 and 1974, and both pursued motifs and textures comparable with those found in *Evening Primrose. The Enclave,* with six or seven sections of music, consists largely of two toccatas for piano with incidental percussion; a four-note motif is prominent, and the harmonic language is sophisticatedly chromatic. *Stavisky* also makes memorable music for its enigmatic, romantic hero (a confidence man whose financial exploits brought down the French government in 1934) out of Ravelian chromatics in its "teasing, troubling musical score" (Sayre 1974), especially in the main theme with its harmonic structure of piled-up thirds very much in the manner of the song "Silly People," cut from *A Little Night Music.* The world of *A Little Night Music,* whose music Resnais used to play to the actors on the *Stavisky* set every day to put them in the appropriate mood, lingered on appositely in *Stavisky:* it is Sondheim's biggest score outside the Broadway musicals (there are forty-five minutes of music) and, seeking to evoke the operettalike high-life world of pleasures and partings, he provided it with several waltzes. One of them, the song from *The Jet-Propelled Couch,* is first heard as a piano trio and utilized in "Salon at the Claridge #1," "Airport at Biarritz," and "Suite at the Claridge"; another, limpidly French, represents Erna. Three discarded songs from *Follies* were also reused as diegetic, largely instrumental music (see chap. 6 for details), but most impressive is the complex fabric of evocative motifs; this includes some bucolic Russian-sounding material and even a fanfare for Trotsky that foreshadows the soldiers' music in *Sunday in the Park with George* and, as Sondheim acknowledged (see chap. 9), as a quasi-symphonic exercise it stood him in good stead for the intricate musical "plotting" of *Sweeney Todd.*

At around the same time as writing music without lyrics for *Stavisky* he was also providing, seemingly for the last time, lyrics without music, for the revival of *Candide* (see Zadan 1990, 162–65 for details). "The Venice Gavotte" was repositioned near the beginning of the show as "Life Is Happiness Indeed" (Sondheim's new lyric stanzas are an object lesson in how to keep vowels moving and consonants to a minimum); "This World" used the music of "Candide's Lament" and replaced Richard Wilbur's lyric; and the "Sheep's Song," its *galant* melodic appoggiaturas forcing an odd ring upon Sondheim's prosody, and "Auto da fé," only part of which is Sondheim's work, were new songs constructed on music discarded from the 1956 production.

Sondheim's next project was his most curious to date: music for Burt Shevelove's English adaptation of *The Frogs,* produced by the Yale Repertory Theatre in the university swimming pool in 1974. Conventional theatrical values can scarcely be applied to this work, given its setting, and it has a flavor and effectiveness all of its own, though it tails off with a diminishing dramatic perspective in the second part with its agon between Shakespeare and Shaw (in Aristophanes' original, the contest is between Aeschylus and Euripides; in each case, the first artist wins and returns to earth with Dionysos to save civilization).

The score is, as it should be, comparable with that of many a Greek play setting from a university pen, in that it is more than incidental music yet less than a musical or opera, and primarily choric. Most of it also avoids any affinity with musical comedy idioms, and indeed the detachment of style is such that in many places one would be hard put to guess that it was by Sondheim. Thus, although the dessicated, ostinato-based texture and well-paced colloquial wit of the *"Prologos"* ("Invocation and Instructions to the Audience," its first part reclaimed from one of the discarded *Forum* openings) are familiar enough, in general Sondheim takes risks with his imagination by keeping as few creative props as possible from his regular milieu, and far from treating the songs as vaudevillian "respites" from a hectic New Comedy action, as he had in *Forum,* in this obeisance to Old Comedy he builds up what can only be described as an authentic world, verbally comic yet ritually strange and impressive through its music, which steers well away from Broadway. The dithyrambic possibilities of choral hymns are well suited to Sondheim's masterly way with repetitive accompaniment figures, and the "*Hymnos*" is tremendous in its cumulative effect; so is the "*Parodos,*" and his ability to base the one on short, chantlike melodic phrases with foreign scale inflections and to endue the other with quartal and semitonal harmonic agglomerations of real toughness and consistency (the choral writing is just plain difficult), modally fluid yet still with enough hidden tonal gravity to ensure kinetic force, is a real achievement. Perhaps the most important point is that it is an achievement without which the still greater idiomatic adventure of *Pacific Overtures,* written the following year, would probably not have been possible. "*Hymnos*" showed the way for "Someone in a Tree."

Other extended parameters in *The Frogs* include the instrumentation (the faithful Tunick scored it for woodwinds, brass, harp, and percussion), the curiously narcotic arioso structure of the "*Parabasis,*" and the use of onomatopoeia in "*Parodos*" and of a sort of auro-visually reflexive text in the short "Travel Music" sections (this verbal accompaniment without a tune, reminiscent of the vamp of "There's Something About a War" from *Forum* [see chap. 3, ex. 3.2d], is a step in the direction of music theater). One might add to the list of new departures the setting to music of a well-known lyric poem by someone else as the climax of the play. The topos with which Shakespeare wins the agon is song itself, embodied in Sondheim's setting of his "Fear No More the Heat o' the Sun." A gem worthy of comparison with some of the finest art song encapsulations of this venerable text (such as Finzi's, with which Sondheim's coincidentally shares certain features), the song is intimately familiar in style and address and yet still in keeping with the harmonic world of the rest of the score with its euphony of fourths and fifths. Why is it so rarely sung?

From the latter half of the 1970s until recently, Sondheim wrote little on the side: the main effort at any point, be it the provision of a new musical or the revision or production supervision of an older one, seems to have been all-engrossing. Two single songs were composed for the cinema: "I Never Do Anything Twice," a suggestive catalog of sexual practices comparable with "Welcome to Kanagawa" (which was written around the same time), appeared in *The Seven per-cent Solution,* a star-studded 1976 film that juxtaposed Sherlock Holmes and Freud, but became better known through *Side by Side by Sondheim;* and a theme tune was supplied for Warren Beatty's 1981 film *Reds,* cleverly and appropriately based on the first eight notes of the "Internationale" (see Sloman 1988, 47) and heard on the soundtrack (mostly at junctures of poignant separation) as a soft-focus piano solo (it was later published as a song, "Goodbye for Now").

For the rest, Sondheim stopped shaving in 1975 and smoking in 1978; suffered a mild heart attack in 1979; gave permission for a fair number of uncanonical and early songs to be fashioned into a revue, *Marry Me a Little,* in 1980; witnessed, even read, the scholarly articles on him that began to appear in 1979 (see Adler 1978–79; Berkowitz 1979; Lahr 1979), followed shortly by a spate of doctoral theses (Adams 1980; Cartmell 1983; Wilson 1983; Gordon 1984; Orchard 1988; Huber 1990); continued giving interviews (the best of all is in Orchard 1988, 632–48) and assisting enquirers; relinquished the presidency of the Dramatists Guild in 1981 but stayed on the council and initiated the Guild's Young Playwrights Festival in 1982; became aware of and periodically visited the British premieres of several of his musicals at the Library Theatre, Manchester, in the early and mid–1980s; was elected to the American Academy and Institute of Arts and Letters in 1983; scaled further heights of public acclaim in 1985 with *Follies in Concert* at Lincoln Center in September and the release of Barbra Streisand's *The Broadway Album,* replete with his songs, to the tune of 3 million copies; wrote a contrafactum of Weill's song, "Jenny," ("Lenny") for Bernstein's seventieth birthday concert at Tanglewood in 1988; enjoyed a new seal of intellectual approval in Britain in 1990 with his appointment as first Visiting Professor of Contemporary Theatre at Oxford University and with the Royal National Theatre's production of *Sunday in the Park with George;* lent his warmth, wit and wisdom to the fight against AIDS whenever his work was used (as it frequently has been) for a benefit event; and caused two-block queues for freezing fans in New York when tickets went on sale for the new compilation *Putting It Together* in February 1993.

Into the 1990s

If *Company* and *Follies* were, above all, musicals for their time, and *A Little Night Music* and *Pacific Overtures* were musicals that showed that high craftsmanship and challenging conceptualization could enjoy commercial success in the case of the former and make their mark despite commercial failure in the case of the latter, then the decade that began for Sondheim in the late 1970s could sustain yet further claims. *Sweeney Todd* established itself as an artifact, authorially integral to a larger than usual extent for a musical, with status in the opera house as well as the repertory theater, while *Sunday* and *Into the Woods,* more than counteracting the failure of *Merrily We Roll Along,* were generally considered to have taken the musical into more profound dramatic territory than many would have dreamed possible, yet without sacrificing its generic attraction. After *Into the Woods,* a work of art of an almost Shakespearian plenitude, one guesses that Sondheim knew he could afford to relax, in the sense of pursuing what he pleased without having to prove himself. He seems to have done so on the one hand by entertaining a broader public than ever before with the *Dick Tracy* songs for Madonna, and on the other by challenging a necessarily narrower one than his career has accustomed him to, beyond the handling of Broadway, with *Assassins.* His two current projects may continue these trends: he is working on a film musical, *Singing Out Loud,* with William Goldman (six numbers, the title song, "Sand," "Lunch," "Dawn," "Looks," and "Water under the Bridge" have been written and the last performed and recorded) on the one hand, and a stage double bill, *Passione d'Amore* and *Muscle,* with James Lapine on the other.

The *Dick Tracy* songs are closest to the *Follies* period numbers in conception, given their late 1930s nightclub settings, and "More" is similar in some ways to Ben's final song in *Follies 1987.* "More" and "Sooner or Later" (which won a Best Original Song Oscar) can be appreciated as well-tailored showpieces for Madonna as the singer Breathless Mahoney; but even within this diegetic function there is subtext, for Mahoney is giving us clues to her identity as No Face—the "more" she wants is to take over the whole city, and the blues element when she claims that "Sooner or Later . . . / I always get my man" hints at her fatal weakness for Tracy, the special agent she must kill if she is to reach her goal. The period pastiche in these songs is nothing new for Sondheim, though the triplet prosody of "Sooner or Later" strikes a fresh stance. It is, however, surprising to hear such a thoroughgoing quodlibet in the verse (and at one point in the words of the chorus) of "More"—Sondheim, presaging the fusion of two Sousa tunes in *Assassins,* sews together short musical and verbal patches from classic popular songs, including Gershwin numbers with naturally linked titles ("I Got Rhythm," "I Got Plenty o' Nuttin'," and "Fascinating Rhythm"). In a way, this complements the cartoon-inspired patches of sharp primary color in the film's visual design. Two other Sondheim songs that appear in the film, "Live Alone and Like It" and "Back in Business," are undistinguished, but Mahoney's third song, "What Can You Lose," played by and sung with pianist Eighty-Eight Keys (Mandy Patinkin), is a different matter altogether, a Sondheim classic of deep personal feeling, melancholy and truthful in its ambivalence about how to deal with unsure or unrequited love: the pain comes in having to make a decision about it. The stream-of-consciousness verbal argument (ending with the inevitably paradoxical decision to do nothing) is meticulously followed through, carried with the sublime simplicity of four-note phrases (based on Sondheim's favorite Ur-motif $\hat{3}$-$\hat{4}$-$\hat{3}$-$\hat{5}$) and intimately resonant harmonies, its two sides hinged on the two stanzas and its train of thought applicable to no less than four of the characters at that moment. All in all, the song is a worthy cousin to "Our Little World," "On the Steps of the Palace," "Children Will Listen," and especially "No More" in *Into the Woods,* though the verbal and musical similarities to all these are so strong that one feels the vein cannot be mined much longer; it is virtually abandoned in *Assassins.*

The comfort of *Assassins* is to see how it connects with so much else that Sondheim has essayed. With its nonlinear plot structure and wealth of short scenes, akin to a revue, it echoes *Company:* the contrasts and variety between scenes that contain no music at all (several of them deliberately crude and slapstick) and those that are all music are kept as sharp as possible, and the chronology runs back and forth between 1865, 1933, 1901, 1981, 1881, 1974, and 1963. As "documentary vaudeville," questioning the constructs of history and stressing the relativity of viewpoints, it bears close comparison with Sondheim's other collaboration with John Weidman, *Pacific Overtures,* and "Something Just Broke," added for the London production, recalls "Four Black Dragons" in its capturing of a historic moment through "street interviews" with ordinary people. As a set of studies in homicidal motivation (and, one might add, in vernacular musics of various sorts), it relates to *Sweeney Todd.* The assassins' confrontation and support of each other across the passage of time affords a similar catharsis to George's understanding of Dot and his artistic heritage in *Sunday,* the positive theme of connection now transformed into a signal for revenge and destruction when the assassins sing "Don't you want to connect? / Then go out and connect!" There is even a thumbnail suite of waltzes, constituting the "Gun Song": a soulful mazurka for Czolgosz, a barbershop quartet, a debonair French waltz for Guiteau, and a frantic Viennese one, hemiola all over the place, for Moore; this (especially the barbershop passage) harks back to the farcical divertissement of the "Cookie" ballet in *Anyone Can Whistle* even more than to *A Little Night Music.* And the assassins' lines in "Another National Anthem" that "If you can't do what you want to, / Then you do the things you can" recall similar ones as far back as *Saturday Night,* Gene's "I don't want to be what I am; / I want to be what I can."

The discomfort of *Assassins* is far more important, however. It kicks over the traces of taste by taking a cold look at America's musical sustenance and the illusory dream it has represented over two centuries (the

Balladeer's various folk idioms are intended as the voice of "the spirit of optimistic America" [Sondheim's phrase], set against the gathering march of the disaffected, though his *Verfremdungseffekt* stance as critical commentator tends to confuse this dialectic in performance and is probably the show's greatest dramatic weakness). The musical styles that Sondheim borrows are raw ones, and he keeps them raw as far as he can while setting himself an impossible conflict of viewpoint, not a new conflict by any means but one sharper than ever before, in that as a good composer he cannot but exercise his reconciling skills upon them. This very living on the edge of taste can be seen as a new depth of integrity in Sondheim's artistic endeavor, and gives rise to a score at once magisterial and submissive, clean and dirty. The submission includes silence: two of the characters, Byck and Moore, have virtually no music of their own, and many of the scenes that are theatrically the most telling, including Czolgosz's meeting with Emma Goldman and his description of his appalling factory job, are wholly spoken. And misfits have misfitting music: from the crude forcing of "Hail to the Chief" into triple time for the carousel waltz of the show's beginning (a conscious or unconscious tribute to Rodgers's similar opening gambit forty-five years earlier)—and even into the rhythm of "America" for Byck's playoff—to its still more ill-fitting, passacaglialike harmonic progression (actually taken from "Unworthy of Your Love") when it returns violently at the shooting of Kennedy, we are faced with some fairly unglamorous musical realities.

Yet we notice these things because of the habitual suavity of Sondheim's technique, and his ineluctably educated musical viewpoint ensures that even here he exalts whatever he pastiches, be it bluegrass in "The Ballad of Booth," a hoedown in "The Ballad of Czolgosz"—(helped subtextually by the chorus's cries of "Big Bill!" one picks up the reference to Buffalo to mean as in Bill, and the conceptualization of the presidential line attendant as a country dance-caller is a stroke of genius)—the folk-pop ballad in "Unworthy of Your Love," or a kind of minstrel show potpourri of gospel hymn and cakewalk in "The Ballad of Guiteau." Nor is the score lacking in artifice. Having chosen "Hail to the Chief" (actually of British nineteenth-century origin, with words by Walter Scott and a tune by the little-known James Sanderson) and Sousa's *El Capitan* march as two presidential données, Sondheim plays with the former's title in a little-noticed pun in "Everybody's Got the Right" (the Proprietor mimics Zangara's Italian accent with the lines "Here, give some / Hail-a to the chief" as he shows him a gun), but more importantly uses its first four notes (the rising steps $\hat{5}$-$\hat{6}$-$\hat{7}$-$\hat{8}$) as an Ur-motif. It permeates the melodic structure of "Everybody's Got the Right," though transferred at first to the "optimistic" (major) scale degrees $\hat{3}$-$\hat{4}$-$\hat{5}$-$\hat{6}$, whose most positive signifiers, $\hat{3}$ and $\hat{5}$, resonate through some of the later songs ("Unworthy of Your Love" begins with them, repeated, and both "The Ballad of Gui-teau" and "Another National Anthem" begin with a $\hat{1}$-$\hat{3}$-$\hat{5}$ arpeggio, with $\hat{6}$ added as a sort of overreaching). One should not make too much of these melodic concordances, but musical sketches suggest that they may not have been entirely a matter of chance or merely the unconscious stressing of connotative scale-degree functions; and the upward sweep of the melody in the chorus of *El Capitan,* as used in "How I Saved Roosevelt," does precisely combine the $\hat{5}$-$\hat{6}$-$\hat{7}$-$\hat{8}$ steps with the $\hat{3}$-$\hat{5}$ cell, only to give way to another Sousa march, *Washington Post,* with a melodic concordance of an even more ebullient upward thrust ($\hat{5}$-$\hat{7}$-$\hat{2}$-$\hat{6}$-$\hat{6}$-$\hat{6}$). The welding of these two 6/8 marches with a simultaneous tarantella for the Italian Zangara is another deft touch; and the sheer tunefulness and harmonic depth of some of the music, such as Booth's nostalgic hymn ("How the Country Is Not What It Was") in the middle of his "Ballad" and Czolgosz's melancholy musing that "It takes a lot of men to make a gun," reminds us how difficult it is to keep sympathy for the assassins at bay when they are projected with Sondheim's persuasive powers.

It is kept at bay, however, and once inside the beguilingly comfortable vaudeville frame song, "Everybody's Got the Right," it is confrontation, even complicity, that we have to face, rather than the promise of assim-ilation. One of the show's many chilling moments comes when the deluded and disaffected Byck sings snatches of "Tonight" and "America" from *West Side Story*, and we realize that when he calls for "*Love songs . . .* They're what the world needs!" he is dragging Sondheim himself into his cultural psychosis, into the guilt of history, as he has attempted to drag Bernstein (who was still alive when this scene was written and to whom he really did send tapes). This moment is the courageous apogee of Sondheim's propensity for self-awareness and self-criticism. We are forced to confront popular music as the opium of the dispossessed, as so much junk food (which also features recurrently in *Assassins*) sustaining countless illusions, countless "lives of quiet desperation." In the Texas School Book Depository scene, as if to nail this point home, the only music used until the very end is the *trouvé* of the Blue Ridge Boys' "Heartache Serenade" on the radio. It is as though the composer can no longer say anything innocent, that his healing way with period styles is an attempt at sympathy and cultural appropriation that will no longer wash, inadequate to the awesome reality of 22 November 1963, when the impotence of the dispossessed and the disaffected suddenly, perhaps for the first time, becomes the power to change history. Even the sense that *Assassins* is somehow not on a par with Sondheim's other musicals not just because of the derogation of the author's "own" musical voice but because it comes across as an incomplete and unfinished artifact, less than a full evening's presentation, can be considered part of its truthfulness: if it feels foreshortened, the fact stands as a warning and a reminder that history will probably afford new opportunities for its scope to be broadened, its episodes to be increased, its cast of characters to be extended.

Chapter 2

The Compositional Process

General Considerations

The musical theater being a collaborative and commercial medium, to understand who wrote what and how and when in a show is a potentially difficult task, not least because a modus operandi that is true for one artist or team may not apply to others. Study of composers' and lyricists' working methods has only recently begun to move from the anecdotal to the systematic, and the results already show obvious differences between, for instance, Frank Loesser's procedures (see Block 1989) and Sondheim's. We are fortunate that Sondheim has himself given accounts of how he writes (see Sondheim 1974 and 1978; Rich 1976; Prince and Sondheim 1979; Freedman 1984; Herbert 1989; Zadan 1990, 229–41), and that he has not only systematically preserved his working material but has also been willing to make it available for study.

Sheldon Harnick has admitted, "I never mastered the knack of getting the right idea the first time around . . . I always took to heart the truism 'Shows are not written, they are rewritten'" (Citron 1991, 176). Sondheim has also had his share of rewrites, and perhaps as a safeguard against too many of them he prefers, generally speaking, to produce a song as late as possible, once it is clear from discussions, from the book, and even from rehearsals what the dramatic moment requires. This demands nerve and a rock-hard creative vision, and is more a product of a brilliant faculty of gestation than of his being, as he has claimed, "lazy" and a "procrastinator" (Zadan 1990, 230). As he points out, "When you've seen the play on its feet with those actors playing those parts that used to exist just on paper, you know exactly what to write for it" (Sondheim 1978, 28). Thus, to take a rather extreme example, *A Little Night Music* went into rehearsal in 1973 with about seven songs—almost half the score— still missing (for further details, see Tunick 1991). The late arrivals included "Send In the Clowns," which arrived two days before the company left New York for the Boston tryout, and "A Weekend in the Country," which was composed *after* the first-act finale had been at least partially blocked on the stage, a process that prompted Sondheim, as Prince recalls, to suggest "that next time we should stage our libretto without any music, show it to him, then let him go away for six months to write the score" (Prince 1974, 179). A ghost of this desideratum had in fact been in existence ever since *Forum,* whereby Prince would first read the script through aloud in his office with Sondheim playing whatever songs were already written, then repeating the process after rewrites with a few actors, and so on, up to four readings; but the suggestion began to take on added reality with the creation of *Sunday in the Park with George* and *Assassins* at Play-wrights Horizons, where, starting from acted readings of the script in front of invited friends, with or without a few songs, workshop perform-ances proceeded to expand as time went on, adding songs as they became available and even adding act 2 only for the last three performances of *Sunday.* In this connection, it is more often than not true to say that his provision of songs, like the production of scenes, starts at the front end of the script, though since he does not date his manuscripts (rehearsal copies *are* dated) it is not always easy to work out exactly when a song was written. Dated typescript drafts of show scripts are a good guide, in that if a lyric is present in the draft it means the song had been written by that point (one can see the *Follies* songs accumulating over a period of five years, for instance).

There are two common starting points to the creation of a Sondheim song. One is the preexistent repertoire of musical motifs (most often accompaniment figures or vamps) that is likely to have been sketched as an aid to setting the tone of a score (the term *score* is used here to indicate the sum total of music in a particular musical). The other is verbal notes, often made during discussion or rehearsal, about characterization, the dramatic situation, what the song needs to accomplish in the depiction of action or attitude, and so on. I shall discuss "A Bowler Hat" from *Pacific Overtures* as an illustration of the compositional process, with addi-tional examples from elsewhere as appropriate.

The preliminary material goes into a file marked "misc." for "mis-cellaneous," Sondheim's term for general sketches usually preceding work on specific songs. He uses two different types of music manuscript paper, and a bifolium with no staves printed on the inside is used as a wrapper or folder for the rest of the material that belongs with it. Further "misc." sketches, written on the other type of paper, loose single sheets, belong inside. Most commonly, the vamps are found on the wrapper sheets, perhaps with further ones on the single sheets as well as verbal and melodic material and song drafts.

Sometimes it is easy to see why musical figures and motifs are a first step. *Follies,* for example, needed its "yearning" figure (the description

Ex. 2.1a

Ex. 2.1b

Ex. 2.1c

is Sondheim's) with the cross-beat triplets (ex. 2.1a) to herald the "beautiful girls" descending the staircase at the beginning of the theater reunion, and an early page of "misc." sketches contains various attempts at it, such as ex. 2.1b. Another, seemingly related page of sketches labeled "Time to Go Home" includes the start of a song again employing triplets, now on the beat, and the opening melodic gesture of "Beautiful Girls" (ex. 2.1c).

Compared with this, some of the *Pacific Overtures* "misc." sketches may not appear immediately identifiable, while one inner leaf is entirely filled with various research notes on Japanese music, in the form of musical notation of scales, melodic patterns, the tuning of its instruments, and so on. However, much of the material on the cover sheet probably does relate to "A Bowler Hat." Three sketches of a waltz figure in 3/4, for instance (ex. 2.2a, i–iii), develop the use of semitone dissonances of the flat sixth and flat second degrees (C-natural and F-natural) over a tonic pedal that, while considerably further transformed, is eventually utilized in the music between the stanzas (see the A-flat and D-flat in ex. 2.2b).

Ex. 2.2a

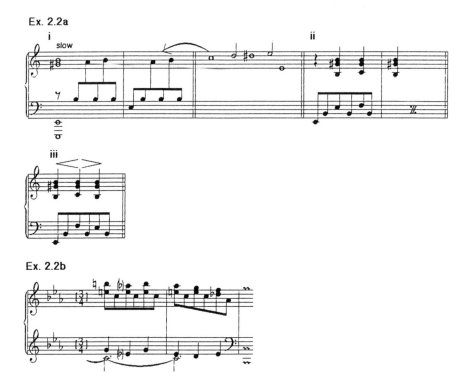

Ex. 2.2b

On the same page, three sketches of a figure with three upbeat eighth notes incorporating an upward fourth (ex. 2.3a, i–iii) seem to foreshadow the song's melodic opening (ex. 2.3b) as well as, perhaps, the subsequent hemiola figure (ex. 2.3c) and a later extension of the eighth notes (ex. 2.3d).

Lyric Sketches

The lyric sheets for "A Bowler Hat" characteristically consist of sketches in pencil on single sides of yellow legal pad paper. Sondheim has described his use of them in the following manner (though in recently commenting on this quotation he points out that the observations about going to sleep are no longer true and that the word processor has taken over at the point of making a clean copy).

> I write lying down so I can go to sleep easily. That's true. I write about ten minutes and sleep for two, on the average. I write on legal pads in very small writing, partly for frugality—I used to write on both sides of the page, and Leonard Bernstein got annoyed because he would be constantly trying to find lyrics and turning the pages over

Ex. 2.3a

Ex. 2.3b

It's called a bow-ler hat.

Ex. 2.3c

The swal-low fly – ing through___ the sky

Ex. 2.3d

You pour the milk be-fore the tea. ____

and over, so I don't do that any more. I find it very useful to use a separate pad for each section of the song.

I do lots of recopying—that's like pencil-sharpening. I get a quatrain that's *almost* right, so I tear off the sheet and start at the top on a clean one with my nice little quatrain which I know isn't right—but this makes me feel I've accomplished something. . . . I use soft lead pencils, very soft. Supposedly that makes the writing easier on your wrist, but what it really does is allow you to sharpen it every five minutes. (Sondheim 1974, 88–89)

There are ten sheets altogether (less than average for Sondheim), culminating in a typed (though annotated) draft of the complete lyric. Of what must be the earliest two sheets, one is headed "BOWLER HAT / . . . Interesting . . ." and contains notes on the contrasting developments in the lives of Kayama and Manjiro, which is what the song is about.

> Kayama becomes an executive
> Manjiro absorbing the ways of a warrior

> Both age—one more traditional

> Manjiro sitting stone still, having tea. K doing scrollwork
> M remains still throughout.

> [etc]

Possibly the heading "interesting" was projected as a refrain word or line.

> Manjiro: Purity, martial arts, poetry, harmony, karma—it's interesting.
> Kayama: Bowler hat, glass of wine—strange, but interesting.

> [etc]

Already on this sheet we find the makings of a list of artifacts, acquisitions, and activities ("pocket watch, spectacles, morning coat, pin-striped suit. Secretary . . . Shipbuilding . . . Other events—wife, etc.") such as so often provide the allusive strength of Sondheim's lyrics. The other preliminary sheet begins to put words into the characters' mouths, or at least thoughts into their heads, beginning with statements probably intended for Manjiro contemplating karma.

> All things in nature fall, scatter, fade
> Life, death, rebirth
> Death is inevitable & beautiful
> Life has no meaning w/o death (white w/o black, etc.)

> [etc]

Occasionally Sondheim will sketch a fragment of rhythmic or melodic notation on his lyric sheets, but the only example for this song, appearing all on its own on the reverse of this sheet, is what was possibly intended as a war cry for the incipient warrior (ex. 2.4). These sketches were not used, for in the song Manjiro remains silent throughout. Farther down the sheet are thoughts for Kayama.

> Fate—look where I've (& it's) come. I was a governor's assistant and I'm getting older.
> A release from rules. My position is whatever I make it. Manjiro can only move within the rules.

Ex. 2.4

Man-ji - ro, Man-ji - ro-san

The playful sounds of words and the rhythms of lyric phrases are also beginning to assert themselves.

Slow litter getting faster—Take a letter [. . .]

A man in a silk kimono, a man in a bowler hat—I think I must get a wife—a wife in a silk kimono
    A bowler hat, a modern man

The next three sheets (sheets 3–5) elaborate on the lists of objects and cultural practices that Kayama is assimilating and on his self-conscious statements about himself, cleverly doubling as the simple phrases he rehearses as he learns English and also French, and they contain almost no phrases attributable to Manjiro. The lists are prodigal.

Amer. doctor	Cravat	Matches
Bowling	British woollens	Magnets
Racing	Umbrella	Telegraph
Tobacco	Bonnets, perfume	Sewing machine
Cigars	Vaccinations	Beer
Tinned ham	Photography	Forks
Piano	Concrete	Binoculars
Billiards	Electricity	Balloons
	Lightning conductor	Bicycles
	Ice cream	
	Lea and Perrins sauce	

Despite the presence of alliteration, rhythmic identity, and association ("Binoculars/Balloons/Bicycles," all with round shapes), very few of these items were used. Conversely, what at first sight appears to be another list in fact represents an agenda of the action and structure of the song.

Book & Brush—letter
Bowler hat
Letter
Bowler hat
Tea & quill—letter
Pocket watch
Letter
Pocket watch (. . . with my bowler hat)
Manjiro ⟶ Typewriter—sword
Morning coat or spectacles or glass of wine
Letter

> Morning coat (he wore a bowler hat)
> Yours sincerely,. . .
> Fade on tableau

This pattern is retained on the stage: Kayama is writing letters with an increasingly Westernized sequence of props (though there is no reference to the typewriter of the sketch) while he sings his internal monologue, and between the six stanzas the reciter reads extracts from them. Presumably, Weidman wrote the prose text of the letters; they refer to objects and events of which there is no sign in Sondheim's sketches. Whether or not the letter-writing scenario had been fixed before Sondheim started working on the song, it provides an effective recurrent metonym for Kayama's career and cultural exchanges, and allows for the interspersal, in the six stanzas of lyrics, of references that strengthen the concept of the cycle or spiral of his life by developing the images of circularity (bowler hat, tea[cup], pocket watch, spectacles [and monocle in the final lyrics], glass of wine)—though Sondheim says that this symbolic imagery was unconscious and points out that a spiral is not the same thing as a circle.

Prosody

Meanwhile, on the same three sheets of sketches, the rhythms of the song are also beginning to assert themselves.

> I bought a bigger house (moved)
> I felt a twinge today
> I learned to swim
> I went to church
> I take cream & two lumps
> I'm taking English lessons—I read "The Critique of Reason"
>
> [etc]

So is the actual prosody of the stanzas.

> I own another   I need
> It's called a bowler hat
> I have no wife.
>   as   dips & sings
> And like a swallow flies
> I fly through (my) life.
>   against the sky
> the swallow flies no more than I
>   As I

I am the swallow flying

[etc]

However, the rhyme scheme is not yet fixed and it is unclear for how many lines the stanza is expected to continue before its symbolic rondeaulike structure is rounded off with the *a* rhyme (the rhyme itself is present in these sketches, e.g., "I must remember that" on sheet 5).

The following four sheets (6–9) are headed "I," "I," "II," and "III." These numerals refer to the fact that each sheet contains sketches of subsequent pairs of stanzas: another subtlety of development has been introduced. This grouping of six stanzas into slightly differing A and B types in alternation accommodates the lines of differing lengths and different rhymes that have been sketched (see ex. 2.5). The point of the alternating stanza types is to provide a structural corollary to the alternation of letter writing and musing that, as we have seen, had already been mapped out. All this is focused on Kayama, though one wonders whether the alternating types of stanza originated in an abandoned idea of having the song consist of alternating statements by Kayama and Manjiro. Whatever its source, the effect is most notable in the second line of each, where Sondheim plots the assonant motifs of "wife" and "wine." It is as though we see two conceptual shapes together: alternation (exchange) and a tragic spiral (women, drink, and the subtextual meaning of the word *career* as applied to Kayama—compare "Then you career from career to career" in "I'm Still Here" [*Follies*]). They are perhaps best illustrated in a diagram (ex. 2.6). Brilliant as Sondheim's utilization of this construction is, it should be pointed out that the model itself is by no means uncommon in song; indeed, it is implicit in any structure in

Ex. 2.5. The Two Types of Stanza in "A Bowler Hat"

Line	A Type No. of Syllables	Rhyme	B Type No. of Syllables	Rhyme
1	6	a	6	a
2	4	b	4	d
3	8	c	6	e
4	6	c	8	e
5	6	b	12	d
6	8	—	8	—
7	9	—	4	—
8	6	a	6	a

Ex. 2.6. The Strophic Plan of "A Bowler Hat"

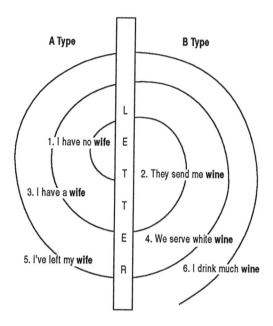

which alternating sections coexist with directional growth such as is afforded by, for instance, increasing orchestration (as in "I'm Still Here").

As for the material of the four sheets of sketches, it appears that what was first sketched on sheet 6 as the first pair of stanzas, with their metric and rhyme format now more or less fixed, generated so much parallel material for the other stanzas that "I" had to be written out again on sheet 7. (Sheet 6 is pretty well covered with additions both on the right of the primary draft and beneath it, and there is a long list of *d* rhymes in the margin—"line/wine/shine/benign/shrine/combine" [etc].) It is also clear that stanza 2 was written onto both sheets 6 and 7 before the decision was made to withhold (until stanza 6) the reference to the pinnacle of Kayama's affluence, the hiring of architects, and to restrict the references to flying to the A stanzas.

> I wear a bowler hat.
> They send me wine.
> The servants fly at my command.
> The house is far too grand.
> I've hired German architects to redesign.
>   from a priest.   from a book
> I'm learning English every day.
> Most exciting.

It's called a bowler hat.

[sheet 7]

Stanzas 3 and 4 seem to have required relatively little effort, for "II" contains few adjustments. "III," however, was more problematic. This should hardly surprise us, given that, in general, in lyric verse a final stanza or stanzas has to carry the burden of both replicating a previous structure and setting the seal on it through some process of closure or culmination. At first there are gaps in stanza 5, surrounded by possible material to fill them in the left-hand margin and on the right of the main text.

                    an opera
               bowler hat
                cutaway   It's called a handkerchief
qualified   It's called a morning coat   They call them spectacles
       I've left my wife

                             There is no wind that sweeps the sky
no samurai   The changes in one's
       More fortunate than I   In dealing with my life As thoroughly as I
contemporary
      life   keeps adjusting to   I've had a pianoforte installed
       One must keep moving with the times. One must accommodate the times
more au   ordered
  courant The Dutch Ambassador is a fool— I've had my photograph
keep pace   He wears a bowler hat.   One steers the middle of the road
adjusting to   I heard some interesting Brahms
   the time

(The reference to "an opera hat" is taken up again at the end of stanza 6, where it generates an impressive list of alternative headgear to the right-hand side of the page—"a stovepipe hat/an Inverness/a derby Hat/ a chimney pot[hat]/boater hat/opera hat/Panama"—before being abandoned altogether for the more symbolically resonant "cutaway.")

Finally, sheet 10 constitutes a complete typing of the lyric in the conventional uppercase script. Even here there are amendments: in stanza 3, at the lines "NO EAGLE FLIES AGAINST THE SKY / AS POWER-FUL AS I" the pun on "EAGERLY" is substituted in pencil for "POW-ERFUL," and there are various other small adjustments and annotations. Two further changes, very minor ones, appeared when the script was published.

Music Sketches

The genesis of the music seems to have taken place at a less even, less craftsmanlike pace, more by trials and then creative leaps. We have a number of preliminary sketches and then suddenly a more-or-less finished product. No doubt this bears out to some extent the traditional view of musical inspiration as a Dionysiac matter; Sondheim himself has contrasted what he sees as the "tiny little craft" of lyric writing with the more formidable technical undertaking of composing music (Sondheim 1974, 65 and 1978, 21–22). But the piano has something to do with it too: musical first or second thoughts and marginalia may well be weighed and chiseled at the keys rather than on paper, for every composer or arranger knows how irritating is the constant management of a pencil at the keyboard, whether it be lodged on the music desk, between the teeth, or behind the ear (Sondheim's preferred method, to judge from the 1972 photograph of him in the *New Grove Dictionary of American Music*). On the other hand, Sondheim keeps music paper by the side of his legal sheets and tries to avoid inventing too much at the piano, given that the fingers tend to fall into familiar patterns at the keyboard (see Rich 1976).

There are four pages of pencil sketches, and then a complete pencil draft of the song. One page of sketches is devoted exclusively to parts of the vocal melody, and another merely contains three measures of unused music labeled "Manjiro?" (Manjiro has no music of his own in the eventual song, though one can argue that the melody of "Poems" on the shamisen at the beginning and in the interludes between the pairs of stanzas represents his traditionalistic presence). The other two pages are mostly taken up with accompaniment motifs, though the first also contains two brief melodic fragments, one of them demonstrating the link between the opening of the vocal melody and the accompanimental vamp by displaying the rhythms of the one and the intervallic angularity of the other (ex. 2.7). Congruently with the "miscellaneous" sketches discussed above, the majority of these sketches are in A minor; the complete draft, on the other hand, is in C minor, the published key of the song. (Sondheim points out that he rarely writes a song in A minor, since his own voice range cannot reach the low dominant (E) that the key entails—in fact it is the very first note—and he likes to sing his own songs, for he records

Ex. 2.7

Ex. 2.8a

Ex. 2.8b

Ex. 2.8c

Ex. 2.8d

Ex. 2.8e

the performances for working purposes.) This page is of the folio type of paper, and thus forms the front of the folder for all the other music sketches; we may assume that it came first, after the "misc." sketches for *Pacific Overtures,* and it also has the title of the song inscribed just above the melody fragment shown in ex. 2.7. The page begins with one measure

Ex. 2.9a

Ex. 2.9b

Ex. 2.9c

of two-stave music in 4/4 with a superimposed rhythmic annotation probably related to ex. 2.4, but all the subsequent two-stave fragments are
sketches toward the accompaniment motifs.

All of these attempts at the primary vamps use too many notes in their
striving for harmonic severity and kinetic motion, although one of them,
possibly the first (ex. 2.8a, i), later appears, with simplification, as the
figure used for the even-numbered stanzas, and the last one (ex. 2.8d),
on the second page, is close to the eventual solution for the odd-numbered
stanzas (compare ex. 2.8e, from the complete draft). We should, however,
also consider how important to the way a song turns out is the *character*
of a vamp: all five of these sketches have strong and highly differentiated
characters—the first is impulsive, the second is dreamy (like a Satie *gymnopédie*), the third and fourth are more capricious (though the fourth is
also slightly gruff or inscrutable). One cannot say that they would have
given rise to categorically better or worse songs, just very different or less
appropriate ones.

The second group of sketches on these pages is for the latter part of
the musical strophe, with its subdominant pedal, and they tend to be
written to the right of the page, in most cases immediately to the right
of the vamps shown in ex. 2.8, suggesting that Sondheim was trying to
keep the two types complementary. The material shown in ex. 2.9c is
close to what is used for the even-numbered stanzas. The third group of

Ex. 2.10a

Ex. 2.10b

Ex. 2.10c

Ex. 2.10d

sketches is for the passages marking time between the stanzas, and they comprise three four-measure spans generally similar to what is found at measures 29–36 in the score.

The melody sketches are less easy to disentangle, for their chronology is a matter of significance where the lyrics, which are not present on the manuscript paper but were presumably in Sondheim's head, are concerned. The sheet begins with a line, complete with chord indications (ex. 2.10a), from the part of the musical strophe whose accompaniment is being worked at in ex. 2.9. This is incorporated into the complete draft of the melody (the version used for stanzas 2, 4, and 6) that begins on the fourth stave of the page (it seems common policy for Sondheim to begin continuity drafts and primary sketches at about this point on a page, thus leaving room for fragments and reworkings both above and below), much as in the score and with the added eighth notes at the end. The only passages requiring adjustment are the two lines of hemiola and their variant (mm. 13–18, 58–63) and the ensuing variant of ex. 2.10a used for the odd-numbered stanzas. At first the sequential consequent in the hemiola lines is pitched too low (ex. 2.10b). In rewriting this, the wheellike turning of the third and fourth measures is extended and enhanced to give the essence of the B version (ex. 2.10c).

This revision begs the big question: how far had the lyrics progressed when the melody was first drafted? Evidently not as far as the stanzaic drafts on sheet 6 (see ex. 2.5), for the material shown in ex. 2.10b contains a total of twenty-four syllables for lines 3–5 of the stanza, and this fits neither the A nor the B type. The revision (ex. 2.10c, omitting the first measure, of course) and its variants seem to have fixed the B type with twenty-six syllables. What follows in the sketches (after a stave devoted to the seventeen-syllable A version of lines 6–7) is a pair of staves that further revise the material shown in exs. 2.10b and c to define the difference between the twenty-syllable A type and twenty-six-syllable B type of lines 3–5 (ex. 2.10d). As can be seen, only a slight further modification of the A type is required before it conforms with what is in the score, and this is duly provided almost exactly in a spare stave nearer the top of the sheet; the definitive B type, on the other hand, emerges without further sketches as an amalgam of the materials shown in exs. 2.10c and d. Nevertheless, despite this repletion of sketches, it is hardly possible to conclude whether the diverging versions of the melody for these lines were what prompted the varying stanza patterns and hence preceded the form of the lyrics, or vice versa; the former seems more likely. At any rate, the two elements were probably proceeding neck-and-neck at this stage in accordance with Sondheim's preference not to "worry so much about the melodic line until I start to get the melodic rhythm of a lyric. . . . *Then* you start filling in the actual vocal line and let the vocal line expand, because you don't want it to be lagging behind the lyric" (Sondheim 1978, 19). We may compare this statement with one by Stephen Schwartz, who voices a similar concern but evidently has to look over the other shoulder.

I handle the lyric first . . . it's important that I get as much of the lyric done as possible right away, because once the music is done, that's it for me. I'm trapped in that form. (Citron 1991, 58)

The Score

For Sondheim, the compositional process ends with the complete pencil draft of a voice and piano copy in short score. That this is what immediately follows from the sketches we have been examining may seem something of a quantum leap, for the accompaniment vamps have to be forged into harmonies for the melody. In this instance, the vamp comprises a minimalist ostinato that needs little varying, and none at all in the bass, until the subdominant figure takes over for lines 6–7 of each stanza; what little additional eighth-note invention there is was presumably written straight into the draft. In some other instances, Sondheim plots a song's harmonies on a separate shorthand sketch, as we shall see.

He is unconcerned with providing a neat manuscript as finished artifact: while professionally clear, his pencil draft is written very much in shorthand, as the rests, key signatures, and repeat markings show (see ex. 2.11a; 2 indicates a repeat of the previous two measures). Similarly, ringed measure numbers are used throughout so that recapitulated figures or passages need not be written out more than once but can be indicated by referring the copyist to previous measure numbers. This particular draft proceeds fairly unproblematically, with only insignificant differences from the final version, until, on the seventh page, a G instead of the E-flat (piccolo part, m. 88 of the published score) leaves the interlude in midair. Sondheim's instructions to the copyist at this point ("Blank page, then Bar (1)-(86), then blank page, then (1)-(67), then I'll give you the end") indicate that he will finish the interlude later. His first attempt at doing so (numbered p. 8), a legacy of the third group of musical sketches referred to earlier (in E major rather than A), is abandoned; another separate sheet, numbered p. 11, with the appropriate measure numbers clearly marked, sets out the end of the interlude as from measure 89 in the vocal score, with the (tied) piccolo E-flat. It links straight back into the next stanza, though the measure numbering in the published vocal score, lacking measures 99–100, suggests that there were once, or were once envisaged, two more measures at this point. (Broadway scores are full of such tell-tale signs of exigency.) Four more additional measures are indicated as an insert on this sheet, marked (36A)-(36D) (mm. 37–40 in the score); they were cut out again in the original cast recording. The ending promised to the copyist is not present—perhaps it was on pp. 9–10, which are lacking (not returned by the copyist?), or perhaps he envisaged putting it there but had to get it into the rehearsal copy by a more expeditious route.

The draft, then, is sent to the copyist, who produces a neat rehearsal copy for the singers and repetiteurs. The orchestrator in due course also sets to work on the composer's draft or a rehearsal copy to produce a full orchestral score. This, however, is not what gets published. The published vocal score (basically in two-stave-plus-voice format) is either a piano-conductor score or something approaching the original piano-and-voice conception. The difference between them may not be great but is worth noting. Until the 1950s, published Broadway scores did not usually include details of orchestration, small-note indications of fills, and so forth, and the musical director of a show would therefore rent a different document, in the form of an unpublished piano-conductor score with orchestral indications. Then the two began to be amalgamated. In the Sondheim canon, for instance, the vocal score of *West Side Story* does not contain orchestral indications, while those of *Gypsy* and all subsequent shows until *Sweeney Todd* do and are thus effectively piano-conductor scores. Simpler piano accompaniments of some of the songs, meanwhile, were (and are still) published separately in "vocal selections" (indeed, for many other composers, especially British ones such as Lloyd Webber, these are all that is published). Interestingly, however, Sondheim has, from *Sweeney Todd* onward, persuaded his publishers to print the vocal scores of his shows according to the layout and detail of his original voice-and-piano manuscripts, primarily for playability, thereby in a sense reverting to earlier practice, though with all the difference in the world between the new artifact's closeness to the composer's musical thought and the old one's pragmatic acquiescences.

A piano-conductor score, in contrast, although still in keyboard format, tends to be several degrees less playable at the piano than the composer's manuscript version, owing to matters such as orchestral chording, additional contrapuntal patterns and riffs, glissandi, percussion beats, "fills" between vocal phrases, and the like. Some orchestrators prepare the piano-conductor score themselves and include it as a part in their full score (for an illustration, see Bennett 1975, 74–77, 80–85); others let it be prepared as a separate job.

What seems extraordinary to a purely classical musician in the overall process is that the orchestrator's full score is seldom a performance document: its primary and often only use is for part copying, after which it reverts, more or less by default (apparently not by right), to the orchestrator from the copying agency, generally without them retaining an archive copy (for accounts of the perilous status of the full score and orchestral performing materials in the Broadway tradition, see Conrad 1988, 21; McGlinn 1989, 29–30). This is because, with the rush of getting a show toward opening night, instrumental changes, cuts, and so on must frequently be incorporated straight into the players' parts, their annotation in the full score presumably being a question of how diligent the orchestrator wants to be with his or her own copy, which in any case has probably had to be built up piecemeal as numbers and routines are prepared in an unpredictable order. Sondheim's regular orchestrator, Jonathan Tunick, besides being extremely neat, *is* diligent, and so is Paul Gemignani, Broadway's leading musical director, who prefers to conduct from Tunick's full scores, which he borrows or copies privately, and which are at least in a classical conductor's format (though often without the lyrics, which he laboriously has to write in). There is evidence that full orchestral scores may soon find their way into the rental material (demand comes from opera company conductors), but although *West Side Story* is about to be the first, no full score of a Broadway musical has yet been published, and this gives a curious and ancient air of guild secrecy to the whole business, despite the appearance of isolated accounts and discussions by practitioners and others of how it all works (see Bennett 1975; Holden 1984; Loney 1984, 339–75; Conrad 1988; Citron 1991, 221–24, 249–53; Pike 1991; Tunick 1991; presumably Hawkins 1989 [which it has not been possible to consult]).

Orchestration

Critical ink is periodically spilled in regret that Broadway composers generally do not orchestrate their own music. The physical labor of producing a full score is enormous (there may be as many as 1,000 pages of full score in a musical), and doubtless many classical composers have found scoring such a chore that even they would willingly relinquish it or delegate its mechanics if they could; indeed, some, for instance Fauré, had others score their music. But that is not the point. Even if ranks could be closed sufficiently to allow Broadway composers time and resources, amid the chaos of preparations for a show, to write their own full scores, it seems a far more remote chance that they could ever be granted the time and resources to test the results. Since the Broadway orchestra is not only out of sight but out of mind to most producers and directors, professional orchestration has to be a highly specialized craft that can produce reliable results with the minimum of fuss (and rehearsal); if the balance of power and responsibility shifted further toward the composer, the creative stakes would be precariously raised in a collaborative world where, for most of the participants' appetites, they are quite high enough already.

That said, Weill orchestrated his own Broadway scores and Bernstein found a way of extending his proprietary control as far as the instrumentation when he composed *West Side Story*, whereas throughout his career Sondheim has chosen not to. Bernstein explains his working procedure in the following manner.

Sid Ramin and Irwin Kostal . . . did more than assist [me], they executed the orchestration. After the others went home at two-thirty in the morning, we had pre-orchestration sessions in which I would indicate exactly what I wanted, note by note, in a shorthand that is intelligible only to orchestrators. They would come back with the score a couple of days later and have a final post-orchestration session at the same time as a pre-session on the next number coming up. So they really executed it in a way without which I couldn't have gotten the score finished. (Guernsey 1985, 51)

This method, clearly dependent on Bernstein's professional expertise as a symphonic composer and conductor, gives some idea of the race against time. Sondheim, in contrast, has summed up his own approach in this way.

I never would talk to him [Jonathan Tunick] in terms of specific instrumentation, except in very minor instances, mostly because I don't consider myself having any expertise in instrumentation. I know a little about it but not much.

But I do know what I want the score to "feel" like. I can remember, for example, telling him on *A Little Night Music* when I first started to write it that I wanted the score to have "perfume"; I wanted it to be "transparent" and just "waft" perfume into the audience. That's the kind of thing that stimulates him. He would much rather work from that than be told, "I want two trumpets, six strings and only one woodwind on the show." . . . Not only do I not have those particular feelings, but it allows him more freedom. . . . And just the way I like each show to feel different than any other show—I don't like repeating myself— . . . each time we sit down to discuss an orchestration we try to think of an entirely different contingent of players and instruments so that it will have its own color and character.

. . . Jonathan . . . does two things . . . which I've never known other orchestrators to do. . . . I write extremely complete piano copy because of . . . my training. So most of the counterpoint—in fact, all of it except for those things that are necessary to hold the orchestra together—[is] written down. . . . Jonathan is restricted by the notes I write. . . . But . . . he listens to me play it on the piano and he tapes everything so he hears the approach . . . where I hit the climaxes and . . . where I'm using rubato . . . he gets much more out of what I have in my head than just the notes on the paper.

Then, he always hangs around rehearsals (which orchestrators almost never do) . . . just soaking in atmosphere, soaking in the dialogue, soaking in what the director is doing. From that, he's able to go home and do very specific coloristic work. (Huber 1986, 23–25)

The first measures of "A Bowler Hat" ought to provide a simple illustration of where the line of Sondheim's authorship is drawn. The dynamic marking (*piano*), metronome mark (absent from the published score), and staccato bass are in Sondheim's manuscript draft of the song

Ex. 2.11a

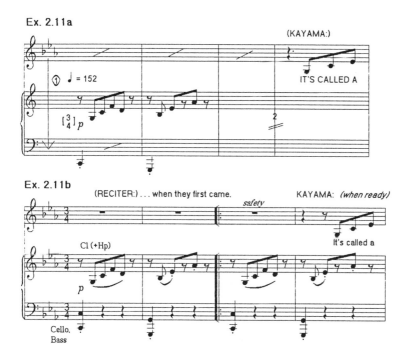

Ex. 2.11b

(ex. 2.11a); the phrasing of the vamp, octave doubling, and orchestral indications are only in the published score (ex. 2.11b), and one might therefore expect them all to be Tunick's. However, Sondheim says that

> I've learned over the last 15 years more and more to notate the phrasing, otherwise Jonathan asks me ... and then I have to tell him.... Jonathan ... has never phrased anything that I didn't specifically either notate or want.

He adds that, in this particular case,

> I put all those slurs in, and the staccato notes, when the copyist made the copy. Jonathan, as he's done in about a third of the songs I've written, literally took my piano copy and wrote "cello, bass, clarinet, harp, etc." In other words, a song as simple as this, and there are numerous others in my canon, doesn't need him to make his orchestration sketch anything but the actual notes that I've written. Obviously the doublings are indeed his.

Sondheim's point is an important one, confirmed by considering the question of small notes. Small notes are generally used in a vocal score to indicate orchestral material that is either unplayable at the piano or has been added by the orchestrator, or both; there are none at all in this song. But even when small notes are present (and they are especially plentiful as idiomatic signifiers in the "pastiche" numbers in *Follies* and other shows), it is difficult to generalize about whether or not Sondheim wrote them, or whether he wrote all the big ones. For instance, he provided the chords for the organ fills in "Company," but he did not supply the haunting solo clarinet introduction to "Send In the Clowns," as the published reproduction of the first page of its manuscript shows (see the dust jacket of Tunick 1991). Nor, as we know from Tunick's own account of his role (see Zadan 1990, 154–59; chap. 5), did Sondheim write the first thematic quodlibet in "Being Alive" or the scalar countermelody in "Losing My Mind" (mm. 29–33 in the score). With a songwriter less authorial than Sondheim, the latter would be but one example of what an orchestrator would expect to add to the product by way of "arrangement" (for an illustration and discussion of the addition of "modest countermelody," see Bennett 1975, 69–87).

A full examination of Tunick's and others' orchestrations of the Sondheim scores is beyond the scope of this book. But some understanding of the instrumental specification of each show is necessary. That each one should be different has already been mentioned by Sondheim as a desideratum and is borne out by the tablulation shown in ex. 2.12. However, the differences were doubtless compounded by practical factors. Budgetary and administrative constraints prevent the Broadway orchestrator from having an entirely free hand in the choice of forces, though Tunick (for one) at least makes a point of knowing not only the exact instrumentation (including doublings) available before he begins scoring, but also the specific players allocated to each chair, so that he can take account of their styles and specialities. There is also, as Tunick points out (1991, 5), a specific minimum number of players that has been negotiated for use in each Broadway theater, and since twenty-five was the legal minimum for the Shubert in 1973 and "the minimum . . . becomes effectively the maximum," he was restricted to that number in *A Little Night Music.* Citron (1991, 253) cites twenty as the minimum at the Alvin, but whether this is a reduction from earlier times or whether the twenty-six players of *A Funny Thing Happened on the Way to the Forum* and the twenty-three of *Company* (see ex. 2.12) were due to a producer's generosity is not clear. To add to the complexity of factors, it has to be borne in mind that the orchestration of a show changes for the original cast recording (numbers of strings are significantly increased) and is sometimes, as with *Forum,* redone for touring and stock usage. The data in ex. 2.12 detail alterations,

Ex. 2.12. Orchestrations of Sondheim's Broadway Musicals

Player	Forum Broadway[1]	Forum Touring	Whistle	Company	Follies 1971	Follies 1987	Night Music	Pacific Overtures	Sweeney Todd	Merrily	Sunday	Into the Woods
Reed 1	?	fl/cl/a sax	fl/pic/a fl	a sax/fl/pic/a fl/cl/E♭ cl	a sax/fl/pic/a fl/cl/E♭ cl[8]	a sax/fl/cl	fl/pic/(/a fl)[9]	fl/pic/(a fl)/rec	fl/pic/(recs)[10]	fl/pic/a fl/a sax/cl	fl/cl/b cl/eng hn/pic/s sax	fl/pic
Reed 2	?	cl/a sax	ob/eng hn/cl	t sax/fl/pic/a fl/cl/b cl	a sax/fl/pic/cl/b cl[8]	a sax/fl/cl	cl/fl[9]	fl/pic/cl/E♭ cl	fl/pic/cl/fl/pic	fl/pic/cl/a sax	fl/ob/cl/eng hn/pic/a sax	cl
Reed 3	?	cl/t sax	cl/E♭ cl/fl/pic/a fl[5]/bar sax	t sax/fl/cl/b cl	t sax/fl/cl/b cl	t sax/cl/[1]	cl/b cl[9]	cl/b cl/fl	b cl/cl/(fl)	cl/E♭ b cl/cl t sax	—	bn
Reed 4	?	b cl/bar sax[2]	bn/cl/b sax	bar sax/ob/eng hn/cl/E♭ db cl	t sax/ob/eng hn/cl[5]	bar sax/cl/b cl	ob/eng hn[9]	ob/eng hn	ob/eng hn/(/cl)	bn/cl/bar sax	—	—
Reed 5	?	(cl/fl)	—	bar sax/bn/cl[3]	bar sax/bn/cl/fl	ob/eng hn[11]	bn/(cl)[9]	bn/cl[5]	bn/(cl)	—	—	—
Hn	3	—	2	2	1	1	1.2.(3)[12]	2	1	1	1	2
Tpt	3	3[4]	3	1/flugelhn.2.3	3	3	2	2	2	2[16]	—	1/pic tpt[16]
Trbn	1	1.(2.3)	1.2/(tuba)	2	3	1	1	1	3	1	—	—
Tuba	—	—	(/trbn 2)	—	—	—	—	—	—	1	—	—
Perc	2	1.(2)	2	2	1	—	1	2	2	2	1(2)[16]	1(2[16])
Kbd	pf	pf[5]	pf/(cel)	elec pf/org	elec pf	elec pf	pf/cel	—	elec org/cel	2	2 pf/cel/synth	2 synth/pf
Gui	1?	—	—	2 acoustic/elec/b	—[13]	—	—	1	—	1	—	—
Harp	1	(1)	—	—	1	(1)	1	1	1	—	1	1[16]
Vn	—	6[6]	—	6	4[14]	6	6	4	6	—	2	2
Va	4	2[6]	—	—	2	—	2	2	2	—	1	2
Vc	2	2[6]	5 [6?]	2	2	2	2	2	2	3	1[16]	1
Db	1	1	1	1	1	1	1	1	1	1 elec	—	1
Other	—	—	accordion	[4 female voices in pit]	onstage pf, db, perc,[15] tpt	—	—	onstage shamisen, shakuhachi,[5] perc	—	—	—	—
Total	26?	26	22 [23?][7]	26	28	22	25	26	26	20	11	15

Note: Instruments described in the vocal score as optional are given in brackets; doublings are separated by a slash. See Music Theatre International 1989–1990 Catalog for rental listings. The options, consolidated largely for touring versions, were not necessarily approved by the orchestrator.

1. The disposition of Reeds, totalling seven, is not known.
2. The rental material includes clarinet in Reed 4.
3. The rental material includes bass clarinet in Reed 5 as an alternative to the bassoon.
4. The rental agent describes the 3d trumpet as optional.
5. This instrument is not listed in the rental material.
6. The strings are described as optional by the rental agent.
7. Tunick questions these figures; he thinks the minimum number of players at the Majestic Theatre was twenty-five at the time.
8. The rental material includes soprano saxophone in Reed 1 (it was used in the opening solo in the Prologue) and omits the bass clarinet in Reed 2.
9. This is the touring version, which in Tunick's opinion is superior; the rental material represents the original Broadway version and includes more ambitious doublings: Reed 1: fl/pic/a fl/cl; Reed 2: fl/pic/cl; Reed 3: fl/pic/cl; Reed 4: ob/eng hn; Reed 5: fl/cl/bn.
10. The rental material includes alto flute in Reed 1.
11. Reeds 3 and 5 were written for one player but played by two.
12. Tunick himself designated the 3d horn optional for the touring version.
13. A guitar is included in the rental material and its use is recommended by Tunick.
14. Tunick recommends six as the minimum.
15. The drummer was also used in the pit during the "follies" sequence.
16. Added for the recording.

often simplifications of the reed doublings, that have occurred between the initial Broadway run and the statutory rental specifications.

The most recent musicals in Sondheim's Broadway canon, *Sunday* and *Into the Woods,* call for strikingly small numbers of players. In *Into the Woods,* this is more than part and parcel of its chamber conception: it is virtually its essence, and Tunick deserves high praise indeed for endowing the score's musical and dramatic potential with such rich resonances—of fairy-tale innocence and warmth à la Humperdinck, pertness of gesture as in the Disney cartoons, containment and purity of solo sonorities (especially wind ones) almost in the manner of Sullivan or Gounod, and neoclassically planar instrumental values as with Stravinsky's chamber scoring. Here if anywhere is a musical that breaks away from the narcissism or nostalgia of the Broadway sound without capitulating to that other narcissism that is rock, and whose sound world, for all that its dramatic world lies generically elsewhere, bears noble comparison with that of the Richard Strauss chamber operas and shares something of the wit and youthfulness of Britten's *Albert Herring* and the magic and refulgence of his *A Midsummer Night's Dream.* Some of these comparisons were undoubtedly in Sondheim's mind when he wrote it, as we shall see, but whether we should have understood and been enriched by them without Tunick is much less certain. One hopes fervently that such a refined sensibility as he and Sondheim achieved here has a future in the musical theater, while taking heart from the fact that Lloyd Webber shortly afterward aimed for something in many ways comparable in the instrumentation and musical tone of *Aspects of Love.*

Sunday's case is rather different. The genesis of its orchestration was not that of the normal Broadway musical, in that it grew (as has that of *Assassins*) virtually by improvisation as the workshop performances proceeded from a starting point of a piano score distributed among three or four musicians. For *Assassins,* the musicians comprised piano, synthesizer, and percussion; Starobin, playing the synthesizer, was able with his increasing familiarity with the score to add layers of color (now fixed as an orchestral score on the cast recording), and one wonders whether this, at the hands of a keyboard player, is what gave rise to the woodwind pairings of *Sunday.* (*Sunday*'s workshop production also included an offstage trumpet, trumpet or rather cornet calls being part of Sondheim's original conception; a horn was substituted on Broadway.) *Sunday*'s two English horns—where are they used?—are a most unusual specification, and Starobin must have been fortunate indeed to have two players who could manage double reed instruments as well as the flute/clarinet family doublings that are common enough. Again, though in a different way from *Into the Woods,* a chamber sensibility is one of the things that results, its frame of reference winging beyond the more obvious affinities with contemporary minimalism to, say,

Ravel's Introduction and Allegro. Its eleven musicians also match Seurat's eleven colors.

Woodwind doublings represent a virtuoso speciality not just on the part of the players but for the orchestrator as well (Bennett [1975, 110] ruefully points out what havoc cuts can play with the orchestrator's calculations about where players change instruments). These doublings became historically necessary as Broadway's harmonic language drew more and more on homogeneous block chords of various kinds, which were influenced by jazz and dance bands as well as classical developments and for which the small number of strings in the pit would not be rhythmically emphatic enough. But although one looks in vain for any recognition of it in the critical literature, they are also there for dramatic reasons. From the Viennese period onward, the woodwinds have inescapably been the "characters" in the classical orchestra, and this has been not only reflected but enhanced in theater usage. Bassoon and oboe, when used at all, are kept solitary creatures, but flutes need to be able to saunter at least in pairs when not in a trio, and in none of the scores before *Sunday* do the resources allow for fewer than three clarinets, while in *Company* as many as five (and five saxophones) can be mustered. Thus the idea of homogeneous choruses of winds is established, just as in a dance band, even if *Company*'s quintupling of family forces is not particularly noticed in terms of block chords (for instance, all five clarinets are in unison on the tenor countermelody of "You Could Drive a Person Crazy"). And the choruses not only interact within the pit (as with any orchestration) but, crucially, with what is happening onstage. Their role is a deeply mimetic one. Time and again, for instance, woodwind or brass fills between phrases of a singing actor's melody show themselves symbolically and wittily analogous to a vocal chorus, group choreography, gestural acting, even lyric rhyme—perhaps the idea actually grew out of the chorus's repetition of the ends of solos in Gilbert and Sullivan and later operetta. Han Duijvendak's recent British studio production of *Company* by Century Theatre was unnerving when it followed this up and actually put the orchestra on the stage: the company of fourteen actors between them played, without a conductor, the entire score and all the instruments, sometimes doubling or swapping among as many as three. What is normally latent, unconsciously symbolic, became manifest, and a whole new dimension of interaction in music theater was opened up.

The phenomenology of theater orchestration cannot be further pursued here, for all that its devices deserve as close scrutiny for dramatic meaning as do those of melody, harmony, words, and dance formations, and this section must close with the isolated observations that *Anyone Can Whistle,* as we shall note, *Forum,* and *Merrily* do without upper strings and thus move one step away from the theater, out of doors as it were and toward the American band sound; that several scores do without violas (doubtless more a technical matter of juggling forces than any kind of statement about character); that *A Little Night Music,* scored as far as possible for "a legitimate operetta orchestra" (Tunick 1991, 6), classically restricts its woodwind options but retains lushness through its strings and horns; and that Tunick put the tuba into *Merrily* in response to Sondheim's prior description of the show's character as frolicsome, youthful, and zany and gave it some audacious solos, though one of them, in "It's a Hit!" is in a passage cut from the vocal score.

Literary Sources

The process followed through in the previous pages with "A Bowler Hat" represents a typical instance of a song's genesis insofar as any single example can be representative. One further matter deserves mention, however: the question of literary sources for lyrics.

Generally speaking, the writer of the book is ahead of the songwriter in the production of copy for a musical. In Sondheim's case, he will have planned and plotted approaches to the material in discussion with the book writer for weeks or months, making and, to a lesser extent, taking suggestions for the placing and routing of songs (without this spadework, collaborators can find themselves moving disastrously in different directions); but he needs to get the *tone* of the approach to the characters from the writing itself. Working with Lapine, he often asks him for a monologue that can be quarried for lyrics. Additionally, and at Sondheim's request, James Goldman's early scripts for *Follies* were rich in descriptive material, partly a sort of stage direction, partly a novelistic attempt to evoke atmosphere and meaning. Conversely, there are undoubtedly occasions when a songwriter wishes to turn into a sung lyric, and does, a speech that the writer of the book intended to be spoken. Three simple examples can be given. Weidman provided dialogue, including the opening line "Pardon me, I was there," to help Sondheim get started on "Someone in a Tree" in *Pacific Overtures.* In *Forum,* the passage "Spell it! . . . F-R-E-E" predated the song "Free" as dialogue in early drafts of the script, along with the words *sing it* as the cue for the song. In *West Side Story,* Tony had the following speech in early drafts of scene 2.

> TONY: It's right outside that door, around the corner: maybe buried under a tree in the park, maybe being stamped in a letter, maybe whistling down the river, maybe—
> RIFF: *What* is?

TONY (*shrugs*): I don't know. But it's coming and *it's* the greatest.

Tony's first clause and the beginning of his last sentence were retained as dialogue, but the phrases *under a tree* and *whistling down the river* were quarried as lyrics in "Something's Coming." (See Schiff 1993, 84 for a variant account.)

These points cannot be further analyzed here, since systematic study of early drafts of the scripts has been beyond the limits of research for this book (the issue is addressed by Citron [1991, 170-77] with respect to other practitioners and the profession in general). What can be shown in detail is what may happen when lyrics arise from the *source* of the script, when the source is a published stage play or screenplay. (Citron also illustrates this process, using a passage from *Oklahoma!*)

Two notable examples of such sources in the Sondheim canon are *Sweeney Todd,* based on Christopher Bond's melodrama, and *A Little Night Music,* based on Ingmar Bergman's film *Smiles of a Summer Night,* whose screenplay is published. This is not the place for a general discussion of how the sources have been adapted, but at least one precise example of lyrics being fashioned out of dramatic dialogue must be given (see also Gordon 1990, 215-16), taken from *Sweeney Todd,* not least because the procedure is not a particularly common one: as has already been observed, lyrics often begin at the point at which the book falls silent.

"By the Sea" in act 2 of *Sweeney Todd* is dramatically efficient because it condenses into one song the play's recurring references to the dream of running a guest house that so clearly motivates Mrs. Lovett's more and more desperate maneuverings right up to her last moments. The song is fashioned from her extended chatter in the first part of act 2, scene 4.

You know, Mr. Todd, we'll be able to pack it in and retire soon. You know, I've always fancied living by the seaside. Open a little guest house, or something, I mean, you could do the odd visitor, just to keep your hand in, like, or you could open a little barber's shop on the front if that weren't enough. . . . Now, what was I saying? Oh, yes, wouldn't it be beautiful by the sea, all that fresh air—and you're partial to a piece of fish for your tea, aren't you? Or a shrimp or two, all done in butter? I say, you like a bit of fish, don't you, Mr. Todd? Well, how about it? We can't go on like this, you know. . . . You living above, like, and us not married. People are beginning to talk. . . . How about a little guest house, then? I'd keep it nice as pie, I would. Warm yer slippers by the fire, fetch you a jug when you wanted one, polish yer razors up regular. You wouldn't want for nothing with me looking after you.

Sondheim's transformation of this is preeminently a matter of expanding isolated words or phrases for purposes of rhyme and refrain. "By the seaside" and "beautiful by the sea" are transformed into the opening phrase "By the sea," which occurs nine times, two end lines of "Down by the sea" plus two of "By the beautiful sea," and three references to "seaside." Sondheim also adds one reference to breakers, one to the English Channel (rhyming with flannel), and a couple to seagulls (which gives rise to Mrs. Lovett's "Hoo! Hoo!" and matching refrains). Bond's two references to fish and one to shrimp are amalgamated with his mention of slippers to provide the "kippers . . . slippers" rhyme (and, by extension, "kippered herring . . . From the Straits of Bering"); "fishies splashing" rhymes with "smashing." Most striking is Sondheim's provision for Mrs. Lovett's glottal Cockney pronunciation. Bond captures her general colloquialism ("you're partial to a piece of fish for your tea, aren't you?"), but it is left to Sondheim to latch onto the sound of the word "butter" in the next sentence and develop it out of context: he rhymes "I'll turn into butter" with "flutter" and "mutter," matches them with "sweater," "letter," and "better" in the previous stanza, and later varies the effect by employing a glottal p in place of the t, rhyming "proper" with "chopper" and bringing back the "kippers" to rhyme with "trippers." Elsewhere, the glottal t is combined with Mrs. Lovett's unlettered penchant for ending sentences with a pronoun or preposition to produce the pun on her own name, "love it," which rhymes with "covet" and is echoed in the second stanza by "quiet," "by it," and "try it" before being transformed in the direction of the punch line, "rest in" rhyming with "Now and then, you could do the guest in," which is a clever contraction of Bond's "I mean, you could do the odd visitor, just to keep your hand in, like." This punch line is also prepared structurally by the vocal melody, which uses a falling third for three of the bisyllables in question and arranges Mrs. Lovett's coarse i vowel so that it falls on the dominant note of the scale, E (see ex. 2.13). (Always with harsh or foreign harmony, the note E is also used for the second syllable of *proper* and *chopper.*) It is also worth noting here that, contrary to Bond's repeated references to Mrs. Lovett's obsession with the capitalist ambition of opening a guest house, Sondheim holds back the word *guest*—and the idea—for this comic climax, first introducing it five lines earlier as a rhyme for nest. The only matter for regret (at least on the part of an author brought up by the sea) is that such skillful handling of character, speech, thought, and structure leaves no room for the development of the number as a geographical

Ex. 2.13

share our kip - pers

week-end trip - pers

guest to rest __ in

do the guest __ in

list song, and we shall never know what conjuring tricks Sondheim might have done with the place names he jotted down among his lyric sketches—Margate, Eastbourne, Brighton, Southend, Clacton, Bognor, Bournemouth, Weymouth . . .

Finally, we may observe that the concentration of context that lyrics demand causes Sondheim to cast the entire song in the future and future conditional tenses, whereas in Bond it is made clear that Mrs. Lovett is trying to recapture a childhood dream, for she introduces the subject in the perfect tense ("You know, I've always fancied . . ."), makes a filial aside in the middle of the speech ("My old mother used to say you could make scrag-end taste like chicken if you was particular with your seasoning"), and refers again to her mother at the end of scene 6 ("My poor old Mum must be turning in her grave. Never mind, Mum, it's worth it to get some of that sea air in me lungs"). Not that this motivation is ignored in the musical: "By the Sea" is introduced by an underscored speech that clarifies it, and Sondheim even takes the trouble to preserve her culinary tip in another song—it appears in "God, That's Good!" as follows.

> Family secret,
> All to do with herbs.
> Things like being
> Careful with your coriander,
> That's what makes the gravy grander—!

Chapter 3

A Funny Thing Happened on the Way to the Forum

Farce as Genre

"Don't you love farce?" Désirée asks in *A Little Night Music*. Sondheim certainly does, and has repeatedly praised the book of *A Funny Thing Happened on the Way to the Forum* for the excellence and intricacy of its comic construction, which appeals to him as pure structure in the same way that his games and puzzles do. "It's really the best farce ever written," he claims, and glories in Gelbart and Shevelove's achievement.

> I think that the book is vastly underrated. It's brilliantly constructed. . . . The plotting is intricate, the dialogue is never anachronistic, and there are only two or three jokes—the rest is comic situation. It's almost like a senior thesis on two thousand years of comedy with an intricate, Swiss watch–like farce plot. . . . It's almost a foolproof piece— it can be done by any high school class or a group of vaudevillians and the play holds up. (Zadan 1990, 68–70)

For him it is all a matter of genre: define the type, understand its parameters, and excel at it. Thus, as we shall see with *Sweeney Todd*, he also admires melodrama, viewing farce and melodrama as complementary theatrical matrixes, two sides of the same coin of a basic generative grammar of motivation and plot. This attitude would seem to fit well with his penchant, already noted, for brilliantly appropriating the latent qualities of projects initiated by others; it also implies that theater can still have stature in the absence of any lofty pretensions either to taste and manners in the case of melodrama or, in the case of farce, to morals.

> What is the moral?
> Must be a moral.
> Here is the moral, wrong or right:

91

> Morals tomorrow!
> Comedy tonight!

This delight in genre has, not unlike much current literary theory, an attractive if telling air of student cleverness about it (and there are two references to students in the Zadan quotation). It can seem immature or disrespectful of tastes and sensibilities, and this is surely one of the things that Sondheim's critics have resented over the years, for it is an abiding feature of his personality and, at least until relatively recently, has given rise to many "too clever by half" verdicts on his work.

But how does one set farce to music? Farce is breathless: singing is the opposite. Citron (1991, 100) sees *Forum* as "the one glorious exception" to an insoluble question. Sondheim's answer (see Zadan 1990, 68, 70; Sondheim 1978, 11–12) is that in *Forum* he was reacting—or was persuaded by Shevelove to react—against the idealistic, integrated model of the musical as taught to him by Hammerstein, the whole basis of which is that characters quite oblivious to the theatrical mechanics of their situation sing their heart out: they do not know that they are singing, but we do, and the exchange, the dramatic contribution, is thereby one of sympathy. That sympathy would be destroyed were the artificiality of the genre to be acknowledged. Farce and melodrama, on the other hand, revel in the artificiality, and playing along with the genre is of course only a first step toward Sondheim's later deconstruction of it. It can be argued (and Sondheim's songs, including "Comedy Tonight" from whose reprise the preceding lyrics are taken, repeatedly support the argument) that in merely adding comic songs to a comic drama and treating them, as he has often pointed out, as "respites" from the action, he has already begun the process of deconstruction.

The sense of dissociation between song and action in *Forum* was perfectly encapsulated by Frankie Howerd in the British production: instead of Senex as Prologus giving a résumé of the situation at the start of act 2, Howerd (Pseudolus) in improvisatory manner counted off on his fingers the songs that had already been sung as a way of recalling where the plot had gotten to. That it was a reminder to himself as an actor, not as a character, made it a perfect addition to the layers of dissociation in the musical.

As soon as a song, like Howerd's routine, stops being about something or somebody and betrays itself, as it were, as being about itself (as all songs must be), it acknowledges the reflexive dimension in (and sometimes between) lyrics and music, and we shall see Sondheim digging ever deeper into this as his career develops. Insofar as "Comedy Tonight" tells us about what we are going to see and hear, it has already begun the process:

it is a song about the show, a simple ploy to put the audience at ease yet at the same time an audacious piece of dissociation, almost like an anticipated rave review set to music. The ploy worked when it saved the show's initial production by being substituted for "Love Is in the Air" as the opening number ("Invocation" had initially been intended for this position but was likewise rejected).

There was, in fact, an unusually large number of cutouts and substitutions in the show as a whole, if one includes in the list those made for the various revivals (see ex. 3.1), and Sondheim (1978, 11–12) blames himself for making the songs, with the exception of "Everybody Ought to Have a Maid" and "Impossible," *too* dissociated in tone or material from the farce, intruding not just on the action but on the style. At this remove the criticism seems overly harsh, given that he succeeded in providing each song with some comic plot of its own, as we shall see.

Plautus, New Comedy, and "Trick" Songs

Most of the songs in *Forum* aim to find their character through crystallizing stock comic situations or manners. So does the book, and it was with this in view that the authors, Burt Shevelove and Larry Gelbart, had trawled Plautus's plays, which, dating from the third and second centuries B.C., are the earliest complete works of Latin literature in existence (some of the material is probably translated from earlier Greek plays, but much of it is original). Gelbart recently recalled the project's long gestation with enthusiasm.

> We began the task of extracting from Plautus a character here, a scene there, and created a considerable amount of new material as connective tissue. Lest it sound like a cut-and-paste project, remember the work took half a decade. . . . What treasure we found in his plays! There they were, running wild in Plautus's pages, appearing for the first time anywhere: the wily slave, the senile skirt-chaser, the henpecked husband, the domineering matron, the courtesan with the hair and heart of gold; page after page of mistaken identity and double meanings. (Gelbart 1989, 25)

Plautus's plays, much of whose contents would originally have been set to music, are Roman successors to the New Comedy of Menander, a comedy of manners that, for all its immediacy, relies on stock responses and is conciliatory rather than satiric. Their lowbrow yet domestic routines and ideals have fueled improvisatory comedy ever since, but they tend to spin out single situations, whereas the heady and frantic mixture with

Ex. 3.1. The Musical Plan of *Forum*

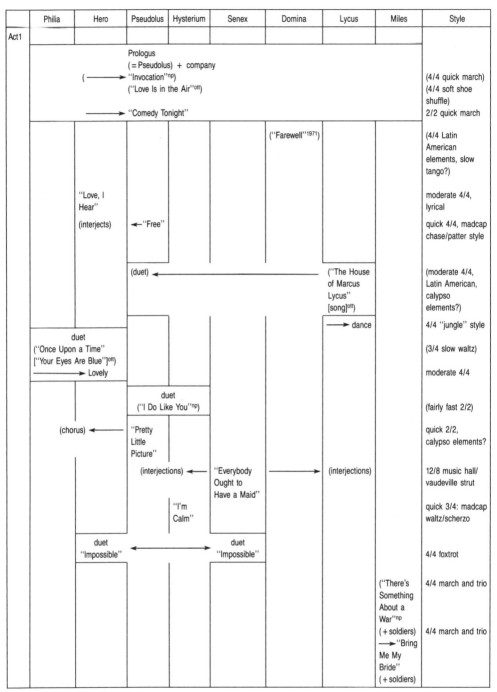

Ex. 3.1.—*Continued*

	Philia	Hero	Pseudolus	Hysterium	Senex	Domina	Lycus	Miles	Style
Act 2						"That Dirty Old Man"			moderate 4/4: plaintive, lyrical, ethnic folky? (lyrical 3/2)
	("Echo Song"ott) → "That'll Show Him" (from act 1)	→ (interjects)							4/4 Latin American, beguine?
			duet "Lovely" (reprise)						
								"Funeral Sequence" (+ girls)	4/4 antique funeral march
			Finale (Pseudolus) + company "Comedy Tonight" (reprise)						

Notes: "Pretty Little Picture" was omitted from the 1971 Broadway and 1986 West End revivals. "The House of Marcus Lycus" was omitted from the 1963 West End production. "Echo Song" was reinstated in place of "That'll Show Him" in the 1971 Broadway and 1986 West End revivals.
npNot performed (rejected in rehearsal).
ottRejected during out-of-town tryout.
1971Written for the 1971 Broadway revival.

which *Forum* climaxes in its chase routines is a more modern development—hence the need to amalgamate sources. Thus the chief action concerning the young man's love for the courtesan and his slave's attempts to help buy her out is taken from the play *Pseudolus* (though similar formulas are found elsewhere), while *Miles Gloriosus* includes the character of that name; the old man returning to find his house apparently haunted is a motif found in *Mostellaria* (*The Ghost*); and so on. The underlying motivation of the slave (however comic) as hero, wishing to be free, is Gelbart and Shevelove's theme, not Plautus's, though Plautus does refer to runaway slaves in a manner that makes one suspect that Sondheim also studied the plays before writing his lyrics.

> If you really want to keep a man from running away, the best way to do it is with food and drink; keep his nose down to a full table; give him anything he asks for, every day; I guarantee he'll never run away then, not even if he's on a capital charge. . . . Food—it's a marvellously effective kind of strait-jacket. . . . (*The Brothers Menaechmus*)

Compare this with lyrics in Pseudolus's song "Free" in the musical.

> Now, not so fast!
> I didn't think . . .
> The way I am,
> I have a roof,
> Three meals a day,
> And I don't have to pay a thing . . .
> I'm just a slave and everything's free.
> If I were free,
> Then nothing would be free . . .

Brecht would have made this thought into a cynical exegesis of mankind's animal servitude; and, indeed, *Sweeney Todd, Forum*'s melodramatic opposite, .erects its philosophy of motivation on the dialectical crux of "who gets eaten and who gets to eat." But here Sondheim prefers to frame the thought as a witty paradox against the overriding sense of the song's title, while keeping the function of political criticism active in the song and thereby ensuring other layers of paradox in due course.

> Can you see me as a voter fighting graft and vice?
> . . . .
> Why, I'll be so conscientious that I may vote twice!
> [Free . . .]
> It's the necessary essence of democracy,
> It's the thing that every slave should have the right to be,
> And I soon will have the right to buy a slave for me!
> Can you see him?
> Well, I'll free him!

It is touch-and-go with Pseudolus's ethics, as one might expect from his dramatic role as pragmatic schemer.

Gelbart and Shevelove's delight in the stock characters and situations certainly rubbed off on Sondheim, whose brief, whether self-imposed or agreed in collaboration, was to supply a portfolio of songs to match, very much along revue or vaudeville lines. The miscellaneous preliminary material for *Forum* includes a list (though not in Sondheim's hand) of different types of song to be considered: "Love songs, Reflective songs, Songs of triumph, Songs of drunken joy, Prayers, Contrasted emotion in song." "Trick numbers" are also referred to in Sondheim's own notes. Naturally the ideas—gimmicks, if you like—changed as they developed. Thus, plans for a song for the "young lover—both miserable & inarticulate—flow of wrong words, etc." were doubtless transformed into the unifying two-note and two-word sighs, with their contrary emotions, of Hero's confessional song "Love, I Hear," while the idea of "wrong words" was perhaps not entirely lost sight of but transferred to the uneducated or just plain stupid Philia ("Lovely is the one thing I can do," she sings, virtually at the limit of her grammatical perceptions). Similarly, the following notes may well have gestated into "Everybody Ought to Have a Maid," but at a considerable remove.

Two Fathers.—Ironic satire on September Song: by the time you've perfected the art of love, it's too late. Or: Giggly remembrances, interrupted phrases—(e.g. Prettiest Girl I ever—darn near broke the chariot—) all left to the imagination.

"Trick numbers" most of them are. In no less than five of them the trick is a reflection of traditional types of improvisation between two characters: Hero punctuates Pseudolus's monologue with the word "Free," with varying intonation and sometimes comic meaning; "Impossible" is a tour de force of structural wit, playing on the similarity of opposites and the characters' constant double takes as they polarize each other; "Echo Song" uses a timeless device, straight in the first stanza and with plays on words and progressive liberties with which part of Philia's phrase is echoed in the second (there is another tiny instance of it in "Lovely"); and the rejected "Your Eyes Are Blue" used third-person dialogue, whose lapses were telltale rather than tale telling, while "I Do Like You" captured the wit and insincerity of the stock friendship routine in its punning title and punning syncopations. The use of more than two characters is the gimmick in "Everybody Ought to Have a Maid," which brings the house down with its simple expedient of additive encores (themselves a macrocosm of the additive phrasing, "maid . . . serving girl . . . loyal and unswerving girl"), as it is also in "Comedy Tonight," whose lists are bandied about between the characters in circuslike parade and given new twists in the Finale. "Lovely" is fuel for one of the oldest and simplest tricks of all when it is reprised between Pseudolus and Hysterium in drag.

   In all these examples (if we count reprise as a structure), the "trick" is in the very building blocks of the music and lyrics, and it may be that this is why the one exception, "That'll Show Him," where the comic effect is outside the song itself (in the frustration Philia's words must produce in Hero and in the intellectual enjoyment her Gilbertian moral logic produces in us), has been unsuccessful in the show. Elsewhere, it is easy to appreciate—and we shall need to study how it is done—just how much grist to Sondheim's mill as a songwriter these trick songs were able to contribute, in that they encouraged him to build a whole song on one initial melopoetic idea—witness the falling sigh in "Love, I Hear" and its opposite, the rising, hysterical breathing (to an inverted interval, the upward rather than downward fourth) in "I'm Calm." "Farewell" was a later addition in a comparable vein, not just a spoof on interminable operatic gesturing but a list song whose virtuoso catalog of technical terms somehow suggests the impressive physical dimensions of Domina herself when she exhorts her family to "scrub my atrium" and "wash my architrave."

The Score and Its Profile

However, none of this tells us much about *Forum* as a score—that is, as a musical entity encompassing variety, shape, and contrast and above all with a stylistic profile. Two decisions seem to have been made fairly firmly and no doubt fairly early: that there would be little "symphonic" development and no wholesale attempt to write in an archaic, pseudo-Roman style. The result was that Sondheim's first consummated Broadway show as lyricist *and* composer marshaled an undemonstrative score, its songs highly crafted but claiming as a whole few pretensions of musical tone or design. Sondheim insists that anything more would have been pointless: "It's just a musical . . . a collection of songs . . . it virtually *has* no musical design." (In contrast, the 1966 film soundtrack, which retains few of the songs, overturned both these decisions: Ken Thorne's score begins with ululating polyphony, presumably on the double aulos, adds whole layers of woodwind arabesques and consecutive fifths and fourths both as separate items and, subtly but pervasively, to Sondheim's music [for instance, in "Lovely"], and includes a lengthy chase sequence in which, as just one of the film's many bizarre "classical" touches, "Comedy Tonight" is turned into a Mozartian pseudo-sonata movement with "Everybody Ought to Have a Maid" as an episodic theme.)

Admittedly there are scattered traces of Hollywood archaism in Sondheim's score, but these are mediated in even the simplest contexts by neoclassical sonorities, and their young composer was first concerned, as we shall see in "Pretty Little Picture," with a certain infusion of dissonance such as is built into the vamp of "Everybody Ought to Have a Maid" like a kind of Mickey Mousing and such as goes more or less unnoticed in the parallel ninths and sevenths of the trio of "Bring Me My Bride." Thus, Miles Gloriosus's fanfares, while based on modally parallel triads, modify some of them to give a fourth-plus-fifth sonority (marked x in ex. 3.2a). Pitch collection x also occurs melodically in the tune of "Bring Me My Bride" (ex. 3.2b), not without a ghost of the theme from *Exodus,* and in the shifting elements of its accompaniment and Phrygian bass figures, both based on parallel fourths (ex. 3.2c). "There's Something About a War," for which this song was substituted, betrays the origin of some of its melodic traits and had a similar but chromatically more exploratory

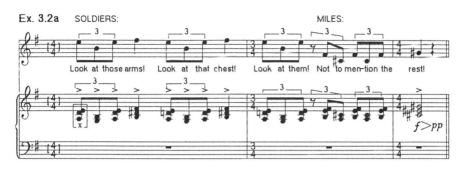

bass pattern and upper accompaniment (ex. 3.2d), fabricating a Prokofiev-like polytonality that must have made the returning melody difficult to pitch and traces of whose parallel thirds survive in the "Left, Right" vamp preceding "Bring Me My Bride." The *x* sonority is also found in the verse of the (first) discarded opening number, "Invocation," which survived as the first section of the opening number of *The Frogs* (see ex. 3.2e). Whether its presence in the ensuing chorus section was more than incidental is doubtful (see ex. 3.2f; this theme was never reused but may

Ex. 3.2d—Continued

Ex. 3.2e

Ex. 3.2f

Ex. 3.2g

well have been the starting point for "There's a Parade in Town" in *Anyone Can Whistle*). More indicative is the fact that a sketch suggests that, at one stage, Sondheim was contemplating not only reprising "Invocation" but apparently ending the whole show on the *x* sonority (ex. 3.2g).

The other obvious example of archaism is in "Funeral Sequence," with its florid, melismatic wailing and Lydian modality (the sharp fourth degree is particularly highlighted when it becomes the new tonic, thus giving a tritonal pivot between the keys of A major and E-flat major).

As for other unifying elements in the music, the initial melodic fourths

Ex. 3.3a

It's my fav' – rite word __ Yes,-- it warms my heart. __ Ev' – ry

love – ly lit – tle let – ter is a work of art! __

Ex. 3.3b

in "Love, I Hear" and "I'm Calm" have already been noted. "Comedy Tonight" and "I Do Like You" also begin with upward dominant-tonic fourths, pointedly repeated in cross-rhythm. There may have been an intentional link between the melody of "That'll Show Him" (originally intended for act 1) and the sketched song "Happy Ending," which was a further attempt at an opening number prior to and in the direction of "Comedy Tonight"; and early sketches for a song called "Take the Acorn" relate melodically to both. But surely the most significant piece of motivic coding was the invention of the sequential running eighth-note figure in Pseudolus's song "Free" (it was composed out as a more graphic but long-winded melodic thread in the abandoned first version of the song— see ex. 3.3a). This figure is present among early "miscellaneous" sketches labeled "chase motifs," and at one point it was intended that the chase scene in act 2 should be accompanied by a complex potpourri of musical reminiscences among which it is linked in by retrograde motion with the eighth-note figure from the melody of "Lovely" (ex. 3.3b). This silent film approach to the score was eventually downgraded, but the running motif remained prominent in the "Comedy Tonight" routine and serves to underline the primacy of the runaway slave idea in the plot, ennobled as the quest for freedom but continually brought low as a comic chase.

The Broadway Matrix and Hispanic Features

If the question of musical unity barely arose, likewise the striving for contrast and variety was not highly developed, and there is little of the highly charged stylistic agenda that later propels *Anyone Can Whistle* and

Follies. A glance at ex. 3.1 shows that most of the songs are in duple or quadruple meter, and there are few extremes of tempo or rhythmic patterning. "Love Is in the Air," as an easygoing soft-shoe number, would have gotten the evening off to an unusually relaxed start in this respect, which was doubtless why the show failed to work until ushered in by its more cocky replacement, "Comedy Tonight," which tips the entertainment model from revue to parade. There is little in triple or compound time, though Hysterium's madcap waltz "I'm Calm," the only song that obviously reflects the farcical pacing of the plot, was originally complemented with the slow waltz "Once Upon a Time," and might have been joined by a 6/8 jig (labeled hornpipe by Sondheim), "The Gaggle of Geese," had the latter ever gotten as far as rehearsal. (It was intended for the point at which Erronius discovers Hysterium and thinks he is his daughter.) Miles Gloriosus's original and replacement marches stand out for their acuity of military pastiche and parody: the trio section of "Bring Me My Bride" is especially endearing, and the lyrics of "There's Something About a War" would have lent a sharp—too sharp—critical edge of satire to the score.

> It isn't just the glory or
> The groaning or the gorier
> Details that cause a warrior
> To smirk . . .
> It's the knowledge that he'll never be out of work!

But the majority of the songs conform to the matrix of the basic Broadway stage walk with its attendant texture of lyrical, often stepwise melody, fourths–marching bass, binding tenor countermelody, and livelier instrumental fills. "Love, I Hear," "Lovely," "Impossible," and "Everybody Ought to Have a Maid" are characteristic examples of the type, which in this show at any rate comes across as essentially a male entertainer's genre, its persuasive smoothness being part of its appeal (this comes home to roost when Pseudolus sings "Lovely" to Hysterium), perhaps because one senses that Sondheim has not yet begun to develop his range of female characters who, as Rose and her daughters had done in *Gypsy,* may be able to appropriate it convincingly. Philia has little satisfactory music to identify as her own, and Domina, in a certain sense the prototype of the Sondheim torch singer, sings music that is outside the stylistic formula and thereby tends to get overlooked. The harmonies and melodic turns of phrase in "That Dirty Old Man" bespeak a rich vein of expression comparable with the blues in their modal flexibility and minor-chord dissonances; it is an extremely fine song musically, verse and all, and is genuinely moving despite the humor.

Ex. 3.4a

Ei - ther some-thing's in the air Or else a change is hap -pen-ing to me.__

Ex. 3.4b

[Moderato con anima]

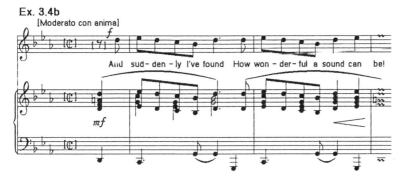

And sud - den - ly I've found How won - der - ful a sound can be!

Ex. 3.4c

[Moderato]

Ex. 3.4d

It is, however, worth noting the extent to which Latin American rhythmic patterns infiltrate the music. Bernstein's score for *West Side Story* was remarkable for its lexicon of types, including the mambo, pasodoble, seis, and huapango ("America"), cha-cha and cachucha ("I Feel Pretty"), and some influence from it may have rubbed off on Sondheim at this stage; certainly Hero's confessional lovesickness contains at least one incidental echo of Tony's (see exs. 3.4a and b). Sondheim's use of Latin American

Ex. 3.4e

Ex. 3.4f

Ex. 3.4g

idioms in *Forum* is incidental too, by no means the dramatically characterizing agent it has to be in *West Side Story*, but their espousal does pinpoint
one of the foundations of his musical style. He simply admits to liking
them, but they are also one of the stylistic loci in other musicals of the
period that has not yet been adequately acknowledged or researched.

It is not possible to distinguish too dogmatically between Latin American and African-American features in Broadway scores. The rhythmic
vamp from "The House of Marcus Lycus" (marked *x* in ex. 3.4c) is one
of several traits that give rise to the convenient label of "jungle" style in

Ex. 3.4g—*Continued*

Ex. 3.4h

Ex. 3.4i

ex. 3.1 (it is borrowed from a term applied to some of Ellington's compositions), but it may seem Latin enough rather than African when, as occurs in the Entr'acte, it is first combined with the motivic tag from the rejected song version of the number (ex. 3.4c—the lyrics were "Hot-blooded, cool-headed, warm-hearted, sly") and then run into a beguine

version of "Lovely" (ex. 3.4d), so labeled here and in the Overture. But further traits are identifiable all the same.

Domina's "Farewell" includes slowed-down tango features and begins with the same sumptuous, guitar-evoking arpeggiated chord based on compound fifths and fourths as the bolero "Liaisons" in *A Little Night Music*. "That'll Show Him" has a markedly Hispanic accompaniment figure with rhetorical fills at the ends of phrases (ex. 3.4e; is it another beguine, or do the fills denote a tango?); the figure is rhythmically identical to that found in augmentation in "Comedy Tonight," which also hints at the cha-cha in the placing of its title phrase. But maybe the point of Sondheim's appropriations is that they are just that, a font of characterizing vamps that, as we have seen, are often the starting point of a song; the point is sharpened when he mixes these accompanimental figures or instrumental gestures with vocal or melodic denotations not necessarily from the same tradition. We should not be surprised at this; new idioms in popular music evolve in precisely this kind of cross-cultural way, often in tandem with dance (though one cannot generalize about which partner, dance or music, sits in front).

Thus African-Caribbean elements also seem to surface in *Forum*, possibly, given the culture's laid-back connotations, as a recourse in the search for songs as "respites." The calypso is spotted here and there, perhaps in the rejected songs "The House of Marcus Lycus" and "I Do Like You," and in the trisyllabic rhyme units with attendant cross-rhythms and octave leaps in "Free" (ex. 3.4f). It also informs "Pretty Little Picture," especially when its cool instrumental melody, which is never sung, above a cross-rhythmic accompaniment is complemented by a vocal melisma that leads into a sort of refrain-coda of eight measures (ex. 3.4g). The complex of rhythmic and melodic coordinates that arises in such a case as this, the most abiding element of which is the almost three-against-four bass rhythm, is a significant pointer to Sondheim's mature style. He is very fond of this rhythm, and of the mesh of pointillistic elements cutting across lyrical ones. However, classical influences should not be lost sight of, and the percussive dissonance found on the third beat of the measure (marked *x* in ex. 3.4g) and developed throughout the song, while perfectly credible as an African-Caribbean reference, suggests that Sondheim's entrée into Latin Americanisms may have been through Milhaud and the French neoclassicists. This song is close to Milhaud's style, itself only a few steps away from that of one of Sondheim's primary mentors, Copland. Copland is at hand elsewhere in the score, for instance in the verse section of "Free" (ex. 3.4h), which also appears at the beginning of the Overture, and in the textural economy, contrapuntal astringency, and concomitant harmonic ellipticality of the rejected song "Your Eyes Are Blue" (the passage in ex. 3.4i, with its canon at the ninth while ambiguously moving from F-sharp major to E major without clearly alighting on B major, is especially notable, and perhaps of more abstract musical interest than the show could sustain).

Refrain and Motif Songs: Structural Ambiguities

Indicative though some of these musical features are, the real achievement of *Forum* lies elsewhere, in the absolute sureness of touch with which Sondheim the composer-lyricist first deploys his double craft on Broadway, in song after song of immaculate construction. It is a matter of building up the musical and lyric structure of each song, unit by unit and layer by layer, in such close parallel that the result offers a more integrated relationship between the two than one would ever expect to find in classical song or opera; indeed, the point is reached at which one no longer necessarily wishes to view the music and the words separately: a syllable becomes a phoneme, hence a *parameter* of an individual note, like pitch or timbre—or vice versa. Cadence and rhyme, incidentally, have always had this mutually explicatory function in song, though it is too seldom recognized or discussed.

To take an elementary example, "Free" is the simplest possible type of "refrain" song. (A refrain song is one in which the title line is the point of arrival; when it is the point of departure, we may call it a motif song. The majority of Sondheim's songs are constructed, in effect, as one or the other type, though the terms and distinctions are not his.) In this case, the one overwhelming idea that justifies the song's existence is Pseudolus's desire to be free; and it is accomplished in one note and one syllable. Pseudolus's antecedents lead always to Hero's consequents (this integration of the dramatic structure as well is also typical of Sondheim's striving for the mutual reinforcement—or witty contradiction—of parameters, almost like a kind of integral serialism). The slave leads, the master follows, though only he can authorize the vital act of freedom. Thus Pseudolus leads the melody first to a cadence on the dominant note (B), which nonetheless has to be supplied by Hero after Pseudolus has deflected it down the octave as well as down to A-sharp. But the real goal for the word must be the upper tonic (a sort of symbolization of the exclamation mark), eventually reached with a fair amount of Beethoven-like repetition and cadential augmentation, the verbal equivalent of which is Pseudolus's insistence that Hero spell it out "the long way" (here the note shares meaning not just on the level of the word or syllable but even the letter); perhaps Sondheim had the psychological program of Beethoven's Fifth Symphony—that is, its concern with destiny and liberty—somewhere at the back of his mind. This upper tonic goal is reached through Pseudolus's climbing scale figures (see *x* in ex. 3.3b), modulating with the help of the A-sharp's enharmonic reinterpretation, but Pseudolus himself only anticipates the note (and the word) in passing; again it is Hero who caps it (literally, if we use the Schenkerian notation that, I hope, clarifies the discussion—see ex. 3.5a). This deals with the chorus, and its antecedent-consequent structure is mirrored in macrocosm when we note that, in the verse, the word *free* is led up to repeatedly but never sung—thus, to identify another point, the verse mediates between dialogue and song, for although Hero speaks the word, its melodic and rhythmic clothing are not yet supplied.

Is this melopoetic structural reinforcement extremely clever or extremely elementary? It is more likely to be found in a nursery rhyme than a *Lied,* but we may nevertheless be wrong to ask this question if the high level of redundancy between music and lyrics that Sondheim's art involves is taken as the initial desideratum not of a double art but of a single one that then goes on to set its own aesthetic agenda when it departs from such unity. Rich ambiguities very soon arise in precisely this context and are mutually influential in his musical and lyric structures; those found in the one will resolve, confirm, or increase those of the other. Ambiguity has interested analysts in both literature and music (see, for instance, Empson on poetry, Dunsby on the music of Brahms), and it is potentially rewarding to journey into the unmapped terrain where they are fused. The problem is that we scarcely have a technical formula for measuring the quantities of ambiguity, the flux and degrees between similarity and difference, regularity and irregularity, fulfillment of expectation and its frustration, that have given rise (in music) to methods of analysis such as Leonard Meyer's "implication-realization" model, let alone an aesthetic one for the qualitative evaluation of their use upon which a great deal of high criticism relies.

Others have taken up this problem, and it may be permissible in the present context to leave some of the presumptions of analysis undefined and its ends unjustified while taking its virtues for granted. Be that as it may, in "I'm Calm" we can see how Sondheim deals with a "motif" song, its title this time of two syllables, and introduces ambiguities virtually from the smallest elements upward.

The constructional cell that forms the title could hardly be more basic: two notes, upbeat dominant to downbeat tonic of double length, form virtually a model antecedent-consequent of tonal grammar (they are anticipated and for a while treated as an ostinato in the pizzicato bass; this suggests that they may also serve an illustrative function, as Hysterium's frantic heartbeat). They articulate two equally basic one-syllable words,

Ex. 3.5a

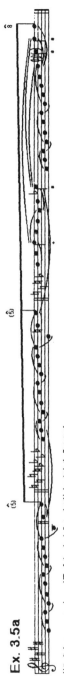

(5) (5) (5) (8)

(All tailed notes are set to the word "Free", though + indicates that this is only in the first strophe and * that it and the other event shown are only in the second. Pseudolus has downward stems. Here upward.)

Ex. 3.5b

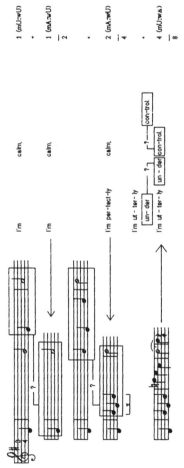

I'm   calm,

I'm   calm,

I'm per-fect-ly   calm,

I'm ut-ter-ly
   un-der   ?   con-trol.
I'm ut-ter-ly un-der con-trol

1 (mU:ʍU)

1 (mA:ʍU)
    2

2 (mA:ʍU)
    4

4 (mU:ʍʌ)
    8

Ex. 3.5c

Ex. 3.5d

[Allegro]

For I'm loved ___ by a pret-ty ___ won - der - ful boy!

though straight away the analysis falls into difficulties if we say that they
are a verbal equivalent of the notes in the form of subject and predicate,
noun phrase plus verb phrase, because, strictly speaking, the verb is elided
into the first word. Still, in other respects the equivalence between the
notes and the syllables seems to hold: they are as closely and as simply
related, grammatically, as they could be, the first is shorter in letters and
phonemes (the second begins with a consonant and masses two end consonants together), and they share an end consonant, analogous in a way
to timbral congruity in the notes (where it would be a matter of end
transient). We can say that until this point, for one measure, there is a
striking unambiguity (U) in and between music (m) and words (w):

$$1 \ (mU{:}wU).$$

The verbal phrase is then repeated exactly, but the musical figure is varied,
being repeated up a tone. How do we decide whether this constitutes
similarity or difference? The question involves thorny logic. Even identical
repetition, like the birth of identical twins, involves a difference in time:
one statement is antecedent, the other consequent; conversely, there is no
such thing as complete dissimilarity, "for events which are perceived
independently have at least that quality in common" (Dunsby 1981, 6;
see 3–9 for further discussion and for the algebraic shorthand that
suggested the system adopted in the present analysis, which is nevertheless
quite different). Here the repetition is rhythmically and intervallically the
same but different in pitch level. Dunsby calls this "reinforcing . . . melodic
non-opposition" (1981, 6), but we may see it as a basic form of musical
ambiguity. It is shown as such in ex. 3.5b, a diagram laid out on
distributional lines (anything in vertical alignment is to be construed as
equivalent, thus vertical "columns" constitute motivic elements; normal
left-to-right and top-to-bottom reading, of the words and music separately,
gives the full sequence of material, ambiguity being represented by the
double appearance of boxed matter). Thus, in this measure, the identical
text resolves the musical ambiguity in the direction of repetition:

$$1 \ (mA{:}wU).$$

The next verbal phrase is an expansion of the first to five syllables, and
it accompanies an expansion of the melodic phrase to five notes occupying
two measures. But how is the melodic phrase expanded—from the first
three notes of the tune (D, G, E), thus as a variant, an intervallic
expansion and rhythmic division of the first *two* measures, the new
stopping point, D, being the equivalent of the earlier A, or as a composing-

out of the initial two-note cell of *one* measure over a greater length of time and greater intervallic range? The structure of the text, with the inserted word *perfectly,* suggests the latter interpretation; thus we listen as follows:

2 (mA:wU)

Then comes a phrase whose text expands to eight syllables, its melody to four measures, cadentially end-stopped after three (in other words, when such a cadence is at hand, what is still heard as a four-measure phrase requires only three poetic feet, a fundamental point of lyrical construction that tends to be ignored by prosodists). Here the music does not seriously encourage more than one interpretation: the phrase is an internal expansion of the previous one, the trope occurring before its final note. This time, however, the verbal expansion is ambiguous: if "utterly" is a reinforcing variant of "perfectly," do we then hear "under," beginning with the same vowel as "utterly," as a further, progressive variation, or as something new? The music suggests the latter, though both words have a descended quarter-note E for their second syllable. Further, do we dissociate "control" from "calm" (it has two syllables and does not rhyme) or seek identity in the presence and positioning of the *c* and the *l* (even though the *c* is one note earlier than in the monosyllabic *calm*)? The music hardly resolves these ambiguities on the smallest level, but on the four-measure level it surely does so in the latter direction, with "utterly under" as a single internal expansion of the verbal motif. Thus, the formula is

4 (mU:wA).

The overall pattern of these quadratically expanding opening phrases is continued, and the next eight measures operate as a single musical unit. However, it is end-stopped after four measures (the dominant pedal in the accompaniment confirms this interpretation while paradoxically lengthening the phrase to twelve measures), and this causes conflict, as we shall see. It is built as a chain of musical motifs sequentially derived from *x* (ex. 3.5b), and like all the other phrases so far it begins on an upbeat quarter note with the word *I.* At its end, the progressive variation away from the motivic fourth with which the song began is redressed with an inverted fourth. The text likewise ties back in to a point nearer to where it started, with the initial grammatical proposition but a different verb ("I stroll") that, rhyming with the previous phrase, emphasizes the cumulative growth of phrase lengths (the number of quarter notes, hence syllables, in each phrase before the final long note has been 1, 1, 4, 7, 13), while being not quite as chainlike as the melody (the chain links are confined to the assonance of the *w* and *u* sounds in "worry . . . where . . . others . . . hurry"). All this is logical enough, but the problem—the ambiguity—is that it conflicts with our expectations of phrase balance in the music and parallelism of metric couplets in the lyrics, and in this respect constitutes irregularity; in fact, it is comic logic, as we can see if we indulge in a little counterfactual analysis. This time we expect the expanding melody to come up with an eight-measure phrase full of quarter notes, rhythmically as shown in ex. 3.5c (this is what Sondheim eventually writes in the instrumental coda to the song); verbally, the parallel expectation is for something like the following, with its increased momentum of poetic feet.

> I'm calm, I'm calm,/I'm perfectly calm,
> I'm utterly under control.
> I haven't a worry,/[I'm not in a flurry,]
> Where others would hurry, I stroll.

In both media, what Sondheim actually gives us at this point is, in contrast, something foreshortened, tripping up to a premature cadence. Thus, in these measures, words and music both exhibit, to a certain extent in mutual reinforcement, another kind of ambiguity, not of two heard meanings but of one heard meaning that goes against expectation. This can be expressed as

$$8 \text{ (mA:wA)},$$

and gives the following overall pattern so far,

$$1 \text{ (mU:wU)}$$
$$+$$
$$\mathit{1} \text{ (mA:wU)}$$
$$2$$
$$+$$
$$\mathit{2} \text{ (mA:wU)}$$
$$4$$
$$+$$
$$\mathit{4} \text{ (mU:wA)}$$
$$8$$
$$+$$
$$\mathit{8} \text{ (mA:wA)}$$
$$16 \, [+4].$$

The Meaning of Song Construction

Such analysis soon becomes exhausting rather than exhaustive. What can we conclude from it?

First, that Sondheim constructs both his lyrics and his melodies very tightly, on small motifs, and that when they run in close parallel this mutual reinforcement enhances our appreciation of his craft. We should not be too pious about this, for at the practical end of the aesthetic spectrum it is the job of a popular composer to build a song around a simple title and find notes to match; this is, after all, one definition of commercial memorability, if it enables the purchaser to remember what the song is called. At the other end, however, Sondheim's parallel structures often leave us marveling at what clever things he does with words and with notes too. This capacity is perhaps at its most striking when he uses parallel ambiguity to close a structure. "I Feel Pretty" from *West Side Story* is a good example: Bernstein had provided a melody whose initial motif stopped short with a Scotch-snap (or rather Hispanic-snap) rhythm; but at the culmination of the tune, the rhythm led on into the final cadence tag. Sondheim managed to match this by transforming the adjective *pretty*, which accompanies the rhythm, into an adverb ("pretty wonderful boy") at this point, while delaying the outcome with ghosts of suspense at the exhilarating *Luftpausen* that the dance tune invites (see the caesuras in ex. 3.5d—for a brief moment we wonder how long the extension will prove, and whether the sense is still adjectival: "pretty one"; or, indeed, in retrospect, "pretty, wonderful boy"). Another Scotch-snap example, more profound in its denotations, is the use of the word *going* in "Good Thing Going" from *Merrily We Roll Along*. While the sense is outgoing, "going on," the melodic motif is an upward $\hat{5}$-$\hat{6}$ musical step of a tone. Musical closure is effected by inverting it, twice, through a downward pentatonic scale to the tonic: $\hat{6}$-$\hat{5}$-$\hat{3}$-$\hat{2}$-$\hat{1}$. Dramatic closure is likewise effected by a parallel reversal of the sense of the word: it becomes "going, going, gone." This is rhyme (in fact, almost a pun) at its most potent, for the difference in sense is huge while the difference in sound is phonemically infinitesimal, involving only a doubling of the letter *g* between the end of one word and the beginning of the next. Given the underlying theme of the loss of innocence, the yoking of this double reversal with the pentatonic scale gains added piquancy.

Second, we conclude that low-level ambiguities in the one medium against low-level unambiguities in the other, while part of the general aesthetic flux, are not of great consequence. Within the regular pattern of their growth over at least the first eight measures, the musical and verbal phrases of "I'm Calm" give the effect of a frictionless unity between melody and lyric, and the low-level ambiguities discussed above are scarcely noticed, tending to counterbalance and annul each other, especially in view of the rapid tempo of the song.

Third, we can demonstrate that low-level ambiguities in the one medium against high-level unambiguities in the other are of much greater consequence. Given the nature of musical, especially strophic, repetition, this applies particularly when high-level unambiguities in the music (exact repeats of sections or strophes) coincide with low-level ambiguities in the lyric (small changes of phrasing, hence large changes of meaning, at parallel points in the metric or stanzaic mold). There are two striking examples of this in "I'm Calm." Musically its form is A A¹ B A², and when the A section comes around for the second time the lyrics are as follows.

> I'm calm, I'm cool,
> A gibbering fool

The first time around the melody there was a comma at this point, and if we supply it again, in expectation, the effect on the sense is comically disastrous, for we need the continuation "... Is something I never become." The other example concerns the chain-link quarter-note phrase (shown in ex. 3.5c). Last time around, the verbal attempt to match the musical repetitions, while never strict in the first place, is broken off in midstream with a sudden fracture of meaning: "let nothing confuse me, or faze me," is followed not by another infinitive but, with a play on grammar, by an aside in the imperative mode, "Excuse me," as Hysterium yawns (the point is emphasized by the breaking up of the phrase into three-note motifs punctuated by the yawns, marked in the score).

The destiny of this third conclusion is quite simple: that while it is the business of music to create ambiguities as a matter of serious taste (we do not normally expect to laugh at a sequence or an interrupted cadence), the business of lyrics is to create wit by similar means. I shall discuss further ramifications of this in due course, including Sondheim's penchant for "list" songs, but since the dissection of humor is commonly perceived as a fool's errand, a halt will now be called.

The Whole Song

It behooves us nevertheless to attempt some kind of analysis of an entire song. Sondheim the composer-lyricist knew uncommonly well what he was doing with structure in the songs of *Forum,* and no better example will be found than "Comedy Tonight." It shares elements of both motif

Ex. 3.6a

and refrain song types, as we can appreciate if we imagine its title to have been "Something": ex. 3.6a shows how the use of the two-note dominant-tonic musical cell starting off alongside this key word makes obvious and unproblematic sense. I have earlier remarked on the motif's immediate repetition in cross-rhythm; it results from its syncopation in measure 1 and offers our first ambiguity, a momentary feeling of triple time. It is surely the melodic equivalent of verbal wit: as incongruity, surprise, anticlimax, the momentary wrong-footing of semantics, musical pun (compare "Weighty affairs will just have to wait" in the lyrics)—call it what you will—it is an essential identifier of the Broadway matrix in both media (I shall return to its implications in chap. 7). As such, it is also our first confirmation that we are witnessing "comedy tonight." In the diagram shown in ex. 3.6b, the antecedent-consequent relationship of these cross-rhythmic initial statements of the two-note cell is shown by the x and y brackets at the lowest (most local) level of structure (a); the same cross-rhythm returns as concomitant to the refrain "A comedy tonight," and at the beginning of the release. The first y phrase, however, as also shown on the second system of ex. 3.6a, is not just a rhythmic reinterpretation of its antecedent x but a positive, "optimistic" expansion of it, upward by one step and one note. Here, effectively, is our second confirmation of joy and comedy, which is therefore in a sense already "familiar," the word to which the extended musical gesture is sung. On the second level of phrasing and structure of both words and music (b in ex. 3.6b), this double "familiarity" is immediately overturned, by the contrasting word *peculiar* and the contrasting downward turn of the melody

Ex. 3.6b

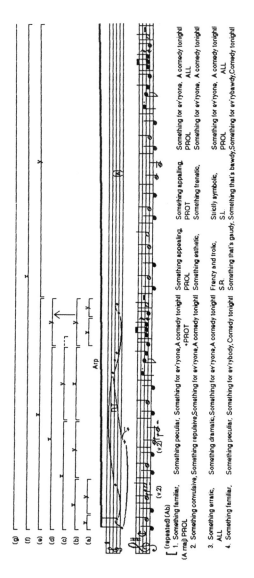

Ex. 3.6b—Continued

(h)

release (new register)

(c)

(b)

(a)

(repeat instrumental)
Nothing with kings, Nothing with crowns, Bring on the lovers, liars and clowns!   New complications,   Nothing portentous or polite,_   (repeat: PROT) Tragedy tomorrow,_   PROL)
PROT   Old situations,   PROL   PROL   ALL   Comedy tonight!
PROL
Nothing with Gods, Nothing with Fate,   Weighty affairs will just have to wait,_   Nothing that's formal,   Nothing that's normal, No recitations to recite!   Open up the curtain,_   Comedy tonight!

/ / / / / / / / / / / / / / / / / / / /
(instrumental)
MILES   DOM   PROL   1ST 1/2   PROL   --- Anything you ask for--- Comedy tonight!
Nothing that's grim, Nothing that's Greek. She plays 'Medea 'later this week!   Stunning surprises,   Cunning disguises,   2ND 1/2   Hundreds of actors out of sight!_   ALL
(Ab)
5:7 No royal curse, No Trojan horse, ‡ And a happy ending, of course!_   Goodness and badness, Man in his madness, this time it all turns out alright!_   Tragedy tomorrow, || Comedy tonight!

(One, Two, Three!)

*ERR
Pantaloons and tunics,
SENEX
Courtesans and eunuchs,
DOM
Funerals and chases,
LYCUS
Baritones and basses,
PHIL   HERO
Pandarers, Phi-
     HYST
lancerers, Cu-
     MILES
Ti-
pidly,   LYCUS
midly,   Mi-   -stakes,
     ERR
Fakes,
     PHIL
Rhymes,
     DOM
Mimes,
     PROL
Tumblers,
grumblers,
tumblers,
bumblers, (now to v.5)

with its new, hollow interval of a third. The fact that we are not dealing with rhymes here actually draws attention to the motivic development and contrast in the music, shown by the lateral columns in ex. 3.6a: it emphasizes the lack of connection between the two verbal sounds, with their different consonants and vowels. The contrast between bright and hollow vowels continues in this way as far as "kings ... crowns" in stanza 1. With their second conjunction, however ("appealing ... appalling"), the overall similarity of sound is increased while the difference of sense is very much greater. Thus, even within such confines as these, particularly when words and notes are yoked, it is never a simple or absolute matter of similarity or difference.

This, if we may pause for a moment to consider what it is we are building up, is why the antecedent-consequent x and y are probably the only serviceable representation of our perception. Neither necessarily dominates the other on any particular level (this rules out representation by a more conventional tree diagram), but they coexist, balance, and complement each other and order each other in time, then join to be governed as a unit by some higher level entity. What happens when words and music set up ambiguities between each other has already been examined; here the attempt is to represent them working together, just as, say, melody and harmony or even pitch and tone color must, toward an overall perception of formal structure that applies to both media, whatever ambiguities and tensions between them have to be subsumed on the way. It may be that the antecedent-consequent pairings and their levels is the only way of doing this.

The reductive representation of the melodic structure of the song, on the other hand, shown on the stave above the actual tune, has little to offer our understanding of the lyrics beyond confirming the role of the refrain, as we shall see, and highlighting the long-term planning (level f in the diagram) of the beginning of the release as a fulcrum of the strophe. (Melodically, this fulcrum sets up the higher octave register, scale degree $\hat{5}$ from which the final structural descent will begin, and everything preceding it can be heard as a kind of preparatory G major arpeggiation, as the diagram shows and as is then repeated more overtly in the return of the A section at the words *old situations;* verbally, it marks the high-level change from the enumeration of "Something"'s [comedy] to that of "Nothing"'s [tragedy].)

To return to our x's and y's, it is obvious that the whole song thrives on them in the lyrics: "convulsive ... repulsive," "formal ... normal," "kings ... crowns," "Something ... Nothing," and so on. Insofar as Sondheim, setting up his opening number, has to be concerned with the contrast between comedy and tragedy, one might expect these two opposites to be kept pretty separate in the song; but, bearing in mind the many different levels of phrasing and structure and the observations made earlier about complementarity, we are in fact hardly concerned whether, for instance, "convulsive" and "repulsive" are to be understood as representing comedy and tragedy or as two aspects of comedy, any more than we are that "gaudy" and "bawdy" do not necessarily contrast at all. The point is that the pairs are immediately and repeatedly synthesized in the verbal phrase "Something for everyone," just as the upward and stepwise movement of the x on level b is simultaneously synthesized with the downward third of its y (see ex. 3.6a) to produce a new structure at level c. This in turn points us forward to what the "something," of which the pairs of adjectives are constituents, is: a comedy; hence at the next level, d, the refrain phrase complements six measures of x with two of y. (Notice that here and elsewhere the structure can be further reinforced or, in some cases, modified by the distribution of characters singing the melody—in this case the Proteans join in at this point in stanza 2.) This y, as ex. 3.6b indicates, has come up from the lower level (b), and refrains or title lines (they may often be equated) have a structural propensity to do this, which is really their object (Citron [1991, 61–62] points out that, as here, the end of the first quatrain is the most common place to find a song's title).

The more there is of straightforward repetition in a musical form, the greater the amount of redundancy of information it conveys structurally. This is why, for instance, on the repetitions of the A section in "Comedy Tonight" the lower levels of x and y pairings are not shown on the diagram: we have no need to be interested in them. The same cannot strictly be said of the lyrics, and it must be admitted that, perhaps inevitably, the diagram somewhat privileges the music in this respect, for there are a few surprises in the way the lyric phrases thwart our expectations. "Frenzy and frolic" suddenly overturns the pattern in the middle of stanza 3 (as does "Goodness and badness" in stanza 5) by cramming the two things enumerated into an a-level x and y, something that happens nowhere else (the consequent that "Goodness and badness" together produce on the next level up, "Man in his madness," is highly satisfying and works well toward the final summing up that the song must accomplish). Further, the structuring of the verbal phrases in the release is significant, for in its second four measures it is allowed to run straight through for the first time in the song. This is true of all four stanzas, and, in the first, attention is drawn to it by the inclusion of the only triple list, that is, one that takes up more than two measures: "Bring on the lovers, liars and clowns!" (the phrase was taken over from "Invocation"; see Sondheim 1974, 69). This gives us, at level c, our first four-measure y (as opposed to the two-measure "Comedy Tonight" refrain that has apparently dominated the structure so far), which in turn encourages us to hear the return of the A section straight through as an eight-measure phrase (level e in the diagram) and thus avoid redundancy of listening (the lyrics in stanza 1, with the unprecedented "Old . . . New . . . Nothing . . ." structural formation, also encourage this).

However, it is not a thirty-two-measure song but a thirty-six-measure one, and the quadratic acceleration just described, which would ordinarily forge the release and return into a sixteen-measure y (level f—this is like a miniature sonata form, in that it is, structurally and historically, binary rather than ternary), is left high and dry by the final four measures (see the question mark at level f in ex. 3.6b). In fact, there has already been an element of undercutting in the music. At the end of the release, the two tied half notes emphasize the fact that their four-measure phrase actually reasserts, after the broader pace with its whole notes, the rhythm as well as the downward third of the song's opening four measures. It is a small ambiguity, but an ambiguity nonetheless because the parallel suggests an x function in place of y, and this is actually the ghost of a way of hearing the phrasing through to the end of the song and thereby accommodating the extra four measures (see the parentheses and question marks at level c moving up to level d).

The virtue of the four-measure extension might appear, therefore, to be that it counteracts the fact that the song's refrain title, permeating the structure effectively enough in the first A section, would have paid diminishing returns after that and would not have been able to compete with the broadening of quadratic span that I have just described as beginning with the release. Nor, to put it another way, would it have been able to accomplish satisfactorily the $\hat{5}$-$\hat{3}$-$\hat{1}$ structural melodic descent down from the high D of the release within a thirty-two-measure AABA structure. But the four-measure extension would seem, on the face of it, to undermine the title in any case, by capping the structure with an epigram of twice its length, "Tragedy tomorrow, / Comedy tonight!" Sondheim has a solution to this, which is, in stanza 4, to insert a cadenza that progressively breaks up the structure halfway through the last four measures, taking it right back to single notes and syllables on an inverted dominant pedal and therefore almost onomatopoeically like an improvised snare drum roll (the number was, after all, staged as a comic circus). This provides the ultimate structural fulcrum (level g), just as it would in a concerto, leaving the way perfectly clear for the $\hat{5}$-$\hat{3}$-$\hat{1}$ descent to follow as the final y and the title refrain therefore to win the day. But this does not happen. Instead, there is a direct return to the release, up a semitone in A-flat, that then goes straight through to the end. (Though it cannot be shown on the reductive diagram, this is a neat way of composing-out the high E-flat at the end of the thirty-two measures.) Having prepared the way for a perfect structural closure of his refrain song, Sondheim frustrates it at the last minute. Perhaps we should have been prepared for this in a number about comedy, and we can almost add it to the list of instances in which the words actually *describe* what the music is doing—I have already noted this occurring in the line "Something familiar . . . ," and the words "Old situations,/New complications" at the return of the A section are another striking example of this profound tendency in Sondheim's songs.

Finally, although there has not been room to present it in ex. 3.6b, we should remember that the real y to "Comedy Tonight"'s x comes when the song is reprised at the end of the show. Senex's pathetic "a tragedy tonight" provides the unforgettable final structural complement—the last joke, if you like—to all that has been going on.

Chapter 4

Anyone Can Whistle

The Motivic Score

There has been no shortage of post mortem discussion of *Anyone Can Whistle*. As a show it failed, in retrospect "a legendary mess" to some (Lahr 1984, 9), "way ahead of its time, in that it was experimental," to others (Sondheim, quoted in Zadan 1990, 82), and provincial revivals have not succeeded in overturning the original negative judgments. But between the backstage anecdotage (see Zadan 1990, 81–92), the legacy of first-night reviews (Zadan 1990, 92–95; Adams 1980, 70–72; Gordon 1984, 475 and 1990, 36–37), and a penetrating study of the dramatic characterization particularly as afforded by the lyrics (Adams 1980, 75–124), the score itself has received little serious scrutiny. Several of its songs have remained familiar, but they need to be grasped in the context of a musical whole that is, generally speaking, as impressive and indicative in its organization as it is ripe in its expression. It is Sondheim's most ambitious score before *Follies,* whose main stylistic premises it exhibits fully fledged, and its concern with a comprehensive musical structure distinguishes it sharply from *Forum.* Uniquely for Sondheim and very unusually for any musical, it is in three acts, with no further division into scenes (again, this is unlike most musicals, with their vestiges of vaudeville structure, but more like a straight play), and this also has a positive bearing on how its musical development is organized.

Sondheim himself has hitherto been the chief commentator on the music.

> *Anyone Can Whistle* is sort of a music student's score. That whole score is based on the opening four notes of the overture, which is a second going to a fourth. All the songs are based on seconds and fourths and the relationship between a D and an E and a C and an F. (Sondheim 1978, 13–14)

Composers are not always ingenuous when it comes to explaining their

Ex. 4.1

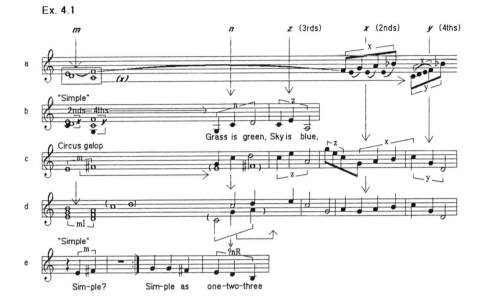

own music, but, in this case, we could not ask for a more helpful lead, as long as we allow for progressive transformation of the intervals Sondheim isolates, for varying levels of derivation, and for the fact that the composer now views his statement as something of an exaggeration.

Act 1

Motivic relationships of a primary order occur in act 1, within the confines of what is best called the "circus" music. These are shown in ex. 4.1, in which all the material has been transposed to give the greatest congruency with Sondheim's C or F major description (the context is ambiguous) of the opening fanfare (it is a semitone lower in the score). The fanfare repeats itself, onomatopoeically suggesting (at least to English ears) the "Roll up!" shouts of a barker and expanding intervallically to cover the scale aggregate of four notes (F to B-flat) indicated as x in ex. 4.1a; horizontalized, the two intervals D–E and F–C offer the same aggregate transposed by a fourth, as shown, and thus also generate the compound fourth, y. The properties of x and y—compound seconds and fourths respectively—are again generated, vertically, when the boxed intervals shown in ex. 4.1a are supplied with a functional tonic-dominant bass (C–G in ex. 4.1b), which is what happens at the beginning of the crucial "Interrogation" scene, the culmination of act 1 (vocal score, p. 57). As so often with Sondheim, Hapgood's melody grows out of the accompaniment motif: the new fourth, G–C, and the new second, C–D, become *n* in ex. 4.1b, the first measure of the tune and the motivic shape that, together with the archetypal scale premise *x,* will give rise to almost all the subsequent melodies in the score.

Hapgood's satirical truism, that "Grass is green, / Sky is blue," could be seen to call for the contrast that is generated between the neoclassically angular cell *n* and the triadic shape *z* that follows it. The circus galop (ex. 4.1c), first heard near the beginning of the overture and emerging triumphant as the instrumental act 1 Finale after Hapgood has announced that "You are all mad," logically develops the four motivic cells from this, and ex. 4.1d shows the melody of "I'm Like the Bluebird" clearly related to it. Both these melodies also contain two-note ostinatos in their accompaniments, comprising the interval of a (major) second (*m*) and presumably deriving from the overture's initial proposition, as shown distributionally in ex. 4.1. In "I'm Like the Bluebird," this figure is inverted (*mI*) and fleshed out to give parallel triads, and whether or not these were consciously derived from *z,* they are of consequence later in the score. Finally, it can be seen that, of the various "Simple" refrains in the "Interrogation" number ("Simple" is set to *m*), one of them, where Cora wittily initiates a waltz ("one-two-three," stemming from Hapgood's "A, B, C"), provides a new twist to *n*—a modified retrograde (ex. 4.1e, *?nR*), to be precise. Much play is made with this as an ostinato, and once again it is amply previewed in the overture, which, we must conclude, is de facto a prime reference point for the score as a whole (we must bear in mind this view, contrary to the conventional dismissal of theater overtures as redundant—it will be equally applicable to *Merrily We Roll Along*).

Partly because of its wholesale presence in the overture the "circus" music of ex. 4.1 has a congruency the demonstration of which is hardly an act of analytical excess. To trace the diffusion of the motivic material in equal detail throughout the remainder of the score, however, would easily lead, despite Sondheim's own invitation, to the situation in which, given the finitude of musical intervals, everything could be derived from everything else in a multiplicity of ways; we should not necessarily know which of the routes was traveled in the composer's mind. However, there are guidelines for perception in the music itself, one of which concerns cutouts. There were three of these in the first act, each rejected song being replaced with another, and in each case both attempts can be seen to have been built on the same motivic material. For instance, whether or not one perceives the accompaniment motif of "Me and My Town" to incorporate a retrograde of the original two-interval version of *x* (see ex. 4.2a, *xR*), it becomes more likely that the melody it generates, Cora's verse "Everyone hates me," was consciously based on *x* when one compares

Ex. 4.2a

Ex. 4.2b

Ev - 'ry-one hates_ me, yes,

Ex. 4.2c

They're storm -ing the wall _ a - gain, ___

Ex. 4.2d

Ex. 4.2e

it with the opening of the melody that (temporarily) replaced it, in the song "The Natives Are Restless" (exs. 4.2b and c). Equally to the point, both songs incorporate the triadic version of *m* in their vamps (exs. 4.2d and e). The second pair of songs in question is the "Miracle Song" and the rejected "The Lame, the Halt, and the Blind"; the latter never got as far as public performance, though its verse survives instrumentally in the "Pumping Music" of the vocal score (No.7, pp. 45–46). Again, accompaniment figures were taken over from the one into the other, the waltz vamp from "The Lame, the Halt, and the Blind," which was also present as punctuation between the lines of its chorus (ex. 4.3a), being reused as a mock a cappella chord sequence in "Miracle Song" immediately prior to its cynical transformation into a robust gospel hoedown (exs. 4.3b and c). The bass of the sequence is again based on *n*, while its religiosity is contingent upon the false relations and parallel motion of the triads erected upon the bass; these are prepared by the ecstatic choral "oohs" of the song's introduction, consisting of the triadic version of the *mI* ostinato

Ex. 4.3a

Ex. 4.3b

Ex. 4.3c

Ex. 4.3d

Ex. 4.3e

(though they are merely unisons on the recording). The principal melodies of both songs are also based on the compound fourth y (exs. 4.3d and e). More obviously still, "A Hero Is Coming" and "There Won't Be Trumpets," which replaced it before being abandoned in turn, are both based on versions of n (which is perhaps better called a generative shape than a motif, since its leaping interval started as a fourth, is here a third, and later in the score grows to a sixth). Both also append the assertive Scotch-snap appoggiatura already heard in "Miracle Song" (marked p in ex. 4.3e and exs. 4.4a and b), and "There Won't Be Trumpets" prominently features m's triads as an ostinato in its accompaniment.

Turning, finally in act 1, to the lyrical episodes in "Interrogation," a

Ex. 4.4a

A he - ro is com - ing __

Ex. 4.4b

There won't be trum-pets

Ex. 4.4c

Ha- ha- ha- ha - ha!

Ex. 4.4d

No, you can't judge a book by its cov - er,__

similar amalgam of *n* and *m* may be perceived in the initial melody and accompaniment of "A Woman's Place Is in the Home," while "You Can't Judge a Book by Its Cover" retrogrades Cora's immediately preceding triadic laughter, substituting a blues third, an ironic touch nicely underlining its protagonist's color (black), which is the subject of the episode (see exs. 4.4c and d).

Act 2

The music in act 2 seems to exhibit third-order derivations from the basic material, in that it contains a good deal of self-conscious "developing variation" within each song. That is, a short motif is stated as the first notes of a melody and is then continuously repeated in various forms, developing before our very ears, as it were, to form the melodic progress of the song, without calling on the older, classical technique of injecting obviously contrasting motifs into the melodic argument. This was a technique Sondheim learned from Babbitt.

The act opens with the simplest example of it, a song ("A–1 March") based almost entirely on stepwise melody. It is probably not fanciful to group the steps so that they span fourths (see the last four measures, vocal score p. 104) and thus relate the material to *x*. "Come Play Wiz Me" seems to develop various versions of the pliable *n* (see ex. 4.5a), again in tandem with *m*'s accompanying triads, but it is probably of

Ex. 4.5a

You wish to play wiz me?_

Ex. 4.5b

FAY:

An - y - one can whis-tle, that's what they say--

? =

[etc.]

Ex. 4.5c

Did a pa-rade __ go __ by?_

Ex. 4.5d

Ex. 4.5e

symbolic significance that, at the song's title phrase, n for the first time turns inward on itself in a new permutation of its constituent intervals (see ex. 4.5a, nP): it is as though we hear Fay's frigidity. The introverting shape then forms the basis of the central song "Anyone Can Whistle," both in the accompaniment and in the first measure of the melody, which collapses as far as a downward seventh (ex. 4.5b). The accompaniment of this, one of Sondheim's finest songs, thereby becomes a study in interlocking thirds and sixths, and it is worth noting that this is for a simple dramatic reason—Fay has just been talking about the contrast between playing the piano by ear and playing the learned, controlled patterns of scales.

> FAY: I can't play the piano by ear. When I was little, my, how I wanted to! My girl friend could. Once I walked into a music store, sat down at a big, shiny grand piano—and I played.

> (*Terrible sounds from pit piano*)

> Well, you can take piano lessons. Use a metronome; learn control and order.

> (*Scales on pit piano, turning into lead-in for the song*)

The "scale" pattern implied by the lead-in is figure a, shown in ex. 4.5b; it may be, however, that the scales themselves were not intended to be played, if the vocal score is authoritative, since (unlike the preceding "terrible sounds") they do not appear in it. In not only risking a song in illustration of (and built on) this inhibition but carrying it off triumphantly, Sondheim achieves the greatness of reflexive irony. He himself does not write songs by ear, so to speak, but by the ordered manipulation of patterns of notes; while on a larger plane it is as though he recognizes that the very act of composition is a substitute for life, an admission of failure; yet the failure becomes his success. It is an awareness to which he will frequently return, most overtly in "Make the Most of Your Music" from *Follies 1987*, where we are to understand that Ben, wounded by the reunion evening's lacerations, returns home and sits at his piano to regain his—significant word—composure.

Cora's central song, "There's a Parade in Town," follows, and here the process of melodic development seems to apply the stepping thirds of a to an extension of the song's primary motif n; the process has worked itself out by the final melodic cadence, which thus neatly illustrates the song's punchline "Did a parade go by?" (see ex. 4.5c). Whether or not coincidentally, this process also affords a permutational variant (marked *?qP* in ex. 4.5c) of the melody of the show's title phrase "Anyone Can Whistle" (marked *q* in ex. 4.5b). The stepping thirds of *a* become syncopated stepping fourths in the central section of "Everybody Says Don't" (ex. 4.5e), and they are immediately inverted in the orchestral fill, but it is less easy to ascertain the origin of the opening section's melody. That it reduces to the figure given in ex. 4.5d is not in doubt, for this, indeed all the material of the song, is exhaustively posited and developed in the subsequent "Don't Ballet"; beyond that, one can only say that it seems to be a free inversion of *a* (*aI* in ex. 4.5d) with *zI* tacked onto the end. Both these songs also use *m* as a triadic ostinato framework for parts of their accompaniment, as indicated in exs. 4.5c and 4.5e.

Act 3

If the music of act 2 focused the motivic derivations by developing them, the act 3 songs appear to diffuse and disperse them. Any relationship between the opening melody of "I've Got You to Lean On" and earlier material would seem arbitrary or obscure; the song's title phrase, however, is set to a clear reiteration of *n* (see ex. 4.6a). "See What It Gets You" literally "take(s) one step" in utilizing the figure *aI* as its melodic frame, now composed out to form a distinct likeness to the *Dies irae* plainsong melody frequently quoted by classical composers and no stranger in Sondheim's later work (ex. 4.6b). Sondheim states that this likeness was not conscious, though we still "see how it gets you down," as Fay points out, with its long, inexorable melodic descent, and note the angry dissonances of the accompaniment, distant cousins to the vengeful chords whose juxtaposition with the *Dies irae* will be a major factor in the characterization of the score of *Sweeney Todd*.

The music of act 3 is completed with the "Cookie Ballet" ("Cora's Chase"), much of whose waltz music appears melodically unconstrained but whose initial (and returning) theme closes in on *n* (see ex. 4.6c), and "With So Little to Be Sure Of." This final song's title phrase is vaguely related to *n*, more specifically to Hapgood's *aI* (compare "Everybody Says Don't"), and by way of general melodic characteristics to the *q* phrase of "Anyone Can Whistle" (see ex. 4.6d). In the score, these melodic compatibilities are strengthened by the fact that all three songs are in C major; the rehearsal copy of "With So Little to Be Sure Of," however, is in D-flat. Perhaps more interesting is the use of a chordal epilogue motif, based on the triads of *m* (the introduction to the song, referring back to "Come Play Wiz Me," reminds us of them) linked up through an inverted *nP* shape (ex. 4.6e). The single oscillating gesture of *m* seems to find its

Ex. 4.6a

final resting place here, to the words "we had a moment, / A marvellous moment." (The cliché of oscillating chords had been used time and again in romantic music, especially by the French, to express the sense of "a marvellous moment.") We have returned, not quite to the essential two notes with which the score began, but to the early $\hat{3}$–#$\hat{4}$ step that arose from it, now in retrograde as Fay sings her last (though she has plenty more to say), to the words *hold me*.

The passage quoted in ex. 4.6e is reminiscent of the instrumental Finale of *West Side Story*, particularly in the use of Lydian modality, reinforced when the bass modulates up a tone in both cases. The tightness and insistence of motivic working in *Anyone Can Whistle*, especially when it is made manifest in the "Don't Ballet," must also have been strongly influenced by the example of *West Side Story*, though it is important to realize that the "Don't Ballet" and much of the dance music for *West Side Story* were written or mapped out by dance arranger Betty Walberg.

The Generic Scheme

The *West Side Story* concordance raises the broader question of stylistic precedents and genres within the score of *Anyone Can Whistle,* and of what the various songs aim to accomplish.

Again the starting point of our investigation needs to be Sondheim's own comments about the work.

> It started a technique for me which I've used a lot since and I intend never to use again, I hope: namely, the use of traditional musical comedy language to make points. All the numbers Angie sang in the show were pastiche—her opening number, for instance, was a Hugh Martin-Kay Thompson pastiche. The character [Cora] always sang in musical comedy terms because she was a lady who dealt in attitudes instead of emotions. I used that technique later in *Company* in "Side by Side by Side" and "You Could Drive a Person Crazy" and a great deal in *Follies. Whistle* was also the first time I ever got to write the music I most like to write, which is highly romantic; for example, the title song and "With So Little to Be Sure Of." (Zadan 1990, 82-84)

Sondheim makes it clear that he is trading in two different types of music in *Anyone Can Whistle,* the pastiche and the romantic. In fact, the use of superannuated popular song styles for schematic purposes was not entirely new to him, since it had occurred in *Gypsy,* as we have seen. More important is to recognize that, for the first type, he does not use the term *parody:* neither here, nor in *Follies,* nor anywhere else, does he distort or fragment his musical comedy models; he borrows them, and honors them in the borrowing, valuing them for what they are and often intensifying them in the process (harmonically, for example). There *is* parody in *Anyone Can Whistle,* stylistically speaking, in the circus music, but this is arguably a third type not identified by the composer and probably influenced by the caricature neoclassicism of *Candide* (compare the beginnings of the overtures of the two works).

A purely musical viewpoint on these classifications emerges as follows. The pastiche numbers adopt the principle of the suite or divertissement, generically a succession of contrasting units based largely on dance or other functional models, their differentiation codified in matters of meter, tempo, melodic character, harmonic rhythm, accompaniment figure, texture, and so on. This idea of a varied "cast" of musical numbers—we might expect a march, a waltz, a foxtrot, a patter song, and so forth— has always been a basic tenet of musical comedy (and is by no means inapplicable to opera); indeed, the integration of its demands with those of both the dramatic cast of characters served by the numbers and the variety of human voices singing those characters is the composer's fundamental challenge. The romantic numbers, in a style that is by implication Sondheim's sole property, are, in contrast, "symphonic." That is, they have dramatic pretensions: they enhance our sympathies and forward the protagonists' aspirations in terms that go beyond the simple generic image. Thus on the one hand Cora's seeing life as a quickstep in which she is supported by her corrupt staff is too static, too social an image to allow for "symphonic" character development, and the borrowing of the music of variety entertainment also implies self-delusion: she is entertaining herself in "attitudes instead of emotions," and her music belongs on the divertissement plane. Fay's "Anyone Can Whistle," on the other hand, generically no further specifiable than as a ballad, is an abstract musical monologue, as is her rejected "A Hero Is Coming." Contrast is still required, both between numbers and within them (just as a symphonic movement requires contrasting themes and a whole symphony contrasting movements), but unity is at a greater premium. The case for the two sorts of music should not be overstated, since even the "symphonic" numbers rely on some kind of popular or functional vamp—a marchlike rhythmic drive in "Everybody Says Don't," for instance—but the distinction is there and is clear enough, though we may often notice it in the lyrics before it becomes apparent in the music. The question is whether Sondheim's romantic music achieves unity of motivation, and if so whether this articulates the aims of the show as a whole.

The circus music, which we may recall served as the gathering point for the musical motifs, does not easily fit either type. It could be seen as an exercise in neoclassicism, implying a possibly cynical detachment from the scenes it accompanies. Both the arbitrary tonic-and-dominant underpinning of initially nonharmonic intervals shown in ex. 4.1b and the melodic caprice shown in ex. 4.1c encourage this view. Or it could be regarded as a special case of pastiche, a "straight" borrowing of a "bent" style (the style being that of the silent film or comedy routine—in short, pantomime). The intense development of the score's initial proposition (x in ex. 4.1a) toward the end of "Interrogation," however (pp. 89–96 in the vocal score), is a serious musical matter.

Cutting across all this is a further genre, represented by the extensive ballet music that adds to the equation by providing an example in miniature of both the main types of music: a symphonic ballet in act 2 and a suite of waltzes (precursor of the overall ground plan of *A Little Night Music*) in act 3. In many respects, the circus music of "Interrogation" in act 1 complements and balances these two essays in choreographic production with a third. Ex. 4.7 shows the overall distribution of musical numbers according to category.

Divertissement Songs

Examining the divertissement music first, we find a striking entrance number for Cora in "Me and My Town." This is one of Sondheim's most skilful pastiches, a soulful, throaty blues exploiting a low female register and correspondingly low bass and chordal textures in the accompaniment. It is a type he will use again, most memorably in "I'm Still Here" from *Follies*. Carlotta is the same kind of battered survivor as Cora, and so is Gussie in *Merrily We Roll Along*. Indeed, the "misc." vamp sketches for *Anyone Can Whistle* include fragments that confirm the similarity between "Me and My Town" and "I'm Still Here" (ex. 4.8a, i) as well as suggesting further subconscious connections between "Me and My Town" and "Anyone Can Whistle," whose vamp as found in the score is followed, in the sketches, by the material shown in ex. 4.8a, ii. The latter is a variant of the main vocal rhythm of "The Natives Are Restless," a song whose unassertive Latin American lilt must have seemed a poor substitute for the harmonic and melodic richness of the blues, used in "Me and My Town" with a sophistication that produces a double modal ambiguity: the song's verse suggests Mixolydian A as well as D major, the chorus Aeolian A as well as the Dorian D that eventuates (though it does not do so unequivocally until the very end of the song, by which time it has modulated up a semitone to E-flat). The "blue" flat seventh of the Mixolydian, Dorian and Aeolian modes is highlighted in Cora's expanding vocal line (ex. 4.8b), and in her final "strut" (fig. 174 in the score) the repeated quarter-note chords of a traditional blues accompaniment are appended. These features, as in the type of cabaret number from which they are borrowed, add a slick irony to the "Cleopatra-like" stance, specified in the script, that Cora's words "Give me my coat. / Give me my crown" confirm (the reference to Shakespeare has already been pointed out by Adams [1980, 89]); that they seem to reappear three years later in a more serious context in Samuel Barber's setting of the original Shakespeare words for singer Leontyne Price in his opera *Antony and Cleopatra* is presumably a coincidence. In the central section of the song, the introversion of the blues is ousted by the highly choreographic Latin American energy of the mambo, at double tempo; the combination of the two in the final section, with the mambo figure as a riff against Cora's original blues melody, is typical of Sondheim and points the way to similar uses of mambo figures decades later in *Merrily We Roll Along*.

Ex. 4.7. The Musical Plan of *Anyone Can Whistle*

	Dance/Scene	Chorus	Cora	Fay	Hapgood	Style — Pastiche	Original
Act 1		"I'm Like the Bluebird"				Neoclassical/circus march?	
			"Me and My Town" ("The Natives Are Restless")			blues/mambo (Latin American?)	
		"Miracle Song" ("The Lame, the Halt and the Blind")				gospel/hoedown (gospel/Spanish waltz?)	
				"There Won't Be Trumpets" ("A Hero Is Coming")			march (alla breve)
	Interrogation				"Simple"	circus (march)?	
		"A Woman's Place"				Latin American	
		"You Can't Judge"				blues	
					"The Opposite"	trite jingle	
Act 2		"A-1 March"				6/8 march	
				duet "Come Play Wiz Me"		foxtrot	
				"Anyone Can Whistle"			ballad
			"There's a Parade in Town"			6/8 march ——▶ ?	
					"Everybody Says Don't"		allegro ↓
	"Don't Ballet"	(by Betty Walberg)					symphonic development
Act 3			"I've Got You to Lean On"			"friendship" quickstep	
					"See What It Gets You"		allegro + allegro recap of ballad
	"Cora's Chase"					ballet waltz sequence	
			duet ("There's Always a Woman")			(Latin American waltz?) ◀——	9/8 scherzo ? ——▶ "insult" duet
				duet "With so Little to Be Sure Of"			moderato love duet

Ex. 4.8a

Ex. 4.8b

Me and my town, __ Bat - tered a - bout,__

Ex. 4.8c

Ze sway of _ my, how you say,_ of my hips, yesss? __

Ex. 4.8d

When-ev - er my world falls_ a - part _____

The crass euphoria of "Miracle Song" (modeled, perhaps on "That Great Come-and-Get-It-Day" from *Finian's Rainbow*) contrasts wittily with "Me and My Town" through a variety of effects, including the "angelic" vocalization on oscillating triads in the introduction and the additive structure of the song, which extends its call-and-response pattern in a pseudo-charismatic succession of different chorus sections ("There's water in a lake," "Come all ye pilgrims," "Come and take the waters") that are in no hurry to wind the form up through recapitulation. The blues are still present, now in the melodic flat thirds, but their underpinning with the cheerfully tonal hoedown harmonies is as nice an irony as the at times almost imperceptible distinction between the language of evangelism and the language of tourism ("Come and take the waters for a modest fee"). Neither irony is invented; both are simply borrowed, and the subject of the song, the fountain, epitomizes the fact that, from the commercial standpoint, there is no real difference between Saratoga Springs and Lourdes.

The remaining divertissement numbers in act 1, the vignettes in "Interrogation," require no further comment. Act 2 sharpens the musical comedy content into two substantial essays on traditional generic mainstays, the 6/8 march and the foxtrot. "A-1 March," which opens the act, is like the A section of a Sousa march, but it is not closed off and merely circles round while its protagonists, the townspeople, are onstage; we have to wait until its reappearance after the scene between Fay and Hapgood for what is in effect its trio section, Cora's sumptuously lyrical "There's a Parade in Town," which finishes the number, much as it would with Sousa, after a return to the earlier section (in fact, the two themes are combined in counterpoint). Implicitly, therefore, this march spans a good deal of the central act of the play. The foxtrot in the interposed scene, Fay and Hapgood's "Come Play Wiz Me," is the only occasion on which the hero and heroine appropriate pastiche, and the message is simple: they need to relax into their role playing (represented by the preeminent social dance of the prerock era) in order to find fulfilment, just as much as Cora needs to break out of hers. Cora's stereotypical "friendship" number in act 3, "I've Got You to Lean On," demonstrates that she fails to do this, falling back instead as she does on the foxtrot's faster, slicker counterpart, the quickstep. The link between the two dance models is most easily perceived in the gliding smoothness of the melodic features, notably the passages of stepwise chromatic movement and the confining of the characteristic quarter-note/eighth-note cross-rhythm to stepwise oscillation (compare exs. 4.8c and d).

Symphonic Songs

If the pastiche music is almost exclusively Cora's, the symphonic (or romantic) music belongs to Fay and Hapgood, who are thereby posited as hero and heroine. Here we face the question of why "A Hero Is Coming" in act 1 was rejected even before reaching rehearsal. Sondheim comments: "Frankly, I don't remember why I changed it, but I suspect it was because it wasn't good enough. I remember liking the tune but thinking the lyric didn't sit very well on the melody." Musically it is one of Sondheim's most impressive songs, and we must regret its loss from this point of view, for it sets up the first movement of the "symphony" in a imposing harmonic arc that holds together not only the contrast between the chorus and the angry verse section (the verse survived intact in "There Won't Be Trumpets," but in "A Hero Is Coming" it sweeps back in at the climax of the chorus with superior logic and effect) but also the unusually symphonic degree of melodic contrast within the chorus itself, subdivisible into the two first-subject motifs (exs. 4.9a and b) and the second subject (ex. 4.9c) of a sonata-allegro complete with tonally adjusted recapitulation. Yet Sondheim is right: there is too much musical

Ex. 4.9a

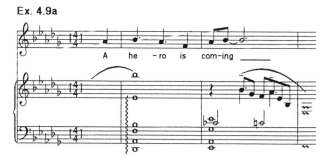

A he - ro is com-ing ____

Ex. 4.9b

You won't know him by his white char-ger

Ex. 4.9c

Tenderly, slightly faster

Ne - ver fear-- he'll be here in time. He - roes don't ap - pear til the nick of

time.

material, and it is too condensed, to allow the lyrics to win through; in fact the song is virtually unsingable. In the production its substitute, "There Won't Be Trumpets," was also cut (see Zadan 1990, 90–91).

The remainder of the "symphony" could be said to consist of a slow movement ("Anyone Can Whistle"), two further allegros ("Everybody Says Don't" and "See What It Gets You") and a final, *moderato* love duet ("With So Little to Be Sure Of"). Both of the allegros contain or give rise to development. In the case of "Everybody Says Don't," this ensues in the form of Betty Walberg's "Don't Ballet," as we have already seen. In "See What It Gets You" it is a matter of cross-reference to other numbers: the opening section turns out to be an antecedent (verse) to a consequent (chorus) in the form of a fast reprise of "Anyone Can Whistle," in which the repeated-note motif of "Everybody Says Don't" is much in evidence in the instrumental fills, as are its slurred cross-rhythms in the accompaniment, while the verse with its frenetic ostinato bass and pungent chromatic harmonies calls to mind that of "A Hero Is Coming" and "There Won't Be Trumpets." Indeed, the symphonic allegros in all three acts share much the same means of expression of angry energy. The elements of Sondheim's musical language, rhythmic punctuation or ostinato against lyrical melody, harmonic warmth against chromatic or diatonic dissonance, are kept skilfully in balance throughout, and it is only in "With So Little to Be Sure Of" that romanticism gets the upper hand, perhaps to the detriment of the score as a whole, for the number is overly long and texturally grandiose without really opening out vocally for the singers. It is worth observing that the discarded (and unfinished) first version of the song demonstrates a potentially richer integration of straightforwardly romantic lyricism with what might be termed neoclassic ironies. Instances of the latter include the parallel-fifths upbeats (extended in mm. 3 and 5 with the unresolved E-flat on the first beat), the prominent fourths in measure 7 (especially on the third beat), and the right-hand E-natural in measure 9 falsely resolving to a D (ex. 4.9d). The B-flat in the first introductory measure of "Anyone Can Whistle" fulfils a similar function, adding a double perspective (a kind of horn call in B-flat) to the otherwise parallel-sixth and -third pattern; so do both the compound-fourth disposition of added-note harmonies in "A Hero Is Coming" (ex. 4.9a) and the song's later chromaticisms (ex. 4.9c), and one could also add the displaced thirds of the fanfares in "There Won't Be Trumpets" to the list of examples (ex. 4.9e). Sondheim has chosen and manipulated his style elements carefully enough to give us the assurance of a purposeful musical language of his own, though its harmonic energy, particularly in "A Hero Is Coming," also seems to owe a positive debt to Gershwin's symphonic idiom.

Ex. 4.9d

[With so lit - tle _____ to be sure of._____]

Ex. 4.9e

[Furioso]

A Score in Search of a Show?

The musical relationships are thus highly satisfactory, but we can be less confident about the dramatic relationship of the symphonic music to the pastiche. In a traditional symphony, the point of contact between the preponderantly abstract material and the referential remnants of the suite is the scherzo; perhaps this was also the case in *Anyone Can Whistle* with Fay and Cora's act 3 "insult" duet, "There's Always a Woman," until it was cut. As a song it was no great loss, and it is as though its potential was eventually reformulated in three different numbers in *A Little Night Music*—the insults resurfaced in "You Must Meet My Wife," the pairing of the women in "Every Day a Little Death," and the frozen tension of confrontation in 9/8 meter in "It Would Have Been Wonderful." But it was the only song that combined Cora and Fay, and without it they lack dynamic interaction. Unlike *Follies*, where the very subject of the musical is the contrast between stage fantasies and realities, and the perception of one in terms of the other, there is no real reason in *Anyone Can Whistle* why the songs of Cora and those of Fay and Hapgood should inhabit the same score. True, the music of "There's a Parade in Town" is so splendidly expansive that for a moment we feel real sympathy for Cora and sense the possibility of dramatic character development (Sondheim had written the song at the request of Angela Lansbury who wanted the role to contain a "noncartoon" song); but by act 3 she is merely recapitulating earlier attitudes and remains throughout a curiously isolated figure with no single musical foil—Schub has no music of his own, her relation with the chorus is oblique, and her interaction with Hapgood peters out after the act 1 Finale.

In fact the show never quite decides who its main characters are. The townspeople and the "Cookies" promise a centrality that they fail to sustain (it is diffused by circus madness of act 1 and further deflected in the ballet sequences of acts 2 and 3, which deny them a vocal focus), and Cora's supporting staff confuse the issue further as a kind of mini-chorus. Musically Cora is well to the fore of her citizens and with her three big numbers threatens to overbalance the show without contributing anything to its development. Hapgood is set up as her adversary in act 1 but fails to confront her thereafter in music, while all his own numbers but one are corporate, and even his one solo, "Everybody Says Don't," hardly squares with his act 1 wizardry, for in it his "espousing of ordinary homilies make this brash non-conformist seem at this moment a trifle jejune" (Adams 1980, 114). It would almost suit Fay better, as is implied by her later adoption of some of its material. Fay, who in any case has more musical numbers (five) than any other character, thus turns out to be the main subject of the symphony, and that her central title song has continued to resonate far beyond the show seems fitting.

We can look forward as far as *Into the Woods* and see a somewhat similar problem there. The Witch has a virtuoso role, like Cora's, yet is not the central character in terms of dramatic development (or even, in act 2, a mechanically necessary one): the Baker is, and like Fay he foils two other characters (his Wife and the Witch) in a way that divides our receptive energy without polarizing it. It is even worth pointing out that while Sondheim has repeatedly dramatized heroic couples with unqualified success (Sweeney and Mrs. Lovett, George and Dot, Fredrik and Désirée), he has never unequivocally isolated a hero or heroine in one of his shows except with negative intent (as with Robert and Franklin Shepard).

In a sense, then, Cora, Hapgood, and the chorus and dancers get in the way in *Anyone Can Whistle*. They do so all the more because of the rich amalgam of musical theater resonances they carry with them. The

Cookies' ballet in act 3 is like a parody of the dream sequence tradition that began with *Oklahoma!,* though Sondheim points out that it is not a dream ballet but "a farcical dance about real events." Cora is in some respects a negative version of Dolly Levi in *Hello, Dolly!* and her central number, "There's a Parade in Town," upstages Dolly's "Before the Parade Passes By" (though this was presumably coincidence, for its rehearsal score carries the same date as the opening night of *Hello, Dolly!* [16 January 1964]. Hapgood's mixed dramatic ancestry is yet more prominent. Musically, his is something of a problem role. He talks too well, at the expense of his singing, and at times he sounds like a Brechtian polemicist (compare Larry Foreman in *The Cradle Will Rock*), at others, in his zany one-liners, like Groucho Marx or other 1930s film comics, without being able to sustain these facets, though the mad comedian in him spills over amply onto the other characters, notably in act 1 (Detmold: "I may be terrible on faces but I never remember a name"). But at the same time he is an Arthurian hero—the references to trumpets, to his arriving "in the nick of time" and to whistling for him as though he were in some sense supernatural make Fay's view of him quite clear. As such he begs comparison with Lerner and Loewe's Arthur in *Camelot* (another role tailored more to speaking than singing; see van Leer 1987, 121); indeed, his quixotic conversation echoes Arthur's (the "opposite of right is wrong" paradox occurs in the act 1 dialogue of *Camelot*).

Once we start thinking about this, it seems extraordinary that Fay's call for a hero in *Anyone Can Whistle* has not generally been taken as a comment on the American reaction to John F. Kennedy's death five months earlier, especially given the Kennedys' own known association with *Camelot* and T. H. White (see Johnson 1991, 19). Its absurdist approach must have put everyone off the scent, and would in any case have alienated them, just as the fantastic approach to his assassination did in *Assassins* nearly thirty years later.

If the Arthurian theme is insufficiently focused, a greater shadow hanging over Hapgood, indeed over the whole musical, is his similarity to Harold Hill in *The Music Man.* The difficulty here is that, unlike Hill, he is simply too honest to convince us. He does not command seventy-six imaginary trombones or "bells on the hill"; he does not sing the big march number or carry the symphonic music. The corporate miracle of a Broadway band and the private one of romance consequently do not quite come together, though neither will they quite go away, for the metaphor of music and its instruments standing for the motivating conditions of life, which had permeated *The Music Man,* recurs in *Anyone Can Whistle,* but in a subdued and negative manner. Hapgood's first entrance, after "There Won't Be Trumpets," takes place to a fanfare "which

NOBODY notices," and in act 2 he produces a trumpet when he tells his story and refers to himself as "the Pied Piper for lunatics"; Cora refers to squeaky flutes and out-of-step marchers in "There's a Parade in Town"; and Fay's observations about piano practice and whistling, seeming to echo Harold Hill's claim in his love scene that the "'think' system [is] as simple as . . . whistling," lead to her say "I'm too unmusical" when Hapgood urges her to "Come with me" in act 3. Something else that nobody notices is the almost symbolic lacuna in the orchestration of the show, which includes no upper strings at all. These emblems are not obvious enough to be more than a poor substitute for the sense of time and place that the depiction of musical activities and the styles of the numbers themselves evoke in *The Music Man,* and all in all we either remain unaware of most of it or perceive it as merely on a par with the pop art ambience of much of the book and a little of the music, that is, as absurdism or cynicism. Cynicism it is not; symbolism for angst and inhibition it may want to be, in which case this is simply not the right score—or the right show—for it, with the exception, as I have suggested, of the song "Anyone Can Whistle" itself. (Even here the message was flippantly received, critics preferring to notch up a quick score about "the lack of a melody I could whistle," thus inaugurating a criticism that has bedeviled Sondheim ever since [see Cartmell 1983, 12], rather than listening to the richness of the music.) We shall see Sondheim making another attempt to match musical instruments with characters, and again not quite seeing it through, in *A Little Night Music,* before eventually exploring the metaphoric equivalences more successfully by layering them in act 1 of *Sunday in the Park With George* at a further remove, with music-as-(visual) art-as-life.

This is one way of articulating the problem of *Anyone Can Whistle:* to see it as a grand score out of step with its book. Sondheim comes to a comparable conclusion through different considerations when, after the explanation of motivic unity quoted at the beginning of this chapter, he acknowledges that

> the fallacy is that the music isn't continuous, so that it doesn't mean anything to the audience's ear *really* . . . the seed doesn't germinate the way it does in a symphony with a continuous spread. It germinates, and then there is dialogue, and then I remind everybody that it's based on the second or fourth . . . it's all too late. (Sondheim 1978, 14)

A final criticism must be that it does not show Sondheim at his most compelling as a lyricist. There are moving lyrics, true enough, and "Anyone Can Whistle" has a timeless quality of intimacy that has made it a

Ex. 4.10

classic. But there are gauche ones too, especially in "With So Little to Be Sure Of": Sondheim has not yet overcome the difficulty of writing (or justifying) a direct love duet, and here one wonders if he was trying consciously or unconsciously to match the expansiveness of "Bess, You Is My Woman Now" from Gershwin's *Porgy and Bess,* given the slight but nagging similarities between the two songs. Overall, there is less scope for his structural wit and integration of lyrics and music in *Anyone Can Whistle* than in *Forum.* There are exceptions, of which the most satisfying is probably the parallel structuring of foxtrot clichés and assumed French phraseology in "Come Play Wiz Me." The material shown in ex. 4.8c includes a prime example of this: the G–F-sharp oscillation is sustained for two measures (appropriately to the genre, as was pointed out), in the first while referring to what it depicts, the dancer's swaying hips, in the second while keeping melodic progress waiting, as it were, as the pseudo-Frenchwoman pretends to search for the next words ("how you say")— there is a complete as well as playful unity between the melodic and verbal trains of thought and once again the words are actually describing what the musical structure is doing. Likewise, at the end of the song, we find the verbal pun—the English phrase as the retrograde of the French— paralleled by the intervallic inversion of the two-note melodic cell, a neat way not just of capping and closing both the melodic and verbal sense but also of resolving the dance's cross-rhythms into simple downbeat patterns with the punning subtext of "agree[ing] . . . in time" (ex. 4.10). This is an interim reminder of Sondheim's double craft at its best. For it to be sustained through a whole score, however, and above all for the scope of lyrics to be harnessed to more epigrammatically critical ends, we have to await *Company.*

Chapter 5

Company

The Concept Musical

Much has been written about *Company*, a fair amount of it by academics (see Berkowitz 1979; Cartmell 1983, 132–76; Bristow and Butler 1987; Hirsch 1989, 85–92; Huber 1990, 101–44; Ilson 1989, 159–77). The received wisdom is that it was Sondheim's first "concept" musical. This term is something of a cliché and has probably outlived its usefulness, not least because it tends toward two meanings. It has primarily to do with the idea of a director's theater (see Cartmell 1983, 94–98; Huber 1990, 1–13), and since director's theater is a condition of our time it is little more than a truism as applied to modern productions, implying a kind of Wagnerian *Gesamtkunstwerk* with music, lyrics, book, set, choreography, lighting, costumes, and direction contributing to an integrated thematic whole whose elements are beholden to each other for style and content rather than to expectations based on their separate or corporate conventions. Inasmuch as it marked the start of the partnership with Harold Prince as director, still relatively fresh from *Cabaret* and *Fiddler on the Roof,* and with Michael Bennett as choreographer and Boris Aronson as set designer, *Company* fits this definition well enough, as it does its extension whereby the director decides what the play is "about" and seeks to have this reflected or stated in all the disciplines and elements of production. *Fiddler on the Roof* is about tradition, exemplified by Russian Jews at the turn of the century; *Company* is about marriage, exemplified by contemporary Manhattan couples and a single man.

But this shades over somewhat paradoxically into the subsidiary meaning. "Content dictates form," as Sondheim himself is fond of saying, and if the script is not preexistent but can be fashioned as the discussion of a topic, "concept musical" can come to indicate a show in which "linear" plot is abandoned or downgraded in favor of vignettes; it becomes a multiple perspective on a subject, like a cubist painting or sculpture (for a comprehensive discussion of how Aronson's set for *Company* consciously explored this comparison, see Ilson 1989, 165–68). Some trace this genre back to Weill's *Love Life* (1948), but as a series of sketches, episodes, or separate stories held together by some common element or character, *Company* had enough other precursors, as well as successors, on the stage, Offenbach's *Tales of Hoffmann* (1880) being as striking an example of the former as was Neil Simon's *California Suite* (1976) of the latter. In this sense it was also effectively a reincarnation of the topical revue, as though the term *concept musical* had come full circle to encompass, say, the 1933 *As Thousands Cheer*, with its "theme" of newspaper headlines, which preceded the various sketches.

These two meanings together have ramifications that are part and parcel of such a fundamental nexus of postmodern cultural exchange that one hesitates to pronounce upon them at all. Sondheim adds the cautionary insistence that Bobby is not so nonlinear that he does not *learn* from the episodes in *Company* (we must consider this later), and that "content dictates form" is a matter of craft, the fitness of means to ends, not a paraphrase of "the medium is the message," down which road lie huge vistas of design doctrine, advertising theory, semiotics, and a world of logos and corporate identity. Nevertheless, *Company* was of its period, as its lettering design reminds us, and as does the celebrated fact that the following year *Follies* "sold more posters than tickets" (Annette Meyers, in Zadan 1990, 181). A musical, like everything else in the 1970s, had to have an immediately identifiable image.

Still, the idea of a multiple perspective and a coherently packaged topic was liberating, and the kaleidoscopic approach has motivated a good deal of Sondheim's work since *Company*, as can be seen in the admittedly abandoned scheme of action replays in *A Little Night Music*, the tangential, variationlike relationship between acts 1 and 2 of *Sunday in the Park with George* and *Into the Woods*, and the chronological shifting back and forth of *Assassins*. *Company* nonetheless differed from all the works mentioned above in that it virtually abandoned plot even within its separate vignettes. This was what made people sit up; it was also what posed the problem we must consider, of whether or not *Company* is still concerned with character development and structural closure, and whether its particular approach, which led to the "concept musical" label, can withstand deconstructive scrutiny.

However we view its generic status, it is a fine score, the uniform trenchancy and poetic edge of its lyrics coupled with the more advanced and differentiated stylistic boundaries of its music lending it a highly developed and distinctive voice that had not yet fully emerged in *Anyone Can Whistle*. It was the work that first won Sondheim his preeminent stature as a composer-lyricist on Broadway, his command of respect and admiration from all and cult adulation from some.

It seemed to fall into place almost at one go, with few cutouts or rewrites, though with some radical shifting around of scenes at the composition stage as the material grew and songs were provided. Once on the stage, the one big problem was the ending, which I shall examine at length later. Other areas requiring reconsideration were the opening, "Have I Got a Girl for You," and "Getting Married Today," details of which will be given in due course.

The Modernist Lyric

Given the urban, contemporary setting, it was important that the tone of the lyrics should be set early in the period of creative gestation. Sondheim has explained how he took it from Furth's dialogue, but the binding image of telephonic conversation must also have been catalytic. This survives strongly enough in the score in the binary rhythmic vamp of the "busy" signal—one beat on, one beat off—that sets the tempo (though in fact it is somewhat speeded up for musical purposes) and motivic pace of the crucial opening number, whose first words in the chorus, set to this pulse, are "Phone rings" (ex. 5.1a). The signal is carefully mimicked in the slurred tenuto-staccato phrasing of the accompaniment, and also governs the intercutting falling third or second, two-eighth-note motif set to the name *Bobby* and its variant diminutives (as a musical diminution, in fact) that serves as a recurrent tag throughout the show (see ex. 5.1b), from the vocal "Overture" to the introduction to "Being Alive" via the various "Bobby-Baby" underscores, the chime of whose title words, as so often with Sondheim, minutely complements the musical two-note motif and its variant propensities. Surviving lyric sketches for an undeveloped song called "Hold Me" demonstrate how an imagined snippet of telephone conversation might suggest a mode of dialogue and a melodic contour to match (the figures are degrees of the musical scale).

7 7 7 7 6   5   6   6 6 65 4   5 55 54 3
Felicia said Johnny may have to go into the hospital anyway.

while a list of "NON-COMMUNICATION non-sequiturs" in the same file reminds us of the negative side of the urban mode of living that *Company* so poetically explores, especially in "Another Hundred People," whose lyrics are, in their own way, second cousins to the verse of Sandburg or Auden. Sondheim must have been conscious of wanting to work within the modernist poetic tradition of fractured experience in *Company*, and although he was not the first to explore it in the genre of popular lyrics— the 1960s beat poets and songwriters such as Bob Dylan and Simon and

Ex. 5.1a

Ex. 5.1b

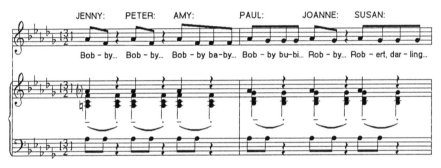

Garfunkel had been there before him in their commentaries on urban alienation—he nonetheless set new cultural sights for the musical by making it aware that it could partake of the great literary theme of the "city of strangers." (See Mulvey and Simons 1990 for a critique of this theme; sadly, their book does not deal with musical theater.) The following lines are from "Another Hundred People."

> It's a city of strangers—
> Some come to work, some to play—
>
> . . . .
> And they find each other in the crowded streets and the guarded parks,
> By the rusty fountains and the dusty trees with the battered barks
> And they walk together past the postered walls with the crude remarks
>
> . . . .
> Will you pick me up or do I meet you there or shall we let it go?
> Did you get my message, 'cause I looked in vain?
> Can we see each other Tuesday if it doesn't rain?
>
> . . . .
> And another hundred people just got off of the train.

They seem to discover images similar to those in Eliot's *Waste Land,* or even to echo them, with their references to the strange city, the crowd, the rain, dirtiness and messages on walls, and dusty and mutilated trees:

[*from* I. THE BURIAL OF THE DEAD]

. . . .
    Unreal City,
Under the brown fog of a winter dawn,
A crowd flowed over London Bridge, so many,
I had not thought death had undone so many.

[*from* II. A GAME OF CHESS]

. . . .
And still she cried, and still the world pursues,
'Jug Jug' to dirty ears.
And other withered stumps of time
Were told upon the walls; staring forms
Leaned out, leaning, hushing the room enclosed.

. . . .
                    'What shall we do tomorrow?
'What shall we ever do?'
                    The hot water at ten.
And if it rains, a closed car at four.
And we shall play a game of chess,
Pressing lidless eyes and waiting for a knock upon the door.

[*from* III. THE FIRE SERMON]

. . . .
'Trams and dusty trees.
Highbury bore me. Richmond and Kew
Undid me.'

(One is even tempted to hear echoes of Eliot's line "What you get married for if you don't want children?" in the *Company* husbands' refrain line "Whaddaya wanna get married for?" from the song "Have I Got a Girl for You," and, many years later, of "What shall we ever do," above, in "Where are we to go? / Where are we ever to go" from "No More" [*Into the Woods*].)

Urban Music

If the lyrics thus pervasively take their tone from the colloquial, casual bleaknesses of urban modernism, the music discovers new pastures, if that is the right word, in rock and, to a certain extent, urban folk music.

Given the undeveloped state of technical analysis of popular music styles, elements are difficult to define except empirically, but the use of repeated notes and repeated chords within firm and slow-moving harmonic changes, a particular bass pattern, and guitar finger-picking figurations are all important rock signifiers and deserve individual scrutiny.

Melodic repeated notes are the unforgettable hallmark of "Company"'s main theme (see ex. 5.1a), characterized by their relentless insistence and exhilarating though forced positivism—we can identify their rise from the third to the fifth degree of the major scale as the motivic and emotional agent in this respect. This interval of a third between major scale degrees $\hat{3}$ and $\hat{5}$ is, of course, the "Bobby" cell in retrograde. We can also see it composed out in various forms in the melodic line of "Another Hundred People," "Being Alive," and the "Whaddaya like" waltz section of "Have I Got a Girl for You"; it may similarly lie behind "The Ladies Who Lunch" and "Marry Me a Little" if we risk stretching the point to abandonment of the repeated notes on $\hat{3}$ and incorporation, instead, of various forms of the "Bobby-Baby" four-note chime ($\hat{5}$–$\hat{3}$–$\hat{5}$–$\hat{4}$). (To risk stretching it further, as Wilson does [see Wilson 1983, 1–58], is to prove nothing other than that all music is based on a limited fount of serial intervals.) Ex. 5.2 shows a tabulation of these relationships, with all the melodies transposed to C major.

Repeated chords also inform the material shown in ex. 5.1a. These emphasize the exceedingly rich harmonic substructure of the movement, and they strike one as being transferred from the rock pianist's rhetorical repertoire rather than the guitarist's: they are the means by which the exploratory harmonic artist sustains effects, probably originating on the electronic organ in gospel music, which rely on suspensions and added notes in the form of simultaneous appoggiaturas. Sondheim's later use of the idiom, actually with piano accompaniment, to depict the earnest and innocent freshness of the young songwriters in "Good Thing Going" from *Merrily We Roll Along* makes us wonder whether 1970 was too early for him to have heard Elton John or Billy Joel, or whether there is a common source. The sound was certainly in the air, and Stephen Schwartz came up with something similar for "Day by Day" in *Godspell* the following year. Harmonically the idiom is highly invigorating, containing as it does somewhere in its background the exultation of church music (rather than the resignation of the blues), and its long unfolding paragraphs, a schematic cross-section of which is given in ex. 5.3a, contribute to the tremendous symphonic effect that this opening number attains. The harmonic foundation is so strong that it is possible to extend a dominant pedal almost indefinitely, which is what Sondheim did on the word *love* so as to remain synchronized with Aronson's moving elevators on the set (see Ilson

Ex. 5.2

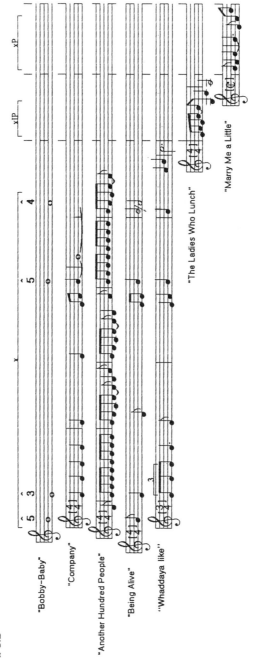

Ex. 5.3a

[etc.]

Ex. 5.3b

Ex. 5.3c

Ex. 5.3d

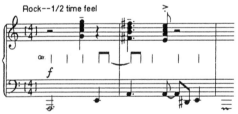

1989, 171). All this applies equally to "Happily Ever After," which in some respects is a more weighty counterbalance to "Company" than "Being Alive."

As for the repeated bass pattern that underpins the idiom, gone is the Broadway bass prevalent in *Forum*. It has been replaced with a rock bass, more of a heartbeat or pulse than a walk, consisting of one long downbeat note, normally the root of the chord, followed by a short upbeat one usually a fourth lower (this means that chords, however complex, tend to be based on root position triads). In the rock tradition it is a conventional matter, rhythmically, of throbbing pedal (bass) drum reiterations, melodically, of bass guitar picking, and, like many other features, may well derive from a Latin American model—the bass pattern of "The Ladies Who Lunch," which is labeled as a bossa nova, suggests as much (ex. 5.3b). The material shown in ex. 5.1a includes the formula, which is equally applicable at slower tempi and in triple time and can also be found in "Someone Is Waiting" (we hear it transformed from a Viennese waltz bass in the link from "Have I Got a Girl for You"), "Another Hundred People," "Being Alive," and "Happily Ever After." The upbeat is sometimes preceded by one or more accessory notes, found intermittently in "Sorry-Grateful," "Happily Ever After," and in the frantic sections of "Getting Married Today," and these eventually lead into the realms of the bass or percussion riff, especially when they are syncopated. "Being Alive" has a tenor ostinato of five eighth notes (see ex. 5.3c), and in the symphonic rock sections of "Tick-Tock," which were written by David Shire (ex. 5.3d), the bass eventually becomes a quasi-improvisatory focus of the music (between mm. 113 and 129 in the vocal score).

Guitar-style accompaniment patterns are a somewhat different matter, as much a folk as rock signifier, comparable to the contemporaneous effects of Simon and Garfunkel and Joni Mitchell. On two occasions, Sondheim sets up a complex mesh of cross-rhythms from the simple French baroque principle of the *style brisé*—that is, the adumbration of a full harmonic texture through the plucking of one note at a time in a variety of registers. This is strictly and fruitfully adhered to in "Another Hundred People" (ex. 5.4a), in which the "alto" part plays in 6/8 or 12/8 against the solid 4/4 underpinning of the bass, while the "tenor" line is like another 6/8 strand out of phase with it and the top line suggests half notes displaced by an eighth-note's distance. "Marry Me a Little" operates similarly, with the 12/8 strand disposed as five dotted-quarter-note pulses plus one eighth note left over (to account for the sixteen eighth notes in every two measures), rhythmically duplicated in melodic counterpoint in the tenor register (ex. 5.4b). The conflicting rhythmic phases are a crucial step on Sondheim's road to a rapprochement with minimalism, especially in the episode sections of "Another Hundred People," where the left-hand pattern repeats rhythmically in phase every measure while the right hand comes around again at only seven eighth-notes' distance (ex. 5.4c). The brittle orchestration makes this passage sound very much like Steve Reich—"it became very busy with lots of bells and woodwinds," Tunick acknowledged, referring to "some of the jabbing sounds [that] . . . I used . . . a lot in *Company*" (Zadan 1990, 157).

There is no one musical style for the songs in *Company*, but the rock influence was made pervasive by Tunick's approach to the orchestration.

Ex. 5.4a

Ex. 5.4b

Ex. 5.4c

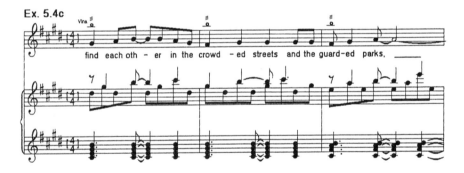

Compared with the standard Broadway sound of *Forum,* with its piano and optional harp, we now have two guitar parts encompassing acoustic, electric, and bass instruments and a keyboard part for electric piano and organ. Tunick should be credited sufficiently.

> The "Company" number was probably the one that I was able to help the most on. The biggest problem with it was getting it to build momentum and the song was always in danger of becoming monotonous, so it needed help in pointing out where sections ended and where new sections began. I tried to bring in new rhythmic elements starting with a quarter-note pattern which, at a certain point, began to skip, then an eighth-note pattern would come in over it. It slowly built to the chorus which I think was very exciting. (Zadan 1990, 157)

Here he is presumably referring to the build-up to measure 40 and again to measure 124 in the score, and is indicating that the material in small notes is his, though not all of it is audible on the original cast recording. Tunick could have said the same about his final build-up in "Another Hundred People," which introduces the "Bobby-Baby" motif (mm. 155–62 in the score); again, though, it is scarcely audible on the recording.

The Score as a Whole

The rock sound aside, other styles in *Company* contribute to a purposeful whole while showing Sondheim sharpening up his command of divergent idioms that stand as contemporary references. Contrary to *Anyone Can Whistle* and *Follies,* these release him from the need to deploy more than the occasional historical pastiche, the main pastiche numbers being "You Could Drive a Person Crazy," a sort of Andrews Sisters routine, and the foxtrot/quick march Broadway production number "Side by Side by Side" with "What Would We Do Without You," which tilts the conventions sideways by appearing at the start of act 2 rather than at the end of act 1. The Latin American undercurrents are strong, and appear in the open as Sondheim's primary vehicle for irony, especially in "The Ladies Who Lunch" (where the idiom is also the categorical way of signifying night club or discotheque culture) and "Little Things." It is interesting to see whither the calypso usage in *Forum* was leading in "Little Things," with its brittle accompanimental dissonances, pointillistically disposed, and its relaxed feminine rhymes. (As in many of Sondheim's list songs, some of the artifacts conjured up, such as "It's making little slips together, trips together, whips together," found no place in the final lyric—couples don't make whips, Sondheim points out—though they survived as far as the backers' audition tape.) The parallel-sixth "Bobby" motifs of the prefatory "Overture" section of the opening number (see ex. 5.1b), with their false relation between A-flat and A-natural, are complemented by and developed into the blues number "Poor Baby" (whose muscular rhythmic introduction prefaces the original cast recording of the whole show, though it is not in the score at that point).

More abstract usages inform "Getting Married Today," a miniature and extremely funny drama whose sections of ecclesiastical pastiche would stand Sondheim in good stead in *Sweeney Todd* and whose patter episodes utilize a driving rhythmic texture, probably of symphonic origin, used again in "The Miller's Son" in *A Little Night Music* and "Your Fault" in *Into the Woods.* This song, with its eventual counterpoint of Paul's and Amy's melodies and choral punctuating "Amen"s (the nearest we come to a love duet in *Company*), was written late in the day and took some effort to get into place; called at one stage "The Wedding Is Off," as such it included quite different music for Amy (though with some of the same verbal phrases), not in a patter rhythm and with an aggressive *martellato* accompaniment suggesting wild church bells, while the draft of "Getting Married Today" lacks the ecclesiastical sections. Sketches seem to indicate that Furth had a hand in shaping Amy's monologue, and Sondheim has explained in detail how he had to reshape her patter and omit the original second verse to minimize the physical difficulty (Sondheim 1974, 76–78).

Suite and symphony reemerge as considerations in the kaleidoscopic "Have I Got a Girl for You," its driving, cross-rhythmic scherzo impulse in the title section (which responds well to Tunick's orchestration and slips virtuosically into a *tre battute* pulse at the words "Dumb! / And with a weakness for Sazerac slings") giving way first to a fast waltz trio and then to the slow waltz "Someone Is Waiting." Originally there was an additional waltz section, "Your hair-do looks great," placed before the fast waltz, but it was cut, along with a conventional recapitulatory structure involving all three sections (ABCBCAC). "Someone Is Waiting" marks Sondheim's appropriation of a distinctive generic archetype of which Copland is also fond (as in the first movement of his Clarinet Concerto), neoclassically detached or alienated in its halting, pendulumlike rhythm ("oom-pah-pah" minus the second "pah") and almost certainly originating in Satie's *Gymnopédies*. Both its emblematic use (to indicate Robert's inability to commit himself) and its connection with Satie are yet more striking in "Barcelona," where even the oscillating imperfect-cadence harmonies are Satie's and where again the number is the static consequent of an extremely dynamic antecedent, in this case the solo dance sequence "Tick-Tock" whose title fixes the pendulum image as thematic.

"Tick-Tock"—in its present shape Shire's work, not Sondheim's, we must remember—brings all these styles together in a surprisingly persuasive symphonic climax. Is this the place for it? Possibly not, for most of the sequence was earlier intended for "Company Overture," a number assembled in rehearsal score as a mixture of the vocal "Company" opening as we now know it with elements of the traditional instrumental overture sequence, and "Tick-Tock" was only inserted as a second act dance sequence at the last minute in Boston. There was at least one other different attempt at an overture number, too, with a cappella–style wordless voices.

One song has not yet been mentioned, though its lyrics have already been quoted in this book's Introduction. "Sorry-Grateful" is surely the key song in the whole score, if one believes that its ambivalences, paradoxes, and lyric epigrams penetrate to the heart of life's bewilderments. It epitomizes the ambiguity between being and becoming that is so central

Ex. 5.5a

Ex. 5.5b

Ex.5.5.c

an aspect of the modern experience, trapped motionless as it is with its oscillating melodic motif of two notes, A–G, G–A (see ex. 5.5a), reversed in tandem with the reversed terms of the song's title (which are immediately reversed again in the assonance "-ry-grateful/Regretful"), while also emphasizing its own sense of an ending by a telescopic series of petites reprises teasing out the ineffable contradiction structured into the lyrics at the cadences.

> You'll always be what you always were, / Which has nothing to do with, /
> > > > > All to do with her
> > > > > [+ cadence motif]
> > > > [+ cadence motif octave higher].
> You'll always be what you always were, / Which has nothing to do with, /
> > > > > All to do with her
> > > > > [+ cadence motif]
> > > > [+ cadence motif octave higher].
> > > > > Nothing to do with, /

All to do with her
[+ cadence motif]
[+ cadence motif octave higher].
[initial motif]

The fall of the cadence itself characterizes the wistful urban style of this song, its vocal line full of the gapped scales of folk music (see *x* in ex. 5.5b) whose angularity in turn seems to give rise to the gently neoclassical use of dissonant harmonic functions within a diatonic framework (the D is the interloper in the second measure of ex. 5.5c, the A in the first measure, encouraged by the recalcitrant F-sharp in the voice part).

"Sorry-Grateful" is a hard number to trump, and if it identifies the paradoxes that are the subject of *Company,* so early in the show, we are likely to be confused rather than enlightened by later perspectives. To a certain extent this is a problem with any great theatrical monologue or song that does not lead to action, but there are other aspects too in which *Company* may appear more of a problem musical than its critical heritage leads us to believe.

The Need for Deconstruction

In short, twenty years later, *Company,* which has never been revived on Broadway or in the West End, exacts a fresh look, despite the fact that its progenitors may seem to have sewn up all there is to say about it themselves in their various interviews and comments. Indeed this is the point: Prince, Sondheim, Furth, and their collaborators produced an artifact so integrated that it is virtually locked into the terms of its discussion. When Sondheim says that "it dealt with the increasing difficulty of making one-to-one relationships in an increasingly dehumanized society . . . it took place in an urban society in which individuality and individual feeling become more and more difficult to maintain. It's the lonely crowd syndrome," he is right, yet uses language very specific to the place, class, and generation in question: a phrase such as *dehumanized society,* even the word *relationships,* is not used by everybody, then or now. It belongs to the very people the show is about.

If the idea thus resists reinterpretation, is it dated? Could D. D. Ryan's 1970 costumes be put back on the stage without seeming as quaint as they do in the photos of the original production? Is the musical in fact still credible? At the same time, though, how is it that we still respond to slang epigrams in the lyrics such as "Marriage may be where it's been, / But it's not where it's at!"? Has nothing moved on in twenty years except clothing?

All this suggests that there may be more paradoxes in *Company* than the one it intentionally addresses, and that a little deconstruction may be in order. It is a fine score, and in many respects represents the center of Sondheim, but identification with its matter and manner, its construct of ambiguities and self-criticisms, has to be balanced against what may seem to be a perverse detachment from its excellence.

Sondheim, Prince, and the writer of the book, George Furth, were all born within four years of each other, and were reaching the age of forty around 1970. To an extent Bobby's and his friends' problems must have been their problems, his life-style theirs (the very word bespeaks the same phenomenon as the concept musical: freedom to choose congruence of matter and manner and, above all, to be aware of the availability of choice). Indeed, Prince has referred to their desire to write "a kind of autobiographical musical" (Zadan 1990, 117). They grew up in an age in which marriage was no longer either economically necessary or economically out of the question to aspiring young people, and no longer the prize to be played for through a long and wearing obstacle course of war, military service, educational or vocational training, family expectations, and financial dependencies. On the contrary, their role as consumers allowed them to wear, as insignia of the liberal conscience, the hardships and dependencies of others as nonfunction or style, a way of dealing with education and acquisitiveness that gave rise to the appropriation of musical styles (jazz, blues, rock, and other minority idioms that in *West Side Story* still retained a large measure of romantic otherness), cuisine, such leisure habits as drug taking, and clothing and hair. In the words of George Melly, the 1960s turned revolt into style. There were plenty of nodal points around the time of *Company* that could be cited, or recited in keeping with the quasi-liturgical lists at which Sondheim excels in his lyrics, such as the Woodstock Festival and gay Stonewall Riots of the summer of 1969.

Such a categorization of dynastic time can easily become glib (we would be unwise to add the moon landing to this list), and there are dangers in speculating on the extent to which the reconstruction of the American dream with the assistance of rock music and its adjuncts after the death of Kennedy helped make *Company* and its audience possible, and the extent to which the aftermath of Vietnam would render it obsolete (and it can be argued that Sondheim's imagery descends very noticeably into darkness for over a decade after *Company*, in different ways, with *Follies, Pacific Overtures, Sweeney Todd,* and *Merrily We Roll Along;* even, perhaps, with *A Little Night Music*); it is also too soon yet to tell how much AIDS has affected our perceptions of coupling and singleness. But it is surely the case that, if its attitudes and modes of discourse capture a moment in time, it is a moment that has perpetuated itself to the present day, at least as a cultural topic. Yuppies are already in full flight in *Company*, in all but name. The phenomenon that *Company* addresses may not be universal in its application—and to the extent that it is not we are again putting our finger on a problem of the concept musical—but it has proved remarkably stable and enduring as an issue. Its postmodernist ways are the ways of Stoppard, Neil Simon, and Woody Allen, of Habitat and Gucci, even, to a degree, of Ayckbourn and the television sitcom. One is tempted to suggest that, instead of the need for Robert to choose marriage once and for all, he might effectively bring his dilemma to a different or varied ironic crux week after week in some serial. There is a real danger, in the lack of "linear development" in *Company*, that the concept musical degenerates into an all-purpose, self-perpetuating formula for domestic comedy. The sharper George Furth's conversational one-liners, the greater the danger. If that is the case, the yuppie is the comic social cliché of our day, just as the middle American family was to the previous generation of scriptwriters and the cockney and the English lord were in Britain before that.

The intention here is not to cheapen Sondheim's achievement but to express a deep need to see it in a more relaxed perspective. On the one hand, his agonized ambivalences about the single and the coupled state hit home as profoundly as ever, and provide a close focus for our assessment of his genius (I have already commented upon this in chap. 1, and can add that it is a major reason gays respond so powerfully to him, and why, in a sense irrelevantly, questions were raised about Robert's sexual orientation in the first reviews and have been raised again since; see Hirsch 1989, 87; Ilson 1989, 174; Zadan 1990, 386–87). On the other hand, Robert's view of the dilemma now seems rather parochial, a result perhaps of an era in which personal fulfilment was couched in narrower terms than it is today; do we really believe that Robert's only "adult" option is to couple, sooner or later, for good and/or ill, or remain a cypher? There are many other worlds impinging on the characters in *Company* that the exclusive dramatic concentration on one issue is in danger of distorting through omission: what about Robert's job, for instance? We know nothing about that, and are reminded of Thom Gunn's comment on popular song conventions: "what lover in a Sinatra song ever *works at a job?*" (Gunn, quoted in Frith 1989, 95). We are not told about his specific abilities, interests, and hobbies. Nor, with the exception of Joanne, do we know or are made to care anything about his friends as individuals. What if one of them became single again, through death or parting? It is going to happen eventually, yet we are denied any conception of it. What about celibacy or conditions of communal life in certain service professions?

Company as a topical revue has no need to consider these things ("characters appear more flat than round" in concept musicals [Huber 1990, 3, quoting Richard Kislan]), but Robert has, if his wishes are to be convincing. The choices open to Robert are applicable, and of consequence, only within a tight social game in which he is caught up; we are not necessarily misanthropic if we prefer not to put one and one together to make two in this instance, or prefer to elevate one of the rejected endings over the canonical one. Sondheim himself recognizes this implicitly in his later musicals, for George in *Sunday* rejects Dot in favor of creative bachelorhood and the characters in *Into the Woods* show a far broader range of dramatic engagement with life's conditions and choices than the cast of *Company*.

The Question of the Ending

It could even be argued, and this is perhaps the simplest view of *Company*'s dialectic, that the question of the ending is all part of the fun: that to leave Robert torn, in his tug-of-war, which was actually staged in "Side by Side by Side," between romantic involvement and realistic detachment (or do we mean romantic detachment and realistic involvement?) is in line with *Company*'s concept, its metaphor, to quote the word beloved of its progenitors. The dilemma may be a critical impasse, an "uncanny moment" (Abrams 1988, 272), but at least it is intrinsically and fruitfully comic, for it thrives on the continual interlocking somersaults and athletic reversals of terms and values performed by Sondheim in many lines of lyrics.

> Good things get better,
> Bad get worse.
> Wait—I think I meant that in reverse.

(The karate escapades of Sarah and Harry are appropriate enough in this scene). Yet we cannot escape from the metaphysical portentousness of the subject as it is expounded to us. There is a temporal dimension to game playing as well as a spatial one, and with every move, every choice in our lives, we create a world of consequences that can never again be uncreated. Furth's lines for Robert in act 1, scene 4 hit the nail on the head.

> ... you can't get out of it ... then—you've always been married. I mean, you can never not have been married again.

This strikes hard, and points to the one-way road between innocence and experience, even between life and afterlife. Hell or heaven is the afterlife we dream of in the singleness of life, and the decision to couple for good or ill becomes our theology, the decision not to our atheism or at least agnosticism. If Robert succeeds in making a wish—and the whole show can be seen as a fantasy taking place in an instant in his mind as he approaches this moment of testimony—he will have become an incarnation of faith.

Given, then, that this is what Robert is faced with in his four final songs ("happily ever after . . . / In hell" are hardly unresonant lines), it may seem futile after all to attempt to defuse the whole issue. Yet one may be bold enough to suggest that if, to continue the theological train of thought, we step back from the concept musical for a moment and decline the scriptural authority of *Company*'s original production, its decisions and solutions and collaborations, we may paradoxically be able to grasp more facets of the conceptual truth by allowing the alternative endings equal validity, to suggest that all four songs ought to be in the score. Perhaps this is a corner that the concept musical was not ready to turn in 1970 but can countenance now; or maybe *Company* should be allowed to mature from a museum artifact (the original production) into a public domain text, complete with its variants and critical apparatus, evidence that is just as liable to undermine the notion of an authoritative text as to establish one.

We cannot pursue this discussion, of course, without being aware of how it looms large in Sondheim's later work. *Follies* was rewritten in 1987 with a different ending, and the comparative status of the 1971 and 1987 versions will be a matter of concern to future scholars and exponents. A periodic adjustment of the ending of *Pacific Overtures* is built into the very plot, since it deals with the history of Japan up to the present, and the present soon becomes history. *A Little Night Music* was originally planned as the dramatization of three alternative outcomes to a situation. And both *Sunday in the Park with George* and *Into the Woods* explore the notion of a perfect ending (at the close of act 1) that turns out to have later consequences, the former somewhat by practical default, the latter with the highest authorial integrity.

There is another side to the issue too. Just as Tippett, in his opera *The Midsummer Marriage,* said that he wanted to cast the plot, for all its mystical overtones, as the traditional comic drama showing the trials and tribulations that a young couple undergo before winning through to marriage (see Tippett 1959, 53–55), so we should not ignore this archetype's significantly different role in the classic novel, in which the comic dimension is less integral and the upshot often more ambiguous. The reason for the difference is partly one of medium. A classic theater audience knows whether or not it is attending "comedy tonight," and the demands of genre are tightly bound up with modes of performance (in opera, the very emergence of the classical style came about historically as a result of the apotheosis of comedy). In the novel, the practice of serialization emphasized the discursive nature of the genre, rendering the unities of time, place, and action far less pressing and even making the reader reluctant to bring their relationship with the characters to any conclusion at all. The author might have no idea what a character's destiny should be, and might even say so to the reader in an authorial aside. David Lodge deals with these matters in his essay "Ambiguously Ever After: Problematical Endings in English Fiction" (Lodge 1981, 143–55), and also points out two factors that have particular relevance to *Company* and the musical. One is that the serial author was subject to consumer feedback.

> There was continual feedback from the audience during the process of composition, and the author was always likely to come under pressure from his friends, his publishers and the reading public at large to provide an ending that conformed to their desires. Dickens first experienced this pressure on a major scale as he approached the end of *The Old Curiosity Shop*, where he described himself as "inundated with imploring letters recommending poor little Nell to mercy." (Lodge 1981, 146)

Lodge also cites Dickens's *Great Expectations,* in which the author's rejected, unhappy ending has been adjudged superior to the canonical happy one. This phenomenon surely bears comparison with what one or more contributors to a musical production would like to put on the stage as opposed to what is found to work in the commercial theater. That an author may be torn between endings and have to opt for one without necessarily wanting to is, presumably, a legitimate possibility within this phenomenon. But Lodge also points out that

> . . . all the examples I have discussed involve a hesitation between—to put it simply—a happy and an unhappy ending, expressed in terms of a love relationship which is or is not sealed in marriage. The marriage knot is the primary symbol of happiness, of the optimistic idea that the nice and the good are one and shall inherit the earth. Conversely, the novelist's refusal to tie the marriage knot between hero and heroine expresses a bleaker and more pessimistic view that life rarely conforms to our desires, or our notions of justice. (Lodge 1981, 149).

Lodge also refers to Frank Kermode's study, *The Sense of an Ending,* which argues that "the history of fiction is the history of a continuous dialogue or dialectic between credulity—our wish to believe—and skepticism—our wish to be told the truth" (Lodge 1981, 149). In *Company*, of course, it is not just the author's problem but the character's: Robert, as a twentieth-century man, is not acting according to outside pressures with which the author has surrounded him and which must be logically resolved (there are none, unless we count his flight from Joanne in the penultimate scene or build up the relationship with Amy), but is himself the author, appropriating the structure of his life as his own creative responsibility. The agonizing choices confronting a novelist are his; his life will go into print, as it were, as a single or married one, and he cannot hold off publication indefinitely. He too must decide between skepticism and credulity. And as with the Victorian or modern novelist's confidential asides, he and his friends share their doubts with the reader, making them his or hers—this is where the songs come in. No wonder *Company* is apt to overwhelm us with its weight of responsibility, conventional literary artifact though it may still be. One may feel that, as a postmodern artifact, it needs some means of escape from that weight, such as is provided by the double ending of Fowles's *The French Lieutenant's Woman* or, virtually by way of improvisation on the stage, by the alternative middles of Ayckbourn's *Sisterly Feelings* (though in a sense Ayckbourn is propounding the opposite view: however we respond to temporal chance or choice, we end up in the same place).

The Four Last Songs

What, then, *are* the alternative endings? Sondheim wrote four completely different songs (though two of them share some of their lyrics). None of them was judged in any technical sense inferior, and Sondheim, commenting on them in his "Theater Lyrics" talk of 1971 (whose published transcript includes the complete lyrics of all four), has said that "they are all songs that for different reasons I like" (1974, 92 see also Sondheim's comments in Orchard 1988, 633–34). Each shows Robert, in his search for happiness, mapping a different route through the life change symbolized by marriage, and ex. 5.6 represents this diagrammatically, chronology being the horizontal axis, fulfilment the vertical. Sondheim explains "Marry Me a Little" as "one of the first songs I wrote for the show. . . . In this version . . . Amy did not get married at the end of the first act, and Robert came to her in the second act and asked her to marry him" (1974, 92). He floats his proposal on a sea of optimism, and the artful and subtle bedding of the voice part upon the accompaniment, with a kind of written-in rubato (see ex. 5.4b), expresses this particularly well.

Ex. 5.6

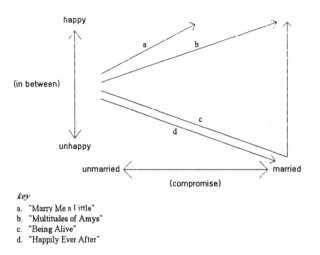

key
a. "Marry Me a Little"
b. "Multitudes of Amys"
c. "Being Alive"
d. "Happily Ever After"

But the optimism only functions because he believes that compromise between complete commitment and a measure of independence is possible.

> Marry me a little,
> Love me just enough,
> Cry but not too often,
> Play but not too rough,
> Keep a tender distance
> So we'll both be free,
> That's the way it ought to be.

This insurance against complete self-abandonment is seen as the shortest route to fulfilment, but the music seems to tell us otherwise, for four times it puts a quartal dissonance in the way of full tonal resolution, ironically on the word *now*. Twice it deflects the melody into a different key; twice it merely obliterates the leading tone at the primary tonal cadence. This song was rejected because "we decided that . . . the audience might not *get* the lie that Robert is telling himself" (Sondheim 1974, 94).

The second song, "Multitudes of Amys," seems straightforwardly romantic: Robert "thinks he is finally in love with Amy" (Sondheim 1974, 94), and the music, which has not been published, thinks so too, being among Sondheim's warmest and most rhetorically full-blooded compositions, cast as it is in the same heady key of D-flat major as "A Hero Is Coming" from *Anyone Can Whistle* and sharing some of its throbbing harmonic sonorities (see ex. 5.7a). This song was rejected because of a changed dramatic situation—we need to be aware that it was not only

Ex. 5.7a

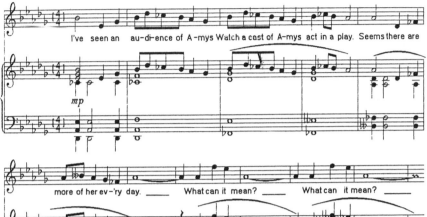

I've seen an au-di-ence of A-mys Watch a cast of A-mys act in a play. Seems there are more of her ev-'ry day. _____ What can it mean? _____ What can it mean? _____

Ex. 5.7b

[Con moto]

Some-one to hold you too close, _____ Some-one to hurt you too deep, _____

Ex. 5.7c

i

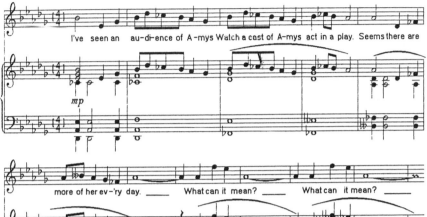

Some-one to crowd you with love,

ii

Some-bod-y crowd me with love,

the last songs that were being switched around as *Company* moved toward the stage: a great deal of the material changed position, Joanne's scene and "The Ladies Who Lunch" coming much earlier in the show at the time of the backers' audition tape and "Someone Is Waiting" coming later, as a lead-in to Robert's focus on Amy (the song's ending, "Wait for me," would have been more effective in this late position).

The third song, "Happily Ever After," was used in the Boston tryout. It goes the other way, and audiences perceived it as "the bitterest, most unhappy song ever written" (Prince, quoted in Zadan 1990, 124), and such, apparently, it is, invigoratingly callous in its jogging 9/8 rock beat that sees the only point in life as an ongoing "little trip" (ex. 5.7b). It views marriage as pure imprisonment and unhappiness, singleness as existential amelioration.

> Waste a little time,
> Make a little love,
> Show a little feeling,
> But why
> Should you try?
> Why not, sure, feel a little lonely,
> But fly,
> Why not fly
> With no one to hold you too close,
> No one to hurt you too deep,
> No one to love you too hard
> Happily ever after?

"Being Alive," the fourth and final song, used in the New York and London productions and present in the vocal score, shares the same starting point and same opening lines as "Happily Ever After," but halfway through there is a change of lyric mode, from the impersonal second-person singular to the first person. It was at an equivalent juncture in "Happily Ever After" that "someone . . ." became "no one . . . ," thus with the knowledge of both songs the transformation is all the more pointed.

> Somebody hold me too close,
> Somebody hurt me too deep,
> Somebody sit in my chair
> And ruin my sleep

This transforms the whole picture, suddenly, from one of rejection to one of acceptance, implying that Robert now wishes for the loss of self-containment, that this will be his happiness rather than his misery.

But will it? Were the authors right to end the show by jettisoning the primary layer of irony and ambivalence that had sustained it all along and had kept Robert moving as a character precisely through his inability to jump through the hoop? This is a classic "happily ever after" ending: we have seen him go through the door at last, and once out of sight he is no longer of concern to us. It is made all the more so because we are spared the skepticism of seeing him attain whatever, or rather whomever, his hard-won ability to wish may eventually procure for him. And the music sews it all up rather neatly: above the solid, slow-moving harmonic framework of repeated choruses, their rock allegiances an adequately balancing endpier for the opening title number, the strings counterpoint, first, the melody of "Someone Is Waiting" and then the tune of "Company" itself (ex. 5.7c, i and ii). As a classic example of "redemptive" cyclic form in the nineteenth-century manner, this is symphonic enough, at little compositional cost; but, at this remove from the aims of *Anyone Can Whistle,* do we really want to believe in a symphonic conclusion? If we note again that, as mentioned in chapter 2, orchestrator Jonathan Tunick was responsible for the first of these two thematic cross-references, and that he gained for it a "Charlie Brown grin" of surprised approval from Sondheim (Zadan 1990, 159), does this just show us one more pair of authorial accomplices in the collusion toward credulity? (Sondheim answers the charge by saying that in fact he considered the quodlibet unsuitable in this context but did not want to obstruct Tunick on this, the first occasion of their working together.)

Let us return to the point made previously, that once we are left alone with Robert in his final song(s)—and his secret birthday wish, his absence from the party, and his extended monologues in song all confirm this aloneness—the authorial voice is essentially his, though urged on in "Being Alive" by the interjections of his friends. But it is not quite as simple as that. Unlike the novelist telling us what happens in the single plane of third-person narrative, there is, as we have already seen, more than one plane of material presented for assessment here, due to the nature of musical theater. Robert's actions may tell us one thing, his words another, his music a third; all of these may hold contradictions or ambivalences within them; and, insofar as he is depicted communicating with us from the stage, he may or may not want to believe himself or want *us* to believe him. Perhaps, paradoxically, what the four songs show us is that we can find plenty of contradictory levels of meaning in any one of them without requiring the lateral spread of all four.

For instance, we have already seen that "Marry Me a Little" is "a lie that Robert is telling himself." Yet he may well *know* that he is telling himself a lie and nonetheless want to use it as his only possible spur to a difficult decision: once he is married, will it matter that he got there by false expectations of compromise? Hence:

Level 1: Hope of positive compromise (lyrics and music);
Level 2: impasse—impossibility or hypocrisy of compromise (guard-edness and naivety of lyrics, checks in music); and
Level 3: subject matter (positive compromise) false, but valid premise as positive catalyst (satisfactory, exhilarating closure of lyrics and music).

"Multitudes of Amys" is similar, but more basic in that there are no contradictions within its structure, only between layers of reception.

Level 1: Robert convinces himself he is in love with Amy (positive lyrics and music);
Level 2: the language is the conventional one of infatuation (romantic lyrics and music), and hence perceived (by us? him?) as artificial, untrue; and
Level 3: infatuation is a self-willed construct nonetheless, thus a legit-imate spur to action (exhortatory, persuasive lyrics and music).

Sondheim said that he viewed "Happily Ever After" not as a bitter song but "as a scream of pain." We may postulate the following.

Level 1: Skeptical view of the impossibility or destructiveness of com-promise indicates painful, hence sincere, rejection of mar-riage (wounding lyrics, vehement music with no respite);
Level 2: this skepticism is cynicism that contaminates and invalidates the selfish existentialism posited as preferable (the angry, demonic urge is present throughout the song in the cast of the lyrics and music—there is no change or counterpoint of mood or mode); and
Level 3: Robert's skillful, even inspired understanding of painful epi-grammatic truths (knowing lyrics, fine, driving music) indi-cate that he has come to terms with both the agony of marriage and the agony of singleness; understanding raises him above the plane of binary action, and no decision is necessary (triple time in music, "ever, ever, ever" repeated in lyrics).

"Being Alive" is somewhat in a class of its own, given, first, that the change of mode affects it in time rather than purely with simultaneous contradictions, and, second, that, as we have already observed, the change "from a complaint to a prayer," as Sondheim puts it—the point at which he actually makes a wish—is effected by the intervention of Robert's friends. Does this make it automatically richer dramatically than the other three songs? It seems existentially more complex too.

Level 1: Change from second-person singular to first person indicates change of heart: negative fear of compromise becomes positive desire for redemption in self-loss (lyrics);

Level 2: repeating choruses undermine this as cynicism, "cyclic" counterpoint undermines it as persuasive or sentimental device (catch-alls and artifices of music: a unified musical structure cannot really change its mind);

Level 3: transcendence arises out of sentimental transformation: the mixture of similar and different elements (new light on lyrics, same music; thematic cross-reference) is the culmination of aesthetic experience Robert is looking for and will find in marriage; and

Level 4: transcendence is delusion: he only sees what he wants to see, and forgets the truths of earlier songs—"Everybody dies," "You'll always be what you always were" (music and lyrics of earlier songs temper or invalidate unitary conclusion).

Finally, we should observe that level 4 applies in a way to all four finales; and that there is a nasty further catch, a level 5: our imperative to applaud whatever Robert sings as his final song. The final decision lies with us, the audience, and insofar as we do not walk out, but applaud, we automatically confirm, validate, and thus in a sense *invalidate* anything on which he decides. That's show business.

Perhaps we should be content that *Company* resists its ending, that it prefers being over becoming. "You can't stay in your thirties forever," Harry says at the beginning of act 2, but the point is that you can: it is a logical conclusion to the tenets of a society based on unlimited consumer choice. This may be why *Company*, which seems to have spawned a whole genre, the "yuppie revue" (whose later exponents include Finn and Maltby and Shire), remains vibrant today, why its vernacular prepositional language minted by people who are "into" things (see the essay "Where It's At: The Poetry of Psychobabble" in Lodge 1981, 188–96) continues to be used after twenty years or more of coinage. Choice of life-style implies, as with contemporary stylistic usage in the arts, that all modes will continue to be valid and available indefinitely in a kind of immortal stasis. We are all preposition without object, all antecedent without consequent, and, unlike classical drama, modern structures can have no recourse to the deus ex machina, for the deus is the machina, the eternal mechanism of city life that New Yorkers are not saved by but worship incessantly as it whirrs and swirls them up and down, side by side, just like the elevators in Aronson's set.

Chapter 6

Follies

The Image in the Mirror

[Folly speaks:] . . . it's even more fun to see the old women who can
scarcely carry their weight of years and look like corpses that seem to
have risen from the dead. They still go around saying "Life is good," still
on heat, "longing for a mate," as the Greeks say, and seducing some
young Phaon they've hired for large sums of money. They're forever
smearing their faces with make-up and taking tweezers to their pubic
hairs, exposing their sagging, withered breasts and trying to rouse failing
desire with their quavery whining voices, while they drink, dance among
the girls and scribble their little love-letters. All this raises a general
laugh for what it is—absolute foolishness; but meanwhile they're pleased
with themselves, lead a life of supreme delight suffused with sweet
fantasy, and owe all their happiness to me. Those who find this too
ridiculous should please consider whether they'd rather spend a life
sweetened with folly like this or go and look for the proverbial beam to
hang from. The fact that such conduct is generally frowned on means
nothing to my fools, for either they don't realize anything is wrong, or if
they do, they find it easy to take no notice. If a rock falls on your head it
does positive harm, but shame, disgrace, reproaches and insults are
damaging only in so far as you're conscious of them. If you're not, you
feel no hurt at all. What's the harm in the whole audience hissing you if
you clap yourself? And Folly alone makes this possible.

—Erasmus, *Praise of Folly*

Follies, like the world of the theater and our participation in it as spectators,
operates between the tragedy and cruelty of self-delusion, Erasmus's "sagging, withered breasts" and "little love-letters," and the exhilaration of
self-preservation and -celebration, for, as Erasmus's Folly acknowledges,
"Self-love . . . is so prompt to take my place on all occasions that she is
rightly called my sister" ([1509] 1971, 94). No one is spared this double
vista, from the chorus girls whose reunion sparked off Sondheim's and
James Goldman's imagination in 1965 to the creators themselves. *Follies*
"was me getting scared about getting older," its codirector Hal Prince

175

stated in 1976 (Ilson 1989, 177). Least of all does the composer escape the critique of projection and survival; Ben, sixteen years after our first reunion with him, is given not a nervous breakdown but these lyrics to usher in and conclude his song at the climax of the "follies" sequence itself.

> What you do is construct yourself
> By the way you conduct yourself.
> You don't have to disclose yourself—
> Compose yourself.
>
> . . . .
>   . . . and,
> Who knows?
> You may even get to like
> What you compose!

The deeply ironic reflexivity of this image, developed, as we have seen, from "Anyone Can Whistle," speaks for itself. What we see depends on the angle of vision. Ben looks at himself and sees someone else, a composer; in *Follies* the mirror, in reflecting the gaze, repeatedly directs it to a third point, and the double vista produces a triangle. Sondheim looks at Ben, but the closer he gets to him the more acute the angle of vision becomes and the more he sees himself (see ex. 6.1a). Or, if we prefer to imagine *Follies* not as angles in space but as accretions, filters, and interfaces along what we think of as the straight line of time—as memory, in fact—we look through the glass to see a different self on the other side of it, younger, older, a fraud rather than genuine, a successful failure. The filter colors, the prism refracts. Do we thereby see more or less of the truth? Do spectacles clarify or distort vision (ex. 6.1b)?

Follies repeatedly sets up these sharp-pointed or mediated linear structures whose corners we turn, whose trajectories we travel, swiftly and in the twinkling of an eye. But its deepest irony is when what we thought was a straight line or a single angle becomes a triangle, when what we construed as the prism of time or choice becomes the mirror of reflexivity. There is no "different" self on the other side of the glass: as the angle sharpens, Ben and Sally realize that the glass is reflecting themselves; Young Ben and Ben are the same person, and so are Young Sally and Sally. "You always are what you always were." In reuniting they can only repeat their folly of thirty years ago, which is what happens during the evening. Their relationship, eternally caught in the other triangles of their friendships and impending or factual marriages (see ex. 6.1c for the basic double triangle on which *Follies* is constructed), is embedded in their characters; there is no free will about it. Each can only sing one song,

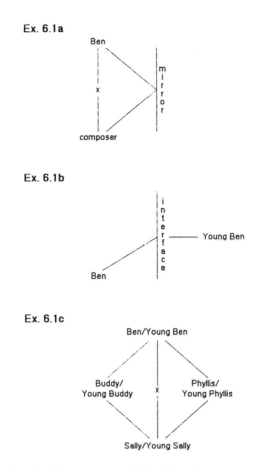

Ex. 6.1a

Ex. 6.1b

Ex. 6.1c

and keep singing it. The song is their folly, forever deluded and forever sustaining.

In a sense, then, *Follies,* particularly *Follies 1987,* belies Sondheim's preoccupation with choice and its consequences, or rather subverts it into an understanding that making a mess of choices or being unable to choose at all is a constant in our character, in itself an essential and predetermined part of our personal music, positive or negative according to self-love, whether or not "you like what you compose." Thus Ben will always desire Sally and hate himself for not loving her, Phyllis will always oscillate between uptown and downtown, Buddy will always oscillate between Sally and Margie, and Sally will always cry over Ben while relying on Buddy.

This teasing out of ideas suggested by the image exploited in the *Follies* "mirror" song, "Who's That Woman?," is doubtless of limited validity. Nevertheless, it is an image to which poets, psychologists, and philosophers have also succumbed. Housman sees the lover's eyes as mirrors in "Look Not in My Eyes"; Lacan has much to say about the "mirror stage";

Schopenhauer, closer to our discussion, asks "Why is it, in spite of all the mirrors in existence, no man really knows what he looks like . . . ?" and continues with this fertile observation:

> A man can only see himself in the glass by looking straight towards it and remaining quite still; whereby the play of the eye, which is so important, and the real characteristic of the face is, to a great extent, lost. . . . A man cannot regard the reflection of his own face in the glass as if it were the face of *some one else*—which is the condition of his seeing himself *objectively*. (. . . When a man sees his own person in the glass the egoistic side of him always whispers, *It is not somebody else, but I myself,* which has the effect of a *noli me tangere,* and prevents his taking a purely objective view.) (Schopenhauer 1897, 155–56)

Here, surely, is the root condition of self-dramatization, of the construction of our personal folly.

Despite the fact that triangles and lines with mediating points can always be resolved into pairs of binary oppositions, it is indicative of the rich texture of *Follies,* in many ways more complex than its predecessors in Sondheim's output of musicals, that triple terms or triple oppositions suggest themselves repeatedly or lead to further enumeration. And through it all it is worth keeping one eye on the idea of folly itself, in all its shades of meaning, for it is with a playing-out of "follies" that the show culminates. Rick Altman helpfully glosses the phenomenon of what he calls "personality disolve" in the musical, though the first part of his definition of it (as given below) might equally apply to the far older and broader political figure of the fool, the jester, in drama.

> This dilemma [of consciousness linked with accountability] is resolved by the introduction of a mode in which certain types of conscious behavior are accorded a special status which frees them from the frightening spectre of accountability. In all of these "make-believe" modes—dream, performance, and role-playing are the most common—an individual gains the right to "play out" personal fantasies without submitting to the judgments normally associated with conscious behavior. The character can say and do what he/she pleases and yet in the eyes of his/her psychic censor it is as if nothing had either been said or done. Like a child playing "dress-up"—like the spectator watching the film—a character can try on a role without actually assuming it. This strategy ultimately permits the recovery of repressed material and thus the merger of submerged and surface components of the personality. By way of make-believe one dissolves into the other. (Altman 1987, 83)

The List Song

The status of song itself within the show demonstrates both its synonymity with folly and the multiple layering to which its identity gives rise. In many respects, "I'm Still Here" is the central song in *Follies*. One of Sondheim's proverbial out-of-town replacements, it was written in Boston when it became apparent that "Can That Boy Fox-trot!" was unsatisfactory because, as Michael Bennett, Prince's codirector, explains, "Yvonne [de Carlo] couldn't do it" (Zadan 1990, 143) and it had "expanded into a seven minute production number which nearly stopped the show every night" (Sondheim and Lucas [1981]). It is a prime example of the "list song," a type that comes into its own in *Follies* more than in Sondheim's previous musicals, even *Company*. (Other examples include Phyllis's "Could I Leave You?" in which her imprecatory list of the "little things" that make her marriage with Ben intolerable gives way to an inventory of the furniture as she anticipates divorce; Sally's list of the minutiae that constitute her life in Arizona; Ben's list of musical terms and devices in "Make the Most of Your Music"; and so on.) Sondheim's notes for his 1971 "Theatre Lyrics" talk include a passage on list songs that does not appear in the published transcript.

List Songs

In a certain sense, most are; refrain with examples. Best is "Let's Do It." But when it has nothing to say, it's a bore. . . . Nothing to say, make a list[.] How you develop it is what counts. . . . I'm Still Here develops through decades but "last year" is what makes it work.

He is eager to make the distinction between "Ah, Paris!" which is a geographical list song with no particular structure or point to it and which he therefore sees as a parody of an earlier genre (to which he himself had contributed in "Philadelphia!" cut from *Do I Hear a Waltz?*), and "I'm Still Here," whose structure says something about Carlotta's character, as we shall see. Be that as it may, the quality of wit is what makes most list songs work, as Cole Porter, the genre's master, understood better than anyone. To a certain extent wit is likely to be invested in rhyme, as with most other types of songs, and rhyme frequently involves the incongruity that is a basic element of so much humor. Thus we enjoy being told by Carlotta about a life so inclusive that it can range from "shanties" to "scanties"; she is no more incongruous than the times she represents, however, whose media embrace both "Amos 'n' Andy" and "Gandhi" ("Gandhi," like most of the other references, is to be understood in the

context of *headlines,* a word which is carefully placed in that it follows up
her reference to stuffing the dailies in her shoes—a classic instance of what
Sondheim means by subtext: "give the actor something to act" [Sondheim
1974, 71]). However, these references are witty not just by means of their
incongruity between sound and sense but because they make us feel clever
when we recognize the phenomena to which they refer (see Swain 1990,
139–40 for a discussion of this factor in *Kiss Me, Kate;* Furia 1990, 6–8 for
a helpful pinpointing of its origins in turn-of-the-century "society verse").
The audience has to identify with the things being listed in a list song,
either because they are the things that make up our own experience (or,
we believe, the things that make up another person's experience, as when
we agree that a person like Ben would own Braques and Chagalls)—in
which case the wit consists in the author having hit the nail on the head—
or because we know that they are among the myriad things that exist out
there in the world: we have heard of them, however faintly, or at least feel
that we ought to have heard of them. This subgenre of list song might be
called the encyclopedia song, or the consumer song when it places the
premium upon possessions and their mode of labeling, which Lodge identifies as the polar concomitant of "psychobabble" (Lodge 1981, 195–96).
Phyllis and Ben treat "Braques and Chagalls" very much as brand names,
and doubtless she would have referred to the "grand" as "the Steinway"
had it rhymed.

"I'm Still Here" is a wonderful encyclopedia song (though, as we have
seen, it suggests the newspaper rather than the encyclopedia as the source
of facts). Some of its references are obvious to all, some can be guessed,
others will tantalize the non-American or younger listener. Amos 'n' Andy
were a radio blackface act current from the mid-1920s; William Beebe
in his bathysphere descended to a record depth of over 3,000 feet in the
ocean off Bermuda in 1934; the Dionne quintuplets were born in Canada,
also in 1934; Brenda Frazier was a society debutante who flaunted a
scandalously luxurious life-style during the Great Depression. Major
Bowes was a talent-spotting radio host.

These references to the 1920s and 1930s conjure up "an entire era,
the time between the two great wars," as one of Goldman's novelistic
stage directions for *Follies* puts it, and most of the unused items listed in
Sondheim's sketches for the song elaborate on this period, for instance
"Shacks," "Public works," "Lines for jobs," "Picket," "Soup kitchens,"
"Wall St. suicides," "Prosperity is just around the corner," "Haile Selas-
sie," "zeppelins," "one World's Fair," "Bobbed hair," "Babe Ruth—40
runs," "Knockknocks," "Garbo," "CCC," "NRA," "FDR," "CCNY,"
"Conser-/Vation Corps," "Bad Swing." In one sense they are enough to
make the song work, to stand, like an old newsreel, as a memorial to the

period of the Weismann Follies (which are supposed to have lasted from 1918 to 1941, 1920 to 1940 in *Follies 1987*). Heard this way, Carlotta is simply singing a song she used to sing years ago. Yet, as Sondheim says, the song "develops through decades." The "Pinko/Commie tool" and other references around it imply the 1950s, and certainly the whole point of the song, heavily underlined by the orchestrated growth of the musical choruses, is to bring us from some distant, remembered past up to the present. Sondheim's intention was that the second chorus, after (and including?) the bridge, should be Carlotta's more recently added material, the gloss on her own past, another layer of survival; and the third chorus adds a further layer—hence the crucial reference to "last year" and the triumphant "at least I was there."

Song as Folly

Carlotta is a survivor, and if she can survive until 1941 she can survive for another thirty or forty-five years. Of course this is what we have been saying about Ben and Phyllis, Sally and Buddy, and it adds another song to the idea of the eternal present while apparently belying it with its panorama of the past, "good times and bum times." This is a contradiction to which we must return. But the most urgent aspect of "I'm Still Here" is its locus as song; it is Carlotta's song, song as Folly, a possession as personal and as indicative of exchange and vulnerability as her body (and perhaps a symbol for it, both aging and ageless), which as female entertainer she gives to the men around her, to the audience, while retaining its identity and dignity, which remain self-communing. There is a poem by Thomas Hardy that conveys and dramatizes this same phenomenon with great power (it too is a lyric, intended in fact or constructed in spirit for setting to music, which has been done more than once, notably by the British composer John Ireland).

Her Song

I sang that song on Sunday,
    To witch an idle while,
I sang that song on Monday,
    As fittest to beguile;
I sang it as the year outwore,
    And the new slid in;
I thought not what might shape before
    Another would begin.

I sang that song in summer,
    All unforeknowingly,

To him as a new-comer
  From regions strange to me:
I sang it when in afteryears
  The shades stretched out,
And paths were faint; and flocking fears
  Brought cup-eyed care and doubt.

Sings he that song on Sundays
  In some dim land afar,
On Saturdays, or Mondays,
  As when the evening star
Glimpsed in upon his bending face,
  And my hanging hair,
And time untouched me with a trace
  Of soul-smart and despair?

Hardy's lyrical tradition is very different from Carlotta's or even Sally's; all the same, we immediately recognize this as a torch song with kinship with "Losing My Mind" as well as "I'm Still Here"; and the inspired coinage of the word *untouched* as an active verb in the penultimate line gives us the nub of *Follies,* the contradiction that time destroys everything yet makes no difference to us at all. Song as lament and song as possession epitomize both terms of the contradiction, and the very nature of song is exposed as tough and "heartless," as we are reminded throughout *Follies* and as Sondheim recognized when he first drew on pastiche in *Anyone Can Whistle* (see Previn 1977).

Similarly, we can both lament and take pride in any kind of high folly. William Empson, in a chapter on "The Praise of Folly" in his book *The Structure of Complex Words,* tells a memorable story.

When M. Hackin discovered what are among the earliest surviving Buddhist statues in the caves of Bamiyan in Afghanistan, at the head of an officially recognized expedition organized like a small army, the occasion was an impressive one, and he found a couplet in English scrawled on one of the more inaccessible of their walls.

If any fool this high samootch explore
Know that Charles Masson has been here before.

This was a deserter from the British Army in India, early in the nineteenth century. . . . The claim of the couplet is that he was a fool; he does not want it forgotten; the assonance of *fool* with *samootch* (cave temple) makes this a remote wild kind of fool to which the adjective *high* can be extended: "Great men do hard things, and the greatest know that it is foolish to do them. Only we, in the secrecy of this place, can rightly say that we are fools." (Empson 1951, 109)

Another gloss on the idea of folly, again not irrelevant to this musical, would be to say that folly is what the Christian understands by the sinner being in a state of grace with God. If the characters in the show are the sinners, their culminating "follies" songs represent the attainment of the state of grace, their potential salvation. The circular platform of *Follies 1987* visualized this well, almost like some ritual elevation of the host; again, as in *Company,* the deus ex machina is recalled yet emphatically absent.

To return to song, woman as sufferer is a necessary and potent concomitant to the region of its identity exemplified above, and its American focus is in the blues. "I'm Still Here" is a blues song in many respects (Carlotta refers to singing the blues), not a twelve-bar blues but still closely indicative of the genre, as well as of jazz in general, in its use of blue notes (the blue seventh and third have been heard even before the voice enters), swing rhythm, repeated pulse, harmonic pace, orchestration and interaction between voice and instruments, structure of cumulative choruses with relieving bridges, and low vocal register. Register is especially worthy of consideration, for it is so low (e-flat to b') that it virtually duplicates that of Roscoe in "Beautiful Girls" (e to a') and where the blues are concerned undoubtedly assists in conveying a song's universal applicability despite the gender of its singer (there remains the converse, however: the throaty register can indicate the arousal of male desire, especially in a striptease context, as in "Ah, But Underneath . . ."). Sondheim exploits a low register for many of his women, in *Follies* and elsewhere. To a certain extent this is a practical matter where singing actors are concerned, for the male and female ranges are not very different from one another in many popular singing traditions (and in any case, according to one school of thought at least, the break between registers occurs at about the same absolute point in the male and female voice); but it is a striking compositional resource nonetheless, in "Broadway Baby" (ranging from g to b-flat'), which is very much a sister song to "I'm Still Here," and in Phyllis's numbers (generally f to b-flat'). Sally's range descends equally far, but she also has to possess a soprano register for the chorus in "In Buddy's Eyes," particularly for the long held d" at the end, and for "Too Many Mornings," in which she reaches as high as g"; this furthers the image of innocent sweetness and romance that she projects and protects. Needless to say, the low register, with its associations of suffering and experience, is avoided in the music for Young Sally and Young Phyllis.

Diegetic Song

If song is both shared experience and personal possession, it matters how this is dramatized, and the issue brings us to the heart of *Follies*. "I'm Still Here" is a diegetic song; that is, as music, lyric, and gesture it is not just engaged as an artificial means of conveying a point to the theater audience or highlighting it for their benefit, though of course it does this; it is an item in the narrative plot—the song is actually happening onstage as part of the real-life story. To put it another way, it is sung by a character who knows that she is singing, and it implies that the other characters onstage know it too, unless they happen to be portrayed as being out of earshot.

Song as part of the narrative is an entirely different concern from that of the "integrated" musical; indeed it often thrusts in the opposite direction. The integrated musical aims to highlight or simply show what a character is going through by musical (for which read also lyrical and choreographic) means: in real life emotions, reactions, or decisions would occur either silently and motionlessly, in the mind, or accompanied by talked or whispered or shouted conversation and gesture or movement, perhaps with laughter or tears or even (to stretch the point) a certain amount of soliloquy (we do not know for certain whether Hamlet actually speaks out loud in order to get his thoughts about "To be, or not to be" straight). To add music to them may convey their nature and truth in an unambiguous or even profound way, but it is a highly artificial way.

The use of diegetic song does not so much reverse this approach as cut across it. It implies a quite different attitude to musical significance and even style, for it does not necessarily matter whether music is trivial or imposing; what matters is that it is actually *there*. Diegetic music plays an important role in film and has been carefully addressed by film theorists (see Gorbman 1987, 20–26 for a clear discussion of it; Palmer, in his more empirical study [1990], refers instead to the distinction between *realistic* and *commentative* music). The use of diegetic music in opera (an issue recently addressed by two leading theorists—see Cone 1989 and Abbate 1991) is far more common, indeed important, than is generally considered, and goes right back to opera's beginnings: the serenade, for instance, is the central event in Monteverdi's *Orfeo*. Wagner used the song contest as a pivotal narrative item in both *Tannhäuser* and *Die Meistersinger,* and there are plenty of diegetic songs (not always vocal) in *Siegfried* and

Tristan and a central role for one in particular in *Der fliegende Holländer.* Above all, perhaps, Bizet's *Carmen* radiates diegetic song, and uses it not just to distinguish the characters but to costume, as it were, whole communities: municipal, military, gypsy, and even urchin groups all have their characteristic music that would actually—or so Bizet and his librettists can persuade us—be heard on the streets of Seville. He sets this up brilliantly from the start of act 1, right down to the provision of a snatch of hummed melody for the captive Carmen.

This does not rule out the use of nondiegetic music, of course, even simultaneously. Indeed, as long as there are both a pit and a stage in the theater, the two have to learn to live together, for the pit orchestra cannot function as a character or prop, but can only mimic a stage band or instrument (such as Beckmesser's lute in *Meistersinger*) or add a nondiegetic layer of its own. It does this on two levels in the third verse of Hans Sach's cobbling song in *Meistersinger,* first by giving him a harmonic accompaniment that he would have to do without in real life, second by counterpointing the motif of Sach's sadness in the horns against his putatively jolly work song melody; the catch is that Eva hears the latter and comments on it without understanding what it is that she hears.

Diegetic music in sixteenth-century Nuremberg or early nineteenth-century Seville is all very well, because it can be believed to represent reality in a culture in which music was out on the streets all the time; the role of music in more recent times, and in the Anglo-American culture that the musical grows to represent and regularly portray, is another matter. *Show Boat* provides the best model. On the one hand, it dramatizes a "primitive" sector of the community, that of the rural black for whom music is still a spontaneous or practical expression as spiritual or work song—the act 1 curtain rises to a black work song, and later Joe sings "Ol' Man River," partly to himself, partly to Magnolia, partly as caller for the responding bargemen who join in, as he idly whittles away with a knife; on the other, it shows white theater folk using music as a very different kind of adjunct to their work. The subtlety occurs when something cuts across the two types. "In Dahomey," purportedly a primitive African song and dance presented at the Chicago Columbian Exposition, turns out to be a fraudulent act by hired urban blacks; more important, Julie knows a blues, "Can't Help Lovin' Dat Man," because she is a half-caste, and her singing of it prefigures her unmasking; thus not just the singing of the song but the recognition of musical and lyric style actually becomes an issue in the plot, and the same can be said when Magnolia has to learn to sing the song in a more up-to-date manner: through the very practicality of its usage it takes on a heavily symbolic role (of the passing of time and the crossing of destinies) in its changing guises as a symbol of entertainment history and, through its effect on its performers and listeners, as an example of possession through memory.

Show Boat is a mixture of what Altman has identified as two of the three subgenres of the musical: the folk musical (in *Show Boat*, blacks are depicted, with their music, in a community that is part of the larger southern way of life and of which the show boat itself is a component), and the show musical, often known as the backstage musical (in which we see behind the scenes to how the nondiegetic music that entertainers present to us is produced, and what it means for them). Both types flourished, in London and at Pinewood as well as in Hollywood and on Broadway, between *Show Boat* (1927) and *Follies,* but the backstage musical had a long way to go from the naive plot mechanics of early sound films or the Ruritanian stages and boudoirs of Ivor Novello's romantic musical plays to the multilayered reflexivity of *Cabaret* or *Follies*. In fact, *Show Boat* itself had set an example of play-within-play hermeneutics that would long remain unsurpassed for richness of dramatic resonance and layering. Right from its opening scene of violent argument within the "happy family," which Captain Andy passes off as an advertising trick, it sets this up, and numbers such as "Ol' Man River" and "Make Believe" offer the director and the audience a variety of viewpoints on how many levels of drama are operating within the song. (For instance, in "Ol' Man River" Joe can be portrayed as pretending to work while disguising a message for Magnolia, on top of which the diegetic verisimilitude of his message can, if the director so wishes, be abandoned in favor of Joe turning it toward us, the audience, in midsong, critically or empathetically as the case may be.) Finally, before returning to Sondheim, we may observe that song as drama is linked etymologically with the idea of *enchantment,* for instance in renaissance theater, where "the playwright must indicate clearly and directly when sounding music ceases to represent earthly entertainment and comes to signify the hidden sounds of the invisible world" (Austern 1990, 196). This brings us right back to the medieval, Boethian distinction between musica mundana, the silent music of the spheres, and musica humana, our imperfect human reflection of it, and suggests a mythic origin for our modern tradition of heard orchestral representation of unheard affects.

Sondheim had made relatively little use of diegetic song or "source music," as his profession calls it, in his own music before *Follies* (though there was plenty of it in *Gypsy*). Only two examples of any consequence from the Broadway musicals spring to mind, for a funeral and a wedding, respectively. The choral layer of "Funeral Sequence" in *Forum* is unambiguous, though even here the superimposed layer of commands by Miles

Ex. 6.2

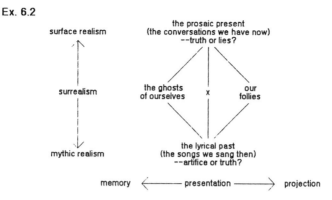

Gloriosus, of which Pseudolus's contributions make a good dramatic joke, is diegetic but (presumably) not musically as opposed to oratorically so (the point is unimportant). The first "Bless this day" section of "Getting Married Today" from *Company* is diegetic, though only as a "split screen" cameo; the second and third sections undermine and (thus somewhat parallel to the *Forum* example) make a joke of this by giving the chorister the "wrong" words—"Bless this bride, / Totally insane, / Slipping down the drain," and so forth.

Sondheim had, however, as we have seen, already explored the idea of two layers of music within a show, differentiated stylistically, particularly in *Anyone Can Whistle,* whose pastiche divertissement numbers juxtaposed and contrasted the representation of those who "dealt in attitudes" with those who propagated the symphonic idea of "sincere" style. What he did in *Follies* was to make the equation between this compositional contrast and the dramatic contrast between characters who think they are talking and characters who know they are singing. It was an obvious step to take, but equally obviously it begs the question, in *Follies,* of whether music constructs myths while conversation tells plain truth, or whether the terms are prey to reversal at some deeper level. This begins to suggest another series of triangles, and it was perhaps for this reason that Sondheim, probably prompted by Prince (who suggested the introduction of the main characters' younger selves; see Ilson 1989, 180–81), was not content to settle for the simple polarization of diegetic and nondiegetic music but permitted it to generate further conceptual compartments, suggesting coordinates across various spectra or axes (ex. 6.2 offers one possible set).

Character Groupings in *Follies*

Before we proceed to examine the differentiated types of music (which amounts to a total of around forty songs written or partly or wholly sketched for the show at various times; see ex. 6.3), it is necessary to see how the feeling for structural permutations and confrontations that the concept of *Follies* encourages is borne out by the different combinations of characters and forces utilized across the show as a whole. This refers primarily to the use of actors on the stage, but it is also worth recognizing that triple terms of reference are at work in one area that ex. 6.3 does not show, namely the orchestra. Here too there is a diegetic/nondiegetic distinction. While we are in the diegetic present, song and dance are accompanied by the stage band (just a piano in *Follies 1987*): Weismann does not have the resources to provide an entire pit orchestra for his reunion. The pit orchestra, therefore, is nondiegetic, and we enter the realm of fantasy or criticism at the inspired moment in "Beautiful Girls" when it takes over from the stage band and raises the music from E major to F major, heightening our experience of the song as it does so. The additional catch is that it is not even a nondiegetic remembrance of a past diegetic sound: the orchestra never sounded like that ("*Follies* is not a recreation of, but a glorification of, every Broadway pit band that ever played . . . it's what you *thought* the pit band sounded like," as Tunick explained [Zadan 1990, 155]). Thus in the diegetic songs the orchestra is already on a par with the ghosts.

To return to groupings on the stage (some of which are evident from the left-hand column of ex. 6.3), we can see that all eight of the main characters (Ben, Sally, Phyllis, and Buddy and their young selves) take part in "Waiting for the Girls Upstairs." "Who's That Woman?" involves seven girls and their seven ghostly counterparts (described as "Memories" in Goldman's original book). Of the four main characters' "follies" songs at the end of the show, one is a solo, one a solo with two supporting girls, another (Phyllis's) a solo with chorus boys (girls as well in *Follies 1987* and *Follies in Concert*), and the fourth (Ben's) a solo with mixed chorus (though the emphasis is on dancing boys in *Follies 1987*). Two numbers that did not survive into the statutory show, "Pleasant Little Kingdom" (which was originally a separate song but later led straight into the central love duet "Too Many Mornings") and "The World's Full of Girls [/Boys]," adopted the procedure of two characters singing, one after the other, the same or similar music to complementary words. There is a good deal of contrapuntal montage, most notably in the duet "You're Gonna Love Tomorrow" that later (very much later in *Follies 1987*) fits together with "Love Will See Us Through" as a quartet or double duet for all four "young" characters (this was substituted for "Little White House" and "Who Could Be Blue?" a double duet whose "second chorus . . . gave a realistic and unpleasant view of the future to counterbalance the idyllic one" [Sondheim and Lucas (1981)], which Prince and Bennett found too lugubrious).

Other ways of scrutinizing and glossing the concept of the duet are also explored. In the diegetic music, for instance, "Rain on the Roof" itself becomes part of a triple montage when it joins (not very convincingly, in contrapuntal terms) with "Broadway Baby" and "Ah, Paris!" early on in the show; "Bolero d'Amour" relieves song with dance; and, most strikingly, "One More Kiss" offers us a love duet between the old lady and her memory, surely the most effective way possible of dramatizing the folly of self-love. As for love between the couples, there is a noticeable tendency away from emphasizing the Sally-Ben relationship as *Follies* grows older. The songs written as early as 1965 or 1966 for *The Girls Upstairs,* long before Prince took the idea on and developed it into *Follies,* included "Pleasant Little Kingdom," "Too Many Mornings," and "It Wasn't Meant To Happen," Sally's "song of seduction in the guise of regret" (Sondheim and Lucas [1981]). "All Things Bright and Beautiful" was written for Sally and Ben but ended up as the instrumental, "Prologue," in 1971 and was cut altogether from *Follies 1987,* and Sondheim's description of how it originally fitted in demonstrates the scale of the changes *Follies* underwent.

> In the original version of *Follies* the show was not a surreal show. . . . I mean the "follies" itself . . . was in fact a show that the women put on for their husbands who were to sit in the front row of the theater . . . and Sally was the galvanizer of it all, and so she was directing all the ladies and getting the costumes out of the storeroom etc etc, and Ben comes on to the stage . . . and he has a bunch of paper flowers, which are one of the props, in his hand, and he presents it to her, and for one moment she forgets the show.

"In Buddy's Eyes," in its original guise as "In Someone's Eyes," included a part for Ben pitted contrapuntally against Sally's and covering some of the sentiments that, it seems, were later siphoned off into his solo "The Road You Didn't Take." A cut section of "Don't Look At Me" also included cyclic counterpoint between Sally and Ben. "Too Many Mornings" was shorn of its antecedent, as I have mentioned, and finally, in *Follies 1987,* we get a duet for Ben and Phyllis, "Country House," brittle and argumentative but not devoid of hidden warmth if one searches deep enough for it in the tonal sequences whose harmonic slenderness may be skeletal but which still have a heart and retain the function of a release

Ex. 6.3. The Musical Plan of *Follies*

Character: Ben	Sal	Phl	Bud	YBn	YSa	YPh	YBu	Pro	Book Song	Ghost Song	Diegetic Song	Follies Song	Style
										"Prologue"1971			
											("Bring On the Girls" [1965])		[?]
								✓			"Beautiful Girls"		[Berlin]
✓	✓								"Don't Look at Me"				SS
✓	✓	✓	✓	✓	✓	✓	✓		"Waiting for the Girls Upstairs" (1965) 1971				SS (foxtrot)
								✓		1971?	"Rain on the Roof"		quickstep [Berlin?]
								✓		1971?	("Chéri"?) "Ah, Paris!"		Broadway galop
								✓		1971?	"Broadway Baby"		blues song [DeSylva, Brown, and Henderson]
								✓		1971?	+ montage		
									1987				
✓									"The Road You Didn't Take"1971				SS
								✓			("Let's Run Away"?) "Bolero d'Amour" (dance) 1971		tango/beguine
✓	✓								("In Someone's Eyes") "In Buddy's Eyes"				SS
								✓		"Who's That Woman?"			foxtrot
✓		✓							"Country House" 1987				SS
								✓			("Can That Boy Fox-trot!") "I'm Still Here" 1971		foxtrot? / blues song
			✓						("That Old Piano Roll")				novelty piano rag /blues
	✓								("It Wasn't Meant to Happen" [1966])				SS
✓	✓								("All Things Bright and Beautiful")				SS (gymnopédie waltz)
✓	✓								("Pleasant Little Kingdom" [1965]) —segue to: "Too Many Mornings" (1965)				SS / SS

(INTERMISSION)

Ex. 6.3.—Continued

Character Ben Sal Phl Bud YBn YSa YPh YBu Pro	Book Song	Ghost Song	Diegetic Song	Follies Song	Style
		"Social Dancing" 1987 ←			
✓	"The Right Girl"				SS
			1987 ←		
	1987 ←				coloratura
✓		"One More Kiss" (1965)			waltz [Friml or Romberg]
✓	"Could I Leave You?"1971				SS (waltz)
? ?				The Folly of Love: "Loveland"1971 "Loveland"1987	[Kern] [?]
✓ ✓		←		The Folly of Youth: "You're Gonna Love Tomorrow" 1971	[Kern/Harburg or Ira Gershwin]
✓ ✓		←		"Love Will See Us Through"	[Burton Lane/ Harburg or Ira Gershwin]
✓ ✓ ✓ ✓				("Little White House" / "Who Could Be Blue?")	[Nacio Herb Brown/ Edens?]
✓ ✓ ✓ ✓		←		+ montage 1971	
✓				Buddy's Folly: "The God-Why-Don't-You- Love-Me Blues"	cartoon/ silent film galop ["Looney Tunes"]
✓ ✓	("The World's Full of Girls" / "The World's Full of Boys")				French galop
✓				Sally's Folly: "Losing My Mind"	[George Gershwin/ Dorothy Fields]
✓ ✓		←		1987 ←	
✓				Phyllis's Folly: ("Uptown, Downtown")	swing
				"The Story of Lucy and Jessie"1971	[Cole Porter]
				"Ah, But Underneath . . ."1987	big band striptease
✓				Ben's Folly: "Live, Laugh, Love"1971	[George Gershwin?]
				"Make the Most of Your Music"1987	production foxtrot
				1987	
✓ ✓ ✓ ✓ ✓ ✓ ✓ ✓ ✓	"Finale-Chaos"1971				

Ex. 6.4a

(see ex. 6.4a, and compare ex. 6.4b, from "Putting It Together" [*Sunday in the Park with George*]).

Two things are absent in all this, however: any structured use of the confrontations between the main characters and their young selves such as is used in "One More Kiss," and, following the loss of "All Things Bright and Beautiful," any "book songs" (nondiegetic, non-"follies"

Ex. 6.4b

music, in Sondheim's own style) for the youngsters ("Waiting for the Girls Upstairs" hardly gives them a chance). This may be felt to be a major weakness of *Follies,* in that it deprives us of the opportunity to judge for ourselves whether the passage of time has changed the characters. What has Phyllis lost in ceasing to be Lucy and becoming Jessie? How different, for Ben, is having "the biggest goddamn limousine" from wanting it? What was Sally like when she was first involved with Ben—did she moon around then too? As long as the ghosts remain ghosts, we never really get to know them, and all the talk about *Follies* being about the loss of youthful idealism cuts little ice without us being able to see it in action. When we do see it, in the "follies" double duet, it appears insipid: deliberately or otherwise, "You're Gonna Love Tomorrow" and "Love

Will See Us Through" are among Sondheim's least personal songs, the pastiche issue notwithstanding, and unlike "Little White House / Who Could Be Blue" they fail to enlist our sympathy for innocence, at least in the choruses (the verses, in line with those of the period they are pastiching, are personable). This may be partly because of the demands of contrapuntal combination, which, although efficient, is here rather anodyne ("Who's That Woman?" and its "Mirror, mirror" section make a much more differentiated and invigorating effect when put together than the double duet does). But it surely applies to the lyrics too. Despite some carefully planted references to their envisaged life-styles and hence to their characters—Young Ben refers to "pundits," a "blue chip" future and his "personal guarantee," Young Sally and Young Buddy to cutting down expenses, burning toast, leaving a light on on the porch and trumping aces—the young protagonists remain rather faceless ingenues in the statutory show. The lyric wit of Young Sally's "We'll stay home nights with the nippers, / You with your pipe, / The dog with your slippers" in "Little White House" and the naive poignancy of the accompanying "Who Could Be Blue?" melody raise her and her situation well above this, invest her with character and enable us to judge in a flash that her folly was there from the start if it never occurred to her that she could not possibly live with Ben rather than Buddy on this basis.

This treatment of the young characters may have been a miscalculation, but it was deliberate. Sondheim points out that, in the 1971 *Follies,* the fact that they were portrayed surrealistically and idealistically, seen only through the eyes of their older counterparts, made him "never want to write anything in the least bit *real* for the younger people." Yet there is nothing additional for them by way of music in the 1987 version, where they are portrayed realistically on the stage, and this seems at odds with Goldman's structures.

Goldman went a certain length in setting up some of the twenty-eight possible pairings between the young and older main characters. He introduced these pairings in three stages in the narrative, first, as one would expect, establishing the mode of dialogue and initial meetings between the "real," older people. All six combinations have been presented by page 20 in the book (p. 31 in *Follies 1987*), before they join together to sing "Waiting for the Girls Upstairs." The second stage, that of dialogue between pairs of ghosts or memories (the young selves), was tightened up considerably in the *Follies 1987* book, for originally it had been casually and confusingly represented too near the beginning of the script; in both versions of the book it overlaps to a certain extent with the first-stage presentations, but is allowed cameos that are less marginal, mostly in the central portions of the narrative, in *Follies 1987*. It is also worth noting that dialogue between Young Buddy and Young Sally does not occur at all in *Follies 1987:* the chronology of her running between Young Buddy and Young Ben is left out of the reckoning rather than somewhat confusingly half-presented. The third stage, effective and climactic in both versions, is when the characters begin to argue with their young selves. In *Follies 1987* this culminates schematically in two concentric circles, of which the inner one rises physically center-stage in the form of a "follies" platform with the "old" characters marooned on it while the young ones, on the outside, gape upward as their futures are elevated before their very eyes. The 1971 culmination, with all eight characters shouting at once, was more abstract and implied a fourth dramaturgical stage of confrontation, in which groups of three characters were involved (see ex. 6.5). This is compensated for to an extent in *Follies 1987* by two slightly earlier passages involving three characters: Ben, Sally, and Young Sally have a triangular confrontation on page 85 and Ben, Buddy and Young Buddy have one on page 91. But they seem something of a residue from 1971, whose crucial exception to the general pattern of pairings was the linking of Ben and Young Sally, which is both a key issue in *Follies* and a key problem. It occurs briefly in both versions, when Young Sally addresses accusing words to Ben at the very point of first reunion. In *Follies 1987,* however, we sense that with the loss of Ben's song of (non-) regret, "The Road You Didn't Take," and of Phyllis's remembrance of her young self in "The Story of Lucy and Jessie" ("Ah, But Underneath...," though cast in the past tense, surely applies to the older Phyllis), Sally is the only character who willingly carries her young self around with her as a prime motivating force (the other young selves become confrontational only as the evening wears on), whereas in the 1971 book the shoe is on the other foot, and it is Ben who sustains the Young Sally: despite his protestations, he wishes he could have the past, and sings "Too Many Mornings" not to Sally but to Young Sally (while Sally gives the vocal response). This is a rich dramaturgical device that surely provides the crux of the plot: Sally's tragedy is that she cannot see that Ben is desiring what she was, not what she is; his is that in resurrecting past desire he sows distress in all four characters, misleads Sally, and causes a breakdown in himself, although it is never quite clear whether

Ex. 6.5. The Three-Character Confrontations in *Follies* (1971)

Buddy ⟶ Young Buddy ⟵ Young Sally
Young Buddy ⟶ Young Sally ⟵ Sally

Ben ⟶ Young Ben ⟵ Young Phyllis
Young Ben ⟶ Young Phyllis ⟵ Phyllis

the breakdown occurs because he hates himself for wounding Sally, because he actually feels he made a wrong choice in marrying Phyllis, or because he resents the facts of life that forced him to choose in the first place when he wanted everything. In *Follies 1987,* on the other hand, it is unclear why he should sing the lyrics of "Too Many Mornings" at all, since they are impossible to construe as sincere when addressed to the older Sally.

Through all this, perhaps too much of Goldman's original dramatic conception is retained for *Follies* to be a "plotless" musical. Before Prince became involved, Goldman and Sondheim had been aiming for the feel of a murder mystery, Sondheim describing it as "a 'who'll-do-it' rather than a 'whodunnit'" and explaining its rationale as follows. "At the end of the first act, the four principals each had reason to kill each other and the second act was who'll do it to whom" (Zadan 1990, 136). In the 1971 version, Ben's breakdown and the subsequent dialogue of denouement between Sally and Buddy both seem to absorb or transform traces of the original melodrama in their apparent and puzzling references to a suicide attempt (Ben shouts out "She said she'd kill herself. I didn't think she meant it . . . ," and as Sally "comes to" after the "follies" she says "I should of died the first time," to which Buddy replies "Cut that out"). Even without this dimension, we need to feel that something has been accomplished dramatically with the four main characters by the end of the evening, but the party setting, which could have set up stronger tensions in a plot for a television or film drama, and could have been handled in a novel by someone like Anthony Powell, tends to dissipate dramatic focus on stage, its "Chekhovian" modality notwithstanding (see Zadan 1990, 135), and with the "follies" as culmination (rather than songs on one of the other planes of conception), it is never sufficiently clear what the dramatic accomplishment is.

This is not to say that *Follies* is a weak or even seriously flawed score, though not all the numbers are necessarily on the same high level of invention and characterization (in particular, "Live, Laugh, Love" was no great loss in *Follies 1987*). On the contrary, it is a very rich one.

The Pastiches

Sondheim's pastiche technique reaches its zenith in *Follies*. It is beyond the scope of this study to trace either *Follies'* exact relationship to Ziegfeld's own shows or to provide a critique of the specific style borrowings in individual songs, though there are plenty of pointers in both directions. The general shape of *Follies,* with its deliberately uncoordinated succession of star turns (moving songs around, as shown in ex. 6.3, was not difficult) culminating in a multiple-number production finale, refers back to the vaudeville tradition; paradoxically, diegetic music—music that is an *item* in the narrative—was a necessity precisely because "vaudeville provided no model whatsoever for the narrative *function* of short comic numbers" (Altman 1987, 202; italics added). Altman also casts light on the spirit of the "follies" finale itself, insofar as it depicts a show business conundrum between individualism and corporate responsibility.

> Life on a vaudeville circuit settled into an uneasy relationship between each act and all the others making up the show. Built into the vaudeville experience, therefore, is an intensified version of the familiar actor/ troupe theatrical dichotomy. On the legitimate stage, competition must be limited to the period of casting, for as soon as the cast is set each person's job depends in part on the performances of the others. If the show folds, everyone is out of a job. In vaudeville, on the other hand, contracts are handed out to each individual act. Individualism and personal ambition perpetually threaten a general ambience of concern and cooperation. In those films which owe the most to the vaudeville tradition . . . we thus find the opposition of individual desire to the good of the group elevated into a major thematic role. (Altman 1987, 202)

While this is not exactly the theme of *Follies,* we do see in Ben's, Sally's, Buddy's, and Phyllis's final numbers an ironic truth of self-denial and self-discipline through the constructs they have created for their own lives, expressed as they are in the impersonal, disciplined routines of a show number (we are, presumably, not supposed to forget that the two women at least have been professional performers and retain the "muscle memory," as Phyllis puts it in the 1971 book, that enables them to get through the "mirror" number at the reunion). It is not dissimilar to the paradox of *A Chorus Line,* where the individuality that we have been sampling in numerous vignettes throughout the evening is destroyed the moment it has triumphed through the auditions, by being suppressed in favor of the precision and mechanical perfection of a row of automatons. We cannot even tell who is who in their chorus line costumes.

The actual style and structure of the "follies" and diegetic songs no doubt came at least partly from study of specific Ziegfeld shows and similar revues or biopics about them. Geoffrey Block (1987, 321) has referred to "Sondheim's incalculable debt to Ziegfeld, *Blackbirds of 1928,* and other revues in *Follies,* " and though Sondheim denies using any particular source as a model (he did study the film *Glorifying the American Girl,* but without finding it particularly helpful), he has been so steeped in both the Broadway and Hollywood traditions since youth that he surely did not need to. Still, he and his collaborators must have had to voice agreement about certain imagery, and a file of *Follies* sketches labeled "Misc./Pastiches" includes a list of ideas written on a sheet of uncharacteristic small notepaper (does this imply that it was scribbled down away from the work desk, maybe at a production meeting?).

No Foolin'—1927
Amer. Indian costume
Yacht Club Boys Sound
Bowed tapshoes
Sunny [tye?] for kick chorus—waving wheat
Tableau w/hymn-like song
Helen Morgan—blues—
Birds—specialty dancer
Girls w/crystal balls or libations
"Loveland"—headdresses

At least some of these ideas came to fruition: "Loveland" is the tableau with hymnlike song (and included the headdresses in 1971); Helen Morgan no doubt lies behind Sally and perhaps behind Carlotta Campion and Hattie Walker as well. There is also a page containing a list of *Follies*-type shows from 1908 to 1931, and in the "General + Misc." file there are notes about Ziegfeld's practices, together with many sketched musical fragments. With his talent as a natural mimic he was soon jotting down musical motifs that suggested the general stylistic ambience. In chapter 2 I discussed how the "yearning" motif of "Beautiful Girls" originated; another example of recognizable but transformed origins can be seen in ex. 6.6a.

Sondheim has given us his own key to the specific style pastiches of individual songs (Zadan 1990, 147; and see ex. 6.3). It would be interesting to try to pin them down further, eventually to specific parallels. The data in ex. 6.3 do not attempt this, but they do include additional suggestions, valid or otherwise. "Rain on the Roof" shares subject matter and manner with Berlin's "Isn't This a Lovely Day?" from *Top Hat* (a number for Fred Astaire and Ginger Rogers); the verbal gist of "Can That Boy Fox-trot!" though not the innuendo, parallels that of Berlin's "You'd Be Surprised," which appears in the film *Blue Skies* but stems from *The Ziegfeld Follies* of 1919 (and also includes the saying "You don't judge a book by its cover," used by Sondheim in *Anyone Can Whistle* and reused in *Follies 1987* as the opening line of Phyllis's "Ah, But Underneath . . . "); the melody of "Little White House" is similar to Roger Eden's celebrated vamp in Nacio Herb Brown's "Singin' in the Rain"; "Live, Laugh, Love"

Ex. 6.6a

Ex. 6.6b

Ex.6.6.c

contains at least two musical suggestions of Gershwin, in its introductory accompaniment, similar to that of "I Got Plenty o' Nuttin'" (this is commented upon humorously by Thomas Z. Shephard in the *Follies in Concert* film documentary), and in Ben's "Me, I like to live, / Me, I like to laugh" refrain, which uses the metric wrong footings of "Fascinating

Ex. 6.6d

The world's full of boys who are wait-ing to be kissed,

Rhythm," though not to the same degree. Sondheim's model for "Losing My Mind" was Gershwin's "The Man I Love." "Broadway Baby," at least at the hands of Elaine Stritch, sounds like a Mae West parody.

Inevitably there are also one or two similarities to more recent musicals, though this is not a built-in part of the concept. Rodgers and Hammerstein's *Allegro*, a major influence on Sondheim, similarly culminates in a song (the title song) using the image of music as life-style, though it is not as clever as "Make the Most of Your Music." *Allegro*'s protagonist shares traits with Ben (he is a successful professional from a small town), and after the title song he is subjected to a dissonant mélange of tunes and fragments from the show as his life seems to crumble around him, as in "Finale-Chaos" from the 1971 *Follies* (whose preceding device of a breakdown in midsong was effectively used earlier in *Gypsy* and later by Robert Altman in the film *Nashville*). "Finale-Chaos" may remind others of the crucifixion collage in *Jesus Christ Superstar*, and it reminds Sondheim himself of his culmination to act 1 in *Anyone Can Whistle*. Finally we may note the technique in *Carousel* of using a ghostly unnoticed character (the dead Billy) as a shadow figure and prompt to the latter-day action, though this aspect of *Follies* was hardly Sondheim's invention.

Other diegetic and pastiche "follies" songs, especially cutouts and sketches, deserve comment. Two of them never reached completion. "Chéri" was sketched for Solange but appears not to have progressed beyond a drafted introduction and voice part, quoting *La Marseillaise* and otherwise somewhat resembling "Ah, Paris!" which superseded it. "Let's Run Away," sketched in a moderately complete two-stave musical draft, referred to "maybe Madrid" in its lyrics, and this may explain the Spanish choice of dance for its replacement, Vincent and Vanessa's "Bolero d'Amour." A further two songs were reused in 1974 in the music to the film *Stavisky* (as well as "Who Could Be Blue?" which became a violin and piano piece in "Salon at the Claridge #2"). The first version of

"Beautiful Girls," entitled "Bring on the Girls," which can be heard on the soundtrack as "Auto Show," is a fine tune (ex. 6.6b), but its lyrics are too direct and lack the mythical dimension of poetic rapture that is so effective in the statutory song (see ex. 6.6c). Only the outer section of "The World's Full of Boys" (ex. 6.6d) is used in *Stavisky* (as "Operetta," both instrumentally and then with the words "C'est moi"), and its *moto perpetuo* Parisian gaiety, attractive enough in its own terms, would doubtless have been a gratuitous follow-up to Solange's solo in *Follies,* from which it is no great loss in musical or dramatic terms (it was envisaged as weaving in and out of the "follies" but was never completed). "Loveland" has gone through two versions (they share the preceding fanfares), of which the 1987 one is richer melodically and harmonically. Its tune gains from beginning with the same rising $\hat{2}$-$\hat{3}$ step as "Beautiful Girls," and the initial chord progression looks back even beyond this, to the "Time to Go Home" sketch illustrated in chapter 2 (see ex. 2.1c).

The Ghost Music

If, so far, it has been relatively easy to pin a pastiche label on the diegetic and "follies" songs, there are nonetheless a few crossovers and connections between them and the "book" songs, largely necessitated by the mediating category of the ghost songs. "That Old Piano Roll," apparently written as a solo for Buddy to dance to with Sally (see ex. 6.7a), seems to straddle three categories: as party music, coming from the stage, its accompaniment is diegetic; Buddy's monologue is not (he would be speaking it, not singing as he dances, in real life); and the fact that the piano roll is "old" and plays ragtime (it is in Sondheim's "pastiche" category) links it as ghost music to the bygone era. Was a pianola to have been present on the stage? Its self-playing keys would have contributed a vivid image to the idea of ghosts, and it seems a pity that it could not be followed through. In the event, the music was retained as the first section of the "Overture" and as various underscores, and it was incorporated into "Social Dancing" in *Follies 1987,* a part real, part surreal number, as Goldman's stage directions rather too archly have to explain.

> (More COUPLES join the dance. . . . The LADIES all wear bits and pieces of old costumes. . . . Though the image is surreal, the GUESTS are in the real world. They are floating on the past, not in it. . . . EACH COUPLE does the dance which was in vogue when they were young—but with a difference. Though the roots are social dancing, it's at one remove, not literal. . . .)

Similarly, in the 1971 book, the trio of songs near the beginning of the

Ex. 6.7a

By the time you get a load - a that sup -er-syn-co-pat-ed co - da, you'll say, 'I think that

old pi - a - no roll's   nice.' __ __

Ex. 6.7b

[Ghostly]

Wait-ing a -round_ for   the   girls up-stairs __

Ex. 6.7c

Ex. 6.7d

Ex. 6.7e

show ("Rain on the Roof," "Ah, Paris!" and "Broadway Baby," plus their montage) make a point of being not quite diegetic, according to the stage directions.

> (And suddenly, abruptly, the stage is clear and dark except for EMILY and THEODORE WHITMAN, who stand quite still for just a beat in a spotlight looking out front as if THEY were about to speak. Instead of speaking, THEY burst into song.)

At the end of "Rain on the Roof" the direction reads:

> (The number goes as quickly as it came, almost as if it never happened. THE WHITMANS stand immobile at one side of the stage. . . .)

In *Follies 1987* this ambiguity between real and surreal is not attempted so early (and is generally downplayed, as I noted earlier): the three songs are set up wholly diegetically by Ronnie Cohen, the pianist, who is armed with all the old music, and Weismann, who simply says "I don't suppose you'd sing for us." This still leaves the problem of the montage, where Goldman does once again suggest surrealism.

(The lighting shifts. The GUESTS freeze in mid-gesture, as if time had stopped. As for THE WHITMANS, HATTIE & SOLANGE, it's not a contest now. They are inside themselves, remembering.)

How effectively the audience can grasp this first juncture of mediation between the three or four worlds that *Follies*'s songs inhabit is debatable.

Another mediating agent is the vamp that introduces "Waiting for the Girls Upstairs" (ex. 6.7b). Marked *ghostly* in the score, it carries rich associations in its rhythm, scoring, texture with sustained tenor, harmony with chromatic appoggiatura chords, and, when the voice enters, a jazzlike shift to IV^7 as the first progression alongside a foxtrot melodic indicator of three cross-rhythmic eighth notes followed by a long note—all these seem to epitomize the vanished Broadway style. Even the silence and retake in measure 2 suggest, in terms of the "till ready" convention, that a singer might have come in at any moment but is no longer there to do so. As so often with Sondheim, accompaniment figures act as unifying features, and variants of this one introduce the choruses of "You're Gonna Love Tomorrow" and "Love Will See Us Through," with an added riff (ex. 6.7c); this is varied further, and slowed down, as the lead into "Ah, But Underneath . . ." in *Follies 1987,* which immediately follows "You're Gonna Love Tomorrow." ("Ah, But Underneath . . ." is itself based on an instrumental idea, a jazz formula of a downward chromatic scale of four notes from the tonic, and this it shares with the two songs it replaced, "Uptown, Downtown" and "The Story of Lucy and Jessie." The chordal basis of "Losing My Mind," on the other hand, is four rising chromatic notes.)

There are two further motivic devices in "Waiting for the Girls Upstairs" representing aspects of memory. One is the haunting little oboe arabesque (ex. 6.7d), the other the soft-edged arpeggio that introduces the vamp (marked *y* in ex. 6.7e), which returns as a lead-in to Buddy's "I remember" section. These two devices have the same harmonic flavor, rich in alternating semitones and minor thirds (in pitch-class terms, 0 1 2 5 6 9 and 0 1 4 5 8). The oboe motif also accompanies one of the subtler underlinings of the theme of *Follies,* when Buddy, in expertly integrated parlando, tries to remember the name of the stage doorman ("what-the-hell-was-his name, you know, the old guy?/*Spoken:* Max! I remember"). The irony is that even at the time, thirty years before, he could not remember it, for a few pages further on Young Buddy sings the same passage (this time the name comes out as Harry). Time changes nothing, and we merely add a layer or a dimension to our mistakes by repeating or compounding them.

The Original Music

To have left until last the music that is unambiguously Sondheim's own stylistic possession is not to belittle it, though its interspersal among the diegetic and other pastiche songs does dissipate its focus, and at one time, at least, Sondheim believed "that there were too many pastiche numbers in the show which hurt the book and subsequently hurt the show" (Zadan 1990, 150). Close observation reveals a firmer consolidation of the style elements of *Company* than might have been suspected.

There are two waltzes. The first, "All Things Bright and Beautiful," which became the "Prologue," is a *gymnopédie* that conveys an innocence or a would-be innocence but whose harmonic dislocation is harder edged than in "Barcelona"; the loss of the lyrics is to be regretted in that they underlined the harmonies and their signification with Ben's references to the primary colors of the flowers (ex. 6.8a), a sort of three-chord trick that is stressed orchestrally at the close of the "Prologue" and looks forward to *A Little Night Music*. (The primary color references to youth might have been motivic: Young Sally and Young Buddy's original duet counterpoised white and blue in its first lines and in the punch line "The only thing blue is the sky"; Phyllis, in remembering her dresses, sings "One of them was borrowed and the other was blue," and in a lengthy speech to Buddy in the original book, refers to choosing the colors of her life with Ben like a painter; Sally, singing to herself in the middle of "Too Many Mornings," mutters "I should have worn green. / I wore green the last time." Similarly, the last of the three chords mentioned above feels motivic in its coloring, consisting, like the "memory" motifs, of minor thirds alternating with a semitone [0 1 4 5 8].) The second waltz is "Could I Leave You," softer and more beguiling exactly as Phyllis is more poised than the inarticulate young Ben, but still with *gymnopédie* elements in the vocal rhythm and occasionally in the accompaniment. This too anticipates *A Little Night Music,* when Phyllis gets into her stride with a scrubbing eighth-note accompaniment as she creates her panorama of past life with Ben (compare Petra's panorama of the future in "The Miller's Son").

The warmer extremes of the stylistic spectrum are represented by violence and romanticism, the former in "The Right Girl," the latter in "Too Many Mornings." "The Right Girl" has a discontinuous vamp slightly reminiscent of that of "Waiting for the Girls Upstairs," and it

Ex. 6.8a

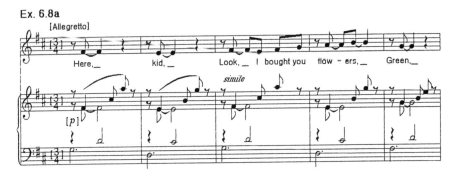

Ex. 6.8b

Ex. 6.8c

Ex. 6.8d

may also remind listeners of some of the music of suppressed or verbally inarticulate energy in *West Side Story*—Goldman's stage directions for Buddy suggest the parallel ("HE has no words for what HE feels, so instead HE bursts into angry dance, leaping down stairs, twisting, tapping without tap shoes all the fury and regret HE is feeling ... "), and the punctuating brass chords in symphonic jazz style, the long instrumental coda (more a symphonic break) and short melodic motif with its clipped third note (exhaustively worked in the "Hey, Margie" sections) also support it (compare the outbusts in "Cool," and *West Side Story*'s celebrated three-note motif). "Too Many Mornings," the central love duet, is as expansive as Sondheim ever becomes; the sketches show him working at this in harmonic terms (see ex. 6.8b). Prefixing the duet with "Pleasant Little Kingdom" would have put its warmth into a deeper perspective, for in this event the nervous detachment of the initial eighth-note motif (ex. 6.8c) gives way intermittently to the romantic "pleasant little thought," within which it loses its staccato poise (ex. 6.8d), before succumbing entirely to desire and remaining only a legato fill, in soft focus on the harp and on a par with memory (ex. 6.8e).

This layered resource of orchestral and harmonic perspective is also broached in three of the songs remaining to be mentioned, "Don't Look at Me," "The Road You Didn't Take," and "In Buddy's Eyes." Sondheim has commented on this aspect of two of them.

> [In "The Road You Didn't Take," Ben] is . . . saying, "Oh, I never look back on the past . . . "; in point of fact, he is ripped to shreds internally. . . . There's . . . a stabbing dissonance in the music, a note in the music that tells you, the audience, that something is not quite Kosher about what this guy is saying. . . . *Follies* contains a lesson in sub-text, a song called "In Buddy's Eyes." It's a woman's lie to her former lover in which she says that everything is just wonderful. . . . Nothing . . . tells you maybe it isn't true . . . although there's something in the orchestration . . . every phrase in that song which refers to Buddy, her husband, is dry, it's all woodwinds. Whenever she refers to herself it's all strings again. (Sondheim 1974, 71)

The second point here refers to the chorus of "In Buddy's Eyes" and applies to the alternating two-bar phrases of the title and "I'm young, I'm beautiful" (though the distinction breaks down at "On Buddy's shoulder"). In "The Road You Didn't Take" what Sondheim refers to is presumably the horn fill (marked x in ex. 6.9a), no doubt meant to suggest a car horn and thus strengthen the traveling image which lies behind the song (and was to be worked out across a whole show in *Merrily We Roll Along,* with its Benlike hero Franklin Shepard); the intrusive F-natural is justified harmonically four measures later, when it is part of a chord (ex. 6.9a, y).

Both these songs help to further style characteristics found in *Company:* "In Buddy's Eyes," every bit as beautiful as "Sorry-Grateful" (though its sentiment is very different), again utilizes rhythmic, harmonic, and melodic traits of Sondheim's "urban folk" idiom—see the reversed Scotch-snap rhythm, compound-fourths harmony and noncadencing melodic leading note in ex. 6.9b. "The Road You Didn't Take" exhibits some of the minimalist sounds of "Another Hundred People" and like that song uses a fluid finger-picking guitar style to float supple vocal declamation in the

Ex. 6.9a

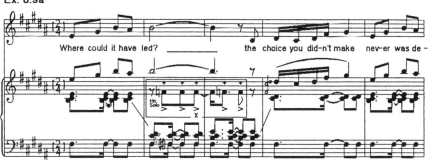

Where could it have led? _____ the choice you did-n't make nev-er was de-

- fined, Was it? ___

Ex. 6.9b

Maestoso

but in Bud-dy's eyes, _____ I'm young, I'm beau - ti-ful. ___

Ex. 6.9c

You're ei - ther a po- et or you're a lov - er Or you're the fa-mous Ben-ja-min Stone.

verse (ex. 6.9c), this being duplicated from Sally's verse to "Don't Look at Me" (both usages, as with "Another Hundred People," symbolize the protagonists' attempts to convey the fancy-free or self-reliant state). The chorus of "Don't Look at Me" also connects stylistically with the title song of *Company* through its use of sharpward-expanding, appoggiatura-based harmonies with micro-cross-rhythmic fills (which in fact influence the vocal melody itself, at the title phrase).

Finally, we may note that the dry, pointillistic style of "Country House" is by no means an idiomatic interloper in *Follies 1987,* much as it reminds us of aspects of *Pacific Overtures* and *Sunday.* We have already traced the Latin American overtones of such writing back to *Forum,* but there are firm traces of it in the 1971 *Follies* as well, particularly in the "Me and Ben" section of "Waiting For the Girls Upstairs" (ex. 6.10a). This song, we have seen, has to mediate between what in this and other instances we may excusably call abstract neoclassicism and Broadway pastiche. In a sense, this is in any case Sondheim's overall stylistic agenda, and in simple devices such as the alternating chords shown in ex. 6.10b, still within the traditional Broadway textural and rhythmic model when they are dressed out a few measures later (ex. 6.10c), but with a compound chord and a "wrong" bass note substituted for the expected dominant seventh (see *x*), they close the gap almost unnoticeably. A similar harmonic procedure is found in "It Wasn't Meant to Happen" (ex. 6.10d).

In Praise of Folly

The dramaturgical gap is not so easily closed. On the one hand, as the apotheosis of Altman's "show musical" category, *Follies* does not really generate its dramatic tension in backstage terms (unlike, say, *A Chorus Line*)—in a sense, the terms are reversed, since the "follies" songs show us what the characters are really like while their "book" songs are full of lies and fantasies. As what Altman calls a "folk musical," on the other hand, namely as a study of marriage and life-style (and as such not so far removed from *Company*), its diegetic songs are too tangential and its "follies" songs placed too near the end to raise the plot, which "cannot sustain serious literary analysis" (Hirsch 1989, 95), above the conversational tedium or jocular slenderness of armchair drama, into which it sinks without the songs' properties of transmutation. Above all, it plays with the two-edged weapon of memory in a way that it cannot quite handle. *Follies 1987,* despite the loss of a final wounding confrontation due to recalcitrant scenery at the climax of the "follies" sequence (see Sloman 1988, 50–51), is at least clearer in its neutrality, if not, as at first appears,

Ex. 6.10a

Ex. 6.10b

Ex. 6.10c

Ex. 6.10d

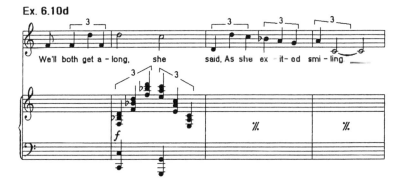

We'll both get a - long,   she   said, As she ex - it - ed smi - ling.

more positive than the original version; but both versions of the show remain ultimately undecided about whether to leave us with a positive or negative image and never reconcile the characters' wish "to do physical violence to the MEMORIES," as the 1971 stage direction puts it immediately before the "follies," with the fact that memory, like song and like folly itself, is an indestructible personal possession. Yet *Follies* somehow thrives in spite of this. It enjoys a robust capacity for survival as a cornucopia of numbers, as a treatise on the classic nature of song itself, presented through its own medium (we should not forget that, in the 1971 version, the theme of the "Loveland" costume for the first showgirl was music). There is nothing novel in this reflexive celebration, for it harks straight back to Busby Berkeley and his production spectaculars involving gigantic grand pianos, wedding-cake orchestras and the like; it is precisely this that Sondheim is acknowledging in "Make the Most of Your Music." And it seems that tiers can continue to be added, mirrors can contribute further reflections, as the work enhances its own built-in classic status, regardless of its practical dramaturgy. *Follies in Concert* in 1985 demonstrated this, and was almost as nostalgic and triumphant a celebration of the era of 1971 as was the original production of 1940, or 1940 of 1908. And so it can continue, each evanescent or uneconomic production contributing something to the "Broadway legend," as London subtitled it in 1987. Perhaps the very art form of the musical has painted itself into a corner of noble failure, of which *Follies* is the epitome, since, as Altman sees it, "all genres eventually become reflexive, self-critical, and often even self-destructive" (1987, 117). Perhaps an unproblematic *Follies* would lose its aura. The ultimate demand of reflexivity is, after all, that *Follies* too should be a folly.

Chapter 7

A Little Night Music

Sondheim's Middle Period

The law of good continuation, of knowing when to repeat and when to do something different, is an aesthetic matter of authorial inner necessity within a literary or musical work of art, but also concerns the commercial side of the artist's relation with the public when applied across an entire output. Perhaps the two facets are historically connected: the cult of the personality of the artist as spiritual leader was contingent upon his salesmanship with the public in the nineteenth century, and the whole idea of an artist having something to say, and therefore needing to find new things to say, to develop, is bound up with that of the market for his or her wares. It is less easy to imagine Bach being sacked by the Leipzig town council for writing cantatas that were too similar to each other than it is to imagine Beethoven losing his audience because the public had grown tired of his message. Or, to look at it another way, the chronology of Beethoven's symphonies and an exegesis of what it means are matters of historical concern partly insofar as they tell a tale of policies, rather like those of a government or statesman. They kept the composer in power, or might on occasions even have satisfied a preference or a need to be in opposition.

The musical, as the art form that plays for the highest commercial stakes of all, can probably never win the power game beyond a certain point. Once an authorial identity is established, be it of director, producer, composer, or writing team, the public and the critics alike make ever more stringent demands in their appetite for novelty on the one hand and the comfort of what they know and like on the other (Sondheim was described as "predictable in his unpredictability" by Benedict Nightingale, a first-night critic of the London production of *Into the Woods* [*Times*, 26 September 1990). Every success makes the next one more difficult. Gilbert and Sullivan eventually had to fail by pulling in different directions along these lines. Perhaps here too art is like government.

Whatever the truest perspective, *A Little Night Music* seems to have

213

begun a new period for Sondheim, and perhaps for Prince as well. It would again be one of mixed success and failure, commercially speaking; artistically, its onset was marked by a turning away from the subject matter of the American present, with its dangers of narcissism, toward the non-American past. There is a relaxed maturity about *A Little Night Music* not because of its traditional tone and European subject matter, but because it takes these for granted and builds impressively on them in terms of sheer technique. It constitutes a tight, commanding generic essay that has little need to question the efficacy of its own material, the validity of its own subject matter, and is thereby as striking for what it leaves out as for what it puts in. Perhaps for the same reason it makes only sparing (though important) use of diegetic music: it must be one of the few waltz-based operettas in the history of the genre without a ballroom scene or any diegetic dancing, their place being taken in act 2 by an extremely immobile and unmusical vehicle of social focus, the dinner table. It thus turns its back on the multiple, contrasted layers of musical signification in *Follies,* and the Liebeslieders, for all their abstraction and surrealism (to which plane dancing is restricted), only sing music and lyrics that complement, extend, and share the material of the central characters rather than oppose it. A single wholesale focus of style and content is also the aim of *Pacific Overtures* and *Sweeney Todd,* which again convey non-American and noncontemporary subjects (though clearly only up to a point in *Pacific Overtures*); thus, in terms of their lyrics, music, and dramaturgy, all three works have to have the courage not just peripherally to explore but to rest on ways and means well beyond what can be seen from Broadway. Nothing in *A Little Night Music* quite matches the audaciousness of the kabuki style in *Pacific Overtures,* though one could argue that its very traditionalism, its being cast as a European operetta, is almost as daring, coming as it does after *Company* and *Follies* had been hailed, at least in some quarters, as signifying the coming of age of the American musical.

There is continuity too, however. *Company, Follies,* and *A Little Night Music* are all traditional comic dramas insofar as they all deal with couples and marriage, with the anguish and identity of love and the self-dramatization to which it gives rise, and they all deal with characters who are articulate about these things. This inevitably affects the lyrics and, to a certain extent, the stylistic matrix of the music. But a more significant factor, one that separates *A Little Night Music* from its predecessors while at the same time making it the outcome of them, is, as I have suggested, the elimination of stylistic opposition between pastiche Broadway styles and an original idiom. This opposition, a musical premise that I have traced from *Anyone Can Whistle* through *Company* to *Follies,* is replaced by integration in *A Little Night Music*. Superficially this appears to be a matter of recognizing, as all commentators have done, that *A Little Night Music* is the apotheosis of a suite of waltzes. True, all the numbers are in triple or compound time, which leaves no room at all for the traditional Broadway march texture (there is not even any attempt to accommodate it to triple meter or to include a 6/8 Sousa march which, after all, was one of its direct ancestors). But this does not mean that everything is pastiche, and in this the numbers in *A Little Night Music* differ from "One More Kiss," the operetta waltz in *Follies*. Despite the many elements borrowed from the great waltz composers and many passages that sound like them, Sondheim has sustained his own divertissement style throughout the score. It is an impossible distinction to ground technically, or even to want to perceive, at every turn, but the maturity of approach does seem to me to be a new achievement and to consist in taking rhythmic and metric archetypes, understanding their connotations, and accommodating them as a framework for one's personal style rather than making them the technical essence of it. The assimilation of Latin American rhythms on the one hand and of the Satie *gymnopédie* on the other has already furnished us with contrasting instances of this. One of Sondheim's own memos for *A Little Night Music,* found in the "Miscellaneous" file, implies others, stylistically wide-ranging.

V[illa]-L[obos]—Parole de Bebe
Beet + Chopin Bagatelles
Bartok Mikrokosmos
Satie

Add the crucial examples of nineteenth-century character genres (such as the polonaise and mazurka as well as the waltz), of which the score of *A Little Night Music* consists, and it can be seen that the overall sensibility of approach is what renders Sondheim, like Ravel, whose influence was doubtless inspirational in this work, not quite a neoclassicist, indeed undoubtedly a neoromantic at times. That the same can be said (though it rarely is) of much turn-of-the-century music, including that of Brahms, the nationalists, and the impressionists, is not our concern here; we can merely register the fact that Sondheim's music shares that uncomfortably comfortable linkage with previous styles that has always been the bugbear of modernism and can hardly be construed as postmodernism where *A Little Night Music* is concerned.

Folly Once More, and Its Motifs

To return to *A Little Night Music* as the successor to *Follies,* it is worth seeing that one of the unused ideas for *Follies,* intended for Sally, was the fragment

Ex. 7.1

of melody given in ex. 7.1. While the phrase as a whole hints in a somewhat ghostly fashion at the climax of "Beautiful Girls," the octave leap and its rhythm more strikingly foreshadow "Send In the Clowns" (so does the key, though only fortuitously when we remember that "Send In the Clowns" was written in E major). Another idea that seems to have been taken into the new show when no place was found for it in the old was a number with parallel texts sketched for *Follies* as "You Would Love My Wife" (though the music for this is quite different from "You Must Meet My Wife"). However circumstantial this transference of material, it may serve to remind us that *A Little Night Music* also has folly as its theme, though it articulates it in affectionate rather than critical and reflexive terms. The theme is enunciated in Hugh Wheeler's book by Mme. Armfeldt as early as the Prologue, when she first refers to the summer night's smiling three times "at the follies of human beings"—first "at the young, who know nothing," second "at the fools who know too little," and third "at the old who know too much."

Ingmar Bergman's screenplay for his film *Smiles of a Summer Night,* upon which the book and frequently the lyrics of *A Little Night Music* are fairly closely based, not only establishes the affectionate mood but plays on particular images of buffoonery. Fredrik really does trip into a puddle and get wet on his way to Désirée's lodgings (in the musical, a somewhat superior touch, Désirée makes up the story of his having fallen into her hip bath and enjoins the comic battle of sex by actually wetting his clothes). Carl-Magnus also falls (from his horse) on his way to Désirée (in the musical his new car has broken down). In the garden pavilion, after Fredrik has seen his wife elope with his stepson, he says to Charlotte in the film, "I look ridiculous," and she comments: "There he sits, the wise lawyer amidst his little catastrophe, like a child in a puddle." In the film we also see Fredrik on his way home in Carl-Magnus's nightshirt, and he meets a policeman.

These references to stock comedy culminate in the recognition that the second of the night's three smiles, the one for the fools, "was particularly broad tonight," as Mme. Armfeldt puts it in the musical. In the screenplay, this poetic motif is Frid's—he says to Petra as they rise from their haystack, "Now the summer night smiles its second smile: for the clowns, the fools, the unredeemable" (Sondheim had intended him to sing this observation, in "Silly People," changing it back to a comment on all three smiles and changing "the unredeemable" to "the rememberers," in line with Wheeler, in the process, but the song was cut), while the very last line in the film is Petra's: "But the clowns will have a cup of coffee in the kitchen." Sondheim's transference of this to his song for Fredrik and Désirée was utterly unconscious and unintentional, and maybe this is why his image of the stage or circus fool in "Send In the Clowns" seems too lightly prepared in the musical to strike home as subtext, though that it is apposite to Désirée's profession as an actress is made clear enough by the reference in the song's reprise not only to farce but to the apogee of the fool in literature.

DÉSIRÉE: Was that a farce?
FREDRIK: My fault, I fear.
DÉSIRÉE: Me as a merry-go-round.
FREDRIK: Me as King Lear.

Structural motifs for Fredrik, the lawyer, are just as lightly handled. There is a deliciously ironic counterbalance to the claustrophobic, bourgeois mood of immorality and decadence in the fact that (as he, a lawyer, is presumably the first to realize) his marriage to Anne is legally null and void in any case given that it is unconsummated, but this is never pointed out to us, nor, presumably, to Henrik, who thus somehow stays on the right side of the law in his "sinning" with his stepmother. Still more to the connoisseur's taste (it has often been commented upon) is the brilliance of Fredrik's first lyric in the musical, "Now," in which, with a lawyer's impeccable binary logic, he runs through all the possibilities of how he might seduce his virgin wife. This is a recurrent Sondheim subtext: as a professional man he is used to weighing decisions and arguments, rather like Ben in "The Road You Didn't Take," acknowledging that "One's life consists of either/or." It is even cast in lawyer's rhetoric ("Then we see / The option that follows of course"). Fredrik executes four layers of mental commands before reentering the circuit, and it is fitting enough that he should break it reflexively by succumbing to the subject of his own discourse, sleep (see ex. 7.2a). All this is accomplished within a single textural span of music, supple and romantically delicate in its harmonic unfolding (in this respect it could almost be a song by Duparc), modulating further and further as Fredrik penetrates his mental maze, until with deft handling of a whole-tone harmonic pivot it is back at the recapitulation (ex. 7.2b), thereby presaging the return to Fredrik's initial proposition. His decision-making logic, ironically petering out in sleep, is a nice foil to the simultaneous chatter of his wife. Frivolous and scatterbrained, and to have been characterized in the song "Two Fairy Tales," had room

Ex. 7.2a

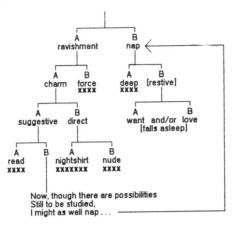

Ex. 7.2b

been found for it, by a story with which she identified about a princess who "lapsed into a coma," "mad / With indecision," she cannot decide what to do or what to wear (in the 1978 film version of the opening "Night Waltz" she actually sings "What shall I wear" as the first line of a new episodic section of music that Sondheim composed for it).

The summer night's three smiles were clearly conceived by Sondheim in terms of three triple-time chords, and in this idea too and its execution there were links with *Follies*. Among the many waltz vamps in the "Miscellaneous" sketches (though not all the sketches are in triple or compound time) there is a page partly of chordal experiment that includes the music shown in ex. 7.3a. There is nothing in the score quite matching the intervallic harshness (0 1 5 7) of the third of these chords, though the long-held dissonance at the beginning of ex. 7.3b, like a stretched-out chromatic appoggiatura to a G-sharp that it never reaches, suggests a parallel. It can be seen that the material shown in ex. 7.3a was incorporated into ex. 7.3b as *x*. In fact this whole passage dates back as far as 1957, when it was used as a subsidiary section of a "French Waltz," intended for Anouilh's *Ring Round the Moon* (see Zadan 1990, 181), whose main section began as shown in ex. 7.3c and whose spare accompaniment, we can observe, also rubbed off on the eventual "Night Waltz" of *A Little Night Music*. Two later variants of the "three Summer Night chords," as Sondheim calls them in the sketches, both in the dark key of D-flat major eventually used in the score, exhibit fuller chordal sonorities: the first two chords in ex. 7.3d are both 0 1 4 8 (the third, 0 2 4 5 8, is rather obviously an appoggiatura chord to the fourth, 0 3 5 8), while the five- rather than four-note chords of ex. 7.3e comprise 0 3 4 5 8, 0 1 4 5 8, and 0 1 3 5 8 respectively. As elsewhere when Sondheim is attempting a dark, romantic musical signification (which I shall discuss further concerning *Into the Woods*), he emphasizes semitones and minor thirds, and this survives into the sparser treatment of the chords (0 1 4 5, 0 1 4, and 0 2 5 8) in the score itself (see the quotation of the opening of "Night Waltz" in ex. 7.3f). Given the acknowledged influence on Sondheim of Ravel's *Valses nobles et sentimentales,* the parallel between the opening of its second waltz (ex. 7.3g, in which all three boxed chords have the structure 0 1 4 8) and Sondheim's sketch (ex. 7.3d) seems especially suggestive. Having surveyed this background to "Night Waltz," the *Follies* connection becomes clearer: the three chords to symbolize the three colors in "All Things Bright and Beautiful" (their sonorities, as shown in ex. 6.8a, are 0 1 3 5 8, 0 3 5 8, and 0 1 4 5 8) are all identical with one or other of the "summer night" chords. We might add that these sonorities fail to find their fullest exploration in the score of *A Little Night Music* as it stands because of the omission of "Silly People," cut during previews of the original production and perhaps the most chromatically complex of all Sondheim's songs; in addition to (and in intricate relationship with) its sensuously dissonant harmonies, its melodic line consists largely of pairs of minor thirds.

Period Tone: The Nineteenth Century

Doing things by threes was a stylish ploy in a conception that already had several others. Bergman had provided much of what was needed in

Ex. 7.3a

Dinner–Death
end of waltz

Ex. 7.3b

[Tempo di Valse]

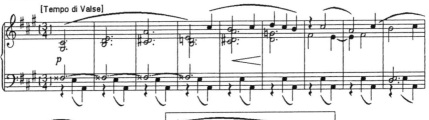

Ex. 7.3c

♩ = 144

[etc.]

Ex. 7.3d

Ex. 7.3e

or

Ex. 7.3f

Ex. 7.3g

Assez lent--avec une expression intense
en dehors

the way of period tone, particularly in terms of his elegant dialogue, which is thoroughly Wildean on occasions. His were lines such as Mme. Armfeldt's riposte to her daughter's suggestion that she may have cheated a little at her game: "Solitaire is the only thing in life which demands absolute honesty"; transferred to a conversation between the old lady and her granddaughter Fredrika (who is not featured in Bergman—there is merely a much younger, silent grandson), this exchange forms the very first lines of dialogue in the musical, in the act 1 Prologue, and Hugh Wheeler capably matches it with further bons mots, such as his opening line for act 2, Mme. Armfeldt's "To lose a lover or even a husband or two during the course of one's life can be vexing. But to lose one's teeth is a catastrophe," with its clear reminiscence of Lady Bracknell. (The Wildean tone did not, however, prevent both Wheeler and Sondheim from enjoying more risqué conceits on occasions, to the extent of lines about Carl-Magnus as "an endless erection / That falls on its knees / When it sees its reflection" in Charlotte's jettisoned song "My Husband the Pig.") Bergman also suggested a comic parallel to Ibsen's *Hedda Gabler* by having Henrik play the piano and attempt suicide in his inner desperation.

It may well be that what Henrik was to be imagined playing—"some stormy passages"—helped Sondheim fix on the nineteenth-century character or genre piece, as found, for instance, in Chopin, as a musical starting point; and he may have picked up on Bergman's Introduction to the published screenplay of *Smiles of a Summer Night*, with its early childhood memory of the apartment next door to his grandmother's in Uppsala, in which a piano "played waltzes, nothing but waltzes." Sondheim certainly decided to develop the diegetic musical content of Bergman's film, and in doing so he transferred Henrik's anger and frustration from the piano to the cello and introduced Fredrika as a young girl practicing exercises on the piano (in which she resembles Marian Paroo's piano pupil Amaryllis in *The Music Man*). As noted in chapter 4, Henrik's cello and Fredrika's piano, which initially appear superimposed (in different keys) as a brief Entr'acte when the scene changes after the act 1 Prologue, are vestiges of an idea, found among the "Miscellaneous" sketches, that never fully took root: "Some characters have instruments: Cello for Henrik, guitar for Petra/Trumpet for K-M, piano for Frederika." In the event Carl-Magnus has military music (a polonaise as his chief song) but no diegetic trumpet, while Petra's guitar, wielded by Henrik in Bergman's screenplay as a telltale prop to his lovemaking with her as Anne and Fredrik return from the theater, is omitted from Wheeler's book, although Petra's solo, "The Miller's Son," suggests a folk style with guitar accompaniment in both its slow and quick sections. (Since there is no guitar in the orchestra, the slow section is accompanied on the harp).

Sondheim's use of the cello in Henrik's early solo, "Later," serves as a prime instance of the sheer musical expertise of *A Little Night Music*. Only what the pit cello imitates (and Henrik, stroke by stroke, mimes) is diegetic, of course—he is alone in the room and we must therefore imagine him practicing either a piece for unaccompanied cello or the cello part of a sonata or character piece with the piano part absent (indeed, the piano accompaniment is initially absent on the original cast recording, as are portions of the later canon mentioned below). Sondheim suggests both these possibilities, for the 3/2 meter of the piece with its feminine cadences could imply a slow baroque sarabande, maybe from a Bach or French solo suite. Yet the piano accompaniment with its steady, somber offbeat chords and ostinato bass pattern also suggests something nineteenth-century, perhaps along the lines of the Fauré *Élégie*, while there is also a hint of Ravel's left-hand piano concerto in the rhythm—see ex. 7.4a. However, the major reference, conscious or unconscious, is surely to Brahms's E minor Cello Sonata (ex. 7.4b). Already, at the beginning, we have three-part counterpoint (plus the accompanying chords) between the cello solo, the bass pattern, and Henrik's vocal monologue, and unlike many other Sondheim instances it is academically scrupulous, at least between two of the parts at any given moment, and normally between all three. This allows the interchange of parts when the first section is repeated (the cello takes over the ostinato figure while the tune migrates to the orchestra) and encourages the canon at the (double) octave that begins, again with a strong French flavor (compare Franck's habitual use of the device) in the *maggiore* section and takes the music to heights of articulateness just as Henrik's verbal oratory becomes so inarticulate with

Ex. 7.4a

Ex. 7.4b

frustration that he punctuates his phrases with physical violence in the form of pizzicato attacks on his instrument (ex. 7.4c). Sketches for the song even include some *alla breve* fugal counterpoint. We have come a long way since Lady Jane's cello number in Gilbert and Sullivan's *Patience*.

Such urbanity makes this a connoisseur's score, and within it a wealth of features can take their place. Tunick's *Rosenkavalier* quotation in "A Weekend in the Country" is matched by the reference to the texture of the same opera's celebrated Trio in the "Now"/"Later"/"Soon" montage and hint of its melody in "Remember?" (ex. 7.4d) and "Perpetual

As I've   of-ten stat-ed,   It's in -tol-er-a-ble

Colla voce

pizz.   arco   pizz.   arco

Colla voce

be-ing tol -er-at-ed.

Ex. 7.4d

[Tempo di Valse]

The pro - pri-e-tress-'s grin, Al - so her glare.

Ex. 7.4e

Agitato

f

Ex. 7.4f

Anticipation"; and there is a generally classical sound in passages such as the introduction to "A Weekend in the Country" (ex. 7.4e—does this remind us of Mendelssohn's "Italian" Symphony, of the second subject of the first movement of Berlioz's *Symphonie fantastique,* or of something else?). On occasions it is even a pianist's score, as we might expect from a composer who plays the instrument expertly and masters his accompaniments to the point of privately recording them as he sings his own songs. Thus "In Praise of Women" not only sounds like a Chopin polonaise but plays like one in its use of fast octaves (ex. 7.4f; compare Chopin's A-flat Polonaise, ex. 7.4g). Tunick (1991, 3–4) knowingly categorizes "Now" and "Every Day a Little Death" as études, pointing out the cross-hand pattern of the latter's accompaniment.

The Waltz and Its Symbolism

Above all, however, it is the use of the waltz and other social dance matrixes that cements the musical structure of *A Little Night Music*. The trinitarian symbolism of its meter is fertile enough. We have noted the three "summer night" chords paralleling Bergman's motif of the three smiles. Not all Bergman's trinitarian invitations were responded to, however—witness Désirée's speech in the diegetic play *A Woman of the World,* which was not taken over into the book of the musical.

Don't forget, Madame, that love is a perpetual juggling of three balls. Their names are heart, word and sex. How easily these three balls can be juggled, and how easily one of them can be dropped.

Nor was the collaborators' original tripartite conception of the action, as a kind of three-card trick emanating surrealistically from Mme. Armfeldt's games of patience, retained.

Our original concept was that of a fantasy-ridden musical. It was to take place over a weekend during which, in almost gamelike fashion, Désirée would have been the prime mover and would work the characters into different situations. The first time, everybody would get mixed up, and through farcical situations, would end up with the wrong partner. Then magically, the weekend would start again. The next time, everything worked out, but Henrik committed suicide. The third time, Désirée arranged everything right but this time when she was left alone with Fredrik, he put on his gloves and started to walk off the stage because she hadn't done anything to make him want her.

The way all this worked was that Madame Armfeldt, who was like a witch figure, would reshuffle the pack of cards and time would revert and we'd be back at the beginning of the weekend again. The characters would then re-form, waltz again, and start over. It was all to be presented like a court masque with a music-box quality. But Hugh Wheeler finally gave up on it. He just couldn't make it work to his satisfaction. (Zadan 1990, 182)

Other tripartite structures may or may not be relevant. Petra's "The Miller's Son," the last new song of the evening, in which she dreams of three possible husbands, may well be a vestige of the original conception, but with the show as it stands it seems unhelpful to posit a precise parallel between her "miller's son," "businessman," and "Prince of Wales" and Frid, Fredrik, and Carl-Magnus respectively, as Mark Steyn does (Steyn 1990). Nor is anything particular made out of the presence of three generations of Armfeldts.

In fact, one might say that couplings, not triplings, are of the essence where nineteenth-century social dance, and the waltz in particular, is concerned; however, as soon as a partner is exchanged and a triangle occurs we are back to three. It is the ambiguity between different arrangements and intersections of two and three that provides the rich texture for the play and, specifically, for its musical construction. Tunick (1991, 3) points out the striking incidence of "duets regarding a third person"—"You Must Meet My Wife," "It Would Have Been Wonderful," and "Every Day a

Ex. 7.5. The Characters in *A Little Night Music*

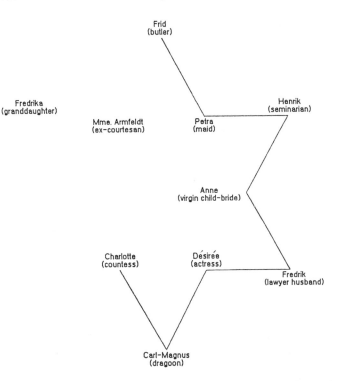

Little Death"—and talks of "the unstable number three drawn to the stable two" as the fundamental motivation behind these songs.

The structure of the plot is actually best visualized as the positions and movements of the ten characters on a dance floor (see Tunick 1991, 2 for an alternative diagram); we can position them in two concentric circles, rather in the manner of *Follies 1987,* say with the men on the outside (see ex. 7.5). This disposition of the characters as in a round dance immediately suggests Arthur Schnitzler's celebrated, once infamous play, *La ronde,* published as *Reigen* in Vienna in 1903 and concerning a sexual chain of ten people; the closeness of the parallel between them and Bergman's characters makes one wonder whether he was familiar with the play or with Max Ophuls's film of it that appeared (with music by Oscar Straus) in 1950, five years before *Smiles of a Summer Night* (see ex. 7.6).

Sondheim's decision to cast *A Little Night Music* as some kind of a suite of waltzes was a natural enough response to the characters' sexual partnerings and the turn-of-the-century European setting. The waltz, linked from the start of its history with bourgeois social and sexual coupling, enjoyed one of its many new leases of life in Edwardian operetta following the enormous success of Lehár's *Merry Widow,* produced in Vienna in

Ex. 7.6. The Characters in *La ronde* and *A Little Night Music*

La ronde	A Little Night Music
Prostitute [....➤	Ex-courtesan (Mme. Armfeldt)]
Soldier ....➤	⎰ Dragoon (Carl-Magnus)
..........➤	⎱
Parlour maid ....:.........➤	Maid (Petra)
Young gentleman.................:.........➤	⎰ Seminarian (Henrik)
...................➤	⎱
Young wife ....:..........:.....➤	Virgin child-bride (Anne)
Husband............:............:....➤	Lawyer husband (Fredrik)
Sweet girl [..............:............:.........➤	Granddaughter (Fredrika)][1]
Poet ....: :	—
Actress ....:.........➤	Actress (Désirée)
Count ....:	—
[Prostitute again]	—
—	Butler (Frid)
—	Countess (Charlotte)

[1]Grandson in Bergman.

1905. Because of the dynamic, swirling properties of its unitary, one-to-
a-bar meter, it had also enjoyed an association throughout the romantic
period of the nineteenth century with the idea of life itself as an uncon-
trolled Dionysian dance, which could further be portrayed as a dance in
the arms of death. This polar identity was the *Lebenstanz* or the *Totentanz,*
to give titles utilized respectively by Delius and Liszt in symphonic dance
or march compositions.

Death is an important undercurrent in *A Little Night Music,* as it is more
obviously in Bergman's dark-toned film. The night's third and final smile
becomes the smile of death at the end, when Mme. Armfeldt expires
(though this does not occur in Bergman, who has the third smile, in the
words of Frid, "for the sad, the depressed, the sleepless, the confused, the
frightened, the lonely"), and she has already helped set this up by referring
to saving the best champagne for her funeral and by her toast "To Life! . . .
And to the only other reality—death!" during the country house dinner.

The Metric Fount: Hemiola

Sondheim's score is not all waltzes, even when so labeled (there were
originally four different songs called "Night Waltz"; "Night Waltz III"

was retitled "Perpetual Anticipation," and the unused "Night Waltz IV," also entitled "Crickets," was a charming, rather English-sounding bar-carolle or contredanse in 6/8). Thus Richard Traubner voices misgivings that are largely unnecessary when he points out "the unlikelihood that any Viennese composer would have written every song in a variant of three-quarter time, as Sondheim proudly did" (Traubner 1984, 420). Rather it is an exhaustive exploration of the ways in which binary and ternary pulses and groupings can be multiplied and compounded. He multiplies three by two, two by three, and three by three in a cornucopia of metric patterns and accompaniment figures, simply omitting the standard two-by-two compound of the Broadway march.

The metrical scheme of *A Little Night Music* is partly a matter of variety, as the rhythms charted and categorized in ex. 7.7 show at a glance. But the vital corollary to the omission of duple compounds is rhythmic ambiguity and flux based on the fact that two and three are both factors of six. In musical terms, this involves the contrast between groupings of six eighth notes into two measures of 3/8 (or one of 6/8) and one measure of 3/4; or of six quarter notes into two measures of 3/4 (or one of 6/4) and one measure of 3/2. It is the latter that normally applies to the standard one-to-a-bar waltz meter of 3/4, where the property arises as a broadening ambiguity when the quarter notes in two consecutive measures are made to sound as though they comprise one measure of 3/2. This, the musical phenomenon of hemiola, is a basic resource of the waltz. Less closely connected with the waltz, but common in Sondheim, is what we may call reverse hemiola, where an established three-beat pulse with duple sub-divisions (e.g., six eighth notes in three-to-a-bar 3/4) is construed as compound time (six eighth notes in 6/8).

Lest we seem to be degenerating into mathematics, it is worth observing that music, and specifically musical time, as the art (or, as the ancients would have it, the science) of number and proportion, must have been very much in Sondheim's mind for him to have made the connection, as many had done before him, between circular dancing, the cyclic unity of musical triple time (in its one-to-a-bar guise, as in the waltz), clock time, and numbers in general. This he did, his web of imagery aided by the Scandinavian setting with its "perpetual sunset," in a mesh of metaphors standing for the anticipations of sexual partnering and perhaps of existential awareness in general. In the statutory score it comes to the surface most clearly in the Liebeslieders' three "Night Waltz" texts ("The Sun Won't Set," "The Sun Sits Low," and "Perpetual Anticipation"); but a broader scheme of reference, perhaps linking with the numeric metaphor of card playing that, as we have seen, was downgraded, had been anticipated. It included a substantial song for Fredrika entitled "Numbers," apparently

Ex. 7.7

Musical Number	Meter	Note Groupings	Tempo Indication	Genre	Vocal Disposition
ACT 1					
"Night Waltz"	3/4	3 dotted half notes, 3 quarter notes (with some eighth notes in accompaniment ----' constant 6, grouped in 4s)	Tempo di Valse	Viennese waltz	Instrumental + vocalise
"Now"	6/8	3 x 2 = 6 eighth notes (constant)	(None)	Tarantella?	Male solo (baritone)
"Later"	3/2	3 half notes (subdivided: dotted quarter note/eighth note ----> constant 12 eighth notes)	Lento	Sarabande/élégie?	Male solo (tenor) + diegetic obbligato cello
"Soon"	3/4	quarter notes + eighth notes in constant hemiola (i.e., 3/2)	Tempo di Valse	Hemiola waltz	Female solo (soprano)
(+ montage)					Trio (preceding voices)
"The Glamorous Life"					
("Piano Practice")	3/4	constant eighth notes	[Tempo di Mazurka]	Exercise/étude	Diegetic piano solo
a)	3/4	quarter notes + dotted eighth note/sixteenth note, triplet eighth notes (in hemiola) ("Piano Practice" eighth-note accompaniment)	Tempo di Mazurka	Mazurka	Female solo (3 different voices/generations in sequence: soprano, deep contralto, baritone)
b)	3/4	triplet eighth-note (later eighth-note) accompaniment, with constant hemiola		Scherzo/fast waltz?	Unison Liebeslieders
"Remember?"	3/4	quarter notes + eighth notes (constant in introduction) with hemiola and displacement of pattern	Tempo di Valse	Folk waltz/Ländler	Male/female duet (mostly in alternation)

Musical Number	Meter	Note Groupings	Tempo Indication	Genre	Vocal Disposition
"You Must Meet My Wife"	3/4	quarter notes + dotted quarter note/eighth note (constant eighth-note accompaniment with implied cross-rhythm from fill); hemiola in episodes	Tempo di Valse--(slow 3)	Slow waltz	Male/female duet (mostly male solo + parlando interruptions)
"Liaisons"	3/2	3 half notes + much quarter-note and some eighth-note/ sixteenth-note subdivision on various parts of the measure	Moderate 3	Slow bolero	Female solo (baritone/parlando)
"In Praise of Women"	3/4	flashy plethora of eighth notes, sixteenth notes, dotted eighth notes and Scotch snaps (smooth B section with constant cross-rhythm in accompaniment: r.h. quarter notes (2 x 3 in eighth-note terms), l.h. dotted quarter notes [3 x 2])	Tempo di Polonaise	Polonaise	Male solo (baritone)
"Every Day a Little Death"	6/8	quarter-note/eighth-note melody (dotted quarter notes in B section); constant 6-eighth-note pulse in accompaniment (assembled from offbeat quarter-note/eighth-note figure)	Moderato	Inégale gavotte/ contredanse?	Female duet (soprano or mezzo + contralto)
"A Weekend in the Country"	6/8	constant hemiola in refrain (Henrik re-interprets it and fits it in as a broader tempo in Part 6); constant eighth notes in accompaniment	Agitato	Gigue/tarantella contredanse?	Tutti finale
	3/4	(Henrik)	Maestoso	Processional waltz	Male solo (tenor)

ACT 2

Musical Number	Meter	Note Groupings	Tempo Indication	Genre	Vocal Disposition
"Night Waltz II"	3/4	half-note/quarter-note melody; hemiola accompaniment (later in voice part)	(None)	Lullaby waltz/ barcarolle?	Liebeslieder (solos in sequence)
"It Would Have Been Wonderful"	9/8	even dotted quarter notes in melody undergo diminution to even eighth notes; mixture of both in accompaniment	Andante--(in 3)	Mazurka/contredanse (Sir Roger de Coverley?)	Male duet (two baritones, mostly in alternation)

Ex. 7.7—*Continued*

Musical Number	Meter	Note Groupings	Tempo Indication	Genre	Vocal Disposition
"Perpetual Anticipation"	3/8	constant eighth notes with some sixteenth notes; displaced patterns in accompaniment	Moderato--(in 1)	Canonic music-box waltz	Female trio (Liebeslieders)
"Send In the Clowns"	12/8 and 9/8	long notes and groups of eighth notes; constant eighth notes in accompaniment (but note Luftpause); duplets appear in fills	Lento	Slow waltz (eighth-note beat) with some 3-"measure" phrases	Female solo (deep contralto)
"The Miller's Son"	(a) 3/4	quarter-note/half-note accompaniment; folklike rhythmic flexibility in melody	Largo	Pseudo-folksong with gymnopédie accompaniment	Female solo (contralto)
	(b) 2/4	melody tends towards constant sixteenth notes but includes tripping cadence rhythm; constant sixteenth notes in accompaniment, but bass already suggesting 3/8	(None)	Contredanse (écossaise/rigaudon?)	Female solo (contralto)
	(c) 3/8	melody in constant eighth notes with double anacrusis; constant sixteenth notes in accompaniment, and 3/8 bass affirmed ("meanwhile" section adds hemiola)	(None)	Fast waltz	Female solo (contralto)

Note: Reprises and the Liebeslieders' compilation "Overture" and vocal setting of "Night Waltz" are not shown

for the opening of the show and also the source of the common time underscoring which remains as no. 22 in the vocal score. This incorporated the "What shall I wear" section of the film version of "Night Waltz" and what seems to be a shadow of the melody of the middle section of "In Praise of Women" (ex. 7.8a), concordant with a note scribbled among the

Ex. 7.8a

Ex. 7.8b

preliminary ideas for the musical: "The word 'time' suddenly at the end of songs. On '6 o'clock.'" Correspondingly, the first lyrics of the film of *A Little Night Music,* set to the first three notes of "Night Waltz," are "Love takes time" (later reversed to "The time love takes").

To return to hemiola, it is an ambiguity or paradox of time in the form of cross-rhythm, but it works with a sense of ease because the smallest units are marked out—the grid in *A Little Night Music* and elsewhere tending to be present as continuous eighth notes or oom-pah-pah quarter notes. When this is no longer the case the situation quickly transforms itself to what is commonly but unhelpfully thought of as syncopation, and we need briefly to investigate it because it is exactly what Sondheim avoids in *A Little Night Music.* Consider ex. 7.8b, which presents the pulse and cross-rhythm of Cole Porter's "Anything Goes"; here the swinging pulse resists subdivision into eighth notes, while the implied compound time that sets in after the first measure of melody also lacks a run of eighth notes at any point. The tension between the two, due to the paucity of points of coordination (we really do hear it as 3:4, not 2:3), is what gives it its irresistible, jaunty Broadway wit. Conversely, although there are occasions in *A Little Night Music* when the 3:4 ratio appears as such, they are only found in the context of running eighth notes; and the occasions on which a quarter-note/eighth-note triple pulse conflicts with itself offer a different situation again from both ex. 7.8b and hemiola—see the accompaniments of "Perpetual Anticipation" and "Every Day a Little Death," where a continuum is established by simply shifting a quarter-note/eighth-note pattern one eighth note backward in consistent displacement (see ex. 7.7).

Hemiola is close to the heart of social dance culture. It is not peculiar to the waltz, being found in the minuet, sarabande, courante, and many other dances of the French baroque, particularly at cadences, those points of gesture that thereby betoken the graceful balance of ambiguity. This in itself is probably a distant courtly echo of the more vigorous use of cadential hemiola in folk dances where it also flourishes and is more likely to be sensed as a correlative to flashes of sexual energy or assertion, even violence. In the waltz it lies somewhere between the two: historically speaking, the waltz certainly signifies and accommodates the supposed licentiousness or at least freewill ardor of bourgeois coupling, and to this extent hemiola, particularly when it is used continuously with the effect of shifting the music into a higher gear, can be heard as articulating a sense of freedom from contractual control, even a sense of ecstasy. At the same time, however, its ambiguity and poise remind us that every society relies on sexual manners, a code of courtship or of flirtation that allows for the flux of response or rejection by framing passion with wit. There is also a sense in which the perpetual motion of the dance is a sublimation of sexual activity rather than a prelude to it. This is what the song "Perpetual Anticipation" evokes, not least in two lines that were drafted but not used: "And waiting for the consummation's / Exciting as sin."

A Little Night Music is a comedy of manners, and Fredrika, like her contemporary Gigi, is being taught her society's manners by a female exemplar who is more detached than her mother would be (in Fredrika's case it is her grandmother, in Gigi's her aunt). It is thus highly appropriate that the rhythmic fount and origin of Sondheim's score should reside in a symbol that signifies, as it did for Fay in *Anyone Can Whistle,* her learning of impersonal control, bearing, and dexterity: piano practice. To be exact, she is attempting to master the smoothness of three groups of two eighth notes each in 3/4 without letting the finger patterns of two groups of three notes impose unwanted 6/8 accents, as the rhythmic notation of "Piano Practice" in ex. 7.7 shows (it is taken not from its first appearance but from that at the opening of "The Glamorous Life," and also shows that after two measures her scalar exercise increases the difficulties of touch further by repeating the finger pattern after *four* notes). Of course this contrasts strongly with Henrik's cello playing, which is personal, disruptive, wild, and emblematic of his rebellion against the sexual manners of the society in which he finds himself. The contrast is underlined by the fact, already mentioned, that we first hear both these diegetic musical symbols simultaneously, in a bitonal relationship to each other.

Something of Fredrika's finger exercises seems foreshadowed in the running-eighth-note accompaniment that develops in the initial "Night Waltz," with its four-note contours (ex. 7.9a) (the connection is suggested

Ex. 7.9a

Ex. 7.9b

Ex. 7.9c

Ex. 7.9d

at the very end of the musical, when the figure is left behind after the waltz like a wisp of smoke, curling upward on woodwind and then muted solo violin until blown away by a single chord on the stage piano—a fitting touch of timbral confectionery whereby Tunick and Sondheim again recall *Der Rosenkavalier* and its ethos). We should also remember that, even earlier in the score than this, the Liebeslieders' warming-up vocal scales are the very first thing we hear. Almost immediately after its first appearance, the rhythmic ambiguity of Fredrika's exercise is complemented, seen in reverse, as it were, in a supple song accompaniment, Fredrik's "Now," the flux of whose quick 6/8 eighth-note continuum is enhanced by being based on a repeating two-note pattern implying 3/4 (this is what the accents indicate in its representation in ex. 7.7). In "Later" the broader meter of 3/2 first introduces the possibilities of a group of twelve rather than six eighth notes; this opening up is not directed toward more complicated cross-rhythms (as discussed previously) but to the very Gallic aesthetic resource of varied and unpredictable distributional groupings, always overshooting a main beat and thus avoiding agogic emphasis, in Henrik's vocal line (see ex. 7.4a). "Soon" develops into that not uncommon phenomenon, the hemiola waltz in which the secondary perspective of 3/2 is sustained rather than incidental, and when these three songs are combined in the trio, our pleasure is as much in hearing the rhythmic combinations—in assessing where the common factor lies—as in the intervallic counterpoint. The factor is the quarter note; thus Henrik's 3/2 reinforces Anne's hemiola, and a second, conflicting level of hemiola is avoided by augmenting Fredrik's patter rhythm into continuous quarter notes (this is appropriate enough, slowed and fuddled as he is by his dream, and in any case may well be a vestige of an earlier version of his song cast in 3/4 with a vocal rhythm in quarter notes). There is even something of a lyric corollary to this rhythmic interplay when the characters steal each other's title words—Henrik sings "Now," Fredrik "Soon," and Anne "Later" on pages 58–59 of the score.

Rhythmic resourcefulness is so basic a component of any musical score made up of contrasting and characteristic numbers that it is unnecessary to comment exhaustively on the admittedly disciplined and special form it takes in *A Little Night Music;* in any case, ex. 7.7 is designed to assist the eye in seeing what the ear hears in this respect. Nevertheless, some procedures and tendencies deserve further comment. It will be noted that the eighth-note accompaniment to "You Must Meet My Wife" (a variant of which, unlikely as it seems, appears to have been considered in the sketches as a possible figure for "Send In the Clowns") again plays with variegated contours—that is, there is an unpredictability about the point at which the rising figure breaks back on itself (see ex. 7.9b), and this begins to echo Sondheim's connection with minimalism as well as Fredrika's exercises. The cross-rhythmic grouping of four eighth notes that, we noted, the piano exercise begins to presage is sensed not only here but in some of the music that was omitted from the score. Charlotte's solo, "My Husband the Pig," whose refrain became the A section of "Every Day a Little Death," had a spirited verse with quick-fire four-note groupings in the fills (as well as melodic contours based on Fredrika's scales; ex. 7.9c); more important, "Two Fairy Tales," a duet for Anne and Henrik, broke the embargo on quadruple time and not only pitted Fredrika's three-eighth-note groupings and the actual tune of her exercise against a metric grid of four (or eight, given the initial barring; it later changes to 2/4, perversely at the point where the voices sing "Now there were three") but compounded the conflict by splitting them up against the grain between the two voices (ex. 7.9d).

Character Dances and Further Rhythmic Resources

In many respects the delightful and informed use of nineteenth-century nationalist dance patterns counteracts this type of rhythmic flux in that they rely on highly characterized and insistent rhythms. There is no mistaking the identity and military association of Carl-Magnus's polonaise "In Praise of Women" (or of its rejected predecessor, "Bang!") or the melancholy solitude of "The Glamorous Life"'s mazurka. The latter, of course, redolent of travel through eastern or northern European wastes— and we should not forget that historically the rise of national dances such as the mazurka coincided with the age of the railway—points up the irony of the song's title. Other dances may be less easy to pin down by title but unmistakable in intention: whether or not "slow bolero" is the best label for "Liaisons," the associations of its bass ostinato and other rhythms (for instance, in the "Where is style?" episode) with Spain or at least Mediterranean luxury are clear and congruent with the guitar-evoking harmony and the text (whose first substantive is the word *villa*) right from the start. It should be admitted, however, that "Silly People" shared some of these marks of identity without suggesting the same evocation; perhaps, in addition to providing a second-act twin to Mme. Armfeldt's first-act number, its rhythmic cast cemented the link between the two characters, mistress and servant.

Some associations may be highly subliminal but nevertheless connected with tradition: "Every Day a Little Death" sounds like a rather dreamy pastoral contredanse in its 6/8 rhythm until, in the "He smiles sweetly" section, we begin to hear, in a broader dimension, the double-upbeat pattern of the gavotte; this is a wonderful touch, for it affects us with the mode of ironic politeness that sets the seal on the scene between the two women and that has been the gavotte's topical province from the eighteenth century to the twentieth (for instance, in one of the confrontations between Othello and Desdemona in Verdi's *Otello*) without our (or even the composer's) necessarily being conscious of the means.

Alongside these clear metrical intentions of *Affekt* runs the strain of ambiguity. Hemiola continues to be present, for instance in the 3/4 vocal rhythm against the 6/8 accompaniment pulse of "A Weekend in the Country" and, conversely, in the 3/2 accompaniment of "Night Waltz II" against its 3/4 melody. Reverse hemiola is effectively used in the B section of "In Praise of Women," the intrusion of the 6/8 pulse of the bass as it cuts across the accompanimental quarter notes being like the slight constriction of a heartbeat as Carl-Magnus lets his imagination dwell on the delights of "Capable, pliable women . . . / Women . . ." (the effect is not unlike that of the dots in the text), while, on a more functional plane, it also signifies the awkward marking of conversational time, the emotional impasse, between Carl-Magnus and Charlotte that it accompanies as a vamp (indeed, the rhythm originally verbalized its own sense of marking time when it formed the accompaniment to the title refrain "Women Were Born to Wait" in the song's first version). Another carefully weighed rhythmic resource is the property referred to above in connection with Henrik's "Later": the varied and unpredictable, or unaccentual, placing of groups of short notes within an otherwise unambiguous or straightforwardly accentual pulse. This, an effect of wit, to use the word in a broad sense, is common to many French dances and some of other nations; in ex. 7.7 it can easily be spotted in the variable placing of groups of two eighth notes and four sixteenth notes in "In Praise of Women" and in the use of eighth-note groups of different lengths in "Liaisons." Its most striking utilization, however, is in "It Would Have Been Wonderful." Here it is set up in the accompaniment rhythm, with its four continuous eighth notes leading away from the main beat rather than up to it. This introduces an effect of patter, of eighth notes wanting to tumble over one another in a continuous cascade, and the humor arises as its rhythmic development depicts the progressive loss of each man's self-control and cool dignity. Originally, as "If," the song began with a different verse section in a smooth, idyllic 9/8 (the opening words were "What a beautiful orderly scene") whose suave four-bar phrases of dotted quarter notes led into the statutory refrain. Here they continue, at first seemingly unaware of the belittling eighth-note rhythm beneath them (ex. 7.10a), but they give way to rhythmic diminution in which the singers get through their lines twice as quickly as they would wish and even, in their confusion, find themselves adding a couple of syllables to the scansion as a stream of eighth notes eventuates (ex. 7.10b); the fact that this filling in of notes is mirrored in the lyrics, which on the first occurrence mutate and parenthesize "bitter" to "better" on the same two notes, is a typically virtuosic piece of structural reflexivity.

The Lyrics and Hemiola

This leads us to a more general consideration of how these rhythmic topics work together with words. We may briefly illustrate the issue by examining the two waltz effects of hemiola and the *Luftpause,* with examples not restricted to *A Little Night Music.*

I have already noted in chapter 2 how a hemiola figure informs two of the central lines of each stanza of "A Bowler Hat" in *Pacific Overtures,* and how in the odd-numbered stanzas it is accompanied by images of flying; in fact its rhythmic onset, giving the metrically floating or soaring

Ex. 7.10a

Ex. 7.10b

effect, and the verb of motion coincide exactly each time (ex. 7.11a). In "You Must Meet My Wife" the element represented by hemiola is water, not air, the process of ungrounded motion drowning rather than flying (ex. 7.11b). Bringing hemiola back down to earth can be an effective melopoetic ploy, as when, in "Cora's Chase" from *Anyone Can Whistle*, the breadth (and breath) of Cora's question is nicely contrasted with the snap finality of her judgement on the "Cookies," with its peremptory eighth notes (ex. 7.11c). (In both these latter two instances the image of elemental motion or atmosphere is matched with related verbal conceits on at least some of the other appearances of its musical figure: in "You Must Meet My Wife" there is a further reference to whims, one to dreaming, and even a plausibly connected one to puffing at cigar ash; in "Cora's Chase," "breathing" is followed up with a misanthropic crescendo of illiberality preceding the same refrain: "moving," "living," "human.")

Ex. 7.11a

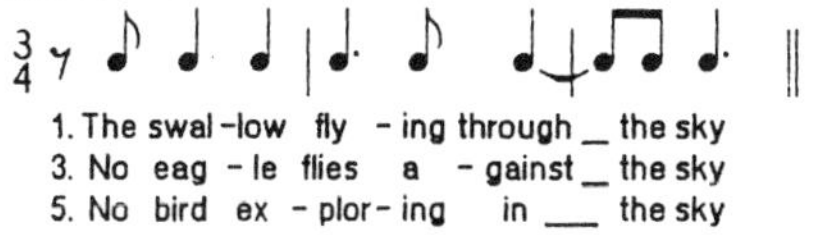

1. The swal-low fly - ing through __ the sky
3. No eag - le flies a - gainst __ the sky
5. No bird ex - plor- ing in ___ the sky

Ex. 7.11b

A sea of whims __ that I sub-merge in, __

Ex. 7.11c

Are they breath - ing? __ Then they're Cook -ies.

Ex. 7.11d

MRS N
Look! Is that __ the moon? Yes. What a love - ly af - ter - noon! Yes. (MRS N)
wait! Is that __ a star? No. Just the glow of a ci - gar. Oh. (MR E)
MRS S
wait... The sun __ is dip - ping.
MR L
Where? You're right, __ It's drop - ping.

Look!... At last! __ It's slip - ping. Sor - ry, my mis-take, it's stop - ping. (MRS S)

Ex. 7.11e

Some-one is wait - ing,
Cool as
Sar - ah,
[. . . Jen - ny.
. . . Warm as
Su - san,
. . . Sweet as
A - my,

Ex. 7.11f

Would I know __ her e-ven if I met her? __

Ex. 7.11g

alternative barring

actual barring

Lock 'em up! Put 'em a - way in the Jar! Time to start get-ting the nets out!

Ex. 7.11h

Ex. 7.11i

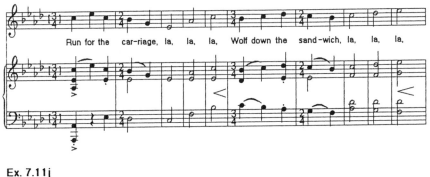

Ex. 7.11j

Another example of deflating hemiola by pulling it up short, with a subtle use of comic anticlimax (and a further reference to a cigar), occurs in *A Little Night Music*'s "Night Waltz II," where romantic references to the moon and a star in hemiola are rudely contrasted with the prosaic, even eighth notes of the lines about the cigar and the afternoon and still more by the lame, monosyllabic word *Oh* with its equally lame end-stopping half note (ex. 7.11d). This is followed by the comic verbal decrescendo from "dipping" (another typical hemiola word in its association with flying or swimming) through "dropping" and "slipping" to the reflexive "stopping," while the overall anticlimax is enhanced by the question-and-answer division of conversation, each reply deflating the atmosphere further until the colloquial "Sorry, my mistake" gives us the verbal "analysis" of the music's structural effect (see ex. 7.11d).

For the opposite effect, of hemiola broadening an otherwise constricted rhythmic proposition, we may turn to "Someone Is Waiting" in *Company*. Here the changing perspective is a mental one, and in the A section of the song Robert is pulled up short by his own impossible demands, as he dreams of an ideal girl, a compound of names and qualities that could never exist in one person, in a dead-end quarter-note/half-note rhythm that gets nowhere beyond his fantasy list (ex. 7.11e). In the B section he pulls himself out of the fantasy by questioning its validity, standing back from the hypnotic 3/4 and taking a deep breath (as it were) with a recuperative structural upbeat of two measures of cumulative hemiola (ex. 7.11f). The sense of a subsidiary upbeat and downbeat (on *know*) within the first two measures of this hemiola lends it an additional sense of rhythmic displacement, and this is a factor that Sondheim sometimes exploits with one eye on the flexible richness of accentuation in speech. The opening section of "Cora's Chase" in *Anyone Can Whistle* offers a good example: it begins with a unit of hemiola delayed by one beat that immediately meshes with one on the beat; the point of overlap itself suggests a 3/4 measure (partly because of the C-sharp chromatic appoggiatura on the word *time*) and consequent irregular barring of the whole phrase (ex. 7.11g).

On one comparable occasion in *A Little Night Music* Sondheim actually employs irregular barring as a result of displaced hemiola. In "The Glamorous Life" the hectic chaos of travel is illustrated with hemiola starting a beat early, as though 5/4 were alternating with 7/4 (ex. 7.11h), and at the lines "Run for the carriage" and "Wolf down the sandwich" the balancing extra beat at the end is lost altogether, as though semblance of 3/4 dignity has finally to be abandoned in the behind-the-scenes confusion of an actress's life; at this point the dignity of a romantic harmonic style is also abandoned and Coplandesque neoclassical counterpoint, no doubt suggested by the metric irregularity, is enjoyed with panache (ex. 7.11i).

One further example of displaced hemiola in *A Little Night Music* may be cited, in "Remember?" (ex. 7.11j). Here it begins two beats early, and given that the pattern of eighth notes in the first part of the phrase lends it the properties of a structural upbeat, the sense of hemiola suggests that the structural downbeat may be heard on the second syllable of the verbal consequent or refrain, "Remember?" rather than, as a kind of notated *Luftpause,* on the eighth-note rest before it. But the ambiguity is gentle, perhaps indicating no more than the softened and inexact memories that are under discussion, and either way the antecedent-consequent nature of the phrase with its one-word refrain acts like the microcosm of a song.

Lyrics and the *Luftpause*

This brings us to discussion of the *Luftpause*. We have already encountered it in chapter 3 in a discussion of the end of "I Feel Pretty" (see ex. 3.5d). It is an archetypal waltz feature, the point of silence or rhythmic hiatus like the moment of stillness and latent energy at the end of a pendulum's swing; it implies the thrill of physical motion, of hovering for a moment

Ex. 7.12a

Five o'-clock. __ Twi-light,

Ex. 7.12b

One more kiss be-fore we part, __ One more kiss and fare - well.__
One more kiss to melt the heart.__ One more glimpse of the past,__
                                          Not with tears or a sigh.__
                                          one more kiss and good - bye.__

Ex. 7.12c

1. Me here at last on the ground, You in mid - air.
2. One who keeps tear - ing a - round, One who can't move.
4. Los - ing my tim - ing this late in my ca - reer?
(3. I thought that you'd want what I want-- Sor - ry, my dear.)

in midair, on the turn, rolling yet poised in suspense, that is part of the waltz's propensity for ecstasy.

The material shown in ex. 7.12a, from "Night Waltz," its *Luftpause* indicated by the grammatical disjunction of the lyrics, illustrates the suspense of waiting for the sun to set so that the night's sexual business can begin. Nobody could mistake this rhythmic effect for hemiola, appearances notwithstanding. In "One More Kiss," from *Follies,* the *Luftpause* is onomatopoeic, expressing the gulp or sob implicit in this pastiche of a sentimental Alpine waltz; if its opening notes remind us of "Edelweiss" from *Sound of Music,* we should note that Sondheim writes the effect into the music and the lyrics rather than, like Rodgers, merely submit to vocal interpretations of crooners, for five out of the six cues for a *Luftpause* are indicated by a rest in the score, five come between a conjunction or preposition and what it governs, and all six illustrate the idea of separation—"we part," "farewell," "the past," "goodbye"—or dissolution—"melt," "a sigh" (see ex. 7.12b).

Sondheim's culminating mastery of the *Luftpause,* however, is in "Send In the Clowns." Whether the decorous need to separate the consonants between "love" and "farce" in stanza 3 (see Citron 1991, 69) should be regarded as a built-in *Luftpause* is doubtful, though the effect does markedly occur at this point in the orchestral reprise of the song (vocal score, p. 228, final measure). But ex. 7.12c indubitably shows how once again effects that anticipate a popular singer's techniques (and that for once actually presaged a hit) are written into the music; once again dependent parts of speech—"in," "who," "my"—are separated in suspense from their consequents; once again the rhythmic suspense, this time with a melodic correspondence too, as the voice slips to the same note an octave lower (i.e., fails to move to its expected destination), illustrates the text: "midair," "can't move," "losing my timing," and "late," with even (we need not doubt, in view of the word's resonances elsewhere in Sondheim which we have noticed) a subtextual meaning of "career" as the ball starts rolling again. Best of all is the variant in the third stanza: here Sondheim plays around with the hiatus, intensifying it by going up to it on the A-flat a beat too early (illustrating the desire of "I want"), and then as it were apologizing for the mistake with the word "sorry" on the same two notes. This almost exactly parallels the effect noted in "It Would Have Been Wonderful" (ex. 7.10b; the same two degrees of the scale are involved), concords with our analysis of "Night Waltz II" (ex. 7.11d), and sets the seal on the irony implicit in the protagonists' situation with its brilliant correlative of reflexive patterning. The song also opens out the waltz perspective of the show as a whole, begins to distance us from it (as Fredrik and Désirée in the bedroom are themselves distanced from the activity elsewhere in the house and garden) by embedding its rhythm and typical melodic gestures in a framework larger than itself, namely the subtle variability of focus of the three- and four-"measure" units (if we are talking in waltz terms) that occasion the alternating 9/8 and 12/8 meter.

The Ending

However, "Send In the Clowns" does not have the last word, any more than "No More" does in *Into the Woods*. The last song before the reprises is Petra's "The Miller's Son," and it is here that Sondheim plays his cards of symbolic signification most fully. We have already observed that too much can be made of its operating by threes, but three sections in each of three strophes it certainly does have, articulating three levels of metric hierarchy (3/4, 2/4, and 3/8, note values remaining constant throughout). The 2/4 section is a marginal exception to the avoidance of duple rhythms in *A Little Night Music*, but this is hardly the point, for even here the duple pattern is undermined by the cross-rhythm in the bass, which facilitates the overall metric modulation from triple time in quarter notes to triple time in eighth notes via this section (see ex. 7.7). Insofar as three-to-a-bar is experienced, at least where the harmonic rhythm of the waltz is concerned, as one-to-a-bar, the effect is that the binary control of 2/4 gives way at both larger and smaller levels to the unitary, circular motion of triple time, tempus perfectum as the Middle Ages saw it. This feeling of perennial, spiraling motion is enhanced by the fact that when hemiola begins to occur in the 3/8 section it reestablishes the 3/4 quarter-note beat that leads back to the initial section, and the clever indicator of this circularity that Sondheim plants for us is the word *meanwhile* that occurs on the quarter-note rhythm at this juncture as well as at the juncture of the 3/4 and 2/4 sections; it articulates the song's philosophy of life as well as its rhythmic structure and might have been its title. Life is process, not goal; the moment is all that can be enjoyed.

It is perhaps a pity that this song, which tends to steal the show, stands rather alone in its level of metric kinesis, and that the only other song (apart from the "Now"/"Later"/"Soon" trio) that is able to balance it by showing three metric perspectives in such dynamic proximity, the alternative version of "The Glamorous Life," was written only for the film and has not been incorporated in the statutory stage show. In this version of "The Glamorous Life" we hear more made of Fredrika's exercises than anywhere else, for their eighth notes in one form or another never let up, except when triplet eighth notes take over as the fourth ingredient of cumulative rhythm; the other three ingredients display an extraordinary deftness yet exhilarating simplicity in their handling of the basic 3/4 pulse, 3/2 hemiola (marked x in ex. 7.13a) and the constant 6/8 counterpulse of the "exercise" eighth notes; rhythms epitomizing all three meters appear in lightning quick progression in the bass fill shown in ex. 7.13b, y.

We may conclude by pausing for reflection from another angle on this treatment of rhythm. The overturning of balanced, fixed relations that the waltz's metric ambiguities, hemiola in particular, propel is certainly a fecund concomitant to the world of sexual comedy and thereby a firm route to artistic success in many an operetta, of which genre *A Little Night Music* is in some senses the epitome. But "in ironic comedy . . . the demonic world is never far away," as Northrop Frye observes, and "a more intense irony is achieved when the humorous society simply disintegrates without anything taking its place" (Frye 1957, 178). This is what happens to a large proportion of the cast at the end of *A Little Night Music* as a result of the characters' waltzing: it is the dance of life insofar as they get the right partners, but the dance of death in social terms, for Henrik betrays his seminary puritanism, Anne loses her virginity and her position and wealth as Fredrik's wife, Fredrik, as he admits, loses his family and must surely lose his clients as a result of being prepared to "sit through all eight performances" of *Hedda Gabler* at Helsingborg for Désirée's sake prior to holidaying in Malmo, and with the breakup of his household Petra may well lose her job, as Frid must presumably lose his with the

Ex. 7.13a

Ex. 7.13b

death of Mme. Armfeldt. Petra may rationalize her sexual future in terms of enjoyment before responsibility, but, as a kind of existential hemiola, underneath there runs the reverse imperative of coupling with Frid primarily for security if one or both of them must look for work. Their world is falling around them as they lie in the grass together; the waltz is a symbol of comic destruction. We shall see it as a symbol of tragic destruction in *Sweeney Todd,* after examining another plot in which a world falls apart, *Pacific Overtures.*

Chapter 8

Pacific Overtures

Consider how the Orient . . . became known in the West as its great
complementary opposite since antiquity. There were the Bible and the rise
of Christianity; there were travellers like Marco Polo who charted the trade
routes and patterned a regulated system of commercial exchange . . . there
were fabulists like Mandeville; there were the redoubtable conquering
Eastern movements, principally Islam, of course; there were the militant
pilgrims, chiefly the Crusaders. Altogether an internally structured archive
is built up from the literature that belongs to these experiences. Out of this
comes a restricted number of typical encapsulations: the journey, the
history, the fable, the stereotype, the polemical confrontation. These are the
lenses through which the Orient is experienced, and they shape the
language, perception, and form of the encounter between East and West.

—Edward Said, *Orientalism*

The Orientalist Tradition

In leapfrogging over his immediate Broadway tradition in *A Little Night
Music,* Sondheim must have been at least partly conscious of what lay on
the other side of his nearest predecessors, conscious of the continuity of
genre between continents and eras nurtured at the hands of most composers for the musical theater. The musical line of descent from Johann
Strauss via Lehár, Romberg, and Friml to Richard Rodgers is a direct
one, not just where the waltz is concerned, but encompassing such gradual
transformations as that of the polka, which roughly speaking liaised with
ragtime and Sousa and gave birth to quickstep and foxtrot textures and
rhythms, all without losing its archetypal function as a stage march.
Indeed, all practitioners in the field need to be aware of their own genre's
stylistic history when, as they frequently are, they are called upon to
pastiche or at least show the terms of reference of an earlier style for
dramatic reasons. Occasionally this is done out of affection that rises above
necessity, as in the Gershwins' song "By Strauss" (their last for Broadway,
as it happened) and in Sondheim's own lyrics, written long before *A Little
Night Music,* for Rodgers' *Do I Hear a Waltz?*

Why is nobody dancing in the street?
Can't they hear the beat?
Magical, mystical miracle!
Can it be?
Is it true?
Things are impossibly lyrical!
Is it me?
No, it's you!

. . . . .

Do you hear a waltz?
Oh, my dear, don't you hear a waltz?
Such lovely blue Danubey music—how can you be still?

. . . .

Roses are dancing with peonies!
Yes, it's true!
Can't you see?
Everything's suddenly Viennese!
Can't be you!
Must be me!

Such continuity resides not just in such basic resources as waltzes and marches. Edward Said's thesis about how the West has constructed the East in an enduring image—and *Pacific Overtures* admirably illustrates his itemization of the "polemical confrontation"—may not be much concerned with how the arts and indeed fashion have exploited the Orient, or at least not with discussing or chronicling it in artistic terms. But it takes little effort for anyone with even a casual engagement with art to cite examples and build up a picture of influence and fascination, from Chippendale's furniture to Whistler's decor, from Nash's Brighton Pavilion to Lord Leighton's paintings. Chinoiserie as a tendency was well established in the eighteenth century (though the French term appeared in English only in 1883), and *japonaiserie* thoroughly penetrated Victorian sensibilities in the last third of the nineteenth century. No doubt some sort of structural separation needs to be upheld between the role of exotic taste in the intellectual arts and exotic taste in design, fashion, and cuisine, for the former has remained alien to many while the latter has been assimilated to the point where it is taken for granted. But with the postmodern phenomenon of universal consumerism (of which Japan is above all the dynamo in the modern world, as the final irony in *Pacific Overtures* conveys), the distinction can be an uncomfortably flimsy one.

Of the arts directly applicable to Sondheim, poetry has probably assimilated Oriental modes of thought and expression, or refashioned them for its own uses, most fully, to the extent that the translated Japanese haiku can hold few aesthetic terrors for the average Westerner and must be at least partly responsible for the descent of twentieth-century free verse into high school creative nonentities and even the pop lyric. Yet music has been in no sense a poor relation in this exploitation; the cult of the exotic, particularly strong in France in the nineteenth century, was a major catalyst in the aesthetic of Debussy and has continued its march through the twentieth century, affecting composers as various as Messiaen and Britten (there is a scribbled reference to "Curlew River," Britten's church parable that transposed Japanese No drama into a British context, among Sondheim's preliminary notes for *Pacific Overtures*). Oriental influence in drama (Said traces it back to Aeschylus's *The Persians*) may be less pervasive, or rather it may be necessary to draw a distinction between *representation* of the Orient as an essence of dramatic conflict (this is, after all, a presence in *Othello*) and aesthetic espousal of it (as in the influence of No on Yeats).

Music and drama in combination have proved a rich field for Orientalism. The eighteenth century liked its "Turkish" music and Mozart enjoyed depicting seraglios on the stage and in the pit; the nineteenth century found gateways to the East in both Spain and Russia, as Bizet's *Carmen* and Borodin's *Prince Igor* bear ample witness. But it may well be that Orientalism's most abiding residence in the performing arts has been in the popular musical theater, perhaps for the obvious reason that it can draw on the allure of music, drama, poetry, decor, costume, humor, gesture, and dance in any desired mixture or proportion. This has long been recognized and has been discussed elsewhere: Engel (1967, 127–33) treats it as part of the general issue of "overlay," the entertainment ingredient in the depiction of time and place, while Swain (1990, 18 and 247–74) devotes ample space to the technical implications of composing an "ethnic" musical.

The issue cuts many ways, but Gilbert and Sullivan nevertheless hit upon something approaching a basic perceptual formula when they wrote *The Mikado,* and it is no use pretending that its shadow does not extend to Sondheim. As a telling example, and with all allowances for differences (Sondheim sees himself expressing "harshness," Sullivan "decorum"), we can appreciate the similarity of the opening gambits of *The Mikado* (ex. 8.1a) and *Pacific Overtures* (ex. 8.1b). Both are informed by homophonic male voices (unison male chorus in *The Mikado,* a solo Reciter, later unison male chorus, in *Pacific Overtures*), a direct address to the audience in the first-person plural, a double ascending upbeat leading to a kind of reciting note (Sondheim's "misc." sketch sheet of Japanese scales, etc., began with examples of this—see chap. 2), an implication of "inscrutable" statuesque

Ex. 8.1a

[Allegro vivace]

If you want to know who we are,_____ We are

gen - tle - men of Ja - pan._____

Ex. 8.1b

[Moderato]

In the mid-dle of the world we float,_____ In the

[f]   mp

mid-dle of the sea.

acting in the short and pithy vocal phrases with long gaps between them, a lack of harmonic progression, and an aggressive 2/4 rhythm descended from nineteenth-century (Western) dance models.

Naturally, Gilbert and Sullivan's designs on the Orient are quite different from Weidman and Sondheim's. *The Mikado,* whose original London run of nearly two years set a new record in the British musical theater, stands at the head of a period in which the allure of the exotic, as I have suggested, was preeminently a matter of color, titillation, and escapism—why else should the Victorian public visit the West End theaters? Scintillating orchestration and, above all, lavishness of costume stimulated the aural and visual senses, while the idea that the East spelled flirtation and sexual libido was never far below the surface, epitomized as it is in the title of Sidney Jones's *The Geisha* (1896). *The Mikado*'s progeny constituted a veritable Cook's tour of Eastern countries, including Edward Solomon's *The Nautch Girl* (1891; India), Lionel Monckton's *The Cingalee* (1904; Ceylon), Leslie Stuart's *Florodora* (1899; the Philippines—though act 2 is set in Wales), Jones's *San Toy* (1899; China), Philip Faraday's *Amasis* (1906; Egypt), and Frederic Norton's *Chu Chin Chow* (1916; Arabia). Some of the ingredients of exoticism survive so robustly in the work of Rodgers and Hammerstein, notably in *South Pacific* (1949) and *The King and I* (1951; set in Siam), that they begin to sound as though they had always been a part of the Broadway style—one thinks not merely of pentatonicism and passages in parallel fourths but of the use of pizzicato strings and glockenspiel in the orchestration, short-winded, simple syntactic structures in the lyrics, repeated notes in the melody and ostinatos and cross-rhythms in the accompaniment of such songs as "I Whistle a Happy Tune" and "Happy Talk." Perhaps it is impractical to separate indigenous from exotic elements at this level.

The second phase of exoticism in the musical theater, however, came hard on the heels of the first, and was already at work in *The Mikado.* This was its use to construct cultural parables, most often comedies or tragedies of conflicting manners. Belasco's play for Puccini's opera *Madam Butterfly* (1904) presents us with the tragedy of different expectations of love, with the irony of the hired girl, the geisha, as the steadfast, romantic partner. *Miss Saigon* retells the story in a Vietnamese setting. The cultural imperialism implied and criticized in such plots is even evident in *Florodora,* whose comic villain, Cyrus W. Gilfain, is the illegal American possessor of the island and its sweated labor manufacturing the perfume with its secret recipe.

The parable need not be couched in geographical realism, however, and the use of the Orient as an alienation technique is what lies at the root of *The Mikado,* since it is a satire on the English, not the Japanese. It functions by looking at a putative "outside" society model to hold the mirror up to one's own, to objectify one's manners by making them seem as alien as the costumes the characters are wearing. Brecht opens up the model to epic and culturally didactic proportions in *The Good Woman of Sezuan,* showing us how cultural logic works by following through the consequences of a foreign story in its own terms. The fact that Oriental stagecraft and narrative are themselves rich in such alienation devices as the use of a narrator or the construction of animal fables adds a dimension to this approach, which resonates in Weidman's two parables embedded in *Pacific Overtures,* the Confucian story about the boy and the grandmother in act 1, scene 3 and the climactic Tale of the Courageous King (which presages the restoration of the Emperor Meiji) in act 2, scene 3.

Pacific Overtures is Brechtian to a certain extent, though the point has been fiercely debated in view of Sondheim's dislike of Brecht's heavy-handedness (see Zadan 1990, 115–17, and the response to the English National Opera production of *Pacific Overtures* in the *Guardian,* 12 and 17 September 1987). It shows us a relentless swath of history and keeps humanistic dramatic sympathy to a minimum while revelling in alienation techniques. Above all, it demonstrates the power of the strong over the weak and the politicization of the individual that this implies. The former is vividly handled in the tableaux of gunboat diplomacy (Kayama and Manjiro's scene beneath the bows of the *USS Powhatan* is a gem) as well as in the episodes of Japanese court life ("When the Shogun is weak, / Then the tea must be strong, my lord," sings the Shogun's mother as she poisons him with chrysanthemum tea), the latter in the developing careers of Kayama and Manjiro and their inevitable final clash.

But for all its acceptance of a moral of guilt as implicit in historical process (it appeared in the bicentennial year and must have evoked memories of Vietnam at a time before they had become commercial big business in films such as *The Deer Hunter*), *Pacific Overtures* enjoys other concerns, and its means of self-awareness and self-criticism, as one would expect with Sondheim, serve to counterpoint against the linear perspective of historical narrative a much more kaleidoscopic one. One facet of the kaleidoscope is the fundamental matter of compositional technique, of how raw material, verbal and musical, is used to give tone and body to a score that is still conceived from the inside as a Western organic whole (indeed, it is more organic than any of Sondheim's earlier Broadway scores, as he has acknowledged: "*Pacific Overtures* was the first time I really tried to interweave themes extensively" [Hirsch 1989, 114–15]; thus we shall examine the use of modal preferences and tonal ambiguities in the music and recurrent motifs arising from them, syllabic patterns in the lyrics, and additive structures in both. The other facet of the kaleidoscope concerns the grafting of resources from the Japanese musical theater onto those of Broadway, and this is a new departure for Western musicals on exotic subjects. It interacts with Sondheim's autonomous creative processes largely in the matter of form, and how it does this and affects his approach to composition will be examined at the end of the chapter.

Pacific Overtures as Historical Pageant

The basic trajectory of the work is relatively straightforward: it charts a tumultuous period of Japanese history, its opening to the West following two hundred years of isolation, by means of a narrator and a choice of characteristic illustrative episodes, some of which are conveyed musically, with a modest dramatic thread in the form of the relationship between Kayama and Manjiro. In fact most of the action occurs between the arrival of the Americans in 1853 and the restoration of the Emperor in 1868; that we come away with a much broader sense of chronicle than this is one of its generic identifiers, for it couches its presentation very much in the manner of a historical stage pageant. The Reciter's opening speech includes the phrase "There was a time . . . ," and right at the end of the show this is picked up in his final statement.

> There was a time when foreigners were not welcome here. But that was long ago. One hundred and twenty years.
>
> *(Pause)*
>
> Welcome to Japan.

His role invites us to watch and reflect upon vignettes being played out, with their cast of many changing characters (the original production "required nineteen actors to play the sixty-one roles in the script" [Zadan 1990, 214], and the revised script for the 1984 off-Broadway production contains a table of how the roles can be distributed among fifteen actors). Some of the vignettes are spoken and mimed (two of these, act 1, scene 8 concerning the diplomatic exchange of gifts and act 2, scene 5 concerning the invention of the ricksha, were omitted from the 1984 script). Others, set to music, offered Sondheim the opportunity for some of his most skillful and characteristic creations, songs cast, appropriately enough in view of the Japanese love of miniature things, as dramas in microcosm. We have already examined "A Bowler Hat" from this standpoint (see chap. 2). "Chrysanthemum Tea" is an equally impressive example, with its own cast of characters, none of whom appears anywhere else in the show and all of whom make their mark unforgettably in the space of a single song (the Shogun without even speaking or singing), their motivations and the consequences of their actions alike established, demonstrated, and fulfilled. Teatime conversation, family tensions, and dynastic history are all in a few lines forged on the anvil of lyric wit into one vengeful perspective as sharp and swift as an arrow.

> Have some tea, my Lord,
> Some chrysanthemum tea.
> It's a tangled situation,
> As your father would agree.
> And it mightn't be so tangled
> If you hadn't had him strangled—
> But I fear that I stray, my Lord.

This musical within a musical even has its own dimension of diegetic music, in the shape of the Shogun's Wife, who "plays the koto and sings, to no one's pleasure," as the stage directions laconically put it.

Sondheim's generic term for what he was doing was "documentary vaudeville" (the phrase occurs among his preliminary notes). His use of episodic history remains close to the spirit and detail of such facts as have survived and could be drawn into his treatment. Perry's gifts really did include a working locomotive, "a machine . . . called a 'train' . . . " (I am not sure about the grain elevator). Furthermore, many of the points made in G. B. Sansom's classic treatment of the subject, *The Western World and Japan* (1950), are the points made in Sondheim's songs, whether or not at the instigation of Weidman: " . . . it cannot be denied," Sansom wryly observes, "that guns spoke with a convincing voice to a people with a long military history" (1950, 257); likewise, he comments that "it seemed absurd to prevent indigent parents from selling their daughters into a profession which served a recognized social purpose; and they were not likely to change that opinion so long as they observed that the brothels in the Treaty Ports were thronged with foreign visitors" (1950, 404–5). Sansom also describes "a song composed for children in 1878."

> It was called the Civilization Ball Song and was designed to impress on young minds the advantages of Western culture. They were to count the bounces of the ball by reciting the names of ten objects deemed to be the most worthy of adoption, namely gas lamps, steam engines, horse-carriages, cameras, telegrams, lightning-conductors, newspapers, schools, letter-post and steamboats. (1950, 401)

Not only did Sondheim use references to such Western "things" in "A Bowler Hat," he actually wrote a song utilizing this idea called "Civilization" or "The Emperor of Japan," to be sung as a children's game song in 12/8 and foreshadowing the rhythms of the "Into the Woods" themes of a decade later. It was to be the final number of the show, depicting the last hundred years of Japanese history using film, puppets, and children's drama with alienation techniques extending to the cast invading the audience; but it could not be made to work dramatically and the idea was completely abandoned.

In the show as it eventuated it is above all the presentation of Kayama and Manjiro that parallels Sansom's technique of offering case studies of characteristic figures in Japan's early years of westernization. Kayama seems to be constructed partly around the figure of Sakuma Shozan (1811–64), perhaps partly around Yokoi Shonan (1809–69). In the following description by Sansom the references to two men rowing out to the American ships, to one of them having been imprisoned for (attempted) breach of territoriality, to communication by poem, and to Sakuma's murder at the hands of patriots all enjoy parallels in *Pacific Overtures,* though the details have been scrambled.

> Among the young men who gathered round Sakuma was a patriot named Yoshida. He, with another adherent of Sakuma, endeavoured to board one of Perry's vessels in 1854, was discovered and imprisoned for an attempted breach of the law which forbade Japanese subjects to leave their country, under pain of death. The police found on his person a farewell poem from Sakuma, who was therefore also taken into custody. . . . He was . . . imprisoned and not released until 1862, then only to be murdered after less than two years of freedom by some anti-foreign fanatics. (Sansom 1950, 273)

Elsewhere Sansom accounts for the "drift into subversive movements" of many samurai who "felt betrayed when they saw that ignorant upstarts with a smattering of English could set up as men of wisdom and earn an easy livelihood" (1950, 413), confirms the aptness of drinking as a dynamic motif in "A Bowler Hat" ("the Japanese visitors to the American ships had already shown, sometimes all too clearly, their enjoyment of stimulating drinks" [295]), quotes Shonan's dictum: "The times are such that we must not be fettered by old maxims" (282) ("One must accommodate the times," Kayama sings), and foreshadows Sondheim's treatment of his subject by acknowledging that Sakuma's career "represents in miniature the intellectual history of the movement which culminated in the opening of Japan" (270).

Character vignette broadens into allegory, however, with the "Lion Dance" and the admirals' song, "Please Hello," and it is here, especially in the use of the five admirals appearing in apt historical order (American, British, Dutch, Russian, and French) in an allegorical divertissement of national styles (or rather caricatures of national styles), that the show's generic kinship with the pageant is confirmed. As "spectacular drama," which "tends to episodic and piecemeal discovery" and moves "toward processional structure," in Northrop Frye's categorization (1957, 289), one wonders whether underlying *Pacific Overtures* is some ancestral link with the American historical pageant movement that was popular from the turn of the century until the early 1920s as a form of community drama (see Prevots 1987, 34–40; Stoner 1991) and frequently revelled in processional exoticism by encompassing the dramatic theme of the assimilation of native American Indian culture into American civilization; one has only to think of the Christian apotheosis of *Hiawatha* and compare it with the commercial one in *Pacific Overtures,* both taking an awesomely broad tone and view as they sweep toward present experience.

The Reflexive Dimension

If this makes *Pacific Overtures* seem somehow rather quaint, there are factors to be examined that lend it, like so much in Sondheim, a deliberate dimension of self-criticism, a "cubism" of perspective (Hirsch 1989, 116) that undercuts and enriches the naïve linear approach. Sondheim has given one explanation of this.

> What we actually did was to create a mythical Japanese playwright in our heads, who has come to New York, seen a couple of Broadway shows, and then goes back home and writes a musical about Commodore Perry's visit to Japan. It's this premise that helped to give us tone and style for the show. (Zadan 1990, 210)

He was looking at himself in reverse, here, of course, given that he and Prince went to Japan, saw a few Kabuki and No plays, and then came home and created their musical. And their Japanese playwright was not so mythical, for *Pacific Overtures* was not the first musical theater piece on the subject of Perry's visit: Japanese composer Kosaku Yamada (1886–1965), who trained in Germany and returned to Japan to found its first major orchestra and opera organizations, had written an opera on the subject, *The Black Ships* (*Kurobune*), in 1940, "in a style reminiscent of Wagner's *The Flying Dutchman* and the late operas of Puccini" (Malm 1977, 207). These ironic layerings are somewhat teasing, and Hirsch comments that "doing the show as an American version of a Japanese impression of how the West had invaded Japanese history and culture wrapped *Pacific Overtures* in a box within a box within a box" (Hirsch 1989, 110); he might have enumerated a fourth box, supplied by the use of an all-Asian cast in the original production.

The reciprocity inherent in the subject is thus catered for: Said's accusatory thesis of Orientalization of the East by the West is answered. At least, it is in part; one might object, however, that the narrative is still in some respects a Western imposition in its very claim to be a drama about Western imposition. Consider the following syllogism in "Chrysanthemum Tea" (and compare Hapgood's interjections in "Simple" from *Anyone Can Whistle*).

PRIEST II: Night waters do not break the moon.
PRIEST I: That merely is illusion.
BOTH: The moon is sacred.
PRIEST II: No foreign ships can break our laws.
PRIEST I: That also is illusion.
BOTH: Our laws are sacred.
PRIEST II: It follows there can be no ships.
PRIEST I: They must be an illusion.
BOTH: Japan is sacred.

Is this an unbiased representation of how a dying Confucianism was failing the historical moment, or is the very polarization of terms, the very creation of a historical dialectic, a prejudicial Western construct? In the ironic context of this song the question thrives; it is only in "Next," perhaps, that it ultimately circumscribes the show's capabilities. "Next," by upholding the dialectic of the turning of tables ("Who's the stronger, / Who's the faster? / Let the pupil show the master!—"), is caught in a vicious circle of guilt and revenge; or to put it another way, perhaps too strongly, it insults the Japanese by apologizing for the tackiness that the West thinks it has bequeathed them. To break out of this impasse (for instance, by acknowledging that factors such as Confucianism and the historical isolationism were not dialectically doomed by the process of historical materialism but accepted as contributory opportunities to a modern destiny that retains its cultural identity and has thus not been imposed from without but shaped from within) would demolish the story.

It is as well to allow for this deconstructivist dead end, much as one must in *Company*, for it is the lot of any ambitious fabric of critical perspectives such as we find in both these musicals. It need not inhibit our appreciation of the terms of reference, and to these we must turn.

Aspects of the Lyrics

Sondheim, with his elemental way with words and mastery of the "tiny little craft" of lyrics, might have guessed that this side of his art would flourish in *Pacific Overtures*.

> Finding the lyric style was much less difficult than I thought it would be: a kind of translator-ese, parable sentences, very simple language with very simple subject-predicate structures, and very little in the way of rhyme. (Sondheim 1978, 10)

> I tried to keep the lyrics haiku-like, and I tried to avoid all words with Latin roots. . . . Romance language roots, to keep it simple but to prevent it from being poesy, as opposed to poetic. Japanese haiku, when translated into English, trembles on the verge of parody: so you have to be very careful about it. And then as the score progresses, the language becomes more Western—as does the music—after the invasion. (Sondheim, quoted in Zadan 1990, 212)

In the first comment he rather throws away the point about "translator-ese." There are in fact two modulations of lyric style implied in what he acknowledges: between the willed simplicity of Confucian poetic utterance and the unavoidable simplicity of phrasing coming from someone learning a language; and between this pupillary style and the patronizing false grammar of someone speaking to a foreigner. There is also a fourth type of speech, the parody of national accent or characteristics, utilized to comic effect for the five admirals in "Please Hello." This last inclusion is nicely ironic, for it shows, when in conjunction with the previous type, that in representing our own speech we descend to self-parody just as much as we parody others in trying to represent theirs. The point is perhaps that modulation across the spectrum of utterance enhances the shifting perspectives in which *Pacific Overtures* is so rich. Thus a line like "I drink much wine" in "A Bowler Hat" may be attributable either to Kayama's feeling for poetic simplicity (the fact could not possibly be expressed in fewer syllables) or to his elementary command of English. Most important to grasp is that all these types will be heavily stylized and declamatory in character. They contribute to a unified lyric mode. They can also be very witty (compare Engel's highlighting of the King of Siam's mode of soliloquy [Engel 1967, 116]).

Grammar apart, a premium is also placed upon single words, even syllables, and this constitutes a kind of lyric pointillism (it goes without saying that, alongside musical minimalism, this will later provide a basic stepping-off point for *Sunday in the Park with George*), in tune with the Japanese feeling for the smallest or simplest elements in a construct. Already in his "Misc. lyrics" sketches and notes Sondheim makes the connection with musical minimalism.

> house building
> It's the brick, not the architecture, the note, not the music
> . . . .
> Silences between sounds

He has also emphasized how conscious he was in *Pacific Overtures* of the importance of the individual note in Japanese music (see Rich 1976). One page of verbal notes is simply headed "*Things,* etc" and includes the following items: "Servants, Sleeves, Mist, Cherry blossoms, petals, Stones, rock, Leaves (falling), Rivers, Seasons, Oars, Tears." Both these conceptions are encapsulated in "Someone in a Tree," without music being mentioned as such (music, unlike poetry, is never conscious of itself in *Pacific Overtures*).

> It's the fragment, not the day.
> It's the pebble, not the stream.
> It's the ripple, not the sea
> That is happening.
> Not the building but the beam,
> Not the garden but the stone,
> Only cups of tea
> And history
> And someone in a tree.

This, of course, is a special kind of list song: history, like the song, consists only of fragmentary events or "moments" strung together (the Baker's Wife in *Into the Woods* returns to this theme), its structure entirely depend-ent upon which ones are recorded, and how. The Reciter has to produce his own history mediating between the incomplete perspectives of space (the warrior underneath the Treaty House could hear imperfectly but not see, the boy in the tree could see imperfectly but not hear) and time (he makes allowances for the failed memory of the old man by invoking the boy, his younger self). The three-dimensional dramatic conceit that results is surely one of the things in *Pacific Overtures* most inspired by exposure to Oriental stagecraft, though the idea of history as fragments was already a tenet of European romanticism, found in Schlegel in the light of classical archaeology (see Daverio 1987, 162–63). Particularly telling is the leverage between the characters in the form of questions and answers, interruptions (both the old man and the warrior intrude upon the scene, beginning "Pardon me"), corrections, and the fact that the boy has to prompt the old man to speak for him, to "Tell him what I see"—he himself no longer exists, he is just a memory in the old man's mind, like history itself. "In one song," as Billington observes, "Sondheim encompasses the fallibility of human memory, the sense that history is a compound of minute particles, the whole philosophic question of whether an event exists if it is unrecorded" (Billington 1987). In fact Sondheim turns the philosophic question on its head when his Old Man exclaims "If it happened, I was there!" as though to say that the past is lost irrevocably when memory fails us, that the disjunction between personal experience and documentation is imponderable. One is further tempted to see a model of the paradoxes of religious faith in this song, even an echo of the Gospel myth, with its four conflicting accounts of Christ's activities and its unforgettable cast of incidental characters hiding in trees and being lowered through roofs to become "part of the event."

The flow of "Someone in a Tree" is, musically and lyrically, a matter of additive structure. The picture of what happened is built up by a complex concatenation of simple statements, including contradictions and corrections; the music, as we shall see, expands by repetition (the lyrics even describe this repetition: "No, we told him that before"—though this is not in the score).

Sondheim and Weidman tend to use the haiku additively as well. Single haiku occur, spoken, from time to time. The following, by Weidman, deliberately negates its own genre by having only sixteen syllables and its long line in the wrong place.

> A gift unearned
> And unexpected
> Often has a hidden price.

Another haiku, by the more dogmatic Sondheim, conforms to the standard pattern of a central line of seven syllables flanked by two lives of five.

> The bird from the sea,
> Not knowing pine from bamboo,
> Roosts on anything.

Many passages in the lyrics approximate to this construction, probably unconsciously—for instance, the pronouncements of the priests from "Chrysanthemum Tea" (quoted previously) can be divided into three groups of three lines of twenty syllables (8 + 7 + 5) each, and indeed are printed thus in the script. The central lines of the odd-numbered stanzas of "A Bowler Hat" also amount to twenty syllables, as we saw in chapter 2, and seem to represent some contained or beleaguered Japanese sensibility amid the gross burgeoning of Western plenty that appears, to the tune of twenty-six syllables, in the even-numbered stanzas.

> The swallow flying through the sky
> Is not as swift as I
> Am, flying through my life.
>
> (20 syllables)

> I take imported pills.
> I have a house up in the hills
> I've hired British architects to redesign.
>
> (26 syllables)

The remaining lines that succeed these in each stanza type of "A Bowler Hat," as we saw, comprise twenty-three and eighteen syllables respectively and can arguably be viewed again as groups of three. The haiku extends itself in Japanese poetry to the waka (a much older verse form), in which a further two lines of seven syllables each are present at the foot of the verse, and it is perhaps this practice of extension that Sondheim reflects here, consciously or otherwise.

The First Observer's comments in "There Is No Other Way" are couched as a repeating pattern of two lines that extends itself to three and gathers syllables toward the refrain line (the Second Observer's interjections are omitted below).

> The eye sees, the thought flies.
> The eye tells, the thought denies.
>
> (13 syllables)

> The word falls, the heart cries.
> The heart knows the word's disguise.
>
> (13 syllables)

> The bird sings, the wind sighs,
> The air stirs, the bird shies.
> A storm approaches.
>
> (17 syllables)

> The leaf shakes, the wings rise.
> The song stops, the bird flies.
> The storm approaches.
>
> (17 syllables)

The song stops, the bird flies.
The mind stirs, the heart replies,
"There is no other way."

(19 syllables)

The word stops, the heart dies.
The wind counts the lost goodbyes.
(SECOND OBSERVER:) There is no other way.

(19 syllables)

A similar additive technique is used in the chorus phrases of "Next," breaking back to a smaller unit to give a double rising curve.

Streams are flowing.
See what's coming
Next!

(9 syllables)

Winds are blowing.
See what's coming,
See what's going
Next!

(13 syllables)

Roads are turning,
Journey with them.
A little learning—
Next!

(14 syllables)

Waters churning,
Lightning flashes.
Kings are burning,
Sift the ashes . . .
Next!

(17 syllables)

Tower tumbles,
Tower rises—
Next!

(9 syllables)

Tower crumbles,
Man revises.
Motor rumbles,
Civilizes.
More surprises
Next!

(21 syllables)

Learn the lesson
From the master.
Add the sugar,
Spread the plaster.
Do it nicer,
Do it faster . . .
Next!

(25 syllables)

If this syllabic growth in "Next" begins to sound ominous, the spoken interjections to which it leads, with their statistics about uncontrollable Western-style effluence, offer an awful substitute for the contained beauty of the haiku, showing just what it has been exchanged for.

This year Japan will export 16 million kilograms monosodium glutamate, and 400,000 tons polyvinyl chloride resin.

(37 syllables)

(Weidman seems fond of this breathless, newsreading mode, for he uses it again toward the end of *Assassins* for cataloging worldwide reactions to the death of Kennedy.) A more comic effect operates in "Chrysanthemum Tea," where the patter monologues of the Shogun's mother drone on for varying lengths of time in a "house-that-Jack-built" manner of adding lines before coming around to a familiar statement, as she awaits the demise of the ruler who is "taking so long" to die. Her basic reciting-note formula around A, cadencing to E before her "Have some tea, my Lord" refrain or release, continues for 21 measures in the Day of the Rat, resuming after the release for a further 13 measures; for 22 measures, resumed for 11, in the Day of the Ox; and for 15 and 10 measures in the Day of the Tiger. Comedy is enhanced in the final stanza, the Day of the Rabbit: it looks as though 13 measures will see the Shogun off and no refrain will be necessary (the first phrase of the *Dies irae* sounds for him in its place); but he twitches, and the monologue is resumed for a further 15 measures before the form runs its course with the refrain and a further 13 measures of patter.

The sense of inventive or competitive play is strong in the Japanese poetic tradition—witness the game of "Poetry cards" played with the ancient *Ogura Hyaku-nin-isshiu* [One Hundred Poems from One Hundred Poets], quatrains with an *abba* rhyme scheme that are well known to most Japanese.

Two sets of cards, the reading cards and the playing cards, consisting of one hundred cards respectively, are used. On the reading card the whole poem is written or printed, while on the playing card only the last two lines are given.

The game is usually played between two parties made up of four or five persons. Each party faces the other with fifty playing cards spread before them on the floor. As the reader recites one of the well-shuffled reading cards, the players try to find and take the corresponding playing card faster than the others. In this way the party that has first finished with their allotted cards wins. (Honda 1956, 103–4)

Sondheim engages the sense of play largely in rounds of poetic permutation, addition, and recurrence; this can easily be appreciated in the passage from "There Is No Other Way" (quoted previously), in which objects are first mentioned twice within a stanzaic unit ("eye" and "thought" in the first one, "heart" in the second, "bird" in the third) and then interwoven and permutated ("bird" recurs in the fourth, and "bird"—with a whole line repeated—and "heart" in the fifth, while in the sixth "wind" is identified with "mind," "song" with the returning "word"); the whole is bound together with one exhaustively explored rhyme.

"Poems" cements all this into one perfect song. Kayama and Manjiro exchange haiku on their journey to Uraga; however, the brief is not only to create a second haiku on the subject supplied by the first, each one in character with its speaker (Kayama is thinking of Tamate, Manjiro of America), but each time, at least at first, to increase the number of syllables by one, from the 14 of the waka extension to the 17 of the haiku.

> Rain glistening
> On the silver birch,
> Like my lady's tears.
>
> > > (14 syllables)

> . . . .
> Rain gathering,
> Winding into streams,
> Like the roads to Boston.
>
> > > (15 syllables)

> . . . .
> Haze hovering,
> Like the whisper of the silk
> As my lady kneels.
>
> > > (16 syllables)

> . . . .
> Haze glittering,

> Like an echo of the lamps
> In the streets of Boston.

(17 syllables)

After this point, the pattern diversifies while the two singers tend to match each other; but the increase begins again, and play on the idea of permutation and recurrence is perhaps even written into the breaking of the exchange when Kayama "can't go" and has to miss a turn, whereupon they both sing together. The song ends with an eleven-syllable recapitulation of all eight nouns forming the subjects of the haiku, seven of them monosyllabic, the remaining one ("Nightingale") pointedly imposing irregularity (which had been reflexively acknowledged in the way its haiku began: "I am no nightingale"); the final syllable is again reflexive: "End."

Multiple Perspectives in the Music

Clearly this additive and permutational verbal technique needs a melodic one to match it, and it is somewhat misleading to attempt this description without reference to the music, for the song is in an ABABAB form with coda that regularizes the irregularities, the B episodes being the long stanzas and the one about the nightingale (see ex. 8.2). As for its melodic progress, it is not surprising to find that the addition of single notes and the permutation of simple intervals are involved. At the risk of going over

Ex. 8.2. The Structure of "Poems"

Singer	Number of Syllables	Subject	Form
K	14	Rain	⌐ A
M	15	Rain	
K	16	Haze	
M	17	Haze	⌐
K	23	Moon	⌐ B
M	23	Moon	⌐
K	16	Wind	⌐ A
M	16	Wind	⌐
K	16	(I am no) nightingale	⌐ B
M	16	(I am no) nightingale	⌐
K	17	Dawn	⌐ A
M	18	Dawn	
K	—	?	
M	—	?	⌐
Both	21	Leaves	⌐ B
Both	26	Sun	⌐
K and M alternating	11	All nouns + "End"	Coda

Ex. 8.3

familiar ground—for this song is in many ways similar to "A Bowler Hat," where we witnessed the gestation of such procedures (see chap. 2)—ex. 8.3 shows, as a distributional melodic analysis, the melodic handling of the syllabic differences involved in all eight exchanges that constitute the A sections of "Poems." The striking thing about them is that, although several of the poems have the same number of syllables, all eight melodic lines are different and a phase-shifting process is generated along with the repeating, expanding, and contracting intervals.

Musically speaking, permutational form is at its most complex in "Someone in a Tree." This song utilizes the outlines of verse-refrain structure but superimposes on it a richly repetitive continuum of motivic patterning, rather like a cubist painting in which abstract patterning creates yet diffuses figurative representation. It consists of two immensely long stanzas. The first begins with a relatively unconstrained verse section based on the motif marked x in ex. 8.4a. The continuum then gets underway, as the old man begins to tell his confused and piecemeal story, with the phrase marked b (see ex. 8.4b), clearly originating in x; phrase a is an incomplete variant of it, and the two phrases repeat and alternate for some time until the boy's exhortation to "Tell him what I see!" introduces what must be thought of as the refrain motif (ex. 8.4c); phrase a follows again, and a new, slower, choralelike phrase appears, expressing the diplomats' dignity ("I see men / And matting"). Then comes the only point of release, phrase c (ex. 8.4b) which reaches the upper tonic F. This phrase is of course merely b with its downbeat portion transposed

Ex. 8.4a

Ex. 8.4b

Ex. 8.4c

Ex. 8.4d

Ex. 8.4e

ABE: Could you wait for a year? We'll a - gree to ex -am-ine it... But la - ter, I fear. There's a drought and a fa - mine.

FRENCH ADMIRAL: A dé-tente! A dé-tente! Zat's ze on-ly thing we want!

up a fifth to give the release effect, but it also undermines the tonal
rhetoric when the two are combined, as they are at measure 134 in the
score. The whole pattern is shown in ex. 8.5 (items of more than one
phrase are indicated in brackets). This must be extremely difficult to learn,
despite the repeated blocks of material. After it the warrior appears and
attempts to start another verse, a step higher in G major, but is for a
while frustrated by the continuation of the previous perspective in F
(phrases *c b c b* are heard); he tries again, and the whole form is then
repeated, the verse in G major but everything subsequent to it in D major.

Ex. 8.5 The Form of "Someone in a Tree"

stanza 1   *b b b*
(verse) *b a b a a b b a a b b b a* (refrain) *a* (refrain) *a* (chorale) *c a b* (refrain) *a* (refrain) *a c b c a c b c c a c b c c c a* refrain

stanza 2   *c b b*
(verse) *b a b a a b b a a b b b a* (refrain) *a* (refrain) *a* (chorale) *c a b* (refrain) *a* (refrain) *a x x x x c c a c b c a c c [c c]* refrain

This time, however, *x* intervenes at the climax to give a different concatenation (ex. 8.5e, stanza 2). We note that *x*, counterpointing *c*, confirms
that the pair of motifs—hence most of the song—is based on a downward
tetrachord (see ex. 8.4d) and, more far-reachingly, that *x*, which with its
greater length and its repetitive insistence begins to feel like an analogue
for Western argument, reappears in "Please Hello," first in diminution
(at the lines [ABE:] "But you can't . . ." [AMERICAN ADMIRAL:]
"Only one little port for a freighter . . ."), then in its original note values
in neat, as it were persuasive, counterpoint (unlike the ensuing cacophony)
with the French Admiral's tune (ex. 8.4e). In "Someone in a Tree," *x*
thus comes to represent the only part of the treaty discussion that we
hear, and is subsequently used as a "negotiation" leitmotif (see Rich
1976).

The double tonal perspective afforded by motifs *b* and *c* in ex. 8.4b is
a crucial aspect of Sondheim's compositional strategy in *Pacific Overtures*.
Being identical but a fifth apart, the more they are equated, or sounded
together in parallel fourths or fifths (which occurs vocally at several points
in the score though only once, momentarily, on the original cast
recording), the more they undermine the distinction between tonic and
dominant, and it is evident from almost any page of the score of *Pacific
Overtures* that the harmony, for the most part avoiding obvious tonal progressions (especially perfect cadences) and often remaining static for long
periods, also tends to do so. It is perhaps hardly necessary to explain
that this accords with our notions of Eastern existentialism, of a sense of
"being" rather than "becoming." The double perspective is particularly
noticeable in "Pretty Lady" (this is also the song in which a double
perspective is used on the stage, in the shape of the wall that we see
from both sides in conjunction with the sailors' repeated entrance). At
measures 56–59 in the score, the tune, at this point being sung in C
major, is duplicated a fourth higher (the parallel fourths are inverted as
fifths on the original cast recording). Without any sense of modulation,
it then simply continues in F major rather than C, the passage of parallel
fourths thus having functioned in one sense analogously to a dominant
or diminished seventh chord in traditional Western tonality, though the

analogy, it must be stressed, does not extend to a sense of direction, which is precisely what is avoided. Similar ambiguity can easily be heard elsewhere in *Pacific Overtures,* for instance in the refrain of "Chrysanthemum Tea," whose melody on its own would suggest A minor but, whose accompaniment not only angles it into D minor, but, with its Phrygian modality, pulls it even lower, toward G minor (see exs. 8.6d and 8.7c). Here, therefore, we have a triple perspective, and the same is true of the refrain of "Four Black Dragons," whose three descending melodic steps are doubled a fourth lower, which simply serves to underline the modal ambiguity already felt in the melody itself—is it $\hat{4}$-#$\hat{3}$-#$\hat{3}$-$\hat{2}$ (the key signature, which in any case tends to change in the middle of it, often but not always construes it thus), $\hat{8}$-#$\hat{7}$-#$\hat{7}$-#$\hat{6}$, its relative minor $^b\hat{3}$-$\hat{2}$-$\hat{2}$-$\hat{1}$, or $^b\hat{7}$-#$\hat{6}$-#$\hat{6}$-$\hat{5}$? Such modal properties and their shifting planes are easier to hear than to explain; ubiquitous as they are in much twentieth-century popular music well beyond the boundaries of *Pacific Overtures,* we lack the terminology to pin them down (I shall return to this point in the discussion of *Into the Woods*).

The Phrygian Matrix and Stylistic Unity

Five fifths piled on top of one another produce the notes of the pentatonic scale, and we are constantly reminded of this in the sonorities of "Someone in a Tree." Further, the superimposition of two fifths without their thirds (i.e., without leading tones) produces an ambiguity between tonic and supertonic, and in fact a pentatonic cluster in the form 0-$\hat{2}$-$\hat{4}$-$\hat{7}$-9 can be shifted up or down a tone without it producing any notes foreign to the key; thus an additional tonal ambiguity may be established between keys a step apart (this is what happens, almost without it being noticed, in "Someone in a Tree" when the warrior enters in G major).

This is not to say that semitone voice leading is avoided in *Pacific Overtures.* On the contrary, it is a vital component of what is probably the central fount of motivic material in the score, namely the group of five notes given in abstract form in ex. 8.6a, i. Various actual uses of this motif are also shown in the example: ex. 8.6b is the opening of "Prayers," a song that, although cut, was "actually the basis of the whole score" (Zadan 1990, 218) (and which bore a ghostly resemblance to "Echo Song," also a song of prayer, from *Forum*); ex. 8.6c shows the same agglomeration of pitches, though with G as well in the accompaniment, in use in an earlier version of the number, called "Prayer" (the title was used for a pair of songs for Tamate and Kayama; this is Kayama's song). Ex. 8.6d is the opening of "Chrysanthemum Tea," and ex. 8.6e is the ostinato of its supplication section.

Ex. 8.6a

Ex. 8.6b

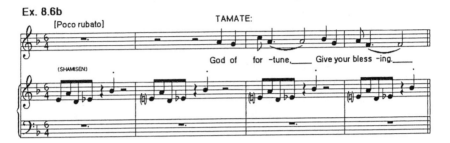

[Poco rubato]

TAMATE:

(SHAMISEN)

God of for -tune,_____ Give your bless -ing._____

Ex. 8.6c

Ex. 8.6d

Ex. 8.6e

4 times

Ex. 8.6f

The cell consists, apart from the E-natural, of two semitones a fifth apart. Thus to the ambiguity of passages a fifth (or fourth) apart is added the ambiguity of whether the upper or lower note of the semitone is the tonic. If the upper, say the E-flat, is tonic, then D is a leading tone and A-natural a raised fourth, implying the Lydian mode or a superimposition of the dominant key. If the D is the tonic, however, then the music is in the Phrygian mode, the only Western mode with a lowered supertonic.

Sondheim utilizes both perspectives, the former for his "Western" music, the latter for much of the Japanese sound. A Japanese Phrygian equivalent, the *in* mode, is used in folk music "as well as most other music after the appearance of the *shamisen* . . . [and produces an] obvious Japanese-like sound by its frequent use of half steps above the root and fifth of the scale" (Malm 1977, 188). However, the Phrygian perspective was not a conscious primary extrapolation on Sondheim's part, for what he was most aware of from his study of Japanese modes was the use of the minor pentachord shown in ex. 8.6a, ii, upon which his periodic lowering of the second scale degree was a creative superimposition. This explains ex. 8.6f, taken from "The Advantages of Floating in the Middle of the Sea" (it seems to represent the Emperor, and reappears in the scene of Kayama's murder, just before the Emperor's resumption of power).

Another account by Sondheim of how he worked toward usable styles takes us in an unexpected direction.

> I was searching for a Western equivalent [of Japanese music], and one day I hit on the correlation between the Japanese scale and the music of Manuel de Falla, a composer whose work I admire a lot. So I just started to imitate him. I took the pentatonic scale and bunched the chords together until they resembled that terrific guitar sound. And I was able to relate to it because suddenly it had a Spanish Western feeling and at the same time an Eastern feeling. It seldom occurs to me to write in minor keys, but because I had to have the feeling of Japanese tonality this afforded me the opportunity to do it. (Zadan 1990, 211)

There appear to be two factors here. One is the "bunching" of the pentatonic scale, and its connection with the "terrific guitar sound" is, historically, that from the time of Scarlatti or earlier added resonance was often given to a triad played on plucked string instruments by filling in the scale step between one of its thirds (usually between the root and third of the chord); this can be heard in any harpsichordist's spreading of arpeggios, and is Couperin's *coulé*. It represents the close position of four of the notes of the pentatonic scale (ex. 8.7a, i). A nonpentatonic sound is achieved, however, if the space between the third and fifth of the triad is filled with a somewhat different, more accentual effect, the simultaneous acciaccatura: this will normally (say, in Scarlatti) be a raised fourth (ex. 8.7a, ii), but may appear as a downward grace note to the root, in major or minor context (ex. 8.7a, iii–iv). This last, the second factor, adds the Phrygian relationship to the minor key.

Historical explanations aside, all that need be said is that in, for instance, "The Advantages of Floating in the Middle of the Sea" Sondheim favors harmonies of close position triads or pentatonic aggregates with added tones and semitones attaching themselves to other notes rather than behaving with voice-leading decorum (see the skeleton given in ex. 8.7b). "Chrysanthemum Tea" makes lighter use of similar resources (ex. 8.7c). However, it is not a particularly new stylistic departure, and harmonic unfolding still enjoys a developmental dimension in ex. 8.7b, at least until it is gainsaid at *x*—as an opening chorus it is not so different in some respects from "Company" (compare ex. 5.3a; other echoes of "Company" can be found in the long crescendos of rhythmic patterning over pedal notes in "Someone in a Tree").

Ex. 8.7 also offers a few passages from Falla that may illustrate the sort of inspiration Sondheim gained from him. Something of the major key *coulé* effect and Phrygian cadences are found in ex. 8.7d, from *The Three-Cornered Hat;* two examples from the piano part of *Nights in the Gardens of Spain* illustrate, respectively, the *coulé* in a minor context and the double semitone sound (F–E, B-flat–A) (exs. 8.7e and f). Ex. 8.7g, from *The Three-Cornered Hat,* reminds us how typically Spanish the Phrygian cadence can be; and finally, ex. 8.7h, also from *The Three-Cornered Hat,* gives us a possible concordance for some of the preliminary vamps for "A Bowler Hat" (compare ex. 2.8b).

The Phrygian property of the double semitone a fifth apart is easy to spot in the score (and in the preliminary sketches—see ex. 2.2a). Apart from the motivic instances already cited in ex. 8.6, it is apparent in the very first vocal notes (B–C) of "The Advantages of Floating in the Middle of the Sea" (see ex. 8.1b—the F-sharp at the end of the first phrase connects up with the F-sharp–G halfstep in the "Kings are burning somewhere" melody to suggest a tonal perspective of B minor in addition to the basic one of E minor). In "Four Black Dragons" the relationship in question is that between the repeated C-sharp–D in the vocal part and the F-sharp–G ostinato in the bass of the accompaniment (see pp. 39–40 in the score). It inhabits the B episodes of "Poems," whose vocal elaboration of an oscillation between D-flat and C is underpinned by

Ex. 8.7a

Ex. 8.7b

Ex. 8.7c

Have some tea, my Lord, Some chrys – an-the-mum tea.

Ex. 8.7d

Ex. 8.7e

Ex. 8.7f

Ex. 8.7g

Ex. 8.7h

G-flat–F, and the fifth note of the motif, G-natural, in the accompaniment. Later in the score it peters out, though the instrumental interludes in "A Bowler Hat" still conclude with Phrygian cadences (see ex. 2.2b).

Its corollary, as we have hinted, is the double leading tone. The leading tone is the most obviously Western feature of the music, and when it first appears unequivocally in the score (in "March to the Treaty House") the shock of vulgarity is considerable, especially when the subdominant trio leads back into the tonic A section with the most blatant dominant modulation imaginable (ex. 8.8a). This is the most fundamental symbol of imposed westernization to be found in the *Pacific Overtures* music, though the gradual process acknowledged by Sondheim can certainly be understood generically as well, operating across the whole of the second half of the score. For instance, the "Lion Dance" includes a cakewalk, possibly as a historical reference to the minstrel show with which the Japanese were entertained on board Commodore Perry's ships; two-step, Gilbert-and-Sullivan patter, Dutch clog waltz, Russian folkdance, and French can-can inhabit "Please Hello"; "A Bowler Hat" is a waltz; "Pretty

Ex. 8.8a

Ex. 8.8b

Lady" utilizes canonic counterpoint and fuses the kind of figurine minuet or mazurka that the song's subject suggests with the melodic wistfulness of a sea shanty that Sondheim had in mind; and "Next," one must assume, represents contemporary utility music of an international facelessness such as accompanies television news programs.

Nonetheless, we should remember Sondheim and Prince's brief to themselves to create the show as though a Japanese writer were trying to ape Broadway. Even in the unaccompanied melody of "March to the Treaty House" (ex. 8.8b) there is something not quite right, for the second B does not rise to C as a leading tone should, and the slurred A-flat-G in measure 3, while evocative enough of high school–cadet vulgarity, still reminds us of the Phrygian relationships, as do several recurrences of it later in the piece and its harmonized return in "Please Hello," where it is underlined by parallel fifths in the accompaniment. Parallel fifths and fourths persist at odd moments in all of the "Please Hello" sections until the French Admiral's, by which time they have (to all intents and purposes) disappeared in the riot of Western manners. They also inform "Pretty Lady," as we have seen. Indeed, if one takes into account the use of fifths and fourths, particularly in the harmonically sparse accompaniments, in "Poems," "Welcome to Kanagawa," "A Bowler Hat," and "Next," it becomes apparent that there is a stylistic unity encompassing the score as a whole that is not subdued by the vector of westernization. These four songs also make use of a minor scale with lowered seventh scale degree, combining elements of the Aeolian (flat sixth) and Dorian (sharp sixth) modes, so this feature too survives right through to the end of the score.

The Kabuki Element

What, then, in view of this stylistic unity, is the position occupied by the kabuki borrowings in the score? Are they merely casual, an extraneous counterpoise to all we have discussed? To a certain extent the answer is yes, and in any case they are not rigidly applied. The shakuhachi comes more from chamber music traditions than from kabuki; some of the dramatic techniques, as acknowledged in the preface to the script, are from the more ancient and austere genre of No, some from bunraku (Japanese puppet theater); the serene and measured recorder melody that introduces Tamate's dance sounds, at any rate to this author's ears, more like gagaku (ancient Japanese court music) than kabuki, just as the frenetic sixteenth-note passages of orchestral music (for instance, the B sections of "The Advantages of Floating in the Middle of the Sea") sound, especially in Tunick's metallophonic orchestration, more like a Balinese than a Japanese continuum. Given that, as we have seen, a prejudicial standpoint is unavoidable when West depicts East, this does not matter in the slightest: documentary vaudeville *Pacific Overtures* may be, documentary ethnomusicology it is not, and Sondheim was quite right to defuse the issue and disclaim too much research by commenting, "I didn't do much . . . how much do you need to know?" (Hirsch 1989, 111). In any case, kabuki itself has assimilated techniques, instruments, and types of song from wherever it pleased, including the No and bunraku traditions.

It should, then, be easy to appreciate how the ethnic borrowings ingenuously offer a second plane of dramatic representation or commentary opposite to that which is present in the singing and the music in the pit, and how they also supply the element of pastiche, create the presence of *objets trouvés,* as foils to the "original" style that constitutes most of the score and has monopolized most of our discussion (note, however, that the terms paradoxically call for reversal: Sondheim's "pit" style is really the pastiche, the onstage music of the shakuhachi, shamisen, vocalization, and improvisatory drums [almost] the genuine Japanese article). As a second plane of material they are analogous to and successors of the Liebeslieder in *A Little Night Music* and the diegetic songs, prompted by the stage band or piano, in *Follies.* Underlying all this one can see how kabuki itself runs parallel to the techniques of Broadway. It is a flamboyant form of musical theater, roughly as old as Western opera, thriving on singing, playing, dance, spectacle, costume, star actors, titillation (the all-male cast is the outcome of a travesty role tradition), and set routines. Moreover, it has its own distinction equivalent to that between diegetic and nondiegetic music, and if it cannot quite match the four musical dimensions of *Follies* it nonetheless cross-cuts between three musical agencies. The onstage vocal and instrumental ensemble of maybe twenty or twenty-five singers and players (*debayashi*) provides the *nagauta*, the "long songs." A smaller downstage-left ensemble, the *gidayu*, supplies narrative music essentially in the form of lute songs as well as declamatory comment and dialogue. The third group is the offstage *geza*, which with its drums and bells as well as the shamisen articulates stereotyped, indicative sound effects (as Malm points out [1977, 204], "similar, less codified techniques are used in Western movie music"). Which is which, in terms of *Pacific Overtures*? It is not possible to say precisely. Malm's comment implicitly equates the *geza* with a Western orchestra providing atmospheric music, but, in the musical, the drums and bells (offstage, according to the script, presumably separated from the onstage shakuhachi and shamisen) do not usurp the orchestra's place (though much of the time Sondheim seems to be at pains to avoid atmospheric underscoring in the pit, nonetheless). The Reciter belongs to the *gidayu*, but Sondheim and Prince separate him from them. The *debayashi* is set out like a Broadway chorus line on the one hand or a pit orchestra on the other but is the exact equivalent of neither and is not recreated in *Pacific Overtures*.

Ritual Form and the Mimetic Interlude

What it is possible to say is that the need for all these elements and ensembles to cohabit dramatically and musically contributes toward an approach to form that is to have a striking influence on some of Sondheim's subsequent shows. We have already analyzed stanzas of virtuosic length in "Someone in a Tree," and they are an important counterpoise to the fact that, in many ways, most of the forms used in the songs in *Pacific Overtures* are repetitive, simple, and clear in effect, with a tendency toward AB cyclic alternation. "The Advantages of Floating in the Middle of the Sea," expressive of the cyclic nature of traditional Japanese life ("Arrange tomorrow like today"), is in the form ABABAA + coda. "Welcome to Kanagawa" consists essentially of verse (V), refrain (R), and suggestive episode (E) in the arrangement VRERERVR (one of the episodes was cut in the 1984 script). "Next" is basically three long stanzas of verse-release format plus a dance break and coda. However, there are often subtleties of detail at work such as we have already seen in "A Bowler Hat" and frequently an interface between sections, motifs, and interludes that belies their linear effect and precludes simple categorization of form:

such is the case with "Four Black Dragons" and the use of material from the verse, not indicated above, in "Welcome to Kanagawa." Moreover, after each A section except the last in "The Advantages of Floating in the Middle of the Sea" comes what may best be described as a mimetic interlude, commanded by the Reciter. (In an earlier version of the song, "We Float," the role of mimetic interlude was apparently greater, for it included the "Lion Dance.") This interruptible and modular approach to form, which eventually and in a somewhat different way gives rise to the immensely long, prefabricated songs in *Sunday in the Park with George* and the extended prologues and epilogues to each act of *Into the Woods,* is at its most noticeable in "Chrysanthemum Tea." During the course of the song we get used to the succession, adopted for each of the stanzas (though it is eventually varied), of koto prelude, verse-refrain monologue, oracular pronouncement, ostinato from "Four Black Dragons," and frenetic pentatonic ritornello, the three latter segments or mimetic interludes all articulated by some form of percussion underscoring whose role, especially where the resonance of bells is concerned, is to assist musical time to free itself from constraints of metrical continuity. Pauses, caesuras, and even "till ready" vamps can act similarly as liberating agents, and the ontological approach is such as to make *Pacific Overtures* a strikingly modern score in its aesthetic. Possibly owing something to Britten (the procedure just described is reminiscent of the formal and temporal planes of the *War Requiem* as well as the church parables), the insertion of mimetic interludes offers a ritual procession of musical events as formal as the court protocol it depicts, or as the tea ceremony itself, and gives us the idea of processional drama or pageant in microcosm. Above all, it is a way of retaining song as a formal event while drawing a greater proportion of the dramatic activity into some kind of musical envelope. It has served Sondheim well since *Pacific Overtures,* for instance in the two complementary songs in *Merrily We Roll Along,* one in each act ("Franklin Shepard, Inc." and "Opening Doors"), which mimic the rituals of typing, composing at the piano, and telephoning as the essence of Frank and Charley's work pattern; it has also helped him resist the all-sung rock styles that, at the time of *Pacific Overtures,* were beginning to dominate the musicals of other composers and lyricists.

Chapter 9

Sweeney Todd

A Piece That Sings

Sweeney Todd is the only one of Sondheim's Broadway scores with a generic description other than "musical" or "musical comedy," being subtitled "a musical thriller." The thriller, defined by *Chambers Twentieth Century Dictionary* as "a sensational or exciting story, esp. one about crime and detection," relies heavily, at least as refined by television and film, not just on an intellectually satisfying plot but on atmosphere and suspense created by the setting and usually by the music as well. By the mid–1970s Sondheim had experience in writing music for television and film, had himself co-written a murder mystery film, *The Last of Sheila,* and had even acted on television. One facet of *Sweeney Todd* is in line with this, for as a complex, dynamic, and satisfying fabric of musical atmosphere, emotional underlinings, and motivic "clues," spun out and woven in the ingratiating way which has recommended itself to countless composers ever since Wagner, it might have been sophisticated film music. Yet music, although often virtually continuous, can rarely be itself in film; the reflexive element, diegetically plotted or calling for applause in the manner of those who "sing . . . on a stage . . . for the sake of the music" (Keller 1987, 20), is normally lacking outside the Hollywood musical. It may be significant that a rare exception, a thriller film score *about* music, was an underlying influence on *Sweeney Todd.*

> When I was fifteen I saw a movie that I adored; I sat through it twice, and I adored it partly because of the story and partly because of the music. The movie was *Hangover Square* (John Brahm, 20th Century, 1945), and it took place in Edwardian times (I was already a budding Anglophile). It concerned a composer who was way ahead of his time but who had the misfortune to be insane. The whole movie revolves around a piano concerto. The composer goes insane when he hears high notes, becomes schizophrenic, goes out, and murders people. Then, when he comes back and isn't insane, he's the most talented, perfect person in the world.

The reason the composer's music was way ahead of its time was that it was composed by Bernard Herrmann, who in 1945 when the film came out was writing movie music ahead of his time. It's easy to see why I identified with the film; I also thought it was the best story that I'd ever come across. The music—a one-movement piano concerto by Herrmann—knocked me out, and I wrote Herrmann a fan letter and asked him if it was going to be recorded. I got a nice reply. Herrmann said it would be recorded by Wallenstein and the San Francisco Sinfonietta. I waited and waited, but a year later it had never come out.

There was one page of the music shown on the screen. It was on the piano of the composer (played by Laird Cregar), and the first time I saw the movie, I sat through it twice so that I could memorize that piece of music. And I memorized it. Several years later the piano concerto did come out on record. Like most film composing buffs, I am a great fan of Herrmann's, and I've always wanted to write an answer to *Hangover Square*. (Sondheim 1980, 10–11)

Sondheim leaves us in no doubt about the importance of this early infatuation, which as a youngster's creative epiphany is a classic of its kind. I have already traced the film's probable influence on two of his other projects (see chap. 1), and although a sustained comparison is beyond the scope of this book, Claudia Gorbman's study of *Hangover Square* and its music (Gorbman 1987, 151–61) suggests any number of parallels between it and *Sweeney Todd,* from the character of the music itself (see her quotation of the organ-grinder's theme and the crowd motif, the one suggesting the *Dies irae,* the other like the accompaniment of "The Ballad of Sweeney Todd" [Gorbman 1987, 176]) to the symbolism of "turning in threes" (155–56) whereby the "three times 'round the Square" hangover cure that explains the film's title, the phone-cranking instruction ("Turn the handle like this, three times") and the organ-grinder's turning handle are all amalgamated in the musical (not in Bond's play) into Mrs. Lovett's instruction to Toby to "put the meat through the grinder three times."

Yet how could he make a thriller musically assertive, give it a musical voice through which to speak, without repeating the film's formula? The answer evidently came nearly thirty years later when he saw Christopher Bond's play *Sweeney Todd* in the East End of London. "It struck me as a piece that sings. . . . It had a weight to it, but I couldn't figure out how the language was so rich and thick without being fruity" (Zadan 1990, 243–44). The reason, as Hugh Wheeler subsequently pointed out to him, was that "Bond had written half of his play in blank verse, but that the lines were not typed out as blank verse." Sondheim's explanation of this continues in the following manner.

All the speeches of the judge, Todd, and the two young lovers are written in iambic meter, and the lower-class characters are given non-metered dialogue. This produces a very subtle effect when you read the play. Beyond the formality of the diction, there is a kind of stateliness in some of the characters that creates an odd juxtaposition with the rag-tag rhythms in the lower-class figures. (Sondheim 1980, 5)

Montagu Slater (1928, 93) had drawn attention to unconscious blank verse in the prose of George Dibdin Pitt in his 1928 Introduction to the script of Pitt's original *Sweeney Todd* play of 1842.

The very first speeches in Bond's play illustrate the blank verse perfectly adequately; they are restored to the layout of iambic pentameters below (Todd's speech ends with an Alexandrine, unless the number of unstressed syllables is construed as immaterial).

ANTHONY: I have sailed the world, beheld its fairest cities,
 Seen the pyramids, the wonders of the east.
 Yet it is true—there is no place like home.
TODD: None.
ANTHONY: What's the matter?
TODD: You are young. Life has been kind to you,
 And fortune smiles on your enterprises.
 May it always be so. My heart beats quicker, too,
 To find myself in London once again,
 But whether out of joy or fear I cannot say.

Mrs. Lovett's "rag-tag rhythms" are also in evidence from the start.

MRS. LOVETT: Are you a ghost?
Todd starts for the door, fearing he has been recognized
Hey, don't go running out the minute you get in. I only took you for a ghost 'cos you're the first customer I've seen for a fortnight. Sit you down.
Todd sits, warily
You'd think we had the plague, the way people avoid this shop. A pie, was it?
TODD: A pie—yes. And some ale.
MRS. L: (*getting the pie*) Mind you, you can't hardly blame them. There's no denying these are the most tasteless pies in London. I should know, I make 'em. (*She puts the pie on the table, then flicks a bit of dirt off the crust*) Ugh! What's that? But can you wonder, with meat the price it is? I mean, I never thought I'd see the day when grown

men and good cooks, too, would dribble over a dead dog like it was a round of beef. (*She goes for some ale*)

Without wishing to repeat the investigation into how Sondheim fashioned lyrics from Bond's play (see chap. 2), these two passages can be used to demonstrate how little he and Wheeler had to change Bond's language and scenario (Sondheim even scribbled Bond's phrase "no place like home" among his music sketches, before altering it to a more highly characterized refrain); indeed, Bond himself, in spite of all the differences in plot and motivation, seems to have taken a delight in retaining details from Dibdin Pitt (such as the lad's finding a hair in a pie in the bake house and winding it around his finger). Yet we can also appreciate how much effort must have gone into every individual decision on what to retain, what to adjust, what to rearrange; what should be sung, what spoken; what rhymed. Compare Bond's opening with that of act 1 of the musical.

> ANTHONY (*sings*): I have sailed the world, beheld its wonders
> From the Dardanelles
> To the mountains of Peru,
> But there's no place like London!
> I feel home again.
>
> I could hear the city bells
> Ring whatever I would do.
> No, there's no pl—
>
> TODD (*sings grimly*): No, there's no place like London.
> ANTHONY (*speaks, surprised at the interruption*): Mr. Todd, sir?
> TODD (*sings*): You are young.
> Life has been kind to you.
> You will learn.

Similarly, much of Mrs. Lovett's speech and train of thought were retained (did the adoption of Bond's reference to "London" as a refrain word in this song suggest the use of it for Anthony and Todd as well?).

> [*singing*] Mind you, I can't hardly blame them—
> (*pouring a tankard of ale*)
> These are probably the worst pies in London.
> I know why nobody cares to take them—
> I should know,

I make them.
But good? No,
The worst pies in London—
. . . .
And no wonder with the price of meat
What it is
(*grunt*)
When you get it.
(*grunt*)
Never
(*grunt*)
Thought I'd live to see the day men'd think it was a treat
Finding poor
(*grunt*)
Animals
(*grunt*)
Wot are dying in the street.

(The unforgettable transmutation of Bond's reference to a dressed cat follows; Bond's dog has been elided.) But two strokes of genius on Sondheim's part have to be admitted: the elaboration of Bond's single reference to stage business (flicking dust off the pie, with its verbal aside) into a virtuoso comic routine of making pastry and squashing bugs, all written into the patter and punctuating rhythms of the song; and the addition of "When you get it" to the comment about the price of meat. The latter sets up the reprise of the phrase as a lead-in to "A Little Priest," where with a delicious pun (a sort of structural reflection of the very idea itself—of how to dispose of the corpse—in all its excruciating comic logic) this tiny inspiration lubricates the fulcrum of the whole plot.

Seems an awful waste.
I mean,
With the price of meat what it is,
When you get it,
If you get it—
TODD (*becoming aware*): Ah!
MRS. L: Good, you got it.

Is *Sweeney Todd* Opera?

Sondheim, then, was faced with an essay cast in the rich texture of traditional dramatic language, its blank verse opposite colloquial prose underlining the direct descent of the play and its type from Jacobean revenge tragedy, indeed from *The Revenger's Tragedy* (see Bond 1991, 4; hardly a live body remains on stage at the end of *Sweeney Todd*, and Anthony's closing speech in Bond's script is as formal as his opening one). It is no wonder that Sondheim's mind turned to opera after seeing the play.

> I remember thinking on my way home that it would make an opera, and I spoke to John Dexter, one of the directors of the Metropolitan Opera, who at that time was directing in the West End in London. In the course of our conversation I asked him if he thought that Sweeney Todd might make an opera, and he said absolutely and that encouraged me to look into the rights for it. That's how it all started. (Sondheim 1980, 8)

When he began his version he evidently got to work just like an opera composer setting a play or libretto to music.

> I started it, trying to write everything myself because it was really all going to be sung . . . it was going to be virtually an opera. I did the first twenty minutes and I realized I was only on page five of Bond's script. So at that rate, the show would possibly have been nine hours long. (Zadan 1990, 246)

At this point Hugh Wheeler was called in to help with the libretto. Being British, he must have been an invaluable intermediary in matters of cultural reference and tone (*Sweeney Todd* is a triumph of the spirit of time and place, as we shall see); however, given that most of the text (about eighty percent, according to Sondheim) is sung, it is impossible to tell just where and how much Wheeler was needed for the supply of material between Bond's script and Sondheim's lyrics. It seems that his greatest contribution was in act 2, for "as we got to work on it," and with Hal Prince involved as well, Sondheim explained, "much of the second half of the piece started to change in shape and in tone and style" (Prince and Sondheim 1979, 23); this seems to have led to tensions between Bond and Wheeler (Bond 1991, 6). The change in "shape" involved altering details of the plot: for instance, in Bond's play when the Judge returns to Todd's parlor he is told that the woman in the chair with her back to him is Johanna; it is in fact the murdered Beggar Woman, left there to terrify him. Perhaps Sondheim, Prince, and Wheeler discarded this unwittingly ironic coup de théâtre on the part of Todd because, swift though the action is at this point, it seems likely that the Judge would have recognized the woman he meets nowhere else in the play and reacted to her as someone more than the "deluded hag who chanced along," thus preempting Todd's own discovery of her true identity.

In fact it does take twenty minutes and sixty pages of piano score for the musical to arrive at the point to which Sondheim refers above, the end of Bond's second scene—a great deal has to be set up and expounded in that time in the way of atmosphere, characterization, and motivation, with musical numbers, themes, and motifs to match, and it can be seen from ex. 9.1 that most of the numbered motifs have been heard by then. In operatic terms, this is not bad going in any case, and a similar rate of condensation of the script would have produced three hours of music, not nine.

As early as 1977 André Previn's interview with Sondheim raised the question of whether he was moving in the direction of opera. *Sweeney Todd* is certainly his biggest and most continuous and integral score; but is it an opera? Some have insisted that it is: Rockwell claimed that "with its mosaic construction, rapidly shifting moods, recurrent leitmotifs and complex ensembles, *Sweeney Todd* belongs on the operatic stage far more deservedly than most of the new operas that jostle for position there" (1983, 217), and Blyton, erecting his whole article "Sondheim's 'Sweeney Todd'—The Case For the Defence" on a similar thesis, ascribed its relative failure on the London theater stage to the fact that "it was heard by the wrong audience . . . it needs to be presented by an opera company like the English National Opera or the Welsh National Opera" (Blyton 1984, 26). More practical manifestations of this conviction were already afoot when these comments were being written, and *Sweeney Todd* was successfully produced by the Houston Grand Opera and New York City Opera in 1984. Opera singers were used in the Manchester Library Theatre's production of 1989, Peter Glossop and Emile Belcourt taking the roles of Sweeney and the Judge. By no means just where Sondheim is concerned, distinctions between musicals and operas are becoming, or being, blurred (see Verdino-Süllwold 1990). One could argue that, instead, they need careful redefinition.

Sondheim himself has taken pains to draw distinctions between what he writes, even in *Sweeney Todd,* and opera, and although his self-confessedly "dogmatic" analyses of operatic values are not particularly helpful (see Herbert 1989, 208–10), some of his comments elsewhere do cast light on generic indicators.

> I've never liked opera and I've never understood it. Most opera doesn't make theatrical sense to me. Things go on forever. I'm not a huge fan of the human voice. I like song, dramatic song. I like music and lyrics

Ex. 9.1. Reprises of Musical Motifs and Numbers in *Sweeney Todd*

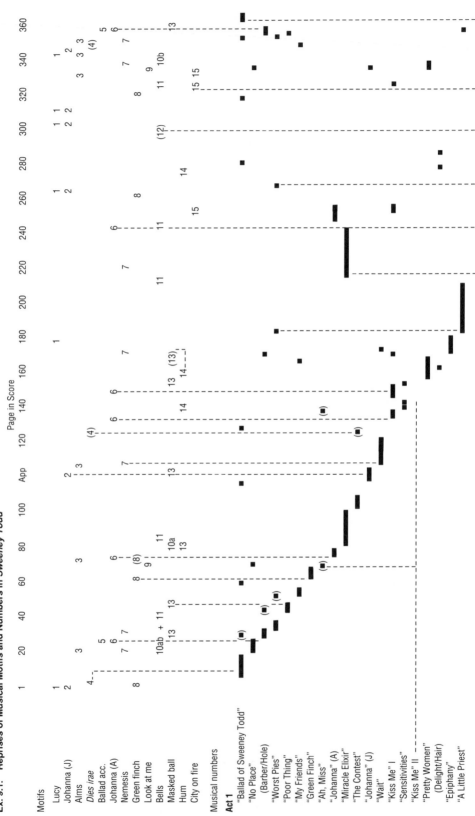

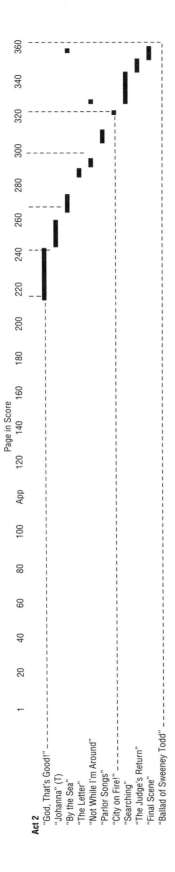

Page in Score

together, telling a story. I am not particularly attracted to performers per se. . . . I like *Carmen,* I like *Bohème,* I like some of *Tosca.* Puccini generally I like best, and the first act of *Peter Grimes,* and *Porgy and Bess,* and *Wozzeck.* That about does it. (Savran 1990, xvi)

One could argue that this shows discrimination rather than incomprehension. Be that as it may, he was happy with *Sweeney Todd* at the New York City Opera because it "is really an operetta, it requires operetta voices, that is to say the needs for the singers are slightly greater than the needs on Broadway but nowhere as great as the needs in grand opera" (Herbert 1989, 210). On the other hand, the degree of musical continuity in *Sweeney Todd* has little to do with operatic pacing, but stems from the need for the score "to function the way 'old movie scores do'" (Hirsch 1989, 124)—Sondheim realized that "the only way to sustain tension was to use music continually, not to let the heat out, so that even if they're talking, there's music going on in the pit" (Zadan 1990, 248).

Sondheim says that there are five spoken sections of the show that he would like to set to music one day. One of them is the ending. The last three minutes of plot involve very little music: after Todd has sung his last word, even the underscoring peters out and leaves the stage to Tobias's last speech and still more to the silence of mime. It remained unsung and unplayed simply because Sondheim did not have time to add music before the production opened. Yet the pacing, although no longer musical, let alone vocal, is wonderful, and the scene is tremendously effective. It is worth comparing it with the conclusion of *Peter Grimes.* Both scenarios, before coming forward into the surrounding frame of a choral ballad, narrow the focus to that of a single, maddened character against the background of a chase (in *Grimes* we still hear the chorus singing his name; in *Sweeney Todd* the lunatics are on the loose, and much of the second act has involved searching, be it Anthony for Johanna, the Beggar Woman for the source of the evil thereabouts, or Todd and Mrs. Lovett for Tobias). But although even Britten has recourse to speech for Bulstrode and Ellen and to silence for Grimes's last action, until then Grimes's scene still holds the stage through his singing, all the more vocal for being unaccompanied. *Sweeney Todd,* even if by authorial default at this point, demonstrates the dramatic potency and rightness of music's self-denial in this genre that is not opera, just as Maria's final speech does in *West Side Story.*

The essential factor mediating between Bond's play as a penny-dreadful thriller on the one hand and Jacobean revenge tragedy on the other, and between the score of *Sweeney Todd* as not really opera on the one hand and not simply film music on the other, is their identity as melodrama. This, "the obverse side of farce," as Sondheim describes it, similarly permits "complications of plot, larger-than-life characters, grand gestures, and nonnaturalistic acting" (Sondheim 1980, 4) within a kinetic structure that can proceed of its own momentum because, as in farce, all of the characters "have one thing they want" (14) and are thus, as representatives of "melodramatic man," "essentially 'whole,'" as opposed to "tragic man" who "is essentially 'divided'" (Smith 1973, 7, paraphrasing R. Bechtold). In Bond's play, the qualities of heightened language, as well as the excitement of the plot, carry forward the audience's empathetic involvement, which is complete; in Sondheim's score it is, in addition, the music that does this, with its heightened role and increased continuity. And although we are to understand melodrama in its current dramaturgical sense, as "a dramatic piece characterized by sensational incident and violent appeals to the emotions" (Smith 1973, 5), it is worth reflecting that Sondheim's exploitation of it in *Sweeney Todd* begins to lead us full circle to the term's historically primary meaning of instrumental music played during (originally between) passages of speech, given the importance of underscoring and instrumental motifs in the score.

Opera is often prime melodrama, of course—"Wagner, Verdi and Puccini still pack Covent Garden and La Scala for operas built upon the most successful melodramas of their day," James Smith points out (1973, 48), referring in passing to *Fidelio, Der Fliegende Holländer, La traviata,* and other plots built on the formulas and attitudes of melodrama such as grandiose or repentant suffering, last-minute salvation, family conflicts, personal triumph, and so on (see also Rahill 1967, chap. 16). Yet we must again stress that Sondheim's way of privileging music within melodrama is not opera's way. The pacing of his sung verbal language remains that of spoken drama, rather than being, as in opera, subservient to the slower and longer-spanned emotional arcs of music. Thus, unlike most opera composers, he does not draw out syllables to unnaturalistic length, nor does he repeat verbal phrases except in a refrain context; the book of *Sweeney Todd* is consequently a good deal fatter than a printed opera libretto. Coupled with this verbal fecundity, he retains wit, colloquialism, and (taking the word in a neutral sense, as building action into the delivery) pantomime as governing *Affekts* in his songs, whose verbal values thereby remain those of the musical theater. Musically, too, the songs still belong there—they are, as ever, cast as ballads, burlesques, marches, waltzes, patter songs, and so forth (Sondheim has described the mixture as "tend[ing] toward a music-hall tradition" [Hirsch 1989, 123]). The one obvious exception is "Green Finch and Linnet Bird," which really is operatic in its overladen verbal language (Johanna uses the word *jubilate*), its touch of coloratura to imitate the birds, and its classical accompaniment figure, untypical of Sondheim—overall it is not unlike the comic opera style

Ex. 9.2

of, say, Menotti in *The Telephone*. This is hardly inappropriate, given that its subject matter is Johanna's petition "Teach me how to sing." Its harmonic scheme is also uncharacteristically discursive in its modulations and couched in terms of recapitulation rather than refrain: it could almost have been written by Prokofiev or Berkeley, and occasioned one of Sondheim's diagrammatic harmonic plans in the course of composition (ex. 9.2). But taking all these factors together, the self-consciously operatic or classical stance in this number (Sondheim refers to its "art song" quality) merely underlines what the work as a whole is not.

Perhaps we can sum up by saying that, as melodrama, *Sweeney Todd* permits the vocal music to enter, cease, or undergo transformation proudly yet unconsciously as the vehicle for the dynamic flux of action and language, rather than have to justify itself surreptitiously or self-consciously with the traditional "cue for a song." It can be there most of the time because the drama, its actions and language and its verbal delivery, move along in the highest gear throughout.

This results in total audience involvement; there is no place for alienation techniques. Concomitantly, it gives rise to a score that is more of a self-sufficient creative document than anything else in Sondheim's output (it is notable that there are no cutouts from *Sweeney Todd* other than the Judge's song and that even this is included in the score as an appendix). It is to the organization of the score that we must now turn.

Diegetic Musical Motifs

Unlike nineteenth-century Seville, nineteenth-century London is not recalled or imagined as a community bursting with spontaneous song and dance; Sondheim's way of evocation could not be the diegetic way of Bizet in *Carmen* (the one character in *Sweeney Todd* who sings a whole number diegetically in public—or whose song is at least representing spoken rhetoric that *ought* to be singing—is the [assumed] foreigner, Pirelli). (*Sweeney Todd* does contain rare instances of diegetic rhyme: in "A Little Priest" the characters *know* that they are creating rhymes, as Sondheim in effect tells us when Todd fails to find one for "locksmith." Sondheim also imagines Tobias's marketplace speech—and presumably its act 2 variant—as containing diegetic rhyme, doubtless composed for him by Pirelli.) But in Victorian London there was plenty of music indoors, particularly in the church and the parlor. Sondheim's gift for stylistic pastiche is never more delightful than in "Parlor Songs": in "Sweet Polly Plunkett" he recalls not only the Sullivan "madrigal" convention with its pert cadences (exs.9.3a and b—shades of "ruler of the Queen's navee" in the words of the latter) but also the rambling melodiousness of eighteenth-century song and even the renaissance madrigal or lute song itself with his touches of Lydian and Mixolydian modality (marked x and y in ex. 9.3c), to which the Dorian mode is added in "The Tower of Bray." (There were more overt madrigal references in the lyric sketches for "Parlor Songs," including "In the garden of life there are thistles & thorns / Falalala . . ." and "A lover lay with his lass / In the grass. . . . ") Modality, also evident in the Aeolian "Ballad of Sweeney Todd," offers a reaching back in time and tradition that parallels the Jacobean elements in Bond; but the more potent and ubiquitous evocation is of London's street sounds and street cries. Most of the musical motifs that comprise the cinematic tissue of atmosphere and narrative are diegetic in the sense of being street sounds, heard or overheard, or personal cries or calls of some kind. The most obvious examples are the Beggar Woman's cry for alms (no. 3 in ex. 9.4) and "City on Fire!" (no. 15), both more-or-less onomatopoeic in the notated tradition of stylized cries. The little figure (no. 14) hummed by the Judge and whistled by Todd in the tonsorial parlor as an exchange of social affability (surely not unmixed with nerves on Todd's part) is day-to-day, environmental music of a different kind (we are presumably not supposed to stop and reflect that Turpin is actually humming a tune from the show). Bell sounds hold pride of atmospheric place. Internalized according to the characters' dispositions, we hear Todd and Anthony's reactions to the city in campanological terms in "No Place Like London," Anthony hearing and seeing the golden radiance of steeple and weathervane (no. 10a in ex. 9.4), Todd some ghostly oppressive echo of what might be a funeral toll (no. 10b) (one of Sondheim's musical sketches for this number is labeled "Bow Bells"). More diegetically superimposed are the repeated uses of the Westminster chimes, complete with acoustic undertones that blossom into apt, Coplandesque neoclassicism of harmony in the St. Dunstan's marketplace scene and its act 2 equivalent, "God, That's Good!" (ex. 9.5). More subtly and perhaps unconsciously woven into the score is a reminiscence

Ex. 9.3a

Ex. 9.3b

Ex. 9.3c

of the rhythm and melody of "Oranges and Lemons" in "Not While I'm Around," again with neoclassically construed undertones (see the consecutive sevenths in ex. 9.4, no. 12), the reference indicative of Tobias's childish innocence and lack of maternal affection.

But the most significant motifs stem from recalled or overheard church and ballroom music, and it is appropriate enough that music of social or spiritual import should accompany the central facts of the plot and even, for the musically acute, be planted so as to suggest its denouement. The prime example of this is the little *inégale* minuet figure (Sondheim labeled it "Gavotte" on one of his sketches) that accompanies the ballroom rape

Ex. 9.4

1. Lucy

2. Johanna (Judge)

3. Alms

4. Dies irae

6. Johanna (Anthony)

5. Ballad acc.

7. Nemesis

8. Green finch

9. Look at me

10. Bells   a.

          b.

11. Bells

Ex. 9.4—Continued

12. Bells

13. Masked ball

14. Hum

15. City on fire

and has been distorted, though without quite losing its classical parallel thirds, to become the Beggar Woman's crazed motif (no. 13 in ex. 9.4); we note that the Judge cannot quite forget it in his postcoital guilt (see p. 385 in the score), and there is a suggestion of it in the rhythmic transformation of the "hum" when Todd nearly gives himself away with the question "As pretty as her mother?"

It is not the only motif functioning as a clue, however. The very first gesture in the score, in the opening organ "Prelude" (it is different on the original cast recording), is a descending scale (no. 1 in ex. 9.4) that Sondheim thought of as representing the singing of "Kyrie eleison" (Hirsch 1989, 123). Its sense of supplication could be said to help set the play up as a melodrama of defeat—which a story about crime more or less has to be if the criminal is the hero—rather than triumph, but it is more specifically associated with Lucy, possibly via Todd's (spoken) rhetorical outcry, taken from Bond's play, "Would no one have mercy on her?" which may well have given Sondheim the "Kyrie" idea in the first place, but chiefly because it is later sung, in "Epiphany," to Todd's cry for vengeance (the opposite of mercy), intoned repeatedly to the words "[Not] one man, no, / Nor ten men, / Nor a hundred can assuage me— / I will have you!" but also sung to the lines "[And I'll] never see Johanna" and "[my] Lucy lies in ashes"; it is this last outcry that remains in the mind, one suspects because it offers a lyric clue to the plot's outcome (Lucy lies in ashes not, as Todd thinks, in the sense of "ashes to ashes," but as a Beggar Woman "picking bones and rotten spuds out of alley ashcans!") or even because "eleison" (mercy) and "Lucy" utilize the same two consonants on the same two notes (if such transformational minutiae seem farfetched, consider "The Story of Lucy and Jessie" in *Follies*). Anthony's intonation

Ex. 9.5

of Johanna's name (or rather of his metonymous "I feel you"), motif 6 (which Tunick's orchestration at first belies), is also embedded in motif 1 (see *x* in ex. 9.4), as Todd's outburst indicates. Both Johanna and Lucy seem to be associated with downward scales, diatonic for Johanna in her purity (see nos. 8 and 9), onomatopoeically chromatic for the fallen Lucy (no. 3). Additionally, the scale of which motif 1 consists is almost immediately inverted in the organ "improvisation" to presage Judge Turpin's repeated gasping of his ward's name (ex. 9.4, no. 2) as he indulges in masochistic pseudopenitence in the form of sexual flagellation, the inversion of the motif indicating his rising lust.

The *Dies Irae*

Even before this, however, an improvisatory extension of the "Lucy" motif (see the passage in square brackets in ex. 9.4, no. 1) has begun to suggest the contours of the *Dies irae,* whose second phrase (see ex. 9.4, no. 4) in any case confirms that the first, of which it is a paraphrase, is built on a downward tetrachord. (This downward scale of a fourth can therefore be considered the root of *Sweeney Todd*'s thematic material.) It is hardly surprising that such a thorough-going symphonic web of musical representation, set in the nineteenth century with a melodramatic stance, should make play with the *Dies irae,* symbol of doom, exploited, among countless other composers, by Berlioz, Liszt, Saint-Saëns, Mahler, and above all Rachmaninoff. Like many of his forebears, Sondheim appreciates that the oscillating pitches of its first phrase can suggest the nightmarish swinging of bells, and he thus adds it to the panoply of his bell evocations. This is evident when we hear the greater part of the first phrase, undisguised though up a third, in the chorus of the "Ballad" (first sung on p. 8 of the score)—especially so when harmonized dissonantly (Blyton [1984, 20] likens this to Weill's male-voice part writing in *The Seven Deadly Sins* when it appears on pp. 128–29 of the score). Sondheim is also aware that Rachmaninoff was capable of basing whole symphonic compositions, such as the Second Symphony, on closely and subtly argued cellular transformations and elaborations of the *Dies irae*'s first four notes (or its first phrase, which is a sequential extension of them), and was particularly influenced by its use in the *Rhapsody on a Theme of Paganini*. We saw in chapter 4 that something of the inexorably descending melodic contour that results from such a composing-out of the motif was unconsciously present in "See What It Gets You" from *Anyone Can Whistle;* in *Sweeney Todd* the process is conscious, perhaps retained in Sondheim's mind after he abandoned the first version of "Chrysanthemum Tea" in *Pacific Overtures,* in which the first two phrases of the *Dies irae* had had a rather more structural role than their episodic one in the statutory version of the song (where only the first phrase appears), being used rather literally as a cantus firmus (in the form of diegetic koto music) holding complicated portions of the music and action together while as many as five characters (the Shogun, his Mother, the two Priests, and two Physicians) all sang different things at once and the onstage shamisen and percussion added their commentary to that of the orchestra. Something of the same binding effect of the plainsong can be seen on pages 317–20 of the score of *Sweeney Todd.*

The first two phrases of the *Dies irae* are heard without concealment or elaboration in the organ "Prelude" (mm. 26–34 in the score); however, this is not played in the original cast recording, which thus conforms with Sondheim's comment that the *Dies irae* "was never actually quoted in the show" (Zadan 1990, 248). Its compositional transformation begins in earnest with "The Ballad of Sweeney Todd": the rondo theme (ex. 9.6b) is built on its essential scale degrees ($\hat{3}$-$\hat{1}$-$\hat{2}$-$\hat{7}$-$\hat{1}$ in the minor) with their sequential building block *x* out of which most of it grows. "No Place Like London" (ex. 9.6c) is a close variant, but with harmonic displacement and therefore disguise, its tonic E-flat, now in a major context, occupying the position of the flat seventh in the Aeolian "Ballad"—in other words, the melody has been shifted up a step.

Now back in the minor, it rises another step to form the motivic material for Todd's "There's a Hole in the World" (ex. 9.6d) and "There Was a Barber and His Wife" (ex. 9.6e), where the upper contour is the dominant of the scale ($\hat{5}$). This melodic contouring matches that of the *Dies irae* statement in the episodic chorus of the "Ballad" referred to earlier, of which, terming it the "first release," Sondheim has said that its transposition "up a third . . . changed the harmonic relationship of the melodic notes to each other" (Zadan 1990, 248). The relative major of this melodic level furnishes the pivot note of the Beggar Woman's "Masked ball" motif (ex. 9.6h) and of Mrs. Lovett's recurrent chatter (whose melodic identifier

Ex. 9.6

is initially set to the words "What's yer rush? What's yer hurry?" in "The Worst Pies in London," ex. 9.6i). Meanwhile, the shape of the *Dies irae* opening has been flattened or generalized into the eerie, brooding oscillation of Todd's "Nemesis" (ex. 9.6f) and inverted to form the "Ballad" accompaniment (ex. 9.6g), these two motifs also relating to each other by a shift of phase (see their vertical tabulation in ex. 9.6). The highlighting of the oscillation, y, is insistent and effective for portraying atmosphere in exs. 9.6f and g and female character in exs. 9.6h and i, while another permutational facet of the basic *Dies irae* four-note motif produces Mrs. Lovett's $z2$, which is also repeatedly present in her conversational monologue "Poor Thing," set to the words "Pretty little thing" and variants of them (ex. 9.6j). The inversion, $z1$, likewise produces offshoots in the initial motifs of "My Friends" (ex. 9.6k) and "Not While I'm Around" (ex. 9.6l). The latter's melodic pivot is on the dominant degree of the major scale, a bright and as it were dogmatic position that it shares with the further variant $z3$ ("Ladies in Their Sensitivities," ex. 9.6m) and that suits the singers (Toby and the Beadle respectively) and their assertions; however, Todd's version of $z3$ in "Pretty Women" (ex. 9.6n) is pitched even higher, as a tonic seventh, as he reaches his climax of murderous anticipation in both act 1 and act 2.

This by no means exhausts the uses of motivic material from the *Dies irae*. For instance, Mrs. Lovett's quick-fire conversational intonation rubs off on the crowd interjections in "Pirelli's Miracle Elixir" and the dialogue in "Kiss Me" ("He means to marry me Monday"), as well as on Todd himself as his delight gathers itself into a waltz in "A Little Priest" ("Mrs. Lovett, / What a charming notion . . ."); and Sondheim himself has pointed out (Hirsch 1989, 125) that the motoric section of "Epiphany" is based on it (the entire first phrase is hidden in an inner part of the accompaniment, though the bass line offers another four-note reflection).

Structural Processes in the Score

Whether or not all this on its own would make for an impressive score, Sondheim's ways of assembling his building blocks also deserve attention; in particular we may consider the use of motivic repetition, transformation, combination, and reprise. "Motif" songs such as "Pretty Women," the two first-act "Johanna"s, "By the Sea," "Pirelli's Miracle Elixir," and so on tend to fuse the two levels of thematic material implied by the tabulation shown in ex. 9.1: short motifs representing clues, depicting surroundings, or introducing characters, which can be implanted all over the score, often between extended numbers, and the set numbers themselves, songs in a word, each responsible for a unified and weighable span of the show. They can repeat a motif kinetically and move away from it for contrast, development, or release. "Refrain" songs, on the other hand, such as "The Worst Pies in London," "Poor Thing," and "Kiss Me," have to work toward a catchy theme without destroying the character built up before it is reached. The distributional analysis of "The Worst Pies in London" (ex. 9.7a) shows how this can be achieved. It is not a strictly neutral diagram, since Mrs. Lovett's $z2$ motif combined with the repeated fragment a out of which it grows is treated as the initial unit (rather than a

Ex. 9.7a

itself) and parameters of contour and inversion as well as this one of
repetition are not applied with absolute strictness. The result is to show
how, within a very close working of material, the unstoppable chatter of
Mrs. Lovett eventually arrives at her refrain—she has a gossip's way of
talking that takes a long time to get to the point, and as an archetypal
gossip works while she speaks. Two particular ploys are evident. One is
that the two-sixteenth-note descent running down the left side of the

Ex. 9.7b

example gradually rises in pitch, starting on C-sharp, D, A, and eventually C-flat as it becomes the two-note core of the "worst pies" refrain (what the example does not show methodically is that it also begins to form into a longer descending scale of four notes—see the eleventh system of the example—that becomes the context for this core). The other ploy is the capricious irregularity of appearances of the extended upward scale before its statements finally catch up with themselves and gather momentum, also rising in pitch, in the refrain (their concomitant augmentation into eighth notes no doubt expresses Mrs. Lovett's running out of "wind").

Another, looser form of motivic transformation can occur when two motifs are put side by side with a connecting thread of *melos*. This Wagnerian procedure tends to signify psychological affinities, either depicting the train of thought or stream of consciousness of a character onstage or showing us, the audience, how to connect our thoughts. (To Engel [1967, 144] it would be an example of "not song" and presupposes an operatic condition.) There is a good instance of it on page 71 in the score (ex. 9.7b), when the two-note "London" chime of Anthony's refrain "No Place Like London" is pointedly repeated on its own and immediately followed by the Beggar Woman's cry starting enharmonically on the same note (E-flat/D-sharp); the affinity is strengthened rhythmically when we reach her eighth-note trochee on the word *woman*. The passage as a whole provides good symphonic continuity while reminding us both of Anthony's humane sympathy and the transformational extremes of London life. As a corollary to this feeling for transition, Sondheim is also at pains to provide connections between accompaniments in *Sweeney Todd*, such as is sensed between "Poor Thing" and "My Friends" and engineered between "Green Finch and Linnet Bird" and "Ah, Miss," and in doing this he shows yet another way of having "each song . . . depend . . . on the last one" (Prince and Sondheim 1979, 27), even if what he meant by this statement was more akin to the web of relationships shown in ex. 9.6.

As for combinations of motifs, there is a good deal of this in "Kiss Me" and the act 2 "Johanna" and "Searching" sequences in particular, though nothing quite on the self-consciously cyclic lines—worked out demonstratively as a kind of symphonic "solution" to a puzzle—that I discussed vis-à-vis "Being Alive" in chapter 5. It is worth noting that, for "Kiss Me" part 2, a 4/4 version of the "Hum" (ex. 9.7c) was sketched as an additional contrapuntal ingredient but not used, and that the sketches also show the "Ladies in Their Sensitivities" countersubject (which is not entirely comfortable harmonically) beginning earlier (in m. 9) and thus proceeding further and Anthony's "Johanna" countermelody reappearing at measure 21 (as in part 1). Another contrapuntal combination not persevered with after being sketched was that of Mrs. Lovett's "Excuse Me" bridge passage (based on Todd's "Nemesis" motif) with the "Alms" motif in "God, That's Good!" (ex. 9.7d). Instead, at the end of the song (pp. 241–42 in the score) Sondheim combined its main theme with the attractive "regal chair" melody that had grown out of the "Excuse me" passage; but this combination, while rhythmically balanced, seems harmonically forced. One cannot help feeling that the "regal chair" tune, generically a march trio, would have best returned in triumph on its own to make a conventional ABAB march structure. One can hardly cavil at Sondheim's deftness elsewhere, however, above all at the denouement of the plot, when Todd discovers that he has murdered Lucy. At this point, three themes are combined: the "Alms" motif forms the orchestral backbone in

6/4 and 9/4, Todd sings the "Lucy" motif to the words "Lucy . . . I've come home again," and Mrs. Lovett cackles away at a reprise of "Poor Thing," retelling her story in an irregular combination of 6/8 and other eighth-note meters. It all works, though Sondheim felt obliged to comment on its unorthodox appearance to his copyist: "(MATTIE—I know this looks weird, but it's the clearest layout I can think of)."

Sweeney Todd's reprise structure is its most outstanding feature. It works on the dual levels of motif and number, though the two interpenetrate a great deal, as my earlier discussion will have suggested and as the vertical lines in the diagrammatic ex. 9.1. show. As the plot accelerates to its catastrophe and the characters' actions and relationships strike home, motivic reprises come thicker and faster even than when they were being set up at the opening, and just as he became engrossed in setting the first twenty minutes of the play to music, so Sondheim "had a better time writing the last twenty minutes . . . than anything . . . since the background music of *Stavisky*" (Zadan 1990, 251). And insofar as it is possible to make a distinction between recurrent motifs and reprises of songs or parts of songs, the latter balance out into something approaching two strategies.

The first is that of concentric narrative frames (see Booth 1981, 63–65 for a discussion of such framing devices in ballad poetry). The outer frame is the "Ballad," heard complete as first (other than the organ "Prelude") and last event and in detached sections from time to time in the course of the show; it thus occupies a position in some ways the converse of that of Senta's ballad in Wagner's *Der Fliegende Holländer* which is heard complete in the middle of the action, a position from which it permeates the score. "There Was a Barber and His Wife," Todd's own narrative ballad, is like a closer focusing of the camera in a film and serves as a second, more intimate frame at each end. Then, respectively, we have the close focus on Mrs. Lovett's profession, character, and story in "The Worst Pies in London" and "Poor Thing," the latter, as we have just seen, being reprised prior to her death, and, closest of all, on Todd's profession as represented by his gleaming razors in "My Friends," reprised after his murder of the Judge. This fourfold closing-in and its reverse process at the end of the evening is highly cinematographic.

The second strategy is that of a parallel rather than mirror image, in that the action of act 2 replicates that of act 1 in a number of respects. Mrs. Lovett's pie shop has replaced Pirelli's booth as the public's nine-days'-wonder (one of the sketches toyed with "The Best Pies in London" as a punchline for the act 2 opening number), and the reprise of "Pirelli's Miracle Elixir" as "God, That's Good!" is a witty touch: Tobias, who opens both scenes, has changed his master but not his tune. "A Little Priest" follows Todd's flashes of epiphany in both acts and concludes his actions with resolve in each case. "Pretty Women" accompanies both of the Judge's visits to Todd's parlor. The melody of "Kiss Me" returns in the act 2 "Johanna" sequence as her incarceration in Fogg's Asylum is shown (in act 1 she was incarcerated in her guardian's house).

The Range of the Score

To sum up, nothing got in the way of Sondheim's organizing the score of *Sweeney Todd* to a self-sufficient degree not attempted with any of his earlier musicals. It is also true that its musical style ranges more earnestly. Blyton (1984, 20) identifies the influence of Stravinsky in the "Nemesis" motif, whose counterpointing of a modal with a chromatic melodic line is certainly a potent and characteristic twentieth-century tool. He also hears Weill in the score (Sondheim does not), as well as Britten and Bliss. Wagner's model of musical flux and representation, as developed by Puccini for purposes of verismo characterization, was as invaluable to Sondheim as it has been to countless other composers for the stage and screen. The later style of Vaughan Williams is suggested in the "Transition Music" between the first two scenes of act 1, while, at the far ends of the spectrum of British music, we have Renaissance and folk references in "Parlor Songs," as we have seen, and music hall breeziness in "Pirelli's Miracle Elixir," "God, That's Good!" and "By the Sea." And while waltz and romantic ballad, both amply represented, are international properties, the Broadway march never appears.

As for the influence of Herrmann, Sondheim has said that "there's a chord I kept using throughout, which is sort of a personal joke, because it's a chord that occurred in every Bernard Herrmann score" (Zadan 1990, 246), and has identified it as a tonic minor triad with added major seventh (pitch collection 0 1 4 8), specifying that the seventh has to be in the bass. It is easy to spot at the very beginning and end of the Judge's song, and is perhaps intended in the final refrain chord of "God, That's Good!" (see, for example, the last measure of p. 219 in the score), but hardly seems pervasive. The very first chord in the score is a minor I$^{\sharp 7}$, and it certainly provides a highly distinctive sonority, one with which the "Alms" music is always imbued. But it is in root position. Conversely, the labeling of a "Sweeney chord" (ex. 9.8a) in the sketches for "The Ballad of Sweeney Todd" does offer the semitone on the bottom, but within a more dissonant sonority (almost the same as the five-note cluster of intervals used in *Pacific Overtures*) that was soon abandoned—the closest approximation to this sonority in the score appears to be in "There Was a Barber and His Wife" (marked *x* in ex. 9.8b). In any case, Herrmann's Piano Concerto chord in *Hangover Square* (quoted in Gorbman 1987, 175)

Ex. 9.8a

Ex. 9.8b

Ex. 9.8c

is a diminished, not a minor triad with added major seventh (0 1 4 7), though its sonority is not very different.

The principle of symphonic contrast is highly developed in "Epiphany," with its extremes of musical articulation, and Sondheim has said that it took

> a month to get the tone of it right. I had to motivate Todd from wanting to kill one man to wanting to kill all men, the moment at which we felt Bond's play was weakest. To demonstrate musically that his mind is cracking I switched between violent and lyrical passages, and had rapid rhythmic shifts, from quick to slow. His murderous vengeance announced to a chugging engine-like theme (the *Dies Irae* disguised) alternates with a keening threnody for his wife and daughter. (Hirsch 1989, 125)

The result, as raw as *The Rite of Spring*'s "Danses des Adolescentes," forms the score's centerpiece, an essay in binary opposition. (As Todd says, "There are two kinds of men, and only two.") Other binary opposites radiate from it, first among them the number's humorous consequent, itself turning the coin from melodrama to farce, in the shape of "A Little Priest." We have already seen in chapter 1 how neatly the refrain of "A Little Priest," with its apprehension of reversing the history of the world by making "those above . . . serve those down below!" (the punning references to the position of Todd's parlor above Mrs. Lovett's shop and, in an earlier line, to "serving . . . up" are intentional), expresses the motivating forces underlying the plot and this particular pivot of it; we might add that its musical segmentation, interrupting Todd's smooth waltz tune with Mrs. Lovett's motivic chatter until the two come together in excruciating counterpoint (ex. 9.8c), sums up the difference between their respectively philosophic (or "moral"; see Mollin 1991, 406–8) and practical preoccupations while making it clear that their partnership is symbiotic. Here, lyrics and music together provide us with our own microcosmic epiphany, in twenty-four measures, as to what the whole thing is about.

This is indeed true if we take the score as a whole, and it is its most operatic aspect: it stands on its own as an aesthetic entity, scarcely needing production values and ingredients for it to be complete.

The Universal Ballad

Perhaps with the benefit of hindsight we can sense Sondheim beginning to pull away from the relationship with Hal Prince in *Sweeney Todd*. From the moment Sondheim fixed his designs on Bond's play it was essentially one man's vision, as an opera score is generally felt to be, and Prince was never fired by the project as Sondheim was. He burdened it with an "alienated" production that it simply did not need, for in effect he added yet another distancing frame to the narrative by dwarfing the stage sets with his surrounding factory, gantry, and hermeneutic drops. Admittedly the direct address to the audience in Sondheim's "Ballad" encourages this, with its mode of moral dialectic ("Sweeney waits in the parlor hall, / Sweeney leans on the office wall," "Isn't that Sweeney there beside you?"), and it seems rather as if Prince and Sondheim edged each other into a corner in which they had never quite intended to end up. Wittke (1980, 314) objected to the "didactic ending," and Hirsch's critique exemplifies the confusion about whether the "Ballad" betokens an alienated or metonymic theatricality.

> At the end of the play the cast pointed to the audience as they pretended to spot Sweeneys everywhere. Although Prince considered this direct address over-obvious, he agreed with Sondheim's view that it "was a valid way of saying that the need for revenge is a universal desire." But are there really Sweeneys all around us? A demonic dispossessed barber fixated on revenge who becomes a serial killer through contempt for his fellow man is surely not a figure of universal resonance. His story is too bizarre to stand the Everyman signification that the creators seem to want to assign it. (Hirsch 1989, 129–30)

The same question could presumably be asked of any murder mystery, and Sondheim's view of the piece undercuts Hirsch: we are, simply, all satisfied by revenge, and "everyone does it, if seldom as well / As Sweeney" (or as Sondheim, we might add). Hirsch nonetheless develops his Brechtian consideration.

> More promising as the moral archetype the show is searching for is the character of Mrs. Lovett, in whose rise to money is a satire and critique of capitalist enterprise such as Brecht and Weill might well have it portrayed in Berlin at the end of the twenties. As a bourgeoise with a criminal soul Mrs. Lovett is moral first cousin to the Peachums in *The Threepenny Opera*, guttersnipes who affect the manners of the moral majority. (Hirsch 1989, 130)

True, *Sweeney Todd* acknowledges a debt to Brecht's source, *The Beggar's Opera*, in such details as its use of the "Ballad" and "Parlor Songs" (Polly Plunkett's name, at least, reminds us of Lucy Lockit's) and in its

Ex. 9.9a

I am the Emp - 'ror of Ja - pan. _____ Is an-y-thing new for my birth - day. _____

Ex. 9.9b

At - tend to the tale of Swee - ney Todd

Ex. 9.9c

It's cer - tain-ly fine for Sun - day... _____

Ex. 9.9d

I must be - gin my jour - ney.

propensity to sing blithely even in the face of deepest distress or gro-
tesqueness (Johanna even makes a point about this: "If I cannot fly, let
me sing"). But the dramaturgical machinery of the plot and the motivic
machinery of the music are surely their own reward in terms of the
audience's aesthetic pleasure, and in the face of such a perfect touchstone
for this as the music shown in ex. 9.8c any further dialectical machinery
is superfluous.

However, there are persistent indicators in Sondheim's work that the
search for some universalizing agent of symbolism beyond the self-satis-
faction of plot mechanics had begun in earnest and would reappear when
the time was ripe. The connecting thread seems to have been the music
of children, in particular the compound-time rhythmic mode of the nursery
rhyme or children's game. The first abortive instance of this had been
the projected "Civilization" finale to *Pacific Overtures* (see chap. 8), with
its sing-song "birthday" tag (ex. 9.9a). This seems to have rubbed off
directly on the sketches for "The Ballad of Sweeney Todd" (ex. 9.9b),
perhaps not surprisingly given narrative balladry's age-old association
with compound meter (the "Hum," "My Friends," and portions of "A
Little Priest" were also initially sketched in compound time). In the first
London production of *Sweeney Todd,* and in the 1984 American opera
productions, the Beggar Woman also sang a fully fledged, narrative lullaby
to her imaginary baby during her dumb-show scene in act 2, to the music

of the 6/8 portion of "Poor Thing" (pp. 48–50 in the score), thereby adding yet another plane to the storytellings. The lyrics were as follows:

> And why should you weep then, my jo, my jing?
> [crooning] oo—oo . . .
> Your father's at tea with the Swedish king.
> He'll bring you the moon on a silver string.
>   [etc]

This additive phrasing before a refrain tag was used again in the context of youthful innocence, to an identical rhythm set as a satirical Irish jig, in the "Bobby and Jackie and Jack" cabaret tune in *Merrily We Roll Along*. The tag returned again in *Sunday in the Park* in the music for the girls and their cardboard-cutout soldier (ex. 9.9c), and, in "Children and Art," Sondheim explored further the approach to universal simplicity as represented not so much by the match of music and lyrics in the nursery rhyme as by the absolute basics of expression used by a child (or an artist) learning a language. Now, with hindsight, we can see that it was all leading to *Into the Woods* (see the tag in ex. 9.9d), where the universal and the childlike could at last take center stage, to the enrichment of Sondheim's art.

Chapter 10

Merrily We Roll Along

The Problem of the Show Musical

On 20 October 1979, at the fifth meeting to discuss their plans for a new musical based on George Kaufman and Moss Hart's 1934 play *Merrily We Roll Along,* Sondheim, Prince, and George Furth—the same basic team that created *Company* a decade earlier—had not yet decided whether to make the hero, a playwright in the original, a composer, violinist, politician, or director. Furth seemed to be talking himself into preferring a composer.

> It's much easier to show the first class talent of somebody if he's a composer. . . . A composer achieves greatness, a director doesn't. You can *demonstrate* the difference between mediocrity and good with a composer, you can't with a director. . . . Composers too often today end up being businessmen. . . . It can be an awfully old story "the symphony composer who ends up writing a musical" . . . i.e., BEGGAR ON HORSEBACK. . . . It's only good if it's freshly observed and original.

Sondheim added later in the meeting: "You're in trouble when you tell a show about show business." At their sixth meeting the following day, presumably having slept on it, he lit the problem from another angle: "A symphony composer who gives up that for a pop song career is a cliché. How do we avoid the cliché? Today [a film composer] is regarded the same as Stravinsky." (The thought was also scribbled down in Sondheim's "Misc. Songs" file—"Pop Groups are 'genius'—where does that leave Stravinsky?"—and surfaced in the end product as Joe Josephson's line, "I'll let you know when Stravinsky has a hit," in "Opening Doors.")

This line of exploration must have seemed a far cry from his last three Broadway musicals, with their virtuoso assurance, ripe for the structuralist decade, of objectivity of terminology and treatment, of content as form, of ambiguities as oppositions, of systems as self-sustaining. *A Little Night Music, Pacific Overtures,* and *Sweeney Todd* could all in a sense be measured

311

by their distance from New York. How was one to measure a musical about a composer of musicals (which was what the hero eventually became)?

Yet the "show musical," to repeat Altman's terminology, was a tried and tested type, one schematic solution to the perennial "cue for a song" problem that every musical must face every moment of its life. Sondheim had borrowed aspects of it in *Follies,* as we have seen, and would have no difficulty in making distinctions between "book" songs and diegetic numbers, on the basis of pastiche or some other method (he opted for a mixture of pastiche and thematic identification in *Merrily We Roll Along*). But it would be difficult to fix the audience's sympathy—and regrets— on Franklin Shepard, for the simple reason that the musical is about the compromise of his talent and we can only measure that talent by transferring it to Sondheim: we hear "Good Thing Going" as a classic of Sondheim's art, not of Frank and Charley's. This applies even more to "Opening Doors." Anyone can hear Frank trying to get "his" motif right as he composes at the piano; what is less noticed by listeners is that his obsession with the quickstep chord progression that will acompany it forms the "symphonic" basis of the entire song as it runs through his subconscious. Diegetically speaking, he suddenly hits on the right chords at the tenth attempt, but that is not the end of the matter, for there are no less than thirty-three different harmonic progressions presented in this rhythm in the course of the song. It is a tour de force, but Sondheim's, not Frank's; conversely, with the arguable exception of Gussie's act 2 opening (in the 1985 version she is seen diegetically singing a verse followed by a sleazy "strut" of "Good Thing Going"), we hear no bad music written by Frank, for Sondheim could hardly have written it without compromising *his* ideals.

Thus we are not able to accept Frank's potential for greatness on the basis of songs he is supposed to have written. At the same time, however, we are unable to reconstruct his character in terms other than his motivating demon, music. His speech as a high school guest is crass and immediately raises questions about his self-awareness (he is more overtly self-hating at this point in the original play). At the other end of the plot, we are initially (or rather finally) presented with him and his human relationships in the rooftop scene, in which his future stature can be indicated only by the speech about his time in the army.

> I lay there and tossed and turned and kept thinking about wasting those two years and then to come back and read this.... But now I get it. I was working too. I *didn't* waste it, Charley. I was writing every spare minute I could find over there. I didn't waste it. Charley, we're going to change the world.

The proof of this pudding will need to be in the eating, for his current stature is merely innocence and naïveté, confirmed in the song that this speech leads into, "Our Time." Yet we never get to the eating—we do not witness any portion of any of Frank and Charley's three successful musicals in its dramatic context, and in any case it is made clear, as an essential part of the plot, that these are potboilers, part of the point of the action being that their collaboration never progresses as far as the show they wanted to write together. And Frank's two "difficult" decisions, which we do witness, agreeing to write the show for Gussie and Joe and going to the first-night party rather than (in the 1981 version, at any rate) following Beth to hospital, can both only be judged as expedients, wise or unwise, in the light of his musical belief in himself, which we are never able to see either justified or misplaced. Characterization is thus somehow forever deferred, and we find ourselves in the deconstructivist's dilemma, in which terms and equivalences cannot be pinned down but keep shifting ground.

Even if Frank's music is not felt to be the sole fulcrum of this deferral, it has to be said that another dramatic pivot, all the talk about dreams and ideals, seems to this author to cut little ice with an audience's sympathies. That this is not merely an Anglican reaction to an American scenario is supported by the fact that the same point was made about the original play in an editorial in *The Stage* in November 1934.

> The theme of the piece . . . is one of those which everybody is familiar with and nobody takes very seriously. That is that young men acquire things called ideals in college, and lose them afterwards. This never was more than half true. It is equally true (and it would make much more stirring drama) that men also acquire a lot of sturdy fighting ideals after they leave college which they never dreamed of when they were busy among their books. (*The Stage* 1934, 23)

Another way of seeing the dramatic problem of *Merrily We Roll Along* is to argue that the dramatic postmortems on Frank's moments of expediency—career of expediency, if we take it from the graduation speech—that are what the reverse-order flashback scenes constitute, need a stronger mechanical prompt. In a different plot they might have received it from, say, a detective or a psychiatrist motivating the character in question to cast his or her mind farther and farther back; and in a sense we, the audience, are being asked to act as psychiatrists in *Merrily We Roll Along,* analyzing what it was in Frank that made him turn out the way he did. The fact that no deeply buried childhood experience or influence is uncovered that would help account for his personal trajectory is perhaps the most unsatisfactory

thing about the plot, compared, say, with that of *Citizen Kane*. But Sondheim disagrees.

> I've always thought that sled trivialized Kane . . . but the point is that
> Frank is the detective—it's not the audience . . . it's Frank who stops . . .
> and who causes the flashbacks. . . . I think it would be wrong to give
> a single reason for his misguidedness: he represents what this country
> is always in danger of . . . which is expediency. . . . It happens in certain
> eras in the country's history, and that's why Kaufman and Hart chose
> to deal with their postwar era, because that's when this kind of syn-
> drome is most prevalent. It's also true of the Eisenhower years, and
> subsequently.

Sondheim recognized from the fourth planning meeting on 9 October
1979 that "Our lead is a cipher . . . there's nothing redeeming in him." Yet
is this Frank's fault? As the Midwest golden boy with the opportunity for
greatness he is the American myth in essence, and insofar as that myth is
preeminently embodied in politics (anyone can grow up to be president),
one person's notion of the stewardship or prostitution of inherent gifts,
which is another's of the elitist values of the academy, scarcely comes into it,
for a politician's job is to make and seize opportunities, to get to the top and
stay there. He cannot exercise influence for good or ill unless he does. This
paradox must have struck the authors from the start, for Furth stated at the
sixth meeting, "Making it [the lead] a politician reaches for the highest ideals of this country. . . . Politics is still the exemplary thing to do with your
life," but added shortly afterward, "Corruption and politics go together. It's
on the nose," and developed the latter thought at the seventh meeting on 1
November.

> Advantage of using a politician is there's a built-in argument that's a
> controversy. The only people who are true to themselves are martyrs.
> Otherwise everyone compromises. "True to yourself" is really Jesus
> Christ. There's something about compromising yourself for a successful
> play. . . . I don't think it's so much . . . there's always another play.

So much for Shakespeare's lines, "This above all; to thine own self be
true [etc]," quoted by both the older and the younger Frank in their high
school speeches as a personal motto (and used in the original play). We
are almost in a position to sympathize with Frank more as the victim
of an unnecessarily guilty conscience than as the fallen idol: to feel that
he has every right to blame society for making him hate himself. In this
light, our tendency to sympathize with Charley may be inappropriate,

and in the original play it is effectively questioned in the restaurant scene when he spins a top, bought for his son, on the floor and Mary (or rather Julia, as she is named here) accuses him of never having grown up. Frank, in contrast, actually has a song entitled "Growing Up" in the 1985 La Jolla version of the musical.

The argument reaches a similar *impasse* if we refer it back to music, for it is popular music that Frank writes—there is never any hint of him being a frustrated symphonist or opera composer—and popular music's first duty is, presumably, to be popular. If only *Merrily We Roll Along* could cast light on how at the same time it might pursue a duty to be good. Anyone who can manage to fix an equation between these two factors will have come up with the philosopher's stone, overcoming the common "fallacy [in terms of opposing attitudes] . . . of a rough correlation between the merit of art and the degree of public response to it, . . . direct in one case and inverse in the other" (Frye 1957, 4). In a sense, *Merrily We Roll Along* shows us the two terms of the equation destroying each other: if Frank's ideal musical has no chance of making or holding the stage in the real world, then perhaps he is right to stop composing rather than continue producing potboilers (though the fact that he forsakes music for film and produces an awful one that, we suspect, is both a critical and commercial flop puts a stop to that line of argument).

"Wait," (as Charley says on television) " . . . because I'm getting in too deep here." Yet it was precisely the same deep water that Sondheim, Prince, and Furth found themselves in when, in what is surely the greatest irony of their careers, *Merrily We Roll Along* seemed to fall prey to the problems underlying its conception rather than make order out of them and closed after sixteen performances. Had they failed artistically because they had failed commercially? Furth later commented to James Lapine, in June 1983, that "Charley is about purity of purpose, dedication, sense of values, the reward of keeping it simple. Prototype would be me (forgive me but I feel that). Steve, you." This is somehow easier to depict in terms of a playwright's values than those of a composer: for some reason there is less of a gap between popular and intellectual theater than there is between popular and intellectual music (the difference is perhaps summed up in the immemorial role of comedy in all kinds of theater as opposed to its habitual absence from music known by definition as "serious"), and thus Charley's integrity can more credibly remain intact throughout what nonetheless must have been a commercial career. All the same, playwrights were among the multifarious names of the living and the dead that cropped up in the creators' preliminary discussions as partial models for Frank's character and career.

Might Sondheim and Prince have included themselves in the list? Given its comprehensiveness, it would begin to look smug if they did not (in Hirsch's words [1989, 135], they "made themselves vulnerable to being accused of looking down from on high at theater professionals who succumb to commerce"); equally it would seem narcissistic if they did. Furth reminded his collaborators, at their third meeting, that

> we deal, in musicals, in a collaborative field so we aren't as true to our own star as the painter, Crale [Crale in Kaufman and Hart's orginal play became Charley]. Someone who doesn't compromise himself is a romantic ideal. That type (as in HORSE'S MOUTH, Jackson Pollock) is crazy, which is a nice character and explains his volatility.

Prince reminded his critics, however, that "People think you set out to iconize yourselves, but you set out to do shows" (Hirsch 1989, 134). Yet their understandable and, in a sense, proper reluctance to identify with the hero, still less with "the suffocating Blob" (Sondheim's term, used at the sixth production meeting, for humankind as party animal) of which by the time of act 1, scene 2 Frank himself, and certainly the drunken Mary, have become a part, is ours too. It is probably not just an Englishman who finds it difficult to extract a guiding and personable metaphor from a bunch of Hollywood sophisticates. Casting all the characters as teenagers in the initial Broadway production was intended to overcome this with a counterbalance of innocence, but the gap was too wide for a Broadway audience to close. The same appears to have been the case with the reverse chronology. Its ironic role is clear enough, and in representing movement in the wrong direction it provides a metaphor for Frank's career. It also complements and acts as a foil to the representation, in the teenage casting, of stasis at one end of the spectrum of experience. This, similarly, offers the metaphorical equivalent of Charley's childlike, maybe childish "consistency" and Mary's unrequited love, both qualities that, while admirable in their constancy, are obstructive and wounding to Frank, who genuinely suffers as a result of Charley's misbehavior on television and Mary's drunkenness at his party. Does anybody really grow up?

The Historical Metaphor

A play, musical or otherwise, is a structure of interlocking and hierarchical problems and metaphors—in short, symbolic actions—and it may be difficult to locate the knife-edge between rich texture and confusion in what results. This is certainly the case with *Merrily We Roll Along*, in which, to judge from Zadan's account of its Broadway production (1990, 269–82), the symbols got in each other's way, just as the collaborators producing them did (the original choreographer, Ron Field, the original leading actor, and the entire wardrobe of costumes were all jettisoned at the last moment). It is generally agreed, however, that the score itself, while not intent on matching *Sweeney Todd* as an authoritative entity able to carry all other production values with it, was not a liability, and it is on this understanding that we shall examine it, though we shall also find that an analysis of it, its later variants (primarily for the 1985 La Jolla production) and its genesis casts light on the show's dilemmas (see Mandelbaum 1990 for a comprehensive account of *Merrily*'s continuing metamorphoses). We might add that the survival of the score has been greatly aided by the fact that, musically speaking, the original performance was, by and large, first-rate, as the compact disk reissue of the cast recording makes doubly clear.

One of the symbolic resources in the plot that may be felt to have been underdeveloped in the musical (it is more pointedly worked out in the original play) is its parallel to the American, or indeed the overall postwar, historical experience. In fact Sondheim's notes reveal that this might have been much more pervasive and overt had the decision not at some point been made to restrict its newsreel or "list song" aspect of remembered facts and artifacts to the 1960 nightclub scene, where it has the advantage of sharpening the likeness between the optimistic youngsters and the Kennedys they are singing and joking about. True to type, they satirize the current affairs of their elders as in countless end-of-year college revues or periodical lampoons (and this was the era when such escapades could yield macrocosmic opportunities for the talented, witness the careers of Tom Lehrer in America and several generations of the Cambridge Footlights in Britain).

> BETH: It's nineteen sixty . . .
> FRANK: And gosh, what a swell year it's been!
> ALL THREE: So many blessings,
>   Such wonders it has brought,
>   You hardly know where to begin:
>   There's Xerox and lasers,
>   The Twist and the "Pill,"
>   A city in Brazil . . .
> BETH: . . . That no one wants to fill . . .
> ALL THREE: Khrushchev stopped screaming
>   And Librium came in.
> CHARLEY: And Nixon didn't win.
> ALL THREE: Goodbye then to Ike and the brass,
>   To years that were cozy but crass.

This approach was originally envisaged for the show as a whole by means of the "Merrily We Roll Along" transitions. These are kept on a ruthlessly short leash in the score, their references restricting themselves to the basic (and, it has to be said, rather tiresome) metaphors of traveling and dreaming. In the sketches, and still to a certain extent in the first preview performances (see Mandelbaum 1990, 17), a history metaphor complemented the geography one. Economic and personal career history characterized the "First Transition," at the end of act 1, scene 2, the fragments comprising the list being punctuated by choral "Bump!"'s in the potholed road (the subtextual pun on "impression" brings this out nicely).

> Bump!
> There's a mortgage.
> Bump!
> A recession.
> Bump!
> Making—
> Bump!
> —A bad impression.
> Bump! Bump!
> What was that?
> The wrong profession.

The "Third Transition," at the end of act 1, scene 4 (which would thus have needed to be updated to 1975 or thereabouts), particularly highlighted the musical's theme of the betrayal of trust and integrity.

> Local hero,
> Bump!
> Name of Spiro,
> Bump!
> Has so many major concerns
> Bump!
> He forgot to file his returns.
> Bump!
> Someone at the Watergate
> Bump!
> Is discovered working late.

The sketches include a list of further references.

> Watergate
> Bangladesh
> Geo. Wallace
> Mexican ill

Ms. (?)
Clifford Irving
Bobby Fischer
PLO (at Olympics)

The "Fifth Transition" (using the numbering of the vocal score, which is different than that of the script), at the end of act 2, scene 1, included the following, which got as far as the stage.

> Cuba has missiles.
> Washington bristles.
> There go the good cigars.

There was also a line about "Pre-fried and freeze-dried and tie-dyed," and there was a sketched list incorporating things British to evoke the post-Kennedy "British invasion."

G.B. denied entry into Common Market
. . .
Beatles
. . .
Great Train Robbery
. . .
Christine Keeler

Sketches for the 1960 "Transition" include a reference to the Berlin wall.

Frank, of course, is Ben in *Follies* all over again, filling us in on the details of the roads he did not take, though likely to end up seedy rather than possessed of Ben's hollow dignity. A further link with *Follies* would have become evident if the wealth of chronicle indicated here had been retained in the "Transition" lyrics, for they would have formed something like a macrocosmic version of "I'm Still Here," its stanzas composed out over the span of a whole score (perhaps the cue was taken from the segments of the ballad in *Sweeney Todd*). Would this have dragged the show down? Possibly—it made for too long an evening at the first preview performances, and in any case the "Transitions" worked less well when the musical was recast with mature actors in some later productions (see Mandelbaum 1990, 21). But as it stands, the "Merrily" music never quite impresses itself firmly enough upon us. The onomatopoeic basic motif (ex. 10.1a, approximating to the rhythm of a year being called out) is apt enough, and genuinely moving with its sense of bright-eyed anticipation and alertness when it occurs for the last time right at the end of

Ex. 10.1a

Ex. 10.1b

Ex. 10.1c

Catch-ing at dreams . . . __   Roll-ing a - long . . . __   Roll-ing a - long . . . __

the show; but the melody remains a utility, not an essence, possibly because, unlike the "journeying" music devised subsequently for *Into the Woods,* and still less like the indefinitely extendable yet fulfilling songs in *Sunday in the Park,* it lacks a satisfying release (any hope of it residing in group I's "Dreams don't die" passage is immediately squashed when group II is superimposed bitonally).

Concordances of the Reverse Narrative

One of the things Sondheim did consider doing with the "Merrily" melody was to present each of its phrases in retrograde (see ex. 10.1b), as though in some curiously diatonic serial segmentation. Was this intended as a counterpoint to the tune in its prime form? It would have fitted snugly. (The phrase *x,* of course, is already inverted in the melody as found in the score to form *xI;* see ex. 10.1c.) It would also have been the converse, microcosmically speaking, of what happens in the show as a whole, where each scene moves in a conventional forward direction but the sequence of scenes is in reverse. In fact one of the weaknesses of the book of the musical is that it makes less of this temporal counterpoint than does the original play, whose every scene ends with a melodramatic event or gesture of some sort (the most violent of these, the iodine throwing at the hero's party, was eventually incorporated into the musical in 1985).

Arranging the elements of a literary or musical narrative as a pure, discrete chronological series is rare outside the theater. Most conventional large-scale musical forms involve some form of recapitulation, and just as for centuries the novel has not only exploited the flashback but devised the frame of a storyteller (whose described presence implies a second one) casting his or her mind back—most novels are still written in the past tense, just as most paintings are still enclosed within a rectangular frame— so opera, particularly in the nineteenth century when it began to take its models not just from theatrical narrative but from the novel, utilized thematic flashbacks and reprises, habitually counterbalancing them with the overture as a series of thematic forewarnings (we note that *Merrily We Roll Along* is Sondheim's first musical since *Anyone Can Whistle* to have a traditional overture of this type). Opera, too, sometimes uses the frame of the storyteller or narrator; Britten's *Turn of the Screw, Billy Budd,* and *Gloriana* are notable in this respect, as are Tippett's *New Year* with its Presenter, Offenbach's *Tales of Hoffmann,* Kodály's *Háry János* and many others. Sondheim himself had already written within a spoken narrative frame in *Pacific Overtures* and a sung one in *Sweeney Todd,* and the Liebes-lieders in *A Little Night Music* have a somewhat comparable function (*A Little Night Music* makes considerable use of fragmentary reprises toward the end, keeping them within the plot). But it is most common for a series of flashbacks, separated or running without interruption, to remain in prime, not retrograde, chronological order. In abstract music, a sonata-allegro recapitulation conventionally keeps the units in the order in which they first appeared, even when wholesale recomposition is involved, and mirror-image recapitulation is something special, thought of as a palin-dromic device. We have already noted how Sondheim moved a little in this direction in *Sweeney Todd.*

Science, on the other hand, long before the doctrine of relativity, was fascinated with time. To understand it would be to be able to manipulate it—hence the theme of aging and its reversal or arrest in Gothic horror. One good example of this is Hardy's poem "The Clock of the Years," in which a Faustian tampering with the fixed law of memory occurs when a man wishes his dead beloved to be remembered as young rather than as he last saw her; the Spirit reverses the clock (to a reversed cycle of fifths in Gerald Finzi's musical setting of the poem) but is "loth to stop it where you will" and conjures up younger and younger images of the girl until her picture is wiped out altogether: "she smalled till she was nought at all." Another instance is Wilde's novel, *The Picture of Dorian Gray.* The standard scientific countdown with its whimsically implicit time reversal apparently originates in Fritz Lang's film *By Rocket to the Moon,* and reminds us that the very existence of the genre of science fiction relies upon the notion of being able to reverse time and know the future, as does that of the Utopian novel (often cast as a dream). There are flickering shadows of both these genres in the rooftop scene of *Merrily We Roll Along,*

the one in the observation of Sputnik and the other in Frank's excla-
mations, "Charley, we're going to change the world" and "we're going
to be able to do . . . anything we can dream of." Nor was Kaufman and
Hart's play the first "experiment" of this sort (the word retains something
of its scientific application) with time in the theater: J. B. Priestley's
reading of philosopher J. W. Dunne's *An Experiment with Time* (1927) and
its theory called serialism led to his group of "time" plays, of which
Dangerous Corner (1932) was the first.

"Art" music developed independent uses for the word *serialism* in the
1920s. On a technical level, music has its own intellectual tradition of
time reversal in the melodic retrograde, stemming from the mensural and
puzzle canons of the Renaissance and after. This, doubtless, was what
was in Sondheim's mind when he wrote the music shown in ex. 10.1b.
Bach wrote retrograde canons, Haydn minuets that go backwards. The
nineteenth century was less interested in such matters, but the twentieth
has witnessed, in addition to the whole paraphernalia of twelve-tone serialism, the use of strict palindrome on a small scale in Messiaen's non-
retrogradable rhythms and on a larger canvas in works such as the
"Praeludium" and "Postludium" of Hindemith's *Ludus Tonalis* and the
last movement of Tippett's Third Piano Sonata. Perhaps most important
is the palindromic interlude at the center of Berg's *Lulu.* This accompanies
a silent film whose latter half shows, as does Lulu's entire career on a
macrocosmic level, how events leading up to and away from the central
point of the action (Lulu's time in prison) mirror each other in reverse.
Film, of course, can actually be run backward.

It is pertinent to dwell on these matters because they are, like the
multiple perspectives of cubism, part and parcel of the modernist legacy
in art. The spoken theater has easily absorbed them; for instance, Pinter's
Betrayal and Churchill's *Top Girls* both plot a love affair backwards, and
Ayckbourn is fond of comparable devices. We have grown to expect conscious and willful technical manipulation, often to the point of virtuosity,
of symbolic modes of experience, and, in this respect, Sondheim has to
be seen, along with Prince, as modernism's chief exponent in the musical.

However, *Merrily We Roll Along,* at least until it dispensed with the opening and closing scenes in the 1985 La Jolla production, is still within the
relatively tame flashback convention. The call of "How did you get there
from here, Mister Shepard?" in the graduation scene makes this clear,
though the reversible terms are a clever ambiguity: "get there from here"
means both "arrive at the past from the present" along the time axis and,
its opposite using the metonymy of space, "progress to the platform from
the audience" (Sondheim does in fact reverse the phrase to "get here from
there" at one point in the show). But narrative models for a reverse-order

sequence of flashbacks are rare, as we have seen, while musically, perhaps the work most analogous to what is required of *Merrily We Roll Along* is d'Indy's *Istar*, a set of symphonic variations that proceeds backward: "Cleverly following the programme from the sixth chant of the Assyrian epic poem of Izdubar, relating the voyage of gradual self-discovery and denudation of the daughter of Sin, the variations are progressively stripped of their ornamentation to reveal their theme at the close" (Orledge 1980, 222); the theme is eventually heard in a heady orchestral unison, entirely unaccompanied.

Merrily We Roll Along is hardly a musical striptease, though its authors should perhaps have bargained for a comparable sense of theatrical disappointment when its callow teenagers finally became their gauche selves in the scene on the rooftop. But Sondheim did attempt something similar to d'Indy's reverse succession of musical events and hence, to a degree, of musical rhetoric.

Musical Planes: Frank and Gussie

There are four planes of music in the show. The first is that of Frank and Gussie, whose relationship forms the central activity of the plot, even its tragedy, for all said and done this is what the flaws in Frank's character amount to, and they strike home in his dealings with Gussie. As if in recognition of this, his musical motif and hers (exs. 10.2a and c) are both based on a returning upward fourth followed by stepwise descent (transposed up an octave in Frank's case, in line with his idealistic optimism— his motif, at least in "The Hills of Tomorrow," has the ring of "a carillon of campus chimes" [Ratcliffe 1990]). One of the dramaturgical miscalculations of the original show (it has been considerably ameliorated in the subsequent revisions; see Mandelbaum 1990) seems to have been that it was difficult for the audience to grasp, from verbal content alone, exactly where Frank had ended up in the first scene unless they remembered two speeches: his acknowledgment to the high school audience, "I've suffered some reverses recently," and his comment in the following scene that he was only going to accept the school's commencement invitation "if my movie flops, my marriage collapses, my life falls apart and I need some good press." Whatever Frank's state of self-awareness in saying this, we were to understand that his marriage to Gussie did fail, but the "EX-MRS. SHEPARD" sweatshirt in the initial production must have looked all too like a desperate dramatic remedy to ensure that the audience got the point.

Most of the cutouts from the original production and rewrites for the 1985 La Jolla version had to do with Frank and/or Gussie. Gussie's musical motif, used in "society" scenes with its blues-based chromaticism stamping

Ex. 10.2a

Ex. 10.2b

Ex. 10.2c

Ex. 10.2d

Ex. 10.2e

Ex. 10.2f

her with something of the femme fatale within the context of a weary society trying to be active, was the basis of the accompaniment to "Darling!" a monologue for her (in the company or presence of Mary, Joe, and a friend called Kate) that was cut from the Polo Lounge scene during previews. Her melodic chatter in this song was a reprise of the "Darling!" passages in "The Blob" (itself cut from the original production) that at

Ex. 10.2f—*Continued*

the same time echoed another cutout, "Honey," in their opening rhythm (see exs. 10.2b, i and ii) and thus linked the two wives; it also used another cocktail snippet of melody heard elsewhere. An earlier version of the song, for Gussie and Kate, was quite different musically, based on independent material and more of a virtuoso patter number (Gussie's nervous gossip was interspersed with kisses). The "Darling" motif also formed the title material of "That Frank," used in the 1985 revival and retained since, essentially a new version of "Rich and Happy" (whose title melody was abandoned) sung about Frank rather than by him.

Frank's musical motif belongs primarily but not exclusively to his diegetic songs (the ones he is supposed to have composed). It is possible that the changes made concerning these numbers were not unconnected with the issue we have already touched on, namely that Frank's status as a composer can never, given the dramatic medium, be entirely clear. Is he a one-song man, his recurrent motif indicating that he has no more tunes in him? Or does the motif represent steadfastness of vision? Do we, the listeners, even have to decide which it is? Whatever the case, there was originally an extra (though minuscule) nightclub number, "Thank You For Coming," presumably designed to show what had happened to the song Joe Josephson did not like ("Who Wants to Live in New York?"; ex. 10.2d), but it should also be pointed out that "Everything's Perfect," an incompletely sketched nightclub number that "Bobby and Jackie and Jack"'replaced, had a chorus that was similarly a waltz but was not based on Frank's motif. There was also a central B section for "The Hills of Tomorrow" that is not in the vocal score though it is in the vocal selections. "The Hills of Tomorrow," again using Frank's motif, represents the song from which all Frank's later compositions are supposed to have sprung, and again we wonder how sophisticated a style it is intended to convey, clever exemplar of a tenor-based, semimodern partsong that it is (while it is not a parody, its voice leadings are somewhat tendentious). It sounds like an imitation of someone such as Leo Sowerby—but is it Frank's or Sondheim's imitation?

Possibly the best musical change made in 1985 and kept thereafter was the composition of an entirely new number, the song "Growing Up" mentioned earlier. It occurs twice, like "Not a Day Goes By," once in each act, and shows Frank musing on what is happening to him, thus in a more sympathetic light than is cast on him anywhere else. It also gives him a generous scene with Gussie. In fact his thoughts here begin to foreshadow the "move on" philosophy of *Sunday in the Park,* and Gussie anticipates some of the maxims and layered thoughts of *Into the Woods* while still conveying her superciliousness.

> You decide on what you want, darling,
> Not on what you think you should.
> Not on what you want to want, darling,
> Not from force of habit.
> Once it's clearly understood, darling,
> Better go and grab it.

The song mixes, with equally positive effect, several of the show's musical motifs. At the beginning, Frank is doodling with "Good Thing Going" at the piano but interpolating Gussie's "Meet the Blob" melody (ex. 10.2e, itself a variant of "Honey" and "Darling!") from the number of that name (see ex. 10.2f). Later Gussie sings her philosophy in a 12/8 version of her motif, and this is followed by a passage in which the original "Good Thing Going" accompaniment is enabled to support not only these two melodies in counterpoint but a variant of the "Rich and Happy" vamp as well (ex. 10.2g). From the score the techniques look a little too self-conscious, but the song works well enough in performance.

The "Merrily" music and that of "The Blob" (the latter the converse of friendship) are on the second plane, choral in the sense of constituting a commentary, abstract in the first case, gossipy in the second. The third plane, sharing some material with the second, is that of the songs connected by the "friendship" transformations, as described below. The fourth concerns Frank's private life with Beth and comprises "Not a Day Goes By," heard complete in both acts, and "Honey," which was cut from the production and whose two stanzas (sung respectively by Beth and Frank with rejoinders from the other) straddled the first of the two statements of "Not a Day Goes By" that occurred in the nightclub wedding scene.

Modular Furniture: The Popular Song Analyzed

The sense of reverse musical structure is concentrated on the "friendship" plane. Sondheim's own account explains how it works.

> Since *Merrily We Roll Along* is about friendship, the score concentrates attention on the friendship of Mary, Frank and Charley by having all their songs interconnected through chunks of melody, rhythm and accompaniment. And since the story moves backwards in time, it presented an opportunity to invent verbal and musical motifs which could be modified over the course of the years, extended and developed, reprised, fragmented, and then presented to the audience in reverse: extensions first, reprises first, fragments first. For example, a release in one song would turn up later—later in the show but earlier in time—as a refrain in another (e.g., "Rich and Happy"/"Our Time"), a melody would become an accompaniment ("Old Friends"/"Opening Doors"), a chorus would be reprised as an interlude ("Like It Was"/ "Old Friends"), and so on, according to the relative importance of the characters' feelings at each point in their lives. Along with this would be the transformation of Frank's hit song from "The Hills of Tomorrow" through his development of it during "Opening Doors," which we actually witness, to its emergence as "Good Thing Going."
>
> In fact, if the score is listened to in reverse order—although it wasn't written that way—it develops traditionally. (Liner Notes, Broadway cast recording)

Ex. 10.3

Elsewhere Sondheim has likened this thematic process, whether or not consciously in accordance with Prince's transformational set and (after the event) the functional sweatshirts worn by the cast, to "modular furniture that you rearrange in a room: two chairs become a couch, two couches at an angle become a banquette" (Zadan 1990, 270). Something of this same approach will become evident in *Sunday in the Park* and, more pervasively, *Into the Woods*.

Perhaps the key phrase in the previously quoted liner notes is "according to the relative importance of the characters' feelings," for its application to the score can tell us something about the psychological anatomy of the Broadway song, a genre to which the music wholeheartedly returns for the first time in a Sondheim show since *Follies*. Ex. 10.3 gives the five musical units that are shifted around and shows them as they *last*—that is, first, plotwise—appear in the score. I shall trace their destinies backward.

"Our Time" is the simplest tune and purest structure in the show, an eight-measure, downbeat refrain (though on its first statement an upbeat is appended), harmonically complete with an (almost) classical four-part imperfect cadence at the halfway point (ex. 10.4a). It caps the downward scalar contour of its verse by descending through an octave, though its final achievement of the tonic is transferred to the upper register. In all these respects it represents rightness and simple fulfilment of the terms at hand, as a refrain should. Its return at the other end of the show, in "Rich and Happy," shows how all these values have been displaced. Frank is singing a thirty-two-measure chorus, a song, based, like "Our Time," on the downward scale as the skeleton of an eight-measure musical paragraph, but now the scale starts from the leading tone, seventh of the

Ex. 10.4a

Worlds to change__ and worlds to win.__

Ex. 10.4b

Who says 'Lone-ly at ___ the top?'

I say 'Let it nev - er stop!' It's

my time com-ing through,__ All my dreams __ com-ing true.__

Gor - geous house,__ gor - geous wife,__ Who wants an - y more from life?__

Skies are beam-ing,

Ex. 10.4c

[Moderato (♩ 84)]

Hey, old friend, Are__ you o - kay, old friend? What__ do you say, old

sempre staccato

[*p*]

sempre staccato

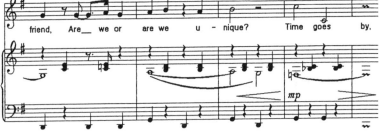

friend, Are__ we or are we u - nique? Time goes by,

mp

mp

Ex. 10.4d

Piu mosso (♩ = 132)

Good friends point out your lies, Where-as old friends live and let live.

tonic chord (it sets off from ex. 10.3, 3, the "Blob" motif, which accompanies it). The "Our Time" phrase appears after sixteen measures, as the release. A release (also known as a "bridge" or "middle eight") should be just what its name denotes, a B passage of emotional comfort, a broadening vision after the repeated rhetorical proposition of the A section, with melodic height (it is habitually at the top of the tessitura) and harmonic depth (often a modulatory sequence based on a cycle of fifths). Frank uses it to persuade himself that, as in the "Our Time" refrain, all is well and not "Lonely at the top." But he overreaches himself when he attempts a third rising sequence (Tunick's trill in the accompaniment seems to underline the point instinctively), significantly to the blinkered transformation of the original words: "It's my time" (in "That Frank" the lyrics are "It's his time / Coming through, / He is hot. / He is due."). This takes the release beyond its statutory function with an extra eight measures and almost strands it in E major, from which it has to make a convoluted harmonic return to the reality of C major (ex. 10.4b). It is an uncomfortable though carefully considered corollary to the modulatory invention in the songs of Kern for which Sondheim had expressed admiration so many years earlier, and accordingly we may feel that the "real" release to "Rich and Happy" never appears, or that it is effectively catered for by the "Best thing that ever could have happened" transition heard in the Overture (p. 8, system 3 in the score).

The "Old Friends" motif (ex. 10.3, 2) originates in "Opening Doors" as the accompaniment vamp to its refrain (p. 203 in the score). It has the rhythmic catchiness of a one-measure riff, its second measure a step lower for harmonic reasons (the context is basically dominant to tonic, despite its melodic appearance to the contrary), and thus suits its function well. Its melodic apotheosis occurs within the convention of climactic dance transformations. The first one, excepting a drafted but unincorporated appearance of the song's ending, "But here's to us—Who's like us? Damn few!" to cap the Kennedy nightclub number, is where it appears as the whirling coda to "It's a Hit!" in the 3/8 meter of a fast waltz, climactic and symbolic of the high point of Frank and Charley's friendship, though not present in the draft of what was originally a more substantial number containing material that would have been all too pertinent when the show itself became a flop (as it is, there is a section of "It's a Hit!" that is on the recording but not in the score). In fact, very early sketches for the "Old Friends" melody were drafted in compound time, as we witness it here. In a typical Broadway production number, a brief waltz break such as this is followed by a proud return to quadruple time for the final "strut" in a proportionally broader tempo, and this is roughly how the song "Old Friends" itself relates to its 3/8 melodic precursor— the friends are using it to demonstrate that they have come through together. Its final appearance, as the verse to "Like It Was," casts it as an emotional reminiscence, offstage as it were, soft and shorn of its Broadway beat, technically a verse but psychologically like an underscore reprise preparing us for the character's "real" song to follow.

The eponymous "Blob" motif (ex. 10.3, 3) is another riff, its three-beat jingle spanning two measures with internal cross-rhythmic repetition before repeating as a unit. As such it is an apt vamp for the mindless party babble that it symbolizes (and that also accompanies it in nonmusical form, prerecorded on tape). Its reappearance in "Rich and Happy" is essentially in a large-scale reprise of the act 2 "Blob" number, but with the significant difference that Frank now bases a main song melody on the motif, duplicating its first two notes (see the last complete measure of ex. 10.4b)—he has succumbed to its values. Its further elevation into a release in "Merrily We Roll Along," discussed earlier, is, if musically problematic, all the more dramatically apt in that its inappropriateness in this role underlines the ironic misbelief that "Dreams don't die."

The material shown in ex. 10.3, 4, first sung to Joe Josephson's "So We'll Do a New Show" patter, is a verse melody—that is, something intrinsically freestanding, new and different but nonetheless melodically somewhat shortwinded and accordingly expected to gel into the broader reaction of a refrain or chorus. It matches the situation the words are describing and attempting to induce—a fresh start for Frank—though the uncertainty of his reaction also seems built in to the uncertainty of its formal consequent: we are not sure whether Charley's "Best thing that ever could have happened" phrase is a refrain for the song as a whole, with "Now You Know" effectively a separate song, or a kind of release within the verse with "Now You Know" as the refrain. Perhaps the distinction is, formally, only one of scale and hence perspective. The question recurs when the music does, in Charley's "Franklin Shepard, Inc." Here the patter has the enhanced momentum of a *moto perpetuo:* it arises not at the beginning of the song but, like a chorus, as the vehicle of its settling down—Frank is in the unquestioning swing of his new career. A variant of the "Best thing" phrase ("He flies off to California") forms the B section not of a thirty-two-measure AABA form but a sixteen-measure AABB one, like a release (or is it, again, a refrain?) that is here to stay, a broadening that is not vision but achievement. From Charley's point of view, of course, this whole context is false and out of control.

Finally, there is the "Like It Was" melody, ex. 10.3, 5, which arises as a double-time "frantic" interlude in "Old Friends" (the implied context is a "friendship" dance routine, and this is the section in which they start arguing). Its derivation by diminution from the "Old Friends" music should be clear from exs. 10.4c and d (the melody falls a step after one measure rather than two, and the bass walks in quarter notes rather than half notes), as should its burlesque character from the accompaniment, with its frenetic, cross-rhythmic sixteenth notes and their chromaticisms. Mary's song, "Like It Was," at least retains the opening phrases of the "Good friends" melody but mellows the accompaniment to a soft harmonic focus of pure nostalgia. As a ballad of regret and as the chorus to her equally nostalgic "Old Friends" reprise it lets the melody go its own way of reminiscence, blossoming inasmuch as it misremembers the past, for Mary departs from the original tune at the line "You and me, we were nicer then," spinning it into an attractive melodic fantasy that bears little relationship to its starting point. (It is one of the loveliest numbers in the score, though it tends to be overlooked.) Yet this process is reflexive, in that she realizes what she has done with the melody: blamed "the way it is / On the way it was. / On the way it / Never / Ever was." (The music is also pastiche insofar as it fits the cocktail lounge over whose loudspeakers it can be imagined wafting, thanks especially to Tunick's jazz combo orchestration highlighting flute, muted trumpets, gentle percussion, and bass.)

Another reflexive touch, and one that bears careful investigation, is the way this macrocosmic compositional critique of a Broadway song's anatomy is also embedded microcosmically in Frank and Charley's "Who Wants to Live in New York?" song, which they perform for Joe Josephson in "Opening Doors." Frank, as we have heard in his diegetic composing at the piano earlier in the number, is obsessed with his "Hills of Tomorrow" motif (ex. 10.2c), and the first half of their thirty-two-measure song, the repeated A section, is relentlessly based on it. But this is too much for Joe: all he wants is a heart-warming release, and he sings a perfectly good eight-measure one as he butts in with "That's great! That's swell!" (its slight similarity to "That Frank" is stronger in the sketches). He does the same thing when he interrupts the end of their B¹ section two measures from the end, just as it is climaxing (after the top F); in fact at this point he provides a perfectly good "refrain" ending—"his" song would presumably have to be called "A Hummable Melody"—to their "motif" song (see chap. 3 for a discussion of these terms), though it is lengthened beyond the quadratic expectation of two measures and has a coda appended. The paradoxes of all this make it a good joke, thanks to its moving in and out of the planes of diegetic and nondiegetic song: in his interruptions Joe unconsciously becomes a good composer while preventing us from witnessing the proofs of good composition in Frank and Charley's song (we shall never hear Frank's release or know what Charley would have rhymed with "noise" in his climax line "But ever since I met you, I . . . "); conversely, what he *thinks* is good composition turns out to be diegetically bad music in the shape of a misremembered (and, on the recording, flat) rendition of "Some Enchanted Evening." The whole process is a delightful example of the conundrum outlined earlier, that of Sondheim the good composer getting in the way of his characters' music. He seems to signal to us that he recognizes this fact, by making "Who Wants to Live in New York?" a sort of verbal paraphrase of one of his own early songs (a good one, to boot), "What More Do I Need?" and by dredging up the old saw about his not writing hummable tunes.

Before leaving this aspect of the score's structure we must observe that Sondheim's description applies it to "verbal motifs" as well as music. "Thank you for coming" is a phrase used by Frank to dismiss an auditioning soprano "before" he makes it the title of a nightclub song. There are some nicely ironic reversed propositions in "Now You Know," notably the tactless Gossip Columnist's "If you want to have weddings, / Then you have to have divorces— / No?" As for the lyrics to the musical passages discussed previously, those of "Old Friends" simply travel with the tune without any pointed or ominous transformations; in contrast, I have already commented on "Our Time" becoming "My time" (via the variant "Your time" at the end of act 1, as discussed subsequently); this too stays with its tune. So does another, easily missed example: Charley's "Best thing that ever could have happened" in "Now You Know," which becomes "Very sneaky how it happens" when he sings it in "Franklin Shepard, Inc."—though without the words one might hesitate to relate the two melodic lines. The lines "We're the movers and we're the shapers. / We're the names in tomorrow's papers," on the other hand, sung by Frank, Charley, and Mary in "Our Time," change their tune when they become "These are the movers, / These are the shapers, / These are the people that / Give you vapors . . ." as Mary misquotes them back at Frank at the other end of the show, during his Bel Air party. The most piquant example of transformed lyrics, however, lies outside the "modular furniture" confines and occurs when an entire song, "Not a Day Goes By," is reprised, phrases such as Frank's intimate "But you somewhere come into my life / And you don't go away" (already given a double edge by Mary's singing it along with him as a torch song) turned into the bitter "But you're still somehow part of my life, / And you won't go away" as Beth confronts him at the divorce trial (because of Sally Klein's vocal difficulties as Beth, this act 1 transformation was reassigned to Frank with his words in the initial production and on the recording).

Stylistic Unity and the Return to Broadway

The second observation is that there are musical cross-references outside the scheme I have been discussing and in addition to Frank and Gussie's music. Not only does the "Blob" motif permeate both the number of that title and "Rich and Happy," but the musical and lyrical fragments of mindless cocktail conversation, and its electronic simulation, are also common to both songs, which may be regarded as a symmetrical pair, one in each act. And toward the end of act 1, before the final strettos of "Now You Know," there is a rich contrapuntal amalgam of various motifs (see pp. 113–15 in the score): the "Merrily" melody acts as a cantus firmus against the "Best thing" refrain and the "So we'll do a new show" verse, followed by the "Our Time" refrain (as "Your time") and, in the orchestra, the "Rich and Happy" motif.

More deeply woven in than this quodlibet, however, are rhythmic and melodic correspondences that bring us to the question of style and to the fact that, in *Merrily We Roll Along,* as will already be clear from some of the preceding musical descriptions, Sondheim has returned to the Broadway model. "Old Friends" uses the standard march matrix, if somewhat austerely (for instance, the F-natural appoggiatura in the held tenor part at the end of ex. 10.4c never resolves). The first verse of "Rich and Happy" has a beguiling instrumental Broadway tenor line, not shown in the score and presumably Tunick's doing, against gently sparkling woodwind scoring of the "Blob" vamp, two octaves higher than printed, which sound like nothing so much as "Singin' in the Rain." Most of the numbers are in quadruple time. Within and across this, the quintessential Broadway cross-rhythm of units of three (see chap. 7 for further analysis of it) is amply evident. Indeed, it is highlighted when it is presented as naked rhythm without melodic contour and used to signify quick-talking New York speech inflections (or the wit that they house) in the context of the lyrics Charley is typing in "Opening Doors." These are bracketed in ex. 10.5a, and their subsequent transfer from diegetic rhythm to orchestral accompaniment is given in ex. 10.5b. The bracket in the second measure

Ex. 10.5a

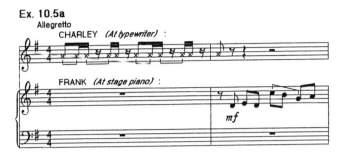

Ex. 10.5b

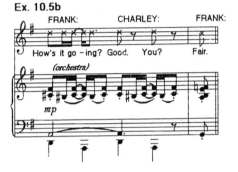

Ex. 10.5c

Ex. 10.5d

i

ii

Ex. 10.5e

Ex. 10.5f

of ex. 10.5a similarly shows the triple-time quickstep cross-rhythm present in Frank's "Hills of Tomorrow" motif, on which he is working (we hear its last note as a downbeat). There are many more examples of this idiom in the score: see the "Rolling along" tag, ex. 10.1c, the second measure of ex. 10.2b, ii, and Beth's pat ending to the first stanza of "Honey." However, cross-rhythm cannot be entirely separated from the contiguous phenomenon of syncopation in its strict sense (that of the time signature's proper rhythm metrically displaced), which in such instances a triple-time unit often sets up (the release of "Good Thing Going," ex. 10.5c, offers a simple example), and the return to the comfort and naïveté of the quickstep and foxtrot is complemented and contrasted with a particularly frenetic repertoire of syncopation. The "Blob" motif generates this, and it can be illustrated in the rebarring of some of the cocktail party conversational jingles (ex. 10.5d). This, if you like, is Hollywood contrasted with New York when "The Blob" reaches the extremely fast tempo (marked *Feroce*) and harsh timbre of its big-band presentation in the "Overture" (there are no upper strings in Tunick's orchestration of the show), where it suggests the hard, aggressive style of cops-and-robbers television music and the slick filming techniques that such music is designed to match, supplemented with a characterizingly crass return to Spanish rhythms in the mambo accoutrement of "Rich and Happy." The possibly intentional interrelationships between some of these energetic rhythmic motifs are proposed in ex. 10.5e. As we read the correspondences vertically they shift in and out of focus and we are struck not just by those of syncopation—all the motifs have some element of it in common, and the "Date" motif is rhythmically identical with the "Blob'"'s first measure—but of melody as well, the upward third apparently functioning as the central pivot on which all the illustrated material except the "Date" motif is hung, while the descending downbeat inflection with which four of the motifs end seems highlighted by the "Blob'"'s being based on it.

It is slightly curious that the downward tetrachord that opens the melody of "Merrily We Roll Along" never firmly ties in with these binding affinities—at least not in the score (it did inform the melody of the first version of "Darling" and the originally drafted ending and discarded B section of "Old Friends"). Despite this, the technical factors evident in ex. 10.5e, which give a highly unified tone to the music (and, because of the rhythms, to the lyrics), may well have originated in the sketches for the show's title song and have worked outward from there; these include a variant of the "Date" motif (ex. 10.5f) labeled "Bel Air—The Good Life," and a note at the top of the same page reads "Sudden changes of speed, dynamics, doubling of beats," which is certainly in accord with the fast, abrupt physicality of this predominating tone. The interpolated "Bump!"'s would have furthered the telegraphic approach, as might a whole series of conversational "Blob" monosyllables drafted for that number.

GUSSIE: Mister Blob. Mrs. Blob.
MR. B: Blob
MRS. B: Blob
GUSSIE: Former Mayor Blob.
MAYOR: Blob.
GUSSIE: And his wife Blob. Mister Shepard.
WIFE: Blob

The Show Song and Its Meanings

Prince and his collaborators aimed to create "the biggest dancing show of their careers" (Zadan 1990, 270), but sustaining its characterization

Ex. 10.6a

Ex. 10.6b

might have become an irritant were it not for some powerful contrasts. The most striking of these is the vein of elegiac romanticism, which sounds fresher than ever before in Sondheim's work and prepares the way for the radiance of *Sunday in the Park* and the simple, primary warmth of *Into the Woods*. "Not a Day Goes By" is an outstanding song in this respect. It commands an exquisite beauty of ellipsis in a haunting sequence of harmony and melody, worthy of Fauré, which once again in a Sondheim song has the courage to describe itself in words (see ex. 10.6a), though we must also remember that it has already recurred, so to speak, with its lyrics transformed into an outburst of pain and anger; and it embeds its subject matter in its form, which cannot come to a close—we recognize the melodic rhetoric of this even if we are unaware of its structural affirmation, a harmonic plane that shifts from G major to A major during the course of the song.

There is a new openness and relaxation about this music, and there is little doubt that writing to characterize youngsters, whatever insoluble problems their presence on stage may have entailed, opened new doors for Sondheim's songwriting. In a sense, however, it was old doors that he was opening, for his brief to himself in the "Misc. Songs" notes was effectively to reconstruct the romantic popular song.

> Lyrical
> First person rather than comment (to avoid irony)
> Simple, energetic, sassy, non-intellectual—if anything exaggerate these
> Moments in the present with just one level
> Risk embarrassment, sentimentality—remember the qualities kids will
>   bring to them
> Kids get younger when they sing

Best of all is "Good Thing Going," its piano introduction the epitome of an adolescent doodler's vamping—a half-understood blues tempo and a half-assimilated folk inflection subsisting above a hand-me-down drone bass (see ex. 10.6b). I have already analyzed the structural goal that Sondheim achieves starting out from this concept (see chap. 3). Yet we also need to note that, at the same time as staying perfectly within the self-imposed brief quoted previously, he allows the song to be appreciated on many different levels that shift back and forth between an intensely private role for the song and a markedly public one, the problem of lack of privacy in modern life being one of the show's themes—"almost every scene unfolds in a public place" (Ilson 1989, 301).

Its first level is as a diegetic depiction of a naïve but deserving hit, a love song written by two young men. On the second level it acts as a microcosm of their friendship and its fate, and thus of the show's overall plot, which they do not recognize but we do. Its third level is that of a potent expression of what all song must ultimately be about, our own self-knowledge, the unspoken or hidden thoughts, desires, and motivations that can never be wholly satisfied except in the death wish of closure that the song's final words so poignantly act out. To the extent that some homoerotic aura (of which they are presumably not conscious) is bound to emanate from the song, given its applicability to Frank and Charley (we cannot be expected entirely to dissociate its love song and friendship levels, especially when they sing it together), it fulfils this role emblematically and in a way that silently acts as a correlative to Mary's largely unspoken and unrequited love for Frank, though it is only fair to point out that the lyric of the song got as far as the typewriter before all references in it to "I" and "her," which was how it was composed, were changed to "we" and "you." In a paradoxical way, reading this kind of personal or subliminal application into it universalizes the song and reminds us that there is also a fourth level to be posited, that of a hit for Sondheim outside the show (the diegetic use of its Frank Sinatra recording over the air in the television studio scene has added a nice depth of reverberation to this level in productions since 1988). But, on the fifth and maybe final level, its very words describe the process of a song becoming a hit ("It started out like a song"), and thus we are brought full circle back to the first level. Yet again the cycle of understanding has proved reflexive, and Sondheim has shown us that in returning, as had been his intention from the start in *Merrily We Roll Along,* to the parameters of "musical comedy in a most traditional way, only with contemporary harmonies" (Zadan 1990, 271), new layers of dramatic meaning are uncovered, new elective affinities established, and new structural fusions achieved.

Chapter 11

Sunday in the Park with George

The Belgian poet Verhaeren described how Seurat would discuss his work "calmly, with careful gestures, while his eye never left one and the slow level voice searched for the slightly professional phrase. . . ." "If I had to describe him in one word," Verhaeren went on, "I would say that he was above all an organizer, in the artistic sense of the word. Hazard, luck, chance, the sensation of being carried away—these things meant nothing to him. Not only did he never start painting without knowing where he was going, but his pre-occupation with his pictures went far beyond their success as individual works. They had no real meaning, in his view, unless they proved a certain rule, a certain artistic truth, or marked a conquest of the unknown. If I understood him correctly, I think that he had set himself to pull art clear of the hesitations of vagueness, indecision, and imprecision. Perhaps he thought that the positive and scientific spirit of the day called for a clearer and more substantial method of conquering beauty."

—John Russell, *Seurat*

The Joyous Synthesis

Having agreed with his new collaborator, James Lapine, that their show should be based on Seurat's *Un dimanche d'été à l'Ile de la Grande Jatte,* Sondheim was seized, we can imagine, with the same excitement that the great painting and its period evoke in us. Recreating a famous painting on the stage was not a novel idea. It went beyond the tradition of the *tableau vivant,* itself common enough in nineteenth-century American theater (see McCullough 1983) and in the concluding tableau of a Victorian melodrama "where characters 'groupe' or 'form picture' as the curtain descends" (Smith 1973, 27), to the not unusual ploy in Victorian Britain of constructing a play out of the story implied by a painting; Frith's *The Railway Station,* for instance, was subjected to such treatment (see Meisel 1983, 377–83; Richards 1988). In these cases the dramatic attraction was generally that "one should make use of the variety that a mixture of classes and occupations can offer," as Zola, writing only a year or two before Seurat began painting *La Grande Jatte,* recommended in his *Naturalism in the Theatre* (quoted in Meisel 1983, 373). It should not surprise us that the same consideration should prove attractive in the musical theater a hundred years later, but the additional prospect of engaging historically with the period, techniques, and artistic biography of neo-impressionism, in which for today's viewer all seems still new yet nothing is threatening, must have been uniquely exhilarating to Sondheim and Lapine.

The more Sondheim found out about Seurat, the more he realized: "My God, this is all about music," pointing out that "Seurat experimented with the color wheel the way one experiments with a scale. He used complementary color exactly the way one uses dominant and tonic harmony. When you start thinking about it, there are all kinds of analogues" (Zadan 1990, 303). And Verhaeren's words about Seurat might justly be applied to Sondheim himself; they certainly reflect his own view of the work of an artistic creator, as we can recognize not just through what we know of him and his methods but through the lyrics he puts into the mouth of his latter-day George, an organizer par excellence, in the song "Putting It Together." Seurat's single-mindedness and integral drafts-manship informed his vision at every stage in his career and in his planning of a painting. As Russell (1965) demonstrates, characteristic forms and motifs would be worked on individually in a multitude of sketches for one big canvas, so that, as we study their generous repre-sentation in the illustrations of Russell's book, each figure or viewpoint has an enhanced life of its own, just like an individual song in a musical; their essences also frequently stretch back into Seurat's previous work, like the conical haystack in *Meule de foin* of around 1883 whose shape, as Russell points out (1965, 110), is replicated in the back view of the nurse in *La Grande Jatte*. Such far-flung connections can be found in Sondheim too, as any devotee will be amply aware; an unlooked-for example might be the similarity of Dot's release in the "Sunday in the Park with George" number (ex. 11.1b) to the opening of "With So Little to Be Sure Of" from *Anyone Can Whistle* (ex. 11.1a). The connection is not arbitrary: the *Sunday* example marks, as we shall see, the beginning of "a continuous and continuing love song that isn't completed until the end of the show" (Zadan 1990, 301), when it becomes the first entirely uncontingent love duet in a Sondheim musical since Fay's and Hapgood's of twenty years before. In fact, Dot and George, serious and for once not bound by the self-detachment or ambivalence that is the familiar hallmark of the dra-matis personae of the Sondheim canon, are the first characters in one of his musicals with whom and with whose conflicts and choices we have complete, fully developed sympathy. Throughout their struggles, mis-understandings, and social confusion this is never in doubt or deprived of its simple, humane grounding through irony and humor, however much

Ex. 11

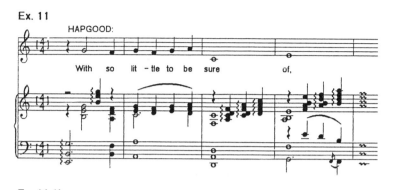

Ex. 11.1b

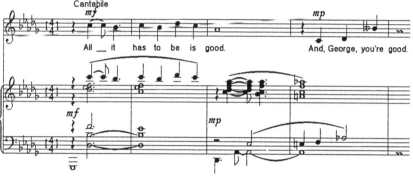

of these there are in their circumstances and surroundings and their reactions to them. (It is curious that' McLaughlin [1991] omits *Sunday* altogether from his survey of society and love in Sondheim's musicals.) *Sunday in the Park* thereby represents a new level in Sondheim's portrayal of humanity, a tighter embrace of artistic truth, and, since it is amply sustained in *Into the Woods,* we should not underestimate Lapine's proprietorship of this achievement, difficult though it is, in a study whose subject is Sondheim, to do it justice or even to separate the contribution of one man from that of the other (for instance, the naming of the heroine was Lapine's happy inspiration).

A lot of things came together in *Sunday in the Park,* and synthesis is undoubtedly the key word, as the very title of "Putting It Together" indicates. E. M. Forster's epigraph in *Howards End,* "Only connect," applies, and the musical shares with Forster's novels something of their striving toward understanding and enlightenment in human relations and aspirations that may only make sense when viewed from beyond the blinkered concerns of specific individuals, generations, epochs, and societies. Hence the love song completed over a hundred-year span; hence also the strong authorial hand that constructs it, giving *Sunday* something of the scope of a huge lyric poem—it was called "A Rhapsody" in one of Sondheim's "miscellaneous" notes for the project, and he has said that he finds Lapine a "poetic" writer and that he could use a good deal of his dialogue as lyrics (Lapine and Sondheim 1984). However much we may feel that "great artists . . . do not convince on the stage" (Russell 1990) or that neither the act 1 nor the act 2 George can entirely escape from the banality of "every Hollywood biopic's favorite cliché, the misunderstood genius who eventually alienates all who love him" (Steyn 1987, 12), we have no difficulty in responding to the lyric as opposed to theatrical expression of truths about art and artists. This is why, as we shall see, it does not really matter how we construe George's creative status at the end of act 2, as long as we accept that he has come through an extended dramatic monologue since the start of the show. Much of the material is cast in his voice as soliloquy—he rarely addresses other characters in song—and this very directness allows Sondheim the author to speak to us at the same time as maintaining George's self-characterization.

In these respects, which Dot's directness and importance enhance rather than destroy, *Sunday* has something of the genre of the romantic long poem about it. With its wit, colloquialism, and fervor it bears a certain comparison with Browning's dramatic monologues about artists (his organist in *Master Hugues of Saxe-Gotha* makes troubled contact with his predecessor rather as the modern George does). With the artist's return to a significant place where he gains inspiration from a companion in the face of creative insecurity it echoes such Wordsworth poems of revisitation as *Tintern Abbey.* *Sunday* also makes shorter poems spring to mind. A member of the audience at Lapine and Sondheim's Boston Museum of Fine Arts lecture on the show (Lapine and Sondheim 1984) pointed out that, given Seurat's interest in classical friezes, the rapt stillness of the figures in the painting and the collaborators' interpretation and capturing of them in the musical, it was reminiscent of Keats's "Ode on a Grecian Urn." George's reflection, that "you watch the rest of the world / From a window" and "you're always turning back too late / From the grass or the stick" to the woman who is waiting, further connects us with Hardy and his treatment of his first wife as he expresses it in "Overlooking the River Stour," regretting that "never I turned my head, alack, / While these things met my gaze / . . . To see the more behind my back."

Sunday invites such comparisons. The need for *connections* is voiced repeatedly in the lyrics, with multiple meanings attached to the word. Dot sings of those who want "bread / And respect / And attention, / Not to say connection" in her first number, contrasting their materialistic motivations with her own desire to be connected, as a model, with posterity in the "more permanent expression" of art, "Something . . . / That's durable / Forever." Later, frustrated by George's preoccupations and lack of attention to her, she contrasts him with Louis, who "makes a connection"—"That's the thing that you feel." Toward the end of act 1 George, finding it difficult to relate to his mother, mutters "Connect, George" to himself as he looks at his sketch of her; his contemporary namesake and descendant in act 2 finds himself having to revert to Dot's materialistic analysis of the term when he recognizes the need for the businessman in the artist.

> Link by link,
> Making the connections . . .
> Drink by drink,
> Fixing and perfecting the design.
> Adding just a dab of politician
> (Always knowing where to draw the line).

Back in the Parisian park, feeling creatively washed out, he describes himself as "attempting to see a connection / When all he can see / Is maybe a tree— / The family tree," the double meaning in fact indicating one of the most important connections of all.

Wagner, Musical Impressionism, and the Synaesthetic Circle

To explore the multifarious terms and levels on which synthesis operates in *Sunday in the Park* is a joyous invitation. To begin with, Seurat's own air was heavy with its sweetness. He lived and worked at a time when cross-pollenation between the arts in Europe was, many thought, leading toward a Utopia of synaesthesia, an enhanced aesthetic response based on the capacity of the senses and values of one art to suggest or combine with those of another. Wagner had proclaimed the *Gesamtkunstwerk* in his music dramas, uniting, so he thought, music, drama, and all stagecraft's other contributory disciplines on equal terms. What he really did was write music of such power that writers and painters were left wondering how they could match it in their own media. Both he and they made a point of flouting the academic conventions of their own disciplines in much the same way that Marxism flouted the traditional disciplines of statehood; we should not forget that the artistic revolution came in the wake of the political ones of 1848–49, in which Wagner was very much caught up (he was exiled and it proved the turning point of his career).

Technically speaking, Wagner could make a chord carry an unprecedented weight of emotion, a chromatic progression of unlimited possibilities of meaning and direction; writers, during the Wagner fever of Paris in the 1870s, looked for comparable ways of enriching the power of individual words and images, of heightening the evocative texture of a poem. Symbolism emerged, at the hands of Baudelaire and Mallarmé, and impressionism in painting achieved similar results with its enhancement of the values, meanings, and ambiguities of light and texture. Nowadays we tend to evaluate the results as complex, multidimensional structures, but at the time the subjective element was what mattered most. The suggestive resonances of a chord, a timbre, a word, a phrase, a rhythm, an image, a shape, a color were to be admitted freely to the individual's powers of reception and response. This was sensuous art, and once the floodgates of the senses were opened all manner of subconscious desires surfaced, to be codified in due course by Freud and Havelock Ellis. By the end of the nineteenth century there was an implicit, all-consuming triple alliance of art, sex, and psychology, even if the war cry was never raised as such. What was raised was a fourth factor in the alliance, that of art for all and for its own sake rather than as the handmaid of dogma; it was becoming a consumer product, concomitant to the vast increase in public leisure that arose in the wake of industrialization. It was no accident that "mon plaisir," as Debussy put it, should be not just a valid aesthetic yardstick by which to measure art but the very subject of so much of it. In a sense, this was what the liberation of the chord from rules of harmonic progression meant: it was being allowed to do what it liked, to play instead of work; and the majority of impressionist and many postimpressionist pictures are similarly on holiday, as it were, with the river, the seaside, the countryside, the circus, the cafe concert, the day off, the park, the theater as their subject matter. *La Grande Jatte* is the apotheosis of this trend.

Alliances are based on shared technical objectives and connections perceived in terms of analogies, and were no new thing in the arts. Louis XIV's absolutism required one set of analogies, based on techniques of rhetoric and ideas of logic and balance in dance, speech, music, philosophy, military and civil protocol, and so forth. Late nineteenth-century European cosmopolitanism and its capitalist consumerism required another set. It all comes down to what are seen to be the appropriate terms of balance and opposition, for strictly speaking an analogy is a ratio.

Let us give what is more than an example, for it is virtually the *fons et origo* of impressionism in music: Wagner's *Waldweben* (Forest Murmurs) in *Siegfried*, part of which is given in ex. 11.2a. He needed to depict, in musical terms, the stillness of a deep forest with sunlight dappling the ground through the leaves. It need hardly be pointed out that, with the possibilities opened up by the use of gas lighting in theaters, the scenic

Ex. 11.2a

portrayal of this effect would be high on the theatrical collaborators' list of things to make the audience aware and appreciative of (it still is), and we should perhaps not even rule out the possibility that the impressionist painters were influenced by what they saw on the stage. But what is the composer to do about it? Wagner's solution was to take unprecedented risks with harmony, by writing the passage as a coruscation of adjacent notes in the strings whose effect is that we are not quite sure whether we are hearing slowed trills within harmonies that are grammatically static beyond the conventions of musical rhetoric, or rapidly oscillating appoggiatura chords whose individual intensity of expression is subservient to the startlingly and sensuously novel harmonic progressions that arise on a larger level when the trilled notes themselves change. Everything is still, yet everything is moving; a dissolution of the senses thereby occurs at this moment of heightened perception. It is, of course, a moment of epiphany or ecstasy for Siegfried, symbolizing his attainment of puberty as he prepares to fight the dragon, cuts himself a pipe on which to play, and wonders what the song of the woodbird means.

The importance of this for the matter at hand should be clear. Wagner showed, in his *Waldweben* passage, that—to introduce a further analogy— the subatomic particles that made up a trill and had never before been thought of as individual entities could be manipulated under a microscope and become immensely powerful once separated; at the same time they contributed to an unprecedented continuity and uniformity of texture. Seurat did the same thing with dots of color and invented pointillism, or divisionism as he preferred to call it, an extension on a more minute level of the brushstroke effects of impressionism. He was the first digital painter.

Ex. 11.2b

Ex. 11.3. **The Synaesthetic Circle in "Sunday in the Park with George"**

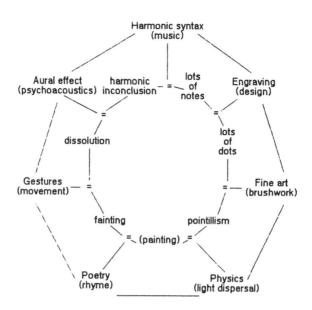

Wagner's harmonic breakthrough, the demonstration that harmonic functions were not absolute but dissoluble into other terms on other levels—terms of rhythm, texture, timbre—has affected music ever since, and much of the note-to-note procedure in *Sunday in the Park* can be easily traced back to it. A good example, in fact the first in the score, comes at the point where, in her title song, Dot sings "But most of all, I love your painting" (ex. 11.2b). Here the very plethora of small notes on the page suddenly suggests the flickering light effects that Seurat and his contemporaries could achieve with their dots. It is impossible to say whether each measure consists of one chord or whether there is harmonic movement within it (for example, from the initial C and E-flat sixteenth notes to their "resolutions" on B-flat and D-flat). As if in recognition of this the music simply fades on this richness of diatonic resonance rather than attempt to resolve it. But Sondheim builds his own composer-lyricist's analogy into the effect as well, in the consequent line, "I think I'm fainting . . ." (Dot's song is about the discomfort of modeling in the hot sun). The rhyme completes the inner cycle of associations and the outer synaesthetic circle and sets the seal of wit on the whole (see ex. 11.3).

Chromatic Theory

This may seem like a sledgehammer cracking a nut, when Sondheim and Lapine's correspondences are planted to be savored and enjoyed within the aesthetics of a musical rather than schematized as though they were a system of knowledge. Yet a system of knowledge was precisely what Seurat aspired to in his paintings, and one of the things that makes them so moving is their witness to positivism, to the fact that his generation could envision a coming together of artistic, political, and scientific values. Whatever tensions may be expressed in the dispositions of human figures in *La Grande Jatte*, it is also a vision of a serene and whole society at play, expressed in terms of a technique of geometry and color that Seurat believed to be the scientific truth. Influenced by the color theories of Helmholtz—who as the preeminent nineteenth-century acoustic physicist also greatly influenced music—and Chevreul, but more closely by Charles Henry, Seurat adopted Henry's doctrines of the union of opposites and the quantification of colors, angles, and spaces for artistic purposes. Henry, with the help of diagrammatic devices such as the chromatic circle (borrowed from Chevreul; see Chevreul 1859, 53, plate 6) and even with specially manufactured aesthetic measuring instruments, believed that everything could be made to complement, to correspond with, everything else, in art and in other areas of life, in a way that science could prove, and apparently "to some," his theories "now seem to foreshadow Planck's quantum theory and the notion of cosmic radiation" (Russell 1965, 193–94). There is a parallel here, perhaps, with current work on fractals using the computer as an aesthetic modulator.

Seurat summarized his understanding of all this in a famous letter to Maurice Beaubourg in 1890.

ESTHETIC

Art is harmony. Harmony is the analogy of contrary elements and the analogy of similar elements of tone, color and line, considered according to their dominants and under the influence of light, in gay, calm, or sad combinations.

The contraries are:

For tone, one more clear (luminous) for one more dark:

For color, the complementaries, that is to say a certain red opposed to its complementary, etc. (red-green, orange-blue, yellow-violet);

For line, those forming a right angle.

Gaiety of *tone* is given by the luminous dominant; of *color*, by the warm dominant; of *line*, by lines above the horizontal.

Calm of tone is equality between dark and light; of color, equality between warm and cold; in line, it is given by the horizontal.

Sad tone is given by the dark tone dominant; in color by the cold dominant; in line by descending directions.

Technique:

Taking for granted the phenomena of the duration of the impression of light on the retina—

Synthesis necessarily follows as a result. The means of expression is the optical mingling of the tones and of the tints (local color and that resulting from illumination by the sun, an oil-lamp, gas, etc.), that is to say, of the lights and their reactions (the shadows), following the laws of contrast, of gradation and of irradiation.

The frame is in the harmony opposed to that of the tones, the colors and the lines of the picture. (Seurat, quoted in Taylor 1987, 541–42)

Like many structural theories from other disciplines, trouble begins the moment one attempts to apply this to music, for the simple reason that music has already been perceived as primarily a structural rather than a representational art for so long that Seurat, presumably consciously, and like Kandinsky after him, has had to do little else than apply its terms and grammatical truisms to his own discipline. Little beyond conventional lay insights are required to appreciate that dominant and tonic harmonies are, as it were, at right angles to one other and that harmony resolves conflicts; that ascending melodic lines instil brightness, descending ones closure or dissolution; and so on. At least, this structural sophistication is true of the parameter of pitch, which has been comprehensively codified and developed from an early period in Western music as melody and harmony. The true analogy for the visual chromatic circle, though not in Seurat's mind or understood by him as far as we can tell by its omission from his terminology, would thus be the harmonic cycle of fifths, one of the deepest structural foundations of classical music, or perhaps some variant of it such as Bartók's complementary tritones. (Skriabin's associative scheme of music with color was, by and large, based on the analogy between the spectrum and the cycle of fifths.) Visual color would be powerful indeed if its disposition by artists could be as integrally conceived as harmonic and tonal structures are by composers.

Chromaticism, Diatonicism, and Pointillism in the Score

How was Sondheim to respond musically to Seurat's theories? He could hardly hope to reinvent the wheel, demonstrating them by the use of musical tools and values that were already his and every other musician's bread and butter—though a desultory attempt at a three-chord tonal equivalent of Seurat's three color pairings is to be found among the "miscellaneous" music sketches for *Sunday* (see ex. 11.5a), and the pure diatonicism that these chords imply did become a schematic issue, as we shall see. But to turn the analogy around, what was to be gleaned from musical uses of the term *color?* A moment's thought would reveal that music uses the analogy of optical color in two different senses: it is applied to timbre or *tone color*—the acoustic wave form of a sound, its overtone structure, normally thought of as a subsidiary attribute as far as the structure of a musical composition is concerned—and to the *chromatic* dimension of pitch. The latter usage presumably came about because musical chromaticism was traditionally thought of as inflection or decoration rather than as structural essence; thus both usages appeal to values of draftsmanship based on line and mass rather than color. Applying the calibrations of the visual chromatic circle to the units of the musical chromatic *scale* rather than the cycle of fifths would give rise to music full of notes a semitone apart. Sondheim commented wryly on the results one might expect.

> Seurat's palette had eleven colors plus white, and he would only mix adjacent colors. At first I thought I'd assign one note of the twelve-note scale to each color and place them in the same way, but then I realized that the entire score would have consisted of minor seconds— an unnourishing prospect. (Ratcliffe 1990)

One hopes that Schoenberg was not attempting an analogy with color theory when he developed twelve-tone composition on this basis, and one wonders even more whether Messiaen's synaesthetic system of color equivalents to the diatonic scale, seemingly based on the chromatic gradations of Rimington's color organ, can be perceptually anything more than arbitrary (see Boulton 1987).

Nevertheless, Sondheim did permit himself a certain amount of travel down the musically chromatic path in *Sunday in the Park*. George's "painting" motif (ex. 11.4a), in its equal-note rhythm and repeated-note melodic character the obvious musical correlative to the repetitive physical act of putting the dots on the canvas (though Sondheim has observed that Seurat's brush technique was more a matter of tiny swirls, not dots), is a vestige of the abortive idea of using adjacent semitones for adjacent colors, and Sondheim has further stated (see Portway and Lee 1990) that act 1, viewed as a whole, can be seen as the resolution of semitonal descent (see *x* in ex. 11.4a) into the radiant diatonicism of "Sunday," the point of resolution being sharply spotlighted by the rather cryptic-sounding disposition of the descent and its simultaneous inversion as dissonant two-part chromatic counterpoint (ex. 11.4b). This seems to have originated, unconsciously, in an unused sketch for *Pacific Overtures* (possibly the very

Ex. 11.4a

Ex. 11.4b

Ex. 11.4c

Ex. 11.4d

Ex. 11.4e

Ex. 11.4f

Ex. 11.4g

Ex. 11.4h

first one; see ex. 11.4c), which would account for its rather strange ritualistic character. His statement suggests that we are to view all pervasive
instances of semitonal chromaticism in act 1 as conducive toward this
point. They include the vamps of "Sunday in the Park with George" (see
the bass and the semitone in the chord of ex. 11.4d), "The Day Off" (ex.
11.4e), and "Everybody Loves Louis" (ex. 11.4f) and the semitonal
descent initiating the main downbeat portion of the melodies of "No Life"
(ex. 11.4g), "Mothers may drone" (a vignette in "The Day Off"), and
"Beautiful" (ex. 11.4h); the "Gossip Sequence" vamp is a variant of the
"Color and Light" motif. Ex. 11.11, which is this author's graphic representation of Sondheim's "love song" music in *Sunday* (see on), shows
semitonal chromaticism, too, in the multiple leads up to a C major point
of attainment.

In act 2, the main chromatic feature to note is the twelve-tone chord
that is built up, one note at a time, in parallel with each spoken tribute
to Seurat in "Eulogies" and that therefore, as well as acting as a stylistic
transition to the modern George, his environment, and his Chromolumes,
it points out to us that there are twelve articulated characters or groups
of characters who constitute the relationships fabricated from the painting—George, Dot, Jules, Yvonne, Louise, the Nurse, the Old Lady, the
Soldiers, the Celestes, Franz, Frieda, and the Boatman (Louis, who never
speaks, would form the baker's dozen). The point of this tone row is that
it is derived, as the "miscellaneous" sketches show, from another that
incorporates a more obvious variant of the fanfare with which the musical
opens (see ex. 11.5b: the act 2 row is sketched on the lower stave).

It is difficult to see anything closely schematic linking or governing
these chromatic usages, and although ex. 11.4g reminds us of Ratcliffe's
description of the "Sunday" horn call (an upward sixth, B to G) as "both
a musical question mark and the first idea from which so much of the
harmonic and emotional storytelling flows," this was not intended as a
connection. It seems more helpful to regard the horn call, which is of
course a primary building block not least because it articulates the title
word *Sunday,* as representative of another prime inspiration, simple diatonicism, and thus to see two different worlds, chromatic and diatonic,
petitioning bitonally for reconciliation in the insistent presence of the
upward sixth shown in ex. 11.4a. The five-note fanfare embedded in ex.
11.5b became, in any case, wholly diatonic and, distancing itself from
the context of a tone row, used instead the idea of free permutation, as
the first two pages of the score, or even its first two measures (ex. 11.5c),
demonstrate.

Ringing the diatonic changes on five notes sounded ritualistic and bell-
like, appropriately enough for Sunday (this was in Sondheim's mind, as
ex. 11.6a demonstrates). It also set up the link with the minimalism of

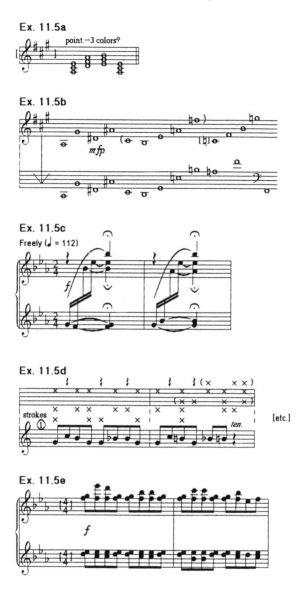

Ex. 11.5a

Ex. 11.5b

Ex. 11.5c

Ex. 11.5d

Ex. 11.5e

Reich and Glass, an influence that Sondheim eagerly acknowledges, right
from the start.

> [Minimalist music] uses the (analogically) pure colors; it uses very
> diatonic harmony . . . in fact I wanted to keep it absolutely pure. . . .
> [At least,] as I worked on the colors of the score . . . it came out to feel
> like that. (Lapine and Sondheim 1984)

But minimalism, the musical equivalent of pointillism, that Sondheim feels gives Reich's music "the same kind of shimmer" as Seurat's painting (Lapine and Sondheim 1984), is also a matter of rhythm. There is a sketch for "Color and Light" (ex. 11.5d) that shows a form of rhythmic counterpoint envisaged as spoken against the music shown in ex. 11.4a— an avant-garde realization of Sondheim's general feeling for dessicated accompaniment patterns as we have traced it through his Latin American preferences and elsewhere; but the texture that eventually grew from the music shown in ex. 11.4a was, although additionally punctuated by offbeat chords, much more akin to a typical Reich or Glass continuum (see ex. 11.5e). Especially in Starobin's radiant and percussive orchestration, passages like this, and the provision of motor rhythm throughout large sections of the score, bring Sondheim fully into the ambit of "process" music. Its pacing, although prepared for to an extent by the long spans of songs such as "Someone in a Tree" in *Pacific Overtures* and even as far back as some of the numbers in *Company,* must have involved considerable risks of judgment; the beauty of "Finishing the Hat," above all, shows how the risks paid off, though it would be wrong not to acknowledge that a lot of contemporary popular music plays much the same game with ostinatos, continuous figuration, and extended structures while somehow hanging on to the traditional AABA song form (the release in "Finishing the Hat" is all-important).

Promenades

If a rhythmic continuum was a primary way of providing *Sunday* with a broad musical canvas while locking it, as we have seen, into the impressionist tradition, there were other structural needs as well. Sondheim's description of the musical's genesis (see Zadan 1990, 296–97) makes it clear that he was conscious from the start that the stage would be peopled with a numerous and diverse procession of characters "out strolling on Sunday." He must also have been aware that Seurat made separate sketches or paintings of many of the figures that eventually appear in *La Grande Jatte,* and some of his own sketches show that he and Lapine thought of these characters in terms of a series of vignettes, a rogue's gallery of portraits past which the audience would stroll, musically speaking, in the course of act 1, just as the characters themselves stroll across the island. These vignettes had to be kept in check and could not all be furnished with songs; nevertheless, the concept developed to the extent of having another of Seurat's paintings, *Une baignade, Asnières,* onstage in a short scene near the beginning as a *tableau vivant* (the boy's song for this vignette, "Yoo-hoo!" was cut and only survives as underscoring). Dot's scene as *Jeune femme se poudrant* is a different matter, more central to the plot and characterization.

Add to this the fact that, as the score and script tell us, "Act 1 takes place on a series of Sundays" and most of act 2 is set in an art gallery where Seurat's painting hangs, and a multiple sense of promenade suggests itself as a guiding stance or action. Sondheim's general notes for the project include a memorandum about act 1 as "Sundays over a year, ending with *the* Sunday. / Everybody tense but pretending to stroll" and a page of notes for the crass conversations of people looking at the painting (promenade conversations in act 1 about George and about each other are, of course, plentiful in the final product). He also sketched a scheme of numbers making the most of promenades.

ROUTINING
    4 Promenades with 3 Interludes?
ACT 1 OPENING—arp. + Sunday—PROMENADE?
    2. DOT—Posing—It's hot up here + Sunday
                      full of info about G
    3. BOYS + BATHERS—"Baignades Asnieres"—Sunday
       (+ J + M: mechanical touch refrain)
    4. PROMENADE?
       OLD LADY + NURSE?
    5. GEORGE—Painting "La Poudreuse"—DUET? Dot's
       complaints
       (+ J + M: mechanical touch; fear of Seurat; M about J = D
       about G)
2nd Sunday 6. PROMENADE. Sunday. Pointillist phrases?
        Celestes—gossip
        /
    7. /\ BOATMAN. (or after #9) Barking keeps people
       away.
    8. CELESTES—Gossip (or after #9)
    9. POINTILLIST TALK—phrases and/or words only.
    10. DOG—Bark—cf. Boatman.
    10A. PROMENADE?—Pointillist
3rd Sunday 11. DAY OFF—F + B, Soldier, Boatman, Jules (anent G)
           Sunday is Salon Day—the salons are free to the
           public

This gives roughly the same order of scenes and vignettes as in the final product, allowing for such changes as the incorporation of some aspects of "The Day Off" into nos. 8-10 and of the Jules and Yvonne component of no. 5 (her name changed from Madeleine) into no. 11. (Is this list incomplete at the end? The addition of a final promenade would have made five, not four). Striking by its absence, however, is any sign of the development of the relationship between George and Dot; and Louis is not mentioned at all. (The song "Everybody Loves Louis" was not even ready for the first workshop performances of *Sunday:* it was added during the run, as were "Beautiful" and "Finishing the Hat"; see Bishop 1991, 3.) Conversely, the envisaged promenades seem to have been downgraded and survive in the score merely as pointillistic underscoring for "Scene Change to Studio" and the like, albeit using the fanfare figures. In fact the sketched scheme more closely anticipates the "Midnight" promenades in act 1 of *Into the Woods*.

But the promenade idea did affect the music, and the obvious correspondence, with Mussorgsky's *Pictures at an Exhibition,* must have been at least subconsciously in mind. One of the "miscellaneous" sketches includes a "Promenade" motif (ex. 11.6a), and while its intervals grew to an upward seventh (ex. 11.6b) and tried a $\hat{5}$–$\hat{3}$ upward sixth (ex. 11.6c) before settling on the $\hat{3}$–$\hat{1}$ one, its rhythm and contour, sounding very like Mussorgsky's "Promenade," were incorporated among (later?) sketches labeled "Promenades" into what became the "Sunday" melody (see *x* in ex. 11.6d) before being abandoned. The "Sunday" melody itself, with two upbeat eighth notes, was drafted among the sketches for "Color and Light" (see ex. 11.6e), and the descriptive reference here to Canteloube's *Chants d'Auvergne* offers another musical correspondence, one that is indeed to be heard in the finished product's serene sensuousness. But the most impressive correspondence in "Sunday," a number that musically comes close to the sensibility of an art song, is surely with Fauré, not so much in the pattering sixteenth-note rhythms of the melody as in the restrained, allusive harmonies. It must be an indirect influence—Sondheim says he has largely bypassed Fauré in his love affair with French music—but he nonetheless shares with him a passionate control, equal to Seurat's in his medium, of elliptical harmony in passages such as the one shown in ex. 11.6f. In particular, the rising C-sharp in the first measure of the example is faced with a falling C-natural in the bass just at the point where it reaches D; secondary dominant and primary subdominant elements are thereby conflated. (Earlier in the song the C-sharp had been wrenched further from its trajectory, directly to a chord based on F-natural.) Four measures further on, C-sharp is withheld entirely, the tension of the withholding building greatly as the progression is twice repeated, and we are denied the resolution for which the dominant thirteenth above A in the bass cries out: the F-sharp does resolve to E, but the D is retained while the bass is lost to B whence it reenters the cycle of fifths and eventually resolves to D for a long dominant pedal. We never hear the C-sharp again in the song.

Ex. 11.6a

Ex. 11.6b

Ex. 11.6c

Ex. 11.6d

Ex. 11.6e

Ex. 11.6f

Ex. 11.6f—*Continued*

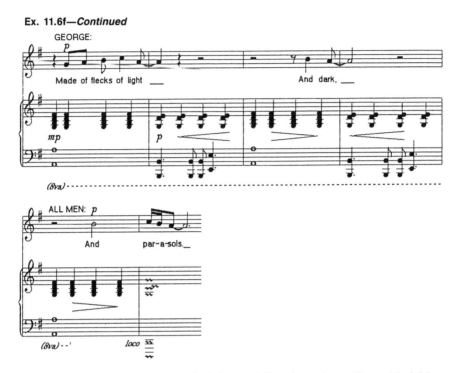

Sondheim's "mimetic interlude" capability (see chap. 8) enabled him to incorporate something of the promenade concept into single songs. In "The Day Off" in act 1, a gently dissonant and tonally parenthetic offbeat chord (marked *x* in ex. 11.4e) is used repeatedly to pull the rhythmic movement up short. I shall return to the onomatopoeic significance of some of its neighboring sonorities, but the ritual function of this chord is somewhat analogous to that of the bell and percussion sounds in *Pacific Overtures,* and when we encounter these points of stasis it is rather as if we have stopped in front of a painting or our glance has been arrested by one of its images—the dogs, the Nurse and the Old Lady, Franz, Frieda and Louise, and the Boatman are all presented in this way, all "on display on Sunday." And as the artist or spectator in front of the frame freezes, the image inside it comes to life: the chord mediates between worlds. For instance, an inversion of it is sustained as a recitative accompaniment when the Nurse begins to sing of her philosophy, and this is the verse of her little song; it gives way to a waltz as she steps out of the frame, as it were, for the chorus. (Similarly positioned and constructed sonorities take on a comparable function as the Witch's "spell" chords in *Into the Woods,* which we can appreciate when she momentarily trances.) Later in act 1 of *Sunday,* at the beginning of "Finishing the Hat," the chord is heard again as George leafs back through his sketches, and it acquires something of the effect of emotion recollected in tranquillity.

In act 2 an obverse process is presented: throughout "Putting It Together" George has repeatedly to sink into some kind of fixed frame, to "freeze" himself into cardboard cutouts in order to be able to converse with the cocktail party "Blob" while keeping his thoughts and aspirations apart and inviolate. Cutouts are an important motif in *Sunday*. The idea of mediation or ambiguity between two-dimensional "scenery" figures and three-dimensional live actors on the stage has already been planted on us in act 1, first in the mixture of the two presented in the *Baignade* scene, then with the routine of the Soldiers, and finally, of course, with the recreation of the painting itself. If it may be interpreted as a continuing metaphor for the question of whether an artist's creations are real or artificial, it also serves the correspondence that Seurat employed no single perspective in *La Grande Jatte* and that the original painting "looks like a stage set" (Sondheim, quoted in Savran 1990, xxvi). Most important, Lapine saw Seurat using the same figures in different places at once in the painting (for example, the two girls appear both fishing and sitting with the flowers), and thus he had to employ cutouts for some of them when he presented the whole painting on the stage. To return to "Putting It Together," here George not only has to conjure up the cutouts as a magician but must keep them in place like a plate-spinning circus performer. Accordingly, the musical emphasis in this number is on continuity, and the applause he (or Sondheim) deserves is, so to speak, for negotiating all seventeen parts of it without breaking the song. There is no obvious parallel or foil to the chord in "The Day Off," though it reappears near the beginning of the number as George's work and "images" are being discussed before his entrance. But, to continue the sleight-of-hand metaphor, his appearance is accompanied by another of Sondheim's three-chord tricks (ex. 11.7a), perhaps to be construed as a kind of magician's gesture (and also as expressing George's nervousness?). Once posited, it can grow into the melodic motif of the song (marked y in ex. 11.7b), and is also suggested by the cross-rhythmic three-eighth-note figure with its upward compound fourth that patterns the accompaniment. The lyrics equate the double leap of the melodic intervals with the doubling of words (including, of course, "Dot by dot"), and at the climax of the song the image of a chain enhances the idea:

> Bit by bit—
> Link by link—
> Drink by drink—
> Mink by mink—

Ex. 11.7a

Ex. 11.7b

while the melodic motif is heard right to the end, even in the final instrumental cadence, where it more or less regains its original rhythmic identity.

Theme and Variation

If this yoking of two identical words and two similar musical intervals represents the smallest level of creative correspondences (and we have seen Sondheim's capacity for such minutiae reaching at least as far back as *Forum*), the largest is represented in *Sunday* by the correspondences between acts 1 and 2. I have traced the provision of large-scale musical correspondences between the acts in *Sweeney Todd* and, to a smaller extent, in *Merrily We Roll Along,* and there will be a more obvious replication still between the extended opening numbers (and parts of the Finales) of acts 1 and 2 of *Into the Woods,* between the two plots they inaugurate and close, and between such other items as the two statements of "Agony" and the Witch's two songs about children ("Stay With Me" and "Witch's Lament"). But it is in *Sunday* that we find the most thoroughgoing correspondences. They affect the music so strongly, of course, because they are such a crucial (though much criticized) part of the dramatic schema, with its two progressive artists and their dilemmas a hundred years apart. Seurat's painting is the central pivot or reflecting surface, for it is built up from nothing but white space during the course of act 1, while at the beginning of act 2 we are told that it is fading, and by the end of the act George has deconstructed himself and his heritage to nothing, has returned once again, in the face of the cultural death he experiences and observes in Paris, to the purity and emptiness of "White. A blank page or canvas." Symbolic of this creative birth and death are the real birth of Marie during the course of act 1 and her death, at the age of ninety-eight, during the course of act 2.

Thus once again, as in *Sweeney Todd,* there is between the acts both this mirror image and an image of parallel. Parallels in the casting are both practical and to a certain extent conceptual. Dot and Marie represent the biological creativity and its imperatives (mistress and family) with which both Georges have to come to terms alongside their artistic freedoms. And one could argue that the parallel casting, in the original production, of the two art establishment figures (Jules in act 1, Greenberg in act 2) and the two severe, critical matrons (George's mother in act 1, art critic Blair Daniels in act 2) was also of schematic significance. Parallels in the music are ubiquitous, as can be demonstrated.

Both acts begin with nervously pointillistic numbers ("Sunday in the Park with George" and "It's Hot Up Here") that share much melodic, accompanimental, and lyric material and could almost be thought of as variants of the same song; both end with the hymn "Sunday." In "Color and Light," George is looking at his canvas and making his painting while Dot is looking in her mirror and making up her body, and thus we also have parallel structures within this song that, with its synaesthetic lyrics and the synaesthetic mise-en-scène (mise, as it were, en Seine), offers an overall parallel to the synaesthetic light sculpture of "Chromolume #7." The first three parts of "Putting It Together" reprise the material of "Gossip Sequence," while part 4 reuses not only a vamp and chord from "The Day Off," as we have observed, but retains the melodic inflections of its part 5 (compare pp. 72–73 and 162–63 in the score). The melodic motif of "The Day Off" (ex. 11.8a) is perhaps parent to the "Art isn't easy" refrain (ex. 11.8b) that arises in part 5 of "Putting It Together" (if so, the con-

Ex. 11.8a

mp

Roam-ing a - round on Sun-day.

Ex. 11.8b

mf

Art is- n't ea- sy-- ___

Ex. 11.8c

p

Fin -ish-ing the hat,

Ex. 11.8d

Put-ting it to - geth-er.

Ex. 11.8e

[Tpt.]

trasting implications of leisure in the one and hard work in the other are a nice touch). "Finishing the Hat" and parts 6 to 17 of "Putting It Together" are the two big "process" songs in the score: the term can be used to indicate both their minimalist musical idiom and the content and mode of their lyrics, and both songs have a present participle in the title phrase and share the musical phrase itself (exs. 11.8c and d), which is a variant of the original fanfares (see ex. 11.5c) whose progeny permeate the whole musical and are especially foregrounded in the horn call found near the beginning of both "Putting It Together" (George's entrance, marked *x* in ex. 11.7a) and "The Day Off" (p. 67 in the score, where it signifies the Horn Player—

though at one stage it was sketched into a fuller paragraph to depict the Soldiers [ex. 11.8e]).

All these parallels work in direct sequence in the score, and all that the shorter act 2 lacks is the series of miniature studies for the minor characters, though there is certainly a parallel between the Old Lady's reflective song "Beautiful," to which the act 1 George responds in the B section and the recapitulation, and Marie's "Children and Art," to which, with a certain poignancy, George in act 2 only responds after her death, remembering its melodic motifs and compound meter in his song "Lesson #8." Finally, and as the climax of each act's dramaturgy, "Move On" parallels George and Dot's duet in act 1, "We Do Not Belong Together," although, true to its title, it also moves beyond it, as we shall see, and is placed later in the sequence of musical numbers.

Many have felt that *Sunday*'s second act is a severe anticlimax, brittle and satirical as it is in its contemporaneity where act 1 reflects the romanticism with which we inevitably imbue the past. But it is important to stress that it was not an afterthought, however labored its compositional history (the workshop production at Playwrights Horizons consisted of act 1 only until the last three performances, when the second act was ready, if with only two songs [see Lapine and Sondheim 1984; Bishop 1991, 3]; even after that, the songs "Lesson #8" and "Children and Art" were not inserted until the end of the preview period on Broadway [Zadan 1990, 311–12]). Sondheim's early aim in collaborating with Lapine was to write "a show made up of a theme and variations, rather than one with a linear story" (Zadan 1990, 296), and the similarity of act 2's musical material to that of act 1 cannot be criticized for poverty of invention when it was a deliberate structural variation or recapitulation, leaving aside the role of "Move On" (to be examined subsequently). At the same time, of course (and this is typical of Sondheim's built-in self-criticism), the whole artistic question of when to repeat and when to do something different, which I raised at the start of chapter 7, is what George's crisis in act 2 is about. References to the idea of variation in the connotatively gratuitous or disturbing context of replication are prominent in the script: George's women in act 1, like Hoffmann's and Lulu's lovers in their respective operas or Rossetti's medieval damsels in *his* paintings, are referred to (by him) in the dialogue as "Variations on a theme," and in act 2 the intended connection between *La Grande Jatte* and the modern George's *Chromolume #7* provokes the following conversation.

> BILLY: Well, I can't say that I understand what that light machine has to do with this painting.
> HARRIET: Darling, it's a theme and variation.

BILLY: Oh. Theme and variation.

Whereas Billy fails to see the connection, George begins to see too much between his successive Chromolumes and suffers a creative blockage, feeling that they have become *merely* variations on a theme. He has been stung by the criticism of Blair Daniels.

> BLAIR: George. Chromolume Number Seven? . . . I was hoping it would be a series of three—four at the most. . . . We have been there before, you know.

The issue, to take it a little further, is the fundamental aesthetic one of *how*, in which terms, to establish the connections between one thing and another: to what extent should the correspondences be repetitions or identities, to what extent transformations, to what extent contrasts? When does one of these distinctions shade into another? How can degrees of similarity or difference be measured or weighed?

The answer, of course, is that they cannot. They can only be felt, perceived, understood as right and fixed in the artist's work, without ever being adequately quantifiable. The artist judges and arranges objects in order to achieve this. Hence Seurat's excision of the tree at the outset of the show, though the diegetic joke when the Old Lady misses it is on a par with the Soldiers' cardboard cutout routine: a sudden collision or fracture between levels of dramatic presentation that some find knowing, others exasperating [Lapine, taking his cue from Seurat's wicked sense of humor, had had a more outrageous early idea for making the soldiers Siamese twins (Lapine and Sondheim 1984]). Hence also the artist's manipulation of the black dog and the four curves of its back and tail to complement the curves between the spokes of the parasol (and in the London production George was shown to turn the dog through 180 degrees, as the lyrics of "The Day Off" suggest):

> If the head was smaller.
> If the tail were longer.
> If he faced the water.
> If the paws were hidden.
> If the neck was darker.
> If the back was curved.
> More like the parasol.

Here again, Sondheim and Lapine's pursuit of correspondences works on more than one level, for Dot has already applied similar lyrics to her own body in "Color and Light."

Toward a Fundamental Aesthetic

One is invited to accept the wealth of correspondences as artistic plenitude more in *Sunday in the Park* than anywhere else in Sondheim's output. It is as relaxed and loose as it is abundant, and doubtless the new creative partnership with Lapine and their close, improvisatory manner of working with each other are the reasons for this; in any case, many of the correspondences are Lapine's, such as the naming of Dot and (presumably) such little production touches as Seurat's provision of pointillistic ants for the dog. The ants get a good laugh in performance, and such correspondences, be they incongruities, sly connections, paradoxes, or profound parallels, are yet again a matter of wit in the musical theater, and it is hardly surprising that Sondheim's lyrics exploit them in their verbal dimensions—through rhyme, assonance, identity, pun, and such other techniques as the deconstruction of figures of speech—as never before. They are everywhere, from Dot remembering her fingernails as she imagines herself "as / Hard as nails" or spraying herself rhythmically with perfume as she muses poetically on George's use of light (thereby subconsciously connecting smell, sound, and vision), to the Celestes spending Sunday when they want to spend money. First and last are the trees: trees in Seurat's picture before the arrival of people, the family tree that connects the two Georges, trees not just removed by the artist but chopped down by the modern Parisians in a narrative motif that points forward to *Into the Woods*.

But the more ventured, the more risked, as the use of the phrase "Always knowing where to draw the line" dares to point out to us in "Putting It Together," triumphantly failing its own test in the process, for it is a tactless figure of speech to use in a play about artists. Similarly, Sondheim enjoys the implantation of French words as a means of sharpening up contrasts or connections while at the same time deliberately letting them expose his own pretensions in putting French impressionism on the stage. In the act 2 cocktail dialogue "new, though" is internally rhymed with "nouveau," and we hear that "tomorrow is already passé"; in the studio Dot counters George's "more red" with "more rouge," this example taking its place among a number of witty shifts in sense that can be regarded as a kind of synaesthetic pun: "More blue . . . / More beer"; "It's getting hot . . . / It's getting orange." These prepare us for the more extended and elaborate synaesthetic metaphors pursued, again at the risk of banality, in the vignettes of Louis the baker and the Boatman. Both characters oppose and confront the artist and his problems. He is unable to apportion or divide his attention ("I am what I do," he says in "We Do Not Belong Together"), he can only make a decision in artistic terms (his answer to "What should I do?" about the problem of his relationship with Dot can only be "Well . . . red"), and he worries about truth and perspective. In contrast, Louis with his culinary art can attain natural complementarity of life and work (distilled into three syllables with their immortal pun, "he kneads me"); the Boatman can enjoy an unambiguous viewpoint, so unlike the artist's ("One eye, no illusion— / That you get with two").

In act 2 the modern George suffers comparable but different problems, again synaesthetically propounded when, in "Putting It Together," he uses words such as *foundation* and *preparation*. These are jargon terms that might apply equally to painting, cookery, chemistry, building, or business management.

> Small amounts,
> Adding up to make a work of art.
> First of all, you need a good foundation,
> Otherwise it's risky from the start.
> Takes a little cocktail conversation,
> But without the proper preparation,
> Having just the vision's no solution,
> Everything depends on execution.

(The ubiquity of these Latin-root terms within a colloquial mode of speech offers a painful contrast with Lapine's linguistic formality and simplicity in act 1, where he avoids contractions such as "it's" in the dialogue so as to give the language something of the flavor of a translation of the period [Kakutani 1984; Lapine and Sondheim 1984].) Lapine also offers a wry comment on the modern artist's relationship with and dependence on money, publicity, and technology—on the sciences, in effect—when he has George's assistant Dennis say "I'm going back to NASA. There is just too much pressure in this line of work."

The biggest artistic liability in the show, however, is the Chromolume. It has to be shown to be a critical failure, which is what precipitates George's crisis. Yet it also needs to be taken seriously if the modern George is to engage our sympathy and interest. It is the same problem as that of Frank in *Merrily We Roll Along* (though now it is accepted that the artist has to progress "Mink By Mink"); this time, however, Sondheim's quandary is not that he cannot write something bad for his hero, but that given that George is an inventor or light sculptor he cannot write anything at all save the inconsequential raw material of motivic cells to be realized electronically. There is thus an embarrassing authorial gap at the very center of the musical; nor does Lapine fill it, for the devices of the electrical short and Marie's unwanted comments on the slide show undermine the

Chromolume with mocking humor rather than support it with contributory wit. There is an enormous difference between this and Sondheim's characterization of the act 1 George, his working methods, his thoughts, and his figures through the witty excellence of song.

Sondheim and Lapine originally wanted a hologram for the act 2 work of art. Finding that the techniques available were inadequate, they used a performance art composition at Playwrights Horizons instead. Sondheim had made an early note to himself about envisaging "Laurie Anderson's version of the Grande Jatte" in act 2 and tried his hand at all kinds of avant-garde sketches for a "Performance art piece," generally using words in a transformatory manner as shown in ex. 11.9a, which was actually used in the workshop performances. This example is all too reminiscent of Gertrude Stein, and the audience found the genre either recondite or ludicrous; Sondheim was wise to abandon the quest. Eventually he concentrated his fusion of syllables and notes into act 1, where it could become a more powerful artistic force as one of the characterizing agents for Seurat. (George's role, as created by Mandy Patinkin, has in any case something of the transdisciplinary verve and virtuosity of the performance artist: in it the singing actor seems to forge his own genre, and one wonders whether Sondheim was influenced by Bobby McFerrin.) Thus the lyric sketches for George's monologue in "Color and Light" began to play with the modulation of one word into another as verbal equivalents of his modulation of color by the mixing of individual specks. One list goes further and also fuses a writer's dots (of punctuation) with an artist's.

speckle
comma
accent
period
fleck
dot
dum
dut
bit
lots
spots
dots
dash
spot
point
stroke
scratch

mark(ing)
touch
stipple.

It continues:

Dab dab dab dab dam Dabba dabba
Drip and drop.

Much of this found its way into "Color and Light," especially part 3, which became a virtuoso patter song for Patinkin, but what is missing in these sketches is any reference to music. This completed the modulation between the three art forms and added a further dimension (a diegetic one, of course) when incorporated into the song as repeated humming syllables ("Bum-bum bum") following the repeated "Blue blue blue" (see ex. 11.9b). (The modulation of sense was extended further, in a kind of pun, when in Part III of "Color and Light" Seurat was made to massage his wrist to the altered syllables "Num-num num.")

The humming syllables are a simple and unpretentious example of what all this was leading to: a proclamation of Sondheim's fundamental aesthetic law, the indivisibility of word and note (or, perhaps more strictly, syllable and note). The proclamation is dramatized using George's art as the subject, as metaphor; or we might say that the equation is solved by adding a term, so that we are dealing with all of the following relationships:

music : words
words : painting
painting : music

We have seen him understanding and developing this law as early as *Forum,* but it can go further than ever before in *Sunday* because the subject matter of the musical grants it permission to be self-conscious.

Its apogee occurs not in "Color and Light," which prepares us for it, but in the dogs' mimetic interludes in "The Day Off," where onomatopoeia is the agent. It is easy to hear the onomatopoeic modulation between word and bark in the dogs' monologues: onomatopoeia is in any case a matter of verbal representation of nonverbal sound through assonance, and all Sondheim does is extend our appreciation of the fact in order to take in the pun. Thus Spot's sentences end with a word that equals a bark—"rough" = "Ruff!" "gruff" = "Grrrruff!" and so on ("And a crack-pot in the bow—wow, / Rough!" is a particularly clever convolution). But much more is involved. The "freeze-frame" harmony (ex. 11.4e, *x*) ana-

Ex. 11.9a

In - ven-tion, in-vent a vis - ion. In-vent a te - le-vis-ion. En-vis-ion the in - ven-tion of the te - le-vis-ion Dot dot dot dot dot dot di - vis-ion dot dot dot dot dot col - lis-ion dot dot dot di - ver - sion. A ver-sion of di - ver - sion.

Ex. 11.9b

[GEORGE:]

mp

(Switches [brushes] quickly)

Blue blue blue blue Blue blue blue blue Ev - en ev - en... Good...

mp

p

p (sotto voce)

Bum-bum bum _ bum-bum-bum Bum-bum bum _

Ex. 11.9c

SPOT: (George)

f (Barks)

Ruff! Ruff! Thanks! The week has been rough!

f

Ex. 11.9d

lyzed earlier is preceded in Spot's verse section by a series of dissonant chords that imitate his barks. Fifi has higher tessitura chords and sparsely textured rhythms for the same purpose (see Spot's in ex. 11.9c, Fifi's in ex. 11.9d—even the names conform to their characterizing vowel and chord sounds, high and bright for Fifi, low and hollow for Spot). The point about the chords is that they can be appreciated as *timbre,* not as harmonic collections of individual notes: when adjacent notes are clustered together (F-sharp, G-sharp, A, A-sharp in ex. 11.9c, *x;* G, A, B-flat, and B-natural in ex. 11.9d, *y*) we begin to hear them as a single sonority without worrying about the individual notes, like a bell's clustered overtones or like any untuned percussion device. This is a truism of contemporary music theory, and Starobin enhances Sondheim's use of these gestures by including percussion in the scoring of the chords. Indeed, Sondheim has understood this aspect of the score from its very first gestures, the piano fanfares (ex. 11.5c), with their shō-like clusterings of notes reminiscent of *Pacific Overtures* and its exemplars in Britten; these he soon furnishes with crotales.

But if there is no need to distinguish the note from the sonority in the chords, in the barks there is no need to distinguish the note from the word, the tone from the phoneme; each is a contributory factor to a single whole, and the gap between music and words has been completely closed. What composers such as Berio managed to achieve with the aid of authors

Ex. 11.10.   The Synaesthetic Circle in "The Day Off"

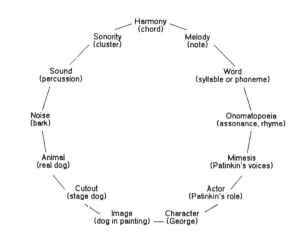

such as Joyce, Sondheim matches in his own humorous, perhaps inconsequential way with the barking of two cardboard cutout dogs, imitated by a musical comedy actor in a sort of vaudeville turn. In doing so he creates a rainbow continuum between virtually all the elements of representation at his and his collaborators' disposal (ex. 11.10). Another synaesthetic circle has been closed.

Sondheim Moves On

Such aesthetic refulgence radiates from act 1 as from the facets of a jewel. By comparison, act 2, "Putting It Together" notwithstanding, lacks luster until redeemed by the love music of George and Dot, which creates the most important set of correspondences in the whole show. Sondheim has described how it works musically.

> The way the score was constructed was based on the relationship of the two central characters. Theirs is a continuous and continuing love song that isn't completed until the end of the show. In the song "Sunday in the Park with George," Dot, in one section, begins a lyrical theme, which is her affection and her love for George. This is picked up later in "Color and Light," and it develops and starts to reach a climax, and just at that point, they break off and they speak. Then in "We Do Not Belong Together" it's picked up and further developed as if it's almost where they left off, and ends with an unrhymed line where she sings, "I have to move on." And when their love is finally consummated, which is the end of the second act, it all comes together and becomes a com-

pleted song in "Move On." "Move On" is a combination of all the themes involving their relationship, including every harmony and every accompaniment; it's where everything culminates. Only it's over a period of four major scenes covering a hundred years. It's one way of threading the theme through time. (Zadan 1990, 301–2)

The material shown in ex. 11.11 will help us see what he means ("Sunday in the Park with George" and "Move On" have been transposed respectively down and up a semitone in the interests of diagrammatic congruence with the C major of the other numbers). The first music in the diagram, the release of "Sunday in the Park with George" (see ex. 11.1b for its full notation), promises a four-square melodic simplicity that is never allowed to work itself out in anything like a thirty-two-measure song, and has already taken a good deal more than 16 measures to emerge. Instead, Dot turns introspective as she contemplates her lover to the accompaniment of the repeated two-chord progression, *x*, that represents George and, as can be seen by reading down ex. 11.11 in vertical alignment, provides the way back into the love music when that music is to be furthered in succeeding numbers. The harmony dissolves in this song at the "fainting" passage analyzed earlier (see ex. 11.2b), having returned to the subdominant with which the release began. A long-term structural bass descent from this subdominant seems implied when we hear the bass E falling to D and thus taking the harmony further in "Color and Light" (see the connecting slurs in ex. 11.11), but we are still pulled up short of a C major cadence, this time on the dominant, where again the music dissolves. The rich chromatic trope enhancing the descent is then transposed up a fourth, along with the "George" chords, as a tension-building preamble to the first chorus of "We Do Not Belong Together," where a C major tonic is at last reached, after which the harmony circles around again using the bass descent from F (see the fourth system in ex. 11.11). The second chorus builds more chromatic tension until released with the refrain line of the song's title on another subdominant (system 5 in ex. 11.11), whence it returns to the tonic with a cycle of fifths elaborating the stepwise bass descent; this process is then repeated and varied for the third chorus, and the song peters out, with the unrhymed line mentioned by Sondheim and with major-minor indecision, at the point of arrival at a fourth tonic. In act 2, "Move On" reaches this point with much less elaboration (see the penultimate system of ex. 11.11), though with the supertonic chord held for a long time. The bass descent and its motifs (built, of course, like all the eighth-note motion shown in ex. 11.11 on *Sunday*'s binding five-note fanfare) come around for a last complete restatement; then, true to its refrain title (which occurs at this point), where

Ex. 11.11

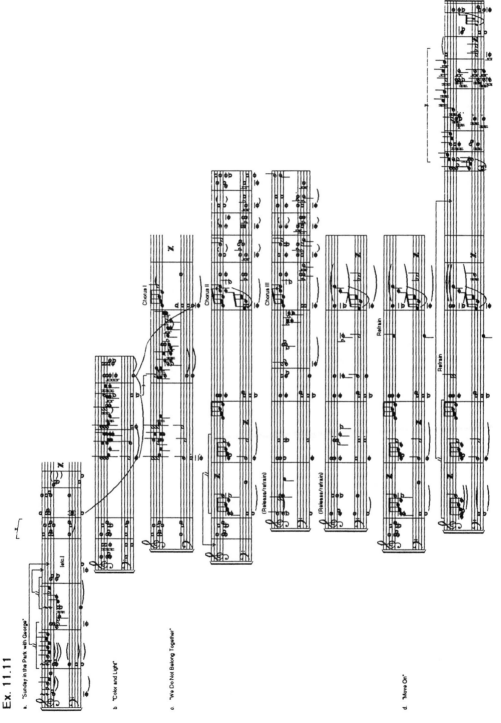

a. "Sunday in the Park with George"

b. "Color and Light"

c. "We Do Not Belong Together"

d. "Move On"

George and Dot sing together homophonically for the first time, in parallel thirds, the song moves beyond them to the chromatic displacements shown at the end of the example before bringing the whole process, indeed the whole score, to rest with the benediction of a plagal cadence, echoing not just the one with which the release of "Sunday in the Park with George" had begun but the mixture of tonic and subdominant triads that had been a conscious presence (see Lapine and Sondheim 1984) as early as the second measure of the score (see ex. 11.5c).

What does all this signify? The necessity of bringing the modern George to this point is not easy to grasp dramatically, though Sondheim, with some signs of impatience, has attempted to explain it.

> If you didn't feel it, you didn't feel it. The attempt is . . . to make you understand his contact with Dot, his connection with his past, which is the past of all of us. Every artist is connected to everybody who's ever painted a picture. If you don't understand that as an artist, you're lost. (Savran 1990, xxiv).

But it is not clear how, in the final scene, George's first acceptance of this continuity—of Marie's insistence on the "tree— / The family tree," which irritated him repeatedly in the art museum—will help him regain his confidence and originality. The lyrics of "Move On" tell us that he does regain it, and that it is a gift from Dot, for he sees "Things I hadn't looked at / Till now: / Flower on your hat. / And your smile." Yet this suggests academic insight into Seurat's inspiration rather than an epiphany of his own, and even if we grasp that he senses an emotional essence being transmitted to him (the hat was the last straw in Seurat's relationship with Dot, though he does not know that) and that this is what causes him to thaw out creatively, it will be difficult for *us* to be moved until we see his next work. Sondheim's "general" notes for "Lesson #8" suggest that it might have diminished this lacuna, for it was meant to accomplish much more than it eventually did. Be that as it may, the catharsis leaves us in any case confused about whether Dot is merely its agent or one of its subjects. Are we simply being told to believe Marie's credo, that "children and art" are the only two things we leave behind, and that Dot and George can therefore meet on equal terms of creativity after a century? This seems too platitudinous, as does the reappearance of George's mother, in a musical that, unlike *Into the Woods*, is not primarily about family relationships. And its being about the relationship of art to posterity is surely further thwarted at this point by the fact that the two artists, unlike the Baker and his father in *Into the Woods*, cannot confront each other (they are played by the same actor). We seem to lose interest in the modern George and want him to merge back into Seurat for the final love duet.

That, however, is the ending's salvation: "Move On" is a love duet. Both music and lyrics soar, and while not exactly operatic (the words surely strike home too conversationally and too deeply for that), they take us beyond anything Sondheim has permitted himself not just earlier in this show but earlier in his output. He has never before given us music as gloriously iridescent as the impressionist harmonies and triumphant vocal lines of the passage condensed at y in ex. 11.11. Ravel offers many such passages, it is true, in works such as *Daphnis et Chloé;* but appropriating them at this dramatic juncture, Sondheim creates something unique. As the tonality loses itself in the shifting figuration the effect is infinitely beautiful and infinitely painful too, for it depicts "ideal states of when you can communicate and when that communication can never take place again" (Zadan 1990, 305). Patinkin is here referring (rather inaccurately—the number had already been written) to a conversation he had with Sondheim about the first act song "Beautiful," a kind of contingent love duet between Seurat and his mother that in some respects complements "Move On" (and which, because of its aesthetic credo, Billington [1990] describes as "the intellectual lynchpin of the show"); but it applies also to this great moment in "Move On," a moment in which Sondheim's music, perhaps for the first time in his career, "heals the characters," as Stephen Oliver said of Mozart's operatic writing. It is a vision of reconciliation, the moment of consummation between George and Dot, even as it tells us that, like a *Liebestod,* such moments belong only to what we can imagine beyond death or can experience through art.

Chapter 12

Into the Woods

A Fairy Tale Musical

Sondheim's creative relationship with Lapine had flourished in 1983 and 1984, and *Sunday in the Park with George* was followed more or less directly by *Into the Woods*. Better still, many of the themes not fully or comprehensibly worked out in the second act of *Sunday* found their proper expression in the second collaboration: once again, as Sondheim has pointed out (Sherrin 1990), the show deals with parent-child and teacher-pupil relationships and with "emotional circularity" between generations.

This time "Sondheim wanted to write a fairy tale 'quest musical,'" Zadan tells us (1990, 337). Rather than merely retell a single tale or invent one, Lapine hit upon the idea of fusing both possibilities by intermingling several classic tales with an original narrative frame. Sondheim, we may recall, had once before plotted two fairy tales in parallel, in the song of that title cut from *A Little Night Music,* a fact that would seem to confirm the view that his songs are often little dramas in miniature; and we shall see how the witty points of coordination of phrase and rhyme in this song find macrocosmic equivalents in the parallel songs of *Into the Woods*. In *Into the Woods* the well-known tales of *Cinderella, Little Red Riding Hood, Jack and the Beanstalk* and (dramaturgically somewhat in the background) *Rapunzel* all appear both as quest stories in their own right and as adjuncts to the central one of a barren couple, the Baker and his wife, who in order to dispel their neighbor the Witch's curse and get a child "go in and mess up everybody else's fairy story" in their need to procure "Little Red Riding Hood's cape, Cinderella's slipper, Jack and the Beanstalk's cow, and Rapunzel's hair" (Zadan 1990, 337). This is act 1. Lapine and Sondheim added a whole extra layer of story and meaning by making act 2 about the consequences of the characters' actions, for "in order to get what they wanted they each had to cheat a little, or lie a little, or huckster a little" (Zadan 1990, 338). What emerged was a faultless plot, complex and farcical in act 1 to an extent not experienced by Sondheim since *Forum,* layered and thus deepened by act 2 both with mechanical expertise (the climax of which is demonstrated in the argument quartet, "Your Fault") and with a spiritual resonance superior to anything Sondheim had hitherto achieved. Whatever worries might remain about the need for act 2 in *Sunday in the Park,* there could be none regarding its pertinence, indeed sublimity, in *Into the Woods.* It makes this musical Sondheim's finest achievement yet.

Musical and theatrical settings of fairy tales have in the past amounted to a not very cohesive legacy. Opera has dealt with them from time to time, as in Rossini's *La Cenerentola (Cinderella)* and Humperdinck's *Hänsel und Gretel* and *Königskinder,* but Humperdinck's efforts to establish fairy-tale opera as a type, though musically and dramatically positive, were not paralleled at the time by more than sporadic attempts by others (for instance, Smyth in *Fantasio,* Stanford in *The Travelling Companion*). Classical ballet, with Tchaikovsky's *Sleeping Beauty* as a crowning glory, made more of the genre. In the vernacular musical theater, pantomime had drawn routinely on fairy stories at least since the eighteenth century; although imported frequently to America in the early nineteenth century, it has remained potent to this day only in Britain, where its traditions of Christmas production, transvestite roles, audience participation, and the transformation scene show no signs of dying out. Pantomime, its songs notwithstanding, remains quite separate from musical comedy, and their coming together, as in Norton's *Chu Chin Chow,* has been rare. In any case, American audiences are more likely to make connections with the musical film, most obviously *The Wizard of Oz,* Disney's pioneering cartoons *Snow White and the Seven Dwarfs* and *Pinocchio,* or Rodgers and Hammerstein's television musical *Cinderella.*

Sondheim, Lapine, and their theatrical team chose to steer more-or-less clear of all this except, perhaps, Disney's musical pertness. Nor did they belabor symbolic language, literary or musical, and there are relatively few dark sayings or riddles in the text (the Mysterious Man's are a recurrent joke) or Wagnerian leitmotifs in the score—"spell" chords, "beans" motifs, and "prince" fanfares all exist and pervade the substructure, but they are worn lightly and are never used to dominate the dramatic or musical pace. Tone, style, and character would nonetheless be all-important.

Few would dispute that fairy tales can be appreciated on multifarious levels of meaning. Alan Dundes, in a recent anthology of literature on *Little Red Riding Hood* (see Dundes 1989, 204–19), charts the history of its interpretation through solar, allegorical, ritual, semiotic, anthroposophical, and psychoanalytic phases. This last, starting with Freud, seems to have remained in the ascendant, though the folklorist or anthropologist is more prone to focus on deep structures and their surface variants in the study of tales of all sorts. Given Sondheim's philosophical bent, however, it is not surprising to find him and Lapine stressing ethical content in their treatment of the fairy tales, though as we shall see they also enjoy structural parallels between them, perhaps with echoes of Propp's pioneering perceptions about their morphology.

This is not to say that Freudian concerns are absent. Bruno Bettelheim's work on them, in his book *The Uses of Enchantment* (1976), which greatly fueled intellectual interest in the fairy-tale genre, was read by Lapine, who also consulted "the writings of Jungian analyst Marie Louise Von Franz, psychologist Eric Fromm, . . . cultural historian Robert Darnton . . . [and] a clinical psychologist" (Mankin 1988, 51). Sondheim appears to have read Bettelheim too, and Mark Shenton's juxtaposition of passages from his book with lyrics from *Into the Woods* in the program for its London production draws attention to ideas and even phrases common to both, such as "trusting everybody's good intentions, which seems so nice" (Bettelheim 1976, 172) and "But he seemed so nice" (Sondheim). Lapine had also written *Twelve Dreams,* a play that "directly reflected his interest in Jungian and Freudian theory, a source he has turned to many times in his career as writer and director" (Mankin 1988, 51). But a certain impatience with psychological abstraction comes across in Lapine's comments.

You can read analysis by someone like Bettelheim who will give you psychological justifications for the moral and personal transgressions presented in these stories. But I started to wonder if there really was any justification. . . . One of my earliest impulses for doing this piece came when I asked a friend of mine who has a little girl if she was going to teach her daughter table manners. And she said: "I don't care about table manners, but I am going to teach my daughter the difference between right and wrong." I was so moved by this and I thought, yes, what's important is trying to teach people that there is a difference— not to give any answers, because obviously that is subjective, just to recognize that there is a difference. (Mankin 1988, 54)

Originally we wanted a public figure, not an actor, to play the Narrator: Walter Cronkite, or Tip O'Neill—someone who disseminated information and points of view. Then when we got rid of him you would see that the news was now being reported by the newsmakers, not the news reporter; decisions were being made by the people, not the politicians. Ultimately, we defined our narrator as a kind of intellectual, a Bettelheim figure; I wanted to get rid of Bettelheim! (Mankin 1988, 55)

In the fairy-tale world, the individual is liberated by his own choices and behavior; in the real world we are more dependent on each other.

If you read Bettelheim, or even the Jungians, they say that the issues presented in fairy tales are about individual or collective psychic development. It seems to me that the real world is about being part of a whole. (Mankin 1988, 55)

Likewise, in Sondheim's music and lyrics, the spelling out of Freudian or Jungian facets is not generally uppermost, and insofar as they are unavoidable in the tales themselves (to which the authors stuck fairly closely once they had chosen their version, be it from Grimm or Perrault), they constitute aspects of the action upon which no comment is offered. The motif of blindness, though presumably connected to the imagery of darkness and light, is not commented upon lyrically. Nor is the fact that many of the women in the story die. It may be significant that an early version of Jack's song of discovery, "Giants in the Sky," in which his description of climbing the beanstalk mounts to a decidedly sexual climax in the music and lyrics, was rejected. In the canonical version there is no reference to climbing the beanstalk, and the clause about the lady giant's breast is shifted back a step so that what now falls on the long line in the melodic spotlight of the returning A section is a less specific statement, in a sense more knowing in its use of the second-person singular, present tense mode of address (the later version is also superior technically, allowing us to get closer to Jack's intimately colloquial persona).

> And I asked for food
> And I asked for rest
> And she saw me fed
> And she made me guest
> And she made a bed of her big soft giant breast
> Up in the sky.
>
> (Rejected Version)

> And she gives you food
> And she gives you rest
> And she draws you close
> To her giant breast,
> And you know things now that you never knew before,
> Not till the sky.
>
> (Canonical Version)

Again, although all adults will recognize the psychosexual implications of Little Red Riding Hood's encounter with the wolf and of the Baker and his wife's strained, childless relationship, such facets are not belabored or highlighted in Sondheim's score—at least, not beyond the provision of a sultry, climactic blues style for the Wolf, somewhat indebted to Ravel's Beast in *Ma mère l'oye,* when he is fantasizing to himself (he uses a more innocent vaudeville style when he is addressing his victim).

However, Little Red Riding Hood's character, like those of her fellow travelers, is sufficiently endowed with comic flaws and paradoxes to make one wonder whether Lapine had popular psychologist Eric Berne's book *What Do You Say After You Say Hello?* (1972) at the back of his mind when he created her. Berne's debunking of the tales' symbolic pretensions into a series of earthy motivations includes questions such as "What kind of a mother sends a little girl into a forest where there are wolves? . . . It sounds as if her mother didn't care much what happened to LRRH, or maybe even wanted to get rid of her" (Berne, quoted in Dundes 1989, 220–21), and Lapine's comments to directors on the show (see Lapine and Sondheim 1990) find him asking cognate questions about his characters and their questionable traits. This was fertile dramatic ground.

As for structural archetypes, these are made evident in act 1, and the dramaturgical interweaving of the main characters' journeys of self-discovery points up their parallels in various ways that include musical cross-referencing: upon their return, Little Red Riding Hood, Jack, Cinderella, and the Baker's Wife all sing songs about what they have learned about themselves that share variants of the same accompanimental vamp and (except for the Baker's Wife's song, "Moments in the Woods," which in any case does not occur until act 2) also share a melodic opening of two short upbeat notes rising from $\hat{3}$ to $\hat{5}$ (exs. 12.1a, b, c and d). Again, all these passages, with the exception of Little Red Riding Hood's, come from a soliloquy cast in the second-person singular and historic present tense, also used elsewhere (for instance, in the Princes' song "Agony"). Sondheim considered going further in using the same material for each of the songs.

> I was thinking of calling all four songs, "I Know Things Now" because the phrase, in fact, occurs in all the songs. I had toyed with the idea of doing four versions of the same songs with different lyrics. You take a look at *The Wizard of Oz* with "If I Only Had a Brain," "If I Only Had a Heart," and "If I Only Had the Nerve." . . . But I wanted to give it some mystery and I think that's why I chose to make each song like variations. (Sondheim, quoted in Stearns 1988, 263)

But even here Sondheim's main purpose is not just to exhibit structural replication but to move toward an understanding of the characters' moral interdependence. The thematic linking of the "real people" in the musical, "almost a symbolic illustration of the show's plea for universal brother-

Ex. 12.1a

[Andante risoluto] [LITTLE RED RIDING HOOD:]

And he showed me things, ma-ny beau-ti-ful things,

mp

legato

Ex. 12.1b

[Andante moderato, non rubato] [JACK:] *mp*

When you're way up high and you look be-low

mp dolce e legato, marcato

Ex. 12.1c

[Allegretto grazioso] [CINDERELLA:]

You think, what do you want?

mf *mp*

sim.

Ex. 12.1d

[Grazioso] Piu mosso, risoluto (♩ = 148)
[BAKER'S WIFE:]

mf

Back to life, back to sense, Back to child, back to hus-band, No one lives in the woods. _

hood" (Stearns 1988, 263), underlines the fact that, to Sondheim just as to Lapine, "eventually, the show is about community responsibility" (Zadan 1990, 338).

Morals and Choices

The distinction between psychological self-fulfillment, which these four songs concern but which *Into the Woods* is not primarily about, and moral growth, which it is very much about, is put succinctly by Little Red Riding Hood, who, despite being a precocious brat, is the first character to reach a mature awareness.

> ... though scary is exciting,
> Nice is different than good.

But she is not sure whether she prefers this state of experience to her previous state of innocence.

> Isn't it nice to know a lot!
>
> ... and a little bit not ....

Or, as Bettelheim puts it, her lyric touches on "the child's ambivalence about whether to live by the pleasure principle or the reality principle" (1976, 171). Understanding ethical distinctions, or the distinction between ethical and psychological fulfillment, means choosing between them, and with ambivalence toward values and the difficulty of choice emerging yet again as a primary theme in a Sondheim musical we can plot its development through his career. Cinderella, whose words *I wish* are the first and last lyrics in the show, is very much in the position of Robert in *Company,* whose birthday wishes (in his case urged upon him by his friends) likewise punctuate the beginning and end of the drama; like him, she cannot bring herself to make the big decision for or against marriage.

> You think, what do you want?
> You think, make a decision.
> · · · · · · · · · ·
> And whichever you pick,
> Do it quick,
> 'Cause you're starting to stick
> To the steps of the palace.
>
> It's your first big decision,
> The choice isn't easy to make.

. . . .

Better run along home
And avoid the collision.
Even though they don't care,
You'll be better off there
Where there's nothing to choose,
So there's nothing to lose.

Unlike Robert, she finds a paradoxical way of solving the dilemma. The idea was Lapine's—Cinderella does not deliberately leave her shoe behind in the folk tale, of which they used Grimm's version (see Opie and Opie 1974, 154)—but the lyric wit is quintessential Sondheim in its opening of the curtain onto another structural layer of logic.

Then from out of the blue,
And without any guide,
You know what your decision is,
Which is not to decide.

You'll just leave him a clue:
For example, a shoe.
And then see what he'll do.

Sunday in the Park, with its positivistic view of artistic creation, achieves a more active attitude toward choice through the voice of Dot.

Move on.
Stop worrying where you're going—
. . . .
I chose, and my world was shaken—
So what?
The choice may have been mistaken,
The choosing was not.
You have to move on.

In *Follies 1987,* on the other hand, the main characters cannot move on, because they all made choices about marriage partners years ago and now regard them as having been the wrong ones. Yet they show us through their songs that it was their flawed characters that led to flawed choices, and all they can do is right them in a sense by sticking by them and constructing their "follies" as personal survival strategies.

In *Into the Woods,* not only does choosing matter, but making the right choice. The dynamics of choice are not self-sustaining, as with the "free" artist or the married couple, but lead to fruitful or damaging consequences for the whole community. Self-interest is a liability, and once wronged, the giant returns and must be appeased or destroyed.

However much the show stresses family and neighborly relationships in order to keep its tone and dramaturgy focused and undidactic, it is impossible not to be drawn toward contemplation of the widest world issues, environmental and political, in response to it. One of the rejected musical sections encouraged this. Before "Your Fault" fell into place, there had been an earlier "argument" quartet, "Have To Give Her Someone," using its accompaniment figure and covering the dialogue found on pages 101–2 of the published script. This then appears to have been curtailed and split up into a short introduction and intercutting episode for a song for the Narrator, "Interesting Questions," of which it formed part, used in the San Diego production prior to the New York opening, that enlarged upon his line "It is interesting to examine the moral issue at question here" while building comic tension toward the point where the group turns upon him as their sacrificial victim. It utilized the polonaise accompaniment that survives as an underscore (no. 18). The Narrator's lyrics included the following lines.

> In tales like these
> Lie subtleties:
> Is it wiser to appease or be defiant?
> And who do you feed to the giant?
>
> . . . .
>
> In tales like these,
> One often sees
> How crisis can be instructive
> Even a little bit seductive.

As I write this, the word *crisis* is ubiquitous in the media, and it is impossible to read these lines without applying them, even the last, to the Gulf War. AIDS has also been invoked as one of the issues underlying the parables in *Into the Woods,* as has the threat of nuclear destruction, which was in the mind of Tony Straiges, the original set designer.

Jim [Lapine] had always talked about the very end of the show being like a polluted L.A. sky. I found a photograph of a burnt-out forest: barren, the sky all red and purple—as if there had been some kind of huge explosion or nuclear disaster. We used this for the final image. This is the most clearly contemporary reference we used, but I think Jim and Steve are dealing visually with a number of serious contemporary issues, of which ecology and nuclear destruction are only a couple. (Mankin 1988, 56)

But Sondheim sees the AIDS parallel as a false premise (it is not a man-made disaster) and, like Vaughan Williams forty years earlier, he prefers to leave the nuclear metaphor unconstrained: " . . . who wants to make a tract? That's not the point" (Stearns 1988, 264).

Musical and Lyric Simplicity

It is certainly not the point of the music and the lyrics, which sparkle or lower with a range of colorings and a simplicity unmatched in Sondheim's earlier work. It is time we examined their style and character, and the methods used to achieve them.

Time and again Sondheim has introduced a musical device, a structure, a phrase, a harmony, maybe just a single note, that manages to dig deeper than the theater pit and that parallels and matches his lyrical aperçus. This is particularly apparent in the simplicity of his recent music, above all perhaps in the penultimate song of *Into the Woods,* "No More." Here the Baker and the Mysterious Man, his father, confront each other for the first time, but not directly, and the recognition of the fundamental irreconcilability, the separation and loss, between two generations in this powerfully and painfully Oedipal scene is expressed not just in verbal reflections and riddles ("They disappoint, they disappear, / They die but they don't") but even more memorably in the harmonic clusters and elliptical, chromatic voice leading of the music. The Baker, at the end of his tether following the death of his wife, seeks release from the problems that the very act of living brings with it; hence the song's title, musically encoded with the simplest possible indicators of closure (equivalents of the "more" governed by the "no"), namely a yoking of leading tone and tonic at the end of the song (ex. 12.2a). In the initial proposition, however (ex. 12.2b), it is as though the gulf between the two primary terms, tonic and dominant, indicated by the leading note *falling* to F, is what has to be acknowledged in the questions and the riddles (Citron [1991, 74–75] sees the whole song as based on this melodic cell). The nagging G-flat–G-natural, then G-flat–A-flat, ostinatos rising chromatically out of the F dominant pedal that underpins the Mysterious Man's monologue, both of which he acknowledges in the last notes of his phrases, aggravate this gulf but do not bridge it (ex. 12.2c). The accompaniment to the Baker's reply in turn tends to undermine the stability of the dominant (though without escaping from it) by twisting ambiguously downward in whole tones (G-flat–F-flat–D, perhaps suggested by the G-flat–A-flat motion discussed above) in a kind of distorted and fragmented parallel tenths relationship with the B-flat–A–F of the voice part (ex. 12.2d). Although it is hardly satisfactory to posit this reading of the passage in isolation

No   more.____

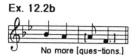

No more [ques-tions.]

Ex. 12.2c

We dis-ap-point, we dis-ap-pear, we die but we don't... __   For -give, though, they won't... __

[etc.]

Ex. 12.2d

No more jests.

Ex. 12.2e

No more ques-tions.   Please. __   No more tests.

Ex. 12.2f

either from the roles that G-flat, A-flat and F-flat play throughout the song (joined by a solitary instance of D-flat near the end) or from the F-flat's alter ego as E natural leading to F, it does give a legitimate diatonic/wholetone conundrum that is a typical neoclassical device, and such devices are used seriously and repeatedly in Sondheim's hands. They are also systematic. For instance, the advent of recognition between father and son in this song is potent, but it is hardly dynamic: it does not lead directly to any acknowledged reconciliation. The sense of paralysis is expressed very early in the music by the rhythmically isolated dissonance at the end of measure 2. This mixes tonic and dominant elements, the latter clarified and released two measures later (ex. 12.2e, *x* and *y*). Significantly, this motive is moving beyond the inhibitions and restraints of verbal communication while highlighting them, the first of the two chords occurring on the nonstructural, inchoate word *please,* the second, with its greater emotional depth of texture, harmony, and dynamics, being purely instrumental. It is as though the Baker cannot communicate with his father in words, yet does so precisely by acknowledging this in his stutterings and silences. Comparing this with the situation between Ben and Phyllis, in the song "Country House" from the 1987 production of *Follies,* we see a similar chord being similarly used to block and yet reveal communication in a closely comparable situation—again the issue is childlessness, and again verbal melody fails (ex. 12.2f).

This is to say that Sondheim knows when a note should fail to resolve, or when a monosyllable should lapse into silence. His lyrics in *Into the Woods* are frequently even more unitary than those influenced by Japanese aesthetic economy in *Pacific Overtures.* Whole passages can be found in which only the odd word has more than one syllable.

It takes trust.
It takes just

A bit more
And we're done.
We want four,
We had none.
We've got three.
We need one.
It takes two.

Do not put your faith
In a cape and a hood—
They will not protect you
The way that they should—

When you're way up high
And you're on your own
In a world like none
That you've ever known,
Where the sky is lead
And the earth is stone.

Given that, in the three examples above, there is a syntactic range from rhymes and parallel clauses only three syllables apart in the first, through gnomic but not particularly cellular epigram in the second, to an extended, breathless subordinate clause in the third, it would be dangerous to generalize much further, though clearly there is homogeneity at work beneath these distinctions, sensed particularly, as I have pointed out, in the use of the present tense and second-person singular mode of address. However, in the first quotation, "list" elements have been pared down to absolute basics ("four," "none," "three," "one," "two"), and there is no room in *Into the Woods* for lists of commodities or even, in the main, lists of qualities. The numbers are of course structural: four ingredients, four fairy tales, three visits to the ball by Cinderella and to the kingdom in the sky by Jack. It seems a shame that a variant reprise of this lyric in the act 2 Finale ("It took three. / Pardon me, / It took four— / It took all of us") was cut after the San Diego production.

Distinctions in the music require more explanation, the types and uses of material calling for an attempt at taxonomy. Like the characters, they group into families, and Sondheim's own way of guiding listeners (see Sherrin 1990) has been to draw attention to three primary founts of material. These are a rhythm, the bright "journeying" quarter-note chord motion that, as an indicator of comings and goings in the woods, informs much of the opening sequence (including, at a different speed, the Witch's patter number) and the vaudeville parts of the Wolf's song; a melody, the five-note "beans" motif; and a chord, for the Witch's spells.

Ex. 12.3

We can also cut the cake the other way and explore the distinction between diatonic and chromatic music, a more schematic and dramatic extension of types that, as we saw, arose in *Sunday in the Park with George.* Light is cast on the fairly brittle but warm and bright diatonicism of the vamps shown in exs. 12.1a to d by Sondheim's comment: "I was responding to the color of the characters. They're primary-colored characters and primary-colored music is called for." Referring to inspiration gained from Stravinsky's *L'histoire du soldat,* he added: "It's a series of little rhythmic adventures.... I wanted something spikey and rhythmically sharp" (Stearns 1988, 263).

The Stravinsky influence should not be made too much of. There may be a hint of *Les noces* in the "Happy now and happy hence" refrain in the act 1 Finale, particularly in Tunick's percussive orchestration, and the solo trumpet usage sometimes dimly recalls that of the cornet in *L'histoire du soldat,* but the affinity is most likely to be sensed in the vamps of ex. 12.1, which can be compared with the soldier's violin motif in *L'histoire* (ex. 12.3—ex. 12.1a is also for solo violin). Nevertheless, the nursery rhyme simplicity of much of the melodic material in *Into the Woods* does encourage Sondheim to take penetrating sidelong glances at tonal materials, very much in Stravinsky's manner. The cadential features of the "Into the Woods" tag itself furnish a good example of this (ex. 12.4): the common currency banality of the melodic cadence is undermined in three respects, first by the parallel triads accompanying the $\hat{3}$-$\hat{2}$ descent, second by the quartal sonority (A-flat, B-flat, E-flat) to which they lead when one expects a tonic chord, and third by the rogue bass line with its chromatic ascent that paradoxically has the effect of creating three tonally independent diatonic dissonances (what the three sonorities, boxed in ex. 12.4, have in common is that two perfect fifths or fourths are embedded in each of them; this also applies to the sister cadence a little later on, at the words "[nor] no one should"). This kind of thing is standard neoclassical practice. One may also appreciate the emulation not so much of Stravinsky as of his warmer French contemporaries, such as Ravel and Milhaud, in the charm and lucidity of Tunick's orchestration, cast, as I

Ex. 12.4

observed in chapter 2, very much as a chamber ensemble (to produce a blues sound out of this, for the Wolf's song, must have been something of a challenge to Tunick).

Beans and Spells

The "beans" motif, initially heard in the underscoring shortly after the Witch's first entrance (marked *x* in ex. 12.5a), is also diatonic and, like the *Sunday* fanfares, forms a five-note pitch collection. Again like the fanfares, it is frequently utilized and repeated; but it tends not to be morphologically developed, though this does not apply to the contrasting paraphrase that immediately follows it in ex. 12.5a, whose thirds are used to propel the song accompaniment's obbligato and intensify the narrative atmosphere. One might also argue that it does not apply when it is later spelled out unmistakably and pantomimically on the xylophone as the Baker counts the five beans into Jack's hand (the sixth, which he keeps for himself, seems to share the pitch of the fifth), for Jack's song of farewell, "I Guess This Is Goodbye"—the only love song in the score, Sondheim points out (see Lapine and Sondheim 1990)—is heavily infused with it in two- and three-note segments.

The "spell" chords, pertaining primarily to the Witch, are highly infused with chromaticism. Their basic formula is a five-pitch collection (the pentachord 0 1 3 4 7; see ex. 12.5b, i), perhaps most simply envisaged as a diminished triad erected above a tonic or pivot note (initially A) plus a first inversion major triad hanging below it, with doubling of the upper E-flat an octave lower to produce the cluster of seconds at the bottom of the chord. This is the chord that accompanies the Witch's various "zaps" throughout act 1—she uses it on the Baker (vocal score, pp. 110 and 148) and the Mysterious Man (p. 119), and it appears, though with a further four pitches superimposed, at our first sight of her bewitched ward Rapunzel (p. 78). It also expresses her loss of powers at the end of act 1 (p. 160),

Ex. 12.5a

Ex. 12.5b

Ex. 12.5c

shame? Who you go-ing to blame this time? Boom! Is-n't quite the same this time!

8vb tone cluster

This time it's Bum-ba-

Ex. 12.5d

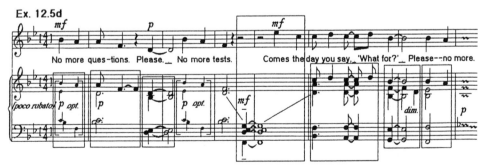

No more ques-tions. Please.__ No more tests. Comes the day you say,_ 'What for?'_ Please--no more.

and on this occasion its third statement is enriched by the addition of a bass note a tritone below the cluster. This addition of a second tritone somewhat reinterprets the sonority, offering it the effect of a dominant seventh without a fifth (A⁷) plus minor triad (D-sharp minor) whose roots are a tritone apart—the hexachord 0 1 3 4 7 9 (see ex. 12.5b, ii). (Jazz musicians might prefer to think of it as a dominant thirteenth with minor ninth and augmented eleventh.) This version of the chord is used, in various transpositions, to accompany the first recitation of the riddle of the magic ingredients (p. 40), the appearance of the beanstalk (p. 94), the solving of the riddle (p. 150), and the Witch's transformation (p. 153). However, the very first two "spell" chords in the score, in the Witch's "rap" song, are something of a textual problem. Occurring at the lines "I should have laid a spell on him right there" and "And I laid a little spell on them—you too, son—," the published vocal score gives them as in ex. 12.5b, iii, with no tritone in the first and with the A-double-flat intensifying the second into a hexachord, both of which sonorities are rather different from those shown in exs. 12.5b, i and ii and more in keeping with those of the song in which they occur, whereas the working rehearsal score retains an A-natural in the first chord, so that it is identical to ex. 12.5b, i, while the second has A-flat, not A-double-flat.

Whatever the correct text (and the vocal score is taken to be correct for the purposes of the table in ex. 12.6), these "spell" chords propagate a sound world highly characterized by certain intervals. Taken together, as ex. 12.6 shows, they produce a preponderance of semitones and major and minor thirds (or their inversions) at the expense of whole steps and perfect fourths and fifths; and tritones are not abundant. It is important to stress that we are dealing (in ex. 12.6) only with the interval content of sonorities, not with their harmonic and textural disposition as chords, but the data are indicative nonetheless, for they provide an index to the intervallic properties from which Sondheim selects the chromatic sonorities that he particularly wishes to stress. This is seen in a sample of chords from the climax of the Witch's original showpiece number, "Boom Crunch!" (it was replaced by "Last Midnight")—see ex. 12.5c for the passage in question. The partitioning of sonorities shown in the example gives eight chords, of which the tetrachord 0 1 4 8—augmented triad with superimposed minor third—is both the most frequently used and the simplest distillation of the elements Sondheim is exploiting: major thirds (of which there are no less than twenty-four in this passage) and the semitone, at the notable expense of the whole step and the tritone (compare the "totals" columns for "Boom Crunch!" in ex. 12.6 with those for "spells").

Statistical sampling can be a dubious business, and this passage is not

Ex. 12.6. Diatonic and Chromatic Motifs and Sonorities in *Into the Woods*

Motif or set	Interval class					
	1, 11 (minor 2nd, major 7th)	2, 10 (major 2nd, minor 7th)	3, 9 (minor 3rd, major 6th)	4, 8 (major 3rd, minor 6th)	5, 7 (perfect 4th, perfect 5th)	6 (tritone)
DIATONIC						
Beans: prime (0 2 3 5 7)	1	3	2	1	3	0
inverted (0 1 3 5 7)	1	3	1	2	2	1
TOTALS	2	6	3	3	5	1
"No More" (0 1 3 6 8)	1	2	2	1	3	1
(0 1 3 5 8)	1	2	2	2	3	0
(0 1 5)	1	0	0	1	1	0
(0 2 3 5 7)	1	3	2	1	3	0
(0 1 3 5 8)	1	2	2	2	3	0
(0 1 3 5 8)	1	2	2	2	3	0
(0 1 5 7)	1	1	0	1	2	1
TOTALS	7	12	10	10	18	2
CHROMATIC						
Spells: rap (0 1 3 4 8)	2	1	2	3	2	0
(0 1 2 3 4 8)	4	3	2	3	2	1
ingredients (0 1 3 4 7 9)	2	2	4	3	2	2
zap (0 1 3 4 7)	2	1	3	2	1	1
TOTALS	10	7	11	11	7	4
"Boom Crunch!" (0 1 4 8)	1	0	1	3	1	0
(0 1 2 4 7)	2	2	2	1	2	1
(0 1 4 8)	1	0	1	3	1	0
(0 1 4 8)	1	0	1	3	1	0
(0 1 4 5 8)	2	0	2	4	2	0
(0 1 2 4 5 8)	3	2	3	4	2	1
(0 1 4 8)	1	0	1	3	1	0
(0 1 4 8)	1	0	1	3	1	0
TOTALS	12	4	12	24	11	2

the whole story. Both "Boom Crunch!" and "Last Midnight" in fact progress from an opening based on bare fifths to a richer, more freely floating harmonic fabric based on thirds. However, nothing in "Last Midnight" is quite as uprooted from its fundamental fifths as the climactic passage from "Boom Crunch!". "Last Midnight"'s development can perhaps be suggested by further samples: measures 29–36, still stressing fifths, offer interval totals of 8, 11, 13, 13, 15, and 5; measures 75–92 give totals of 8, 7, 7, 11, 10, and 3; and the extraction of rhetorically weighted chords leading up to the climax (mm. 139, 155, 159, 163, 165, 173, and 177–80) give 12, 5, 13, 20, 14, and 5 (comparatively close to the distribution in "Boom Crunch!"). The grand interval total from all these samples, the "Boom Crunch!" one included, is 40, 27, 45, 68, 50, and 15.

We can apply the same analysis to diatonic motifs and songs. The "beans" motif gives a slightly different diatonic pentachord when subjected to inversion, which occurs pointedly and sententiously near the end of the show, at the central section "People make mistakes" in the song "No One Is Alone" (this inversion has been foreshadowed near the end of act 1, molded before our very eyes, as it were, out of the prime form of the motif in a cantilena placed high in the orchestral texture as Rapunzel's Prince's sight is restored). Contrary to the spells, these diatonic motifs (0 2 3 5 7 and 0 1 3 5 7) exploit major seconds (or minor sevenths) and perfect fourths and fifths, and if we seek the acme of Sondheim's diatonic earnestness and examine the opening of the song "No More," already scrutinized for more rhetorical purposes, we can see that a reasonable partitioning of perceived sonorities (i.e., accepting, as part of the neo-classical aesthetic, that horizontal and vertical events are no longer rigidly exclusive dimensions of a single perspective; see ex. 12.5d) yields, over the distance of the first seven chords or events, similar preferences within a norm of diatonic pentachords: there are as many as twelve major seconds or minor sevenths and eighteen perfect fourths or fifths in the totals row for "No More," in addition to a consonant admixture of thirds. Tritones are almost completely avoided, and most striking of all is the way Sondheim takes care to place a single semitone within every sonority.

These two songs occur, or occurred, one after the other, and highlight the fact that the diatonic and chromatic musical worlds are differentiated more metaphysically in *Into the Woods* than in Sondheim's earlier scores. We must, however, remember that, as discussed earlier, chromatic confrontation is soon added to the agenda in "No More"; and Sondheim (Lapine and Sondheim 1990) says that the counterpoint that appears with the diatonic "beans" motif on page 40 of the score transforms it into the chromatic pitch collection of the "spell" chord that immediately follows (this is not actually the case—the former collection is 0 1 3 4 6 8, the latter 0 1 3 4 7 9). Still, the Baker, for all his weakness and perplexity, is a creature of the light, just as the Witch, for all her human discourse, not to mention temper, is a creature of darkness (her very disappearance relegates her to the shadows). Both worlds exist side by side, and to recognize them as neighbors is to recognize them as coexistent within the human psyche. "Man must recognize the 'light' and the 'shadow' in his own personality. . . . 'It is the only truth I shall ever say,'" as Ian Kemp has commented, glossing and quoting another major twentieth-century musical dramatist, Tippett (Kemp 1980, 5). The lyrics of *Into the Woods* are full of references to light and darkness. Early on, for example, Little Red Riding Hood's recounting of her experience inside the Wolf, "down a dark slimy path," leads to the following somewhat obvious generalization.

> So we wait in the dark
> Until someone sets us free,
> And we're brought into the light,
> And we're back at the start.

At the end of the story, in "No One Is Alone," the lines "Hard to see the light now. / Just don't let it go," spoken by Cinderella and the Baker, are complemented by "Hold him to the light now, / Let him see the glow" when the musical section returns, sung by the Baker's Wife. Enclosing all is the "Into the Woods" chorus, whose release near the beginning of act 1 has the words "The way is clear, / The light is good," whereas when it returns to conclude act 2 the lines are "The way is dark, / The light is dim," shortly followed by a not unhumorous exchange: "The light is getting dimmer . . . / I think I see a glimmer—" (the humor is enhanced because we remember that originally this music was sung to the lines "I sort of hate to ask it, / But do you have a basket?"). The music also finds symbols for darkness in addition to the chromatics. A case in point is the frequent use of the extreme flat key of G-flat (and even on one occasion of C-flat), much beloved of the nineteenth-century romantics (see Macdonald 1988).

It is important to appreciate that the two worlds are articulated by particular musical styles, not merely the abstractions of intervals, sonorities and harmonies and the associations of keys. Both "Boom Crunch!" and its highly impressive replacement, "Last Midnight," are not just waltzes but a particular type of waltz, French and Ravelian in their *gymnopédie* rhythm and rich chordal texture on the one hand, infused with the kinesis of the jazz waltz on the other. Sondheim himself, in a letter to the author written around the time he was working on *Into the Woods*, draws a further distinction.

> The reason, incidentally, for the preponderance of the two specific colors ("dark" versus "romantic") of the waltzes that you bring attention to is the pervasive influence in my writing of Ravel, particularly *La Valse* (dark) and the *Valse nobles et sentimentales* (romantic).

Tunick picks up on the Ravel influence in his orchestration of "Last Midnight," with its bassoon solos and string harmonics; it seems to this author, however, that the "dark" harmonies of "Boom Crunch!" and "Last Midnight" stem from both the Ravel works, not just *La valse*. But certainly the musical box confectionery of "Any Moment" and the demonic momentum of "Last Midnight" are worlds apart as waltzes.

No doubt further confirmations of contrasted harmonic worlds could be sought and found in material from other songs and other characters. The Wolf, for instance, enjoys a quite different form of complex chromatic harmony in his blues passages. So do the Stepsisters in some of their more gruesome moments, though they also perforce inhabit Cinderella's diatonic world.

Pentatonic Innocence and Children's Games

There is a third harmonic, or rather intervallic, world, one of innocence rather than these positive and negative poles of experience. Before analyzing it we must enumerate the third recurrent motif, a fanfare with a somewhat *Petrushka*-like sparkle (ex. 12.7a). It primarily represents the royal family, but both this and the "beans" motif are used for other purposes too. For instance, Rapunzel's vocalise is the latter, while the former is also the very first tune we hear (ex. 12.7b), sung by Cinderella not so much as a fanfare indicating her dreams of a royal life but as the initial generating snippet of communal melodic tags in 12/8. Its rhythm, and the fact that, like the "beans" motif, it forms a nonchromatic pitch collection spanning a downward minor seventh, are the features that matter. The downward seventh appears everywhere, including the opening melodies of "Agony," "A Very Nice Prince," "Hello, Little Girl," and "Giants in the Sky" and the "Don't you know what's out there in the world" section of "Stay With Me," the first two based on the fanfare and the last two on the "beans" motif, though the effect of such widespread use is to minimize the distinction between them. The lower note of the seventh in the fanfare is the sixth scale degree, and, insofar as it is perceived as a melodic substitute for the lower dominant, there are mild neoclassical forces at work here; this property also links it with the "Into the Woods" tag itself (see ex. 12.8), with its insistent lower $\hat{6}$ usage, particularly at the end of the second measure. One might add that the $\hat{5}$–$\hat{6}$ downward seventh had been a Sondheim fingerprint as early as "Anyone Can Whistle."

Recurrent degrees of the scale in association with intervallic shapes have always been a strong guiding force for Sondheim where the unifying of melodic cells is concerned, doubtless because their relative tensions are a

Ex. 12.7a

Ex. 12.7b

[Brightly]

I wish...   More than an-.y – thing...

Ex. 12.7c

Ex. 12.7d

Shiv-er and quiv-er, lit–tle tree,   Sil–ver and gold throw down on me.

Ex. 12.7e

Childishly

(repeat indefinitely)

matter of inflection that complements the rhetoric of speech (cadence and
rhyme are similarly complementary). They are certainly a significant
feature of the melodic web of *Into the Woods,* and the primary-sounding $\hat{5}$–
$\hat{6}$–$\hat{7}$–$\hat{8}$ ascent of the "Into the Woods" phrase itself is widely present,
repeatedly occurring in the jaunty accompaniment (see ex. 12.7c; the E-flat
$\hat{8}$ is "understood"). In general, however, scale degrees are not that cut-
and-dried in these tags. Cinderella's initial "I wish . . ." proposition trans-
poses the fanfare up a fourth, so that the melodic seventh is now from
the tonic down to the supertonic, and the reason for this ambiguity of
placement, which thoroughly permeates the entire "Opening" number
and other music of the show and is doubtless one of the factors that

confuses people, as Tunick claims in a passage to be quoted subsequently, is that these "innocent" snatches of tune are constructed on a pentatonic frame—our third harmonic world in *Into the Woods*. As such they hardly need or respond to their notes being placed in a particular order as melodic themes, for the intervals of the pentatonic scale, devoid of semitones, are easily construed as a single sonority, although Sondheim does tend to avoid one of the five notes and, conversely, by no means excludes semitones in his melodies as passing notes between the pentatonic coordinates. The point about the pentatonic pitch collection is that it can be positioned at three different levels within any diatonic "key," as ex. 12.8 shows (all the material has been transposed into C major or A minor for the purposes of this chart)—hence the variable placements of motifs and their perceived variants within one column or another, as the arrows in ex. 12.8 suggest. The pitches D, G, and A are common to all three positionings, which may be why the harmony tends to be based on a supertonic, dominant or submediant triad—the opening chord of *Into the Woods* is a mixture of all three, and Cinderella's "forest" music tends toward impressionistic stasis on the supertonic (see ex. 12.7d).

Like those of other modal music, such properties, highly ambiguous to the tonal mind, encourage the idea of a pivot note rather than a tonic. The obvious corollary to their use in *Into the Woods* is the universal children's games tag (ex. 12.7e), of which Van der Merwe has written:

> What is the key of this little tune? Is it in C major or A minor [or, he might have added, F major or D minor]? The question is absurd. Being repetitive, it has no need to be in any key. Its miniature mode of three notes has no tonic, and can be conveniently described as atonic. (Van der Merwe 1989, 102)

In evoking the world of children's games—and this accounts for the high proportion of compound time in the score—Sondheim is in his element, for just as repetitive melodic jingles such as these accompany the stochastic exchanges of children in the playground ("I'm the king of the castle," for instance), here they can accommodate minute examples of Sondheim's punning, game-playing mind in the lyrics. "The woods are just trees, the trees are just wood" sings Little Red Riding Hood, bandying the word back and forth. Most pervasive is not just the additive structure of ritual lyrics after the manner of "the house that Jack built" but, within such additive processes, the play on alternating subject/predicate clauses and infinitive phrases, one or the other fitted to each pair of notes. Sondheim scores in the game by introducing puns and phrase structures that cut across the basic model.

Ex. 12.8

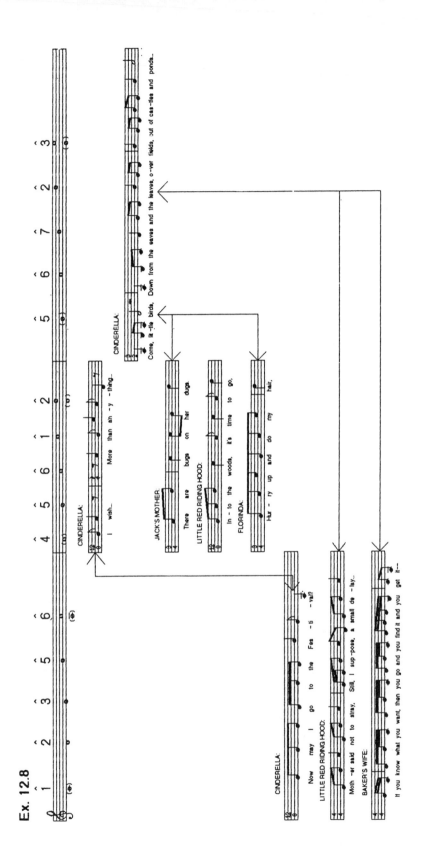

Subject/Predicate Clause	*Infinitive Phrase*
. . . it's time	to go
I hate	to leave
I have	to[,] though . . .
I must	be[-] gin . . .
	to where
I am . . .	

He had used exactly the same technique in "Love, I Hear" in *A Funny Thing Happened on the Way to the Forum,* for the different dramatic purpose of characterizing Hero's sighing inarticulacy (the double pun on "to/too" and "day/weak" is especially delicious).

I pine	
I blush	
I squeak	
I squawk	to[-] day
I woke	too weak
	to walk . . .

There are preechoes of this technique, and of this particular song, in both a lyric by Burt Shevelove himself that Sondheim has said he admires very much, "I'm in Trouble" from *Month of Sundays* (see Sondheim 1974, 70), and in Vernon Duke and Yip Harburg's song "I Like the Likes of You" from *Ziegfeld Follies of 1934,* which exhibits both the impassioned stammered phrases of "Love, I Hear" and the reversals of terms in "I Do Like You."

The Music of a Community

We are now in a position to consider some of the consequences of the types of material available. We can assert that for the primary, "good" characters (that is, excluding the Witch), taken individually, there is not the traditional emphasis on motivic title or refrain songs, which tend to be associated rather with the Wolf ("Hello, Little Girl"), the Witch ("Last Midnight" and her three solos involving the refrain "Children won't/will listen"), and the Princes ("Agony"). Duets and ensembles are an exception to this, as demonstrated by "It Takes Two," "Your Fault," "No More," and "No One Is Alone," the last three occurring as act 2 gathers musical momentum with its "group scenes" (Sondheim, quoted in Mankin 1988, 60). Core material in a title or refrain song has to be very firmly "owned" by the character singing it, and the material has to have a high stylistic profile. This is not quite the case in *Into the Woods,* where the core material can crop up, memorable in the manner of a jingle (Sondheim uses the term *ditty*), anywhere in a song, can be broken off, and tends to be shared between the characters, as in the case of the vamps illustrated in ex. 12.1 and the tags of ex. 12.8. Sondheim's comment on his intentions in this respect, that he wanted "ditty writing—a lot of 16-, 32-, and 64-measure songs" (Stearns 1988, 263), has been elaborated by Tunick.

> The entire score for *Woods* was thought of structurally as one big song. The melodic material consists of fragmentary, rhythmic and very catchy phrases that weave in and out. I think this confuses some people. They hear what appear to be independent melodic fragments weaving in and out, when in reality they are all part of the development of a much larger musical composition. (Mankin 1988, 62)

Sondheim has offered the following further explanation.

> There are certain themes in *Woods* that come out of nowhere and go nowhere—songs or song ideas that are never finished. In this respect, *Woods* is closest to *Merrily We Roll Along,* in that I decided to use musical ideas not as developmental *leit motifs,* but in the functional way you would use modular furniture. The same theme becomes an inner voice, an accompaniment, a counterpoint. It may be fragmented, but it is not really developed. (Mankin 1988, 60)

This is true. For instance, in addition to the examples already discussed, there are transferences of the "beans" motif into an accompaniment figure, first for "I Guess This Is Goodbye" and then, immediately following it, for a quite different song, "Maybe They're Magic" (in which it also "becomes an inner voice" in diminution in m. 6); it becomes a countermelody in "No One Is Alone." There are also numerous examples of solo numbers left uncompleted: Jack's Mother never has a whole song to herself, and her lovely "Jack, Jack, Jack" melody breaks off before the A section has time to return (until it was cut out, this also occurred in the act 2 "Opening" as a duet with her son); the Wolf's blues twice gets as far as its subdominant second line, and moves up a tone on its third attempt, each one in a different key, but never completes a harmonic paragraph; the Baker's Wife offers a tempting harmonic vista for one measure in her song "Maybe They're Magic," at the title line, but fails to elaborate on it; both of the quick 2/4 numbers, "Ever After" in act 1 and "Your Fault" in act 2, lead into something else. And the "ditties," tossed back and forth as a variety of modular units, account for a great

Ex. 12.9a

Ex. 12.9b

Ex. 12.9c

deal of the music, particularly in act 1. The material shown in ex. 12.8, incidentally, offers only a sample of this, with the pentatonic consideration uppermost, and there is plenty more: the "sensitive, clever, / Well-mannered, considerate" intercutting, first heard on the original cast recording (though it is not in the vocal score) sung by the Baker's Wife during her first encounter with Cinderella, is later transferred to "Agony" and, ominously, in view of the Wife's indiscretion in act 2, to "It Takes Two"; and the eighth-note continuum figure evoking the ball in 6/8 in act 1 is brought back in 3/4 for the Baker's Wife's encounter with the Prince in act 2.

But it is not all fragments and frustration, and the counterbalances are what make this Sondheim's most refulgent score to date. Even the "ditties" are satisfyingly grouped into strong, assertive rhythmic entities, in 12/8 for the general questing and youthful kinesis headed by Little Red Riding Hood, 3/2 (mostly) for Cinderella's communing with her mother and with nature and 3/4 for her and Jack's Mother's domestic concerns, and 4/4 for the Baker and his wife's squabbling about the beans. And there is a potent distinction between these harmonically static or neutral melodic tags and the wonderfully memorable tunes, particularly releases, that break out from time to time, especially in the "knowing" songs, where warmth and strength are generated very much by traditional methods of harmonic progression (the paradox of presenting them without their harmonies illustrates this in the selection given in ex. 12.9). Best of all, the Witch's song, "Stay With Me," tantalizingly impotent in the passion of its incomplete chorus to the words "Who out there could love you more than I?" fulfils its latent force, like a miniature version of the love music spanning the whole of *Sunday*. The opening motif, to the lines "What did I clearly say? / Children must listen," returns as the "Witch's Lament" in act 2. Now regretful rather than vehement, the melody, to the words "No matter what you say, / Children won't listen," soars at the heart-breaking lines "Children can only grow / From something you love / To something you lose," on which word it breaks off, as the bass, which was just beginning to open up, jabs frustratedly at repeated A's (in an earlier, rejected version of the song, it continued from this point to a bitter conclusion). At the end of act 2 this point is reached again, but now the harmonic horizon is extended through a cathartic cycle of fifths leading to the relief of the dominant: "Children Will Listen," and so will we, to an effect that is so simple and so masterly.

The Achievement

Sondheim wrote a great deal of music for *Into the Woods*, "more . . . for this show than . . . for any other, with the exception of *Forum*" (Mankin 1988, 64). Melodically, as must be amply evident from the preceding discussion, the starting point of this music is the jingle, whose essence is the very property that critics have so often been reluctant to grant him, hummability, though doubtless even this virtue will be construed as poverty of invention or intellectualization by some. But it reaches far beyond workaday materials, and it may well be that a not insignificant practical part of the reason for so many incomplete songs is that Sondheim's musical and lyric inspiration was flowing more fully than ever, providing him with more material than could be used. Of the many cutouts, several have already been referred to. We may note more. The original version of "Maybe They're Magic" included a rich additional section for the Baker's Wife, led into by her harmonic opening up to the words of the title. Cinderella had a short, simple waltz, "Just Like Last Night," in which she recalled the ball (it remains in the score, transferred to the Baker's Wife in act 2 as an introduction to "Moments in the Woods"), and a much more significant and extended one in her subsequent song, "Back to the Palace." "Second Midnight," a long musical number about the problems of bringing up children (placed near the end of act 1) included quite new melodic and lyrical material constructed upon the "Into the Woods" vamp, "Children Will Listen" complete except for its final dominant (its appearance here seems utterly premature in comparison to the canonical act 2 solution), and a long, independent section, in effect a separate song, cast as a duet and beginning with the lines

> How do you say to your child in the night,
> Nothing's all black, but then nothing's all white?

The idea of this section, and some of its material, was saved instead for act 2 and "No One Is Alone," but it deserves independent life outside the show. The act 1 Finale included a version of the "So Happy" section eventually transferred to the beginning of act 2 that made more of the waltz passages by setting more of them to words. And "Your Fault" was reprised with a different set of lyrics as "The Plan," an excited quartet of plotting how to kill the giant. But there can be no doubt that the score and book in their published form constitute an authoritative text, with the exception only of "Our Little World," the song written for Rapunzel's first visit from the Witch in the London production (it shows the human, diatonic side of the Witch and complements "No More," some of whose material it shares, as a duet for mother and daughter).

Into the Woods is a radiant work, whose lyrics cohabit perfectly with Lapine's prose (indeed, Hudson Talbott's retelling of the plot as an illustrated children's book [1988] is able to draw on both throughout, seamlessly) and convey far-reaching issues such as can rarely if ever have been treated in musicals before. The dramatic poetry of "Last Midnight" resonates vividly with its agnostic vision of humankind left on its own in the garden, scrabbling about "Separate and alone, / Everybody down on all fours." The music reaches heights of characterization, dramatic pacing and sheer beauty in the wonderful sequence of four songs toward the end ("Your Fault," "Last Midnight," "No More," and "No One Is Alone"), which leave us confident that Sondheim's powers are still on the increase. It may not be impertinent to close this book with an observation about "No More." This song surely breaks through to a new level of truth, ultimately beyond the reach of wit and irony and professionalism of technique, in its final section; the Baker's choked phrases, such as "All the children ... ," let go of discursive meaning, risking sentimentality but achieving something much more profound. Earlier in the song, the Baker and his father confront each other for the first time. Twenty-five years before, Sondheim had scribbled a pencil note to himself to depict the ironic conundrum of "Like father, like son," and he did so, expertly and wittily, in "Impossible" from *Forum*. Now, no doubt unconsciously echoing his earlier brief, he set the words to music, at the only point in the show when the two men sing together. This time there are no verbal puns, just the simple musical device of a melodic line inverted against itself to convey the idea of the mutually reflected image, to the ghost of the same rhythm as "Impossible." Whence comes such continuity? Sondheim, whose career had begun when he found a substitute father for his own absent one in

Oscar Hammerstein, and for whom therefore there may well be a deeply personal catharsis at work in this song, should have the last word.

> Your father may be dead . . . but you're carrying around not only his genes but some of his thoughts. . . . The whole show is about what is passed down to us by our parents.

Selective List of Sources

I have not included details of the published vocal scores of Sondheim's Broadway musicals, or of their published scripts and the texts of other plays, poems, and so forth, except where they include editorial substance. All quotations and statements from Sondheim in the text without a bibliographic attribution are from conversations with or taped comments and letters to the author.

Abbate, Carolyn. 1991. *Unsung Voices: Opera and Musical Narrative in the Nineteenth Century*. Princeton.

Abrams, M. H. 1988. "The Deconstructive Angel." In Lodge 1988, 264–76.

Adams, Michael C. 1980. "The Lyrics of Stephen Sondheim: Form and Function." Ph.D. diss., Northwestern University.

Adler, Thomas P. 1978–79. "The Musical Dramas of Stephen Sondheim: Some Critical Approaches." *Journal of Popular Culture* 12:513–25.

Alexander, Marguerite. 1990. *Flights from Realism: Themes and Strategies in Postmodernist British and American Fiction*. London, paperback 1989.

Altman, Rick, ed. 1981. *Genre: The Musical: A Reader*. London and New York.

Altman, Rick. 1987. *The American Film Musical*. Bloomington, Indianapolis, and London, paperback 1989.

Anderson, David J. 1988. "Theatre Criticism: A Minor Art with a Major Problem." Ph.D. diss., Ohio State University.

Aston, Elaine, and George Savona. 1991. *Theatre As Sign-System: A Semiotics of Text and Performance*. London and New York.

Austern, Linda P. 1990. "'Art to Enchant': Musical Magic and Its Practitioners in English Renaissance Drama." *Journal of the Royal Musical Association* 115:191–206.

Babington, Bruce, and Peter W. Evans. 1985. *Blue Skies and Silver Linings: Aspects of the Hollywood Musical*. Manchester.

Banfield, Stephen. 1992. "Sondheim, Stephen (Joshua)." In *The New Grove Dictionary of Opera*, ed. S. Sadie, 4:450–52. London and New York.

Barkin, Elaine, and Martin Brody. 1986. "Babbitt, Milton (Byron)." In *The New Grove Dictionary of American Music*, ed. H. W. Hitchcock and S. Sadie, 1:102–7. London and New York.

Barricelli, Jean-Pierre. 1988. *Melopoiesis: Approaches to the Study of Literature and Music*. New York and London.

Beckerman, Bernard. 1990. *Theatrical Presentation: Performer, Audience and Act*. New York and London.

411

Bennett, Robert Russell. 1975. *Instrumentally Speaking*. Melville, N.Y.

Bennett, Susan. 1990. *Theater Audiences: A Theory of Production and Reception*. London.

Bergman, Ingmar. 1960. *Four Screenplays of Ingmar Bergman*. Trans. L. Malmstrom and D. Kushner. New York.

Berkowitz, Gerald. 1979. "The Metaphor of Paradox in Sondheim's *Company*." *Philological Papers* 25:94–100.

Bernstein, Leonard. 1982. *Findings*. London.

Bettelheim, Bruno. 1976. *The Uses of Enchantment: The Meaning and Importance of Fairy Tales*. New York and London.

Billington, Michael. 1986. "Pacific Conquest for Sondheim." *Guardian*, 3 May.

Billington, Michael. 1987. "An Individualist on Broadway." In English National Opera Program Book for *Pacific Overtures*. London.

Billington, Michael. 1990. "The Creation Conundrum." *Guardian*, 17 March.

Bishop, André. 1991. "Introduction." In *Sunday in the Park with George*, 1–5. New York.

Bishop, André. 1991. "Preface." In *Assassins*, vii–xi. New York.

Block, Geoffrey. 1987. Review of *American Musical Revue: From the "Passing Show" to "Sugar Babies"* by Gerald Bordman. *American Music* 5:319–21.

Block, Geoffrey. 1989. "Frank Loesser's Sketchbooks for *The Most Happy Fella*." *Musical Quarterly* 123:60–78.

Blyton, Carey. 1984. "Sondheim's *Sweeney Todd*—The Case for the Defence." *Tempo*, no. 149: 19–26.

Bond, Christopher. 1974. *Sweeney Todd: The Demon Barber of Fleet Street*. London.

Bond, Christopher. 1991. "Introduction." In *Sweeney Todd*, 1–9, New York.

Booth, Mark. 1981. *The Experience of Songs*. New Haven.

Bordman, Gerald. 1986. *The American Musical Theatre: A Chronicle*. Rev. ed. New York.

Boulton, Paul. 1987. "An Outline of the Relationship between the Term *Colour* and Music with Special Reference to Messiaen." B.A. diss., Keele University.

Bradbury, Malcolm, and James McFarlane, eds. 1976. *Modernism: A Guide to European Literature 1890–1930*. London.

Bristow, Eugene K., and J. Kevin Butler. 1987. "*Company*, About Face! The Show That Revolutionized the American Musical." *American Music* 5:241–54.

Britton, Andrew. 1978. "*Meet Me in St. Louis:* Smith, or the Ambiguities." *The Australian Journal of Screen Theory* 3:7–25.

Brylawski, Samuel S. 1986. "Sondheim, Stephen (Joshua)." In *The New Grove Dictionary of American Music*, eds. H. W. Hitchcock and S. Sadie, 4:258–60. London and New York.

Cartmell, Dan J. 1983. "Stephen Sondheim and the Concept Musical." Ph.D. diss., University of California, Santa Barbara.

Chevreul, M. E. 1859. *The Principles of Harmony and Contrast of Colours*. Trans. C. Martel. London.

Citron, Stephen. 1985. *Songwriting: A Complete Guide to the Craft*. New York, paperback 1990.

Citron, Stephen. 1991. *The Musical: From the Inside Out*. London.

Cone, Edward T. 1974. *The Composer's Voice.* Berkeley and Los Angeles.

Cone, Edward T. 1989. "The World of Opera and Its Inhabitants." In *Music: A View from Delft,* 125–38. Chicago.

Conrad, Jon Alan. 1986. "Taking Stock of Sondheim." *Opus* 2, no. 4: 30–35.

Conrad, Jon Alan. 1988. "Broadway Orchestration." Typescript.

Current Biography. 1973. "Sondheim, Stephen (Joshua)." *Current Biography Yearbook,* 386–89.

Cushman, Robert. 1977. "Stephen Sondheim." In *The Hansen Treasury of Stephen Sondheim Songs,* 4–7. New York.

Daum, Raymond, ed. 1983. "The Reminiscences of Stephen Sondheim." Oral History Research Office, Columbia University. Typescript.

Daverio, John. 1987. "Schumann's 'Im Legendenton' and Friedrich Schlegel's *Arabeske.*" *Nineteenth Century Music* 11:150–63.

Davis, Sheila. 1985. *The Craft of Lyric Writing.* Cincinnati.

Delamater, Jerome. 1981. *Dance in the Hollywood Musical.* Ann Arbor.

Driver, Paul, and Rupert Christiansen, eds. 1989. *Music and Text.* Contemporary Music Review, vol. 5. Chur and London.

Dundes, Alan, ed. 1989. *Little Red Riding Hood: A Casebook.* Madison, Wis.

Dunsby, Jonathan. 1981. *Structural Ambiguity in Brahms: Analytical Approaches to Four Works.* Ann Arbor.

Elam, Keir. 1980. *The Semiotics of Theatre and Drama.* London and New York.

Engel, Lehman. 1967. *The American Musical Theater: A Consideration.* New York, 1967.

Engel, Lehman. 1977. *The Making of a Musical: Creating Songs for the Stage.* New York.

Empson, William. 1930. *Seven Types of Ambiguity.* London.

Empson, William. 1951. *The Structure of Complex Words.* London, paperback 1985.

Erasmus, Desiderius. 1971. *Praise of Folly* [1509]. Trans. B Radice. Harmondsworth.

Esslin, Martin. 1987. *The Field of Drama: How the Signs of Drama Create Meaning on Stage and Screen.* London.

Feuer, Jane. 1982. *The Hollywood Musical.* New York and London.

Fordin, Hugh. 1977. *Getting to Know Him: Oscar Hammerstein II.* New York.

Freedman, Samuel G. 1984. "The Creative Mind: The Words and Music of Stephen Sondheim." *New York Times Magazine,* 1 April, 22–32, 60.

Freud, Sigmund. 1960. *Jokes and Their Relation to the Unconscious* [1905]. Trans. J Strachey. Harmondsworth.

Frith, Simon. 1989. "Why Do Songs Have Words?" In Driver and Christiansen 1989, 77–96.

Frye, Northrop. 1957. *Anatomy of Criticism.* Princeton.

Furia, Philip. 1990. *The Poets of Tin Pan Alley: A History of America's Great Lyricists.* New York.

Furth, George. 1979. *Merrily We Roll Along.* Typescript of production meetings with Sondheim and Prince.

Furth, George. 1983. Letter to James Lapine. June.

Gelbart, Larry. 1989. "Musicals Then." *Opera Now,* August, 25.

Gelbart, Larry. 1991. "Introduction." In *A Funny Thing Happened on the Way to the Forum,* 1-10. New York.

Goldstein, Richard M. 1989. "'I Enjoy Being a Girl': Women in the Plays of Rodgers and Hammerstein." *Popular Music and Society* 13, no. 1: 1-8.

Gorbman, Claudia. 1987. *Unheard Melodies: Narrative Film Music.* Bloomington, Indianapolis, and London.

Gordon, Joanne L. 1984. "The American Musical Stops Singing and Finds its Voice: A Study of the Work of Stephen Sondheim." Ph.D. diss., University of California, Los Angeles.

Gordon, Joanne L. 1990. *Art Isn't Easy: The Achievement of Stephen Sondheim.* Carbondale and Edwardsville, Ill.

Guernsey, Otis L., Jr., ed. 1985. *Broadway Song and Story: Playwrights/Lyricists/Composers Discuss Their Hits.* New York.

Hartman, Charles. O. 1991. *Jazz Text: Voice and Improvisation in Poetry, Jazz, and Song.* Princeton.

Hawkins, Roy B. 1989. "The Life and Work of Robert Russell Bennett." Ph.D. diss., Texas Technical University.

Hawkins, Harriett. 1990. *Classics and Trash: Traditions and Taboos in High Literature and Popular Modern Genres.* Hemel Hempstead.

Herbert, Trevor, ed. 1989. "Sondheim's Technique: Stephen Sondheim Interviewed by Trevor Herbert." In Driver and Christiansen 1989, 199-214.

Hirsch, Foster. 1989. *Harold Prince and the American Musical Theatre.* Cambridge.

Hirst, David. 1985. "The American Musical and the American Dream: From *Show Boat* to Sondheim." *New Theatre Quarterly* 1:24-38.

Hischak, Thomas. 1991. *Word Crazy: Broadway Lyricists from Cohan to Sondheim.* New York.

Holden, Stephen. 1984. "How the Music Gets That Special Broadway Sound." *New York Times,* 29 January.

Holmberg, Carl B. 1984. "On the Rhetoric of Popular Song: 'Y'ain't Juzz Whizzlin' "Dixie""" *Popular Music and Society* 9, no. 4: 27-33.

Honda, H. H., trans. 1956. *One Hundred Poems from One Hundred Poets.* Tokyo.

Huber, Eugene R., ed. 1986. "A Conversation with Stephen Sondheim." Typescript.

Huber, Eugene R. 1990. "Stephen Sondheim and Harold Prince: Collaborative Contributions to the Development of the Modern Concept Musical, 1970-81." Ph.D. diss., New York University.

Ilson, Carol. 1989. *Harold Prince: From* Pajama Game *to* Phantom of the Opera. Ann Arbor.

Johnson, Haynes. 1991. "Kennedy's Farewell to Camelot." *Guardian,* 14 August.

Kakutani, Michiko. 1984. "How Two Artists Shaped an Innovative Musical." *New York Times,* 10 June.

Keller, Hans. 1987. *Criticism.* London.

Kemp, Ian. 1980. "Tippett, Sir Michael (Kemp)." In *The New Grove Dictionary of Music and Musicians,* ed. S. Sadie, 19:1-11. London and New York.

Kerman, Joseph. 1952. *Opera as Drama.* New York.

Kermode, Frank. 1967. *The Sense of an Ending: Studies in the Theory of Fiction.* New York.

Kivy, Peter. 1988. *Osmin's Rage: Philosophical Reflections on Opera, Drama, and Text.* Princeton.

Klensch, Charles. 1948. "Undergrad-penned 'Rainbow' Gives Biz to Local Yokels." *Williams Record,* 8 May.

Koestenbaum, Wayne. 1989. *Double Talk: The Erotics of Male Literary Collaboration.* New York.

Krasker, Thomas, and Robert Kimball. 1988. *Catalog of the American Musical: Musicals of Irving Berlin, George and Ira Gershwin, Cole Porter, Richard Rodgers, and Lorenz Hart.* Washington, D.C.

Lahr, John. 1979. "Sondheim's Little Deaths: The Ironic Mode and its Discontents." *Harper's,* April, 71–78.

Lahr, John. 1984. "Stephen Sondheim." In *Automatic Vaudeville: Essays on Star Turns,* 5–21. New York.

Lapine, James, and Stephen Sondheim. 1984. *Sunday in the Park with George.* Boston Museum of Fine Arts Lecture.

Lapine, James, and Stephen Sondheim. 1990. *Into the Woods: A Conversationpiece.* Music Theatre International Production Video. New York.

Lester, Joel. 1989. *Analytic Approaches to Twentieth-Century Music.* New York and London.

Lewine, Richard, ed. 1977. "Symposium: The Anatomy of a Theater Song." *Dramatists Guild Quarterly* 14, no. 1: 8–19.

Lodge, David. *Working with Structuralism: Essays and Reviews on Nineteenth- and Twentieth-Century Literature.* London, 1981, paperback 1986.

Lodge, David, ed. 1988. *Modern Criticism and Theory: A Reader.* London and New York.

Lodge, David. 1990. *After Bakhtin: Essays on Fiction and Criticism.* London and New York.

Loney, Glenn, ed. 1984. *Musical Theatre in America: Papers and Proceedings of the Conference on the Musical Theatre in America.* Westport, Conn.

McCullough, J. 1983. *Living Pictures on the New York Stage.* New York.

Macdonald, Hugh. 1988. "♯♭♮♮." *Nineteenth Century Music* 11:221–37.

McGlinn, John. 1989. "The Original *Anything Goes*—A Classic Restored." In *Anything Goes: First Recording of the Original 1934 Version,* 29–34 (EMI Records Ltd.). Hayes.

McLaughlin, Robert L. 1991. "'No One Is Alone': Society and Love in the Musicals of Stephen Sondheim." *Journal of American Drama and Theatre* :27–41.

Malm, William. 1977. *Music Cultures of the Pacific, the Near East, and Asia.* 2d ed. Englewood Cliffs, N.J.

Mandelbaum, Ken. 1990. "How Did You Get to Be Here, Mr. Sondheim? *Merrily We Roll Along* to Washington, D.C.: Analysis and Review." *Theatre Week* 3, no. 29: 16–22.

Mandelbaum, Ken. 1991. *Not Since "Carrie": 40 Years of Broadway Flops.* New York.

Mankin, Nina, ed. 1988. "The *PAJ* Casebook #2: *Into the Woods.*" *Performing Arts Journal* 11, no. 1: 46–66.

Meisel, Martin. 1983. *Realizations: Narrative, Pictorial, and Theatrical Arts in Nineteenth-Century England.* Princeton.

Middleton, Richard. 1990. *Studying Popular Music.* Milton Keynes.

Mollin, Alfred. 1991. "Mayhem and Morality in *Sweeney Todd.*" *American Music* 9:405–17.

Mordden, Ethan. 1976. *Better Foot Forward: The History of American Musical Theatre.* New York.

Mordden, Ethan. 1981. *The Hollywood Musical.* New York.

Morley, Sheridan. 1990. "Side by Side with the Sondheim Art." *Sunday Times* [London] *Magazine,* 4 March, 66–70.

Mulvey, Christopher, and John Simons, eds. 1990. *New York: City as Text.* New York.

Music Theatre. 1989. *Music Theatre International 1989–1990 Catalog.* New York.

Olesen, Walter. 1986. Private communication to Paul Salsini, 24 March.

Opie, Iona, and Peter Opie. 1974. *The Classic Fairy Tales.* London.

Orchard, Lee F. 1988. "Stephen Sondheim and the Disintegration of the American Dream: A Study of the Work of Stephen Sondheim from *Company* to *Sunday in the Park with George.*" Ph.D. diss., University of Oregon.

Orledge, Robert. 1980. "Indy, (Paul Marie Théodore) Vincent d'." In *The New Grove Dictionary of Music and Musicians,* ed. S. Sadie, 9:220–25. London and New York.

Osolsobě, Ivo. 1974. "Musical as a Potential Universal of Human Communication." English-language abstract in *The Theatre Which Speaks, Sings, and Dances: Semiotics of the Musical Theatre.* Prague.

Osolsobě, Ivo. 1981. "A Letter from the Other Side: To [the] *Musical Theatre in America* Conference: Wassenaar, March 23, 1981." Typescript.

Osolsobě, Ivo. 1984. "Vienna's Popular Musical Stage as a Semiotic Institution." In Proceedings of the 2nd Congress of IASS/AIS, Vienna, 1979, ed. J. Bosk. *Semiotics Unfolding* 3:1739–51.

Osolsobě, Ivo. N.d. "On the Three Frontiers of Theatrical Freedom: The Liberated Theatre of Voskovec and Werich in Prague, 1927–38." Typescript.

Palmer, Christopher. 1990. *The Composer in Hollywood.* London and New York.

Perrin, Edwin N. 1949. "'All That Glitters' Shiner for Cap and Bells, Cast: 'Rainbow' Tops Latest Musical." *Williams Record,* 23 March.

Peyser, Joan. 1987. *Leonard Bernstein.* New York.

Pfister, Manfred. 1988. *The Theory and Analysis of Drama.* Cambridge.

Pike, John. 1991. "Michael Starobin: A New Dimension for *Assassins.*" *Show Music* 7, no. 3: 13–17.

Plautus, Titus Maccius. 1964. *The Rope and Other Plays.* Trans. E. F. Watling. Harmondsworth.

Plautus, Titus Maccius. 1965. *The Pot of Gold and Other Plays.* Trans. E. F. Watling. Harmondsworth.

Portway, Bob, and Anthony Lee, producers. 1990. *Sunday in the Park with Stephen.* BBC "Omnibus" Television Program, 20 March.

Previn, André. 1977. "The World of Stephen Sondheim." Interview, "Previn and the Pittsburgh," Channel 26 Television Program, 13 March.

Prevots, Naima. 1987. *Dancing in the Sun: Hollywood Choreographers, 1915–1937.* Ann Arbor.

Prince, Harold. 1974. *Contradictions: Notes on Twenty-Six Years in the Theatre.* New York.

Prince, Harold, and Stephen Sondheim. 1979. "On Collaboration between Authors and Directors," ed. G. Cryer. *Dramatists Guild Quarterly* 16, no. 3: 14–34.

Propp, Vladimir. 1958. *Morphology of the Folktale.* Bloomington.

Rahill, Frank. 1967. *The World of Melodrama.* University Park, Penn.

Ratcliffe, Michael. 1990. "Putting It Together." In Royal National Theatre Program Book for *Sunday in the Park with George.* London.

Rich, Frank. 1976. "Someone in a Tree." CBS "Camera Three" Television Program, 28 March.

Richards, Jeffrey. 1988. "Sir Henry Irving, The Victorian Theatre and the Spirit of the Age." Paper presented at the Social History Conference, York.

Rockwell, John. 1983. "Urban Popular Song, the Broadway Musical, the Cabaret Revival and the Birth Pangs of American Opera: Stephen Sondheim." In *All-American Music: Composition in the Late Twentieth Century,* 209–20. New York.

Rodgers, Richard. 1975. *Musical Stages: An Autobiography.* New York.

Russell, John. 1965. *Seurat.* London and New York.

Russell, John. 1990. "Colour and Light." In Royal National Theatre Program Book for *Sunday in the Park with George.* London.

Said, Edward. 1978. *Orientalism.* London.

Salsini, Paul. 1991. Interviews with Irwin Shainman, Jean Bryant, and Helen Kelley. Typescript.

Salsini, Paul. 1992. *"Evening Primrose."* Typescript.

Salsini, Paul. N.d. "Early Sondheim Musicals." Typescript.

Sansom, George B. 1950. *The Western World and Japan.* London.

Savran, David. 1990. "Stephen Sondheim: An Interview with David Savran." *Sunday in the Park with George,* text of the musical, ix–xxvi. London.

Sayre, Nora. 1974. "Belmondo at His Best in Resnais Creation." Review of *Stavisky. New York Times,* 30 September.

Scher, Steven P. 1992. *Music and Text: Critical Enquiries.* Cambridge.

Schiff, Stephen. 1993. "Deconstructing Sondheim." *New Yorker,* 8 March, 76–87.

Schopenhauer, Arthur. 1897. "Psychological Observations." In *Essays,* trans. Mrs. R. Dircks, 143–67. London and Felling upon Tyne.

Schuller, Gunther. 1968. *Early Jazz: Its Roots and Musical Development.* New York.

Schuller, Gunther. 1989. *The Swing Era: The Development of Jazz 1930–1945.* New York.

Shainman, Irwin. 1987. "Saluting Sondheim: The Maestro of Musical Theater." *Berkshires Week,* 1 November, 10–11, 14.

Sheren, Paul, and Tom Sutcliffe. 1974. "Stephen Sondheim and the American Musical." In *Theatre '74,* ed. S. Morley, 187–215. London.

Sherrin, Ned. 1990. "Interview with Stephen Sondheim." "The Late Show," BBC Television Program, 24 September.

Slater, Montagu, ed. 1928. *Sweeney Todd: The Demon Barber of Fleet Street,* by George Dibdin Pitt. London.

Sloman, Tony, ed. 1988. The Sondheim *Guardian* Lecture." *BIASED: Newsletter of the Sondheim British Information and Appreciation Society,* Spring-Summer, 34–61.

Smith, James L. 1973. *Melodrama.* London.

Sondheim, Stephen. 1974. "Theatre Lyrics." In *Playwrights, Lyricists, Composers on Theatre,* ed. O. L. Guernsey, Jr., 61–97. New York.

Sondheim, Stephen. 1978. "The Musical Theater." *Dramatists Guild Quarterly* 15, no. 3: 6–29.

Sondheim, Stephen. 1980. "Larger Than Life: Reflections on Melodrama and Sweeney Todd." In *Melodrama,* ed. D. Gerould, 3–14. New York Literary Forum.

Sondheim, Stephen, and Craig Lucas. [1981]. "Notes on the Songs." In *Marry Me a Little* (libretto). New York.

Sponberg, Arvid F. 1991. *Broadway Talks: What Professionals Think About Commercial Theater in America.* New York.

Stage. 1934. "The Editor Speaks His Mind: What Is the Play About?" *Stage,* November, 23.

Stearns, David Patrick. 1988. "Making Overtures: Stephen Sondheim Talks to David Patrick Stearns." *Gramophone,* August, 263–64.

Steyn, Mark. 1987. "A Funny Thing Happened to Sondheim." *Drama,* no. 165: 11–13.

Steyn, Mark. 1990. "Seventies Sondheim on Broadway." BBC Radio 3.

Stoner, Thomas. 1991. "'The New Gospel of Music': Arthur Farwell's Vision of Democratic Music in America." *American Music.* no. 9: 183–208.

Suskin, Steven. 1986. *Show Tunes 1905–1985.* New York.

Suskin, Steven. 1991. *Opening Night on Broadway: A Critical Quotebook of the Golden Era of the Musical Theatre, "Oklahoma!", 1943 to "Fiddler on the Roof", 1964.* New York.

Sutcliffe, Tom. 1987. "Sondheim and the Musical." *Musical Times* 128:487–90.

Swain, Joseph P. 1990. *The Broadway Musical: A Critical and Musical Survey.* New York.

Talbott, Hudson, adapted and illus. 1988. *Stephen Sondheim and James Lapine: Into the Woods.* New York.

Taylor, Joshua C., ed. 1987. *Nineteenth-Century Theories of Art.* Berkeley.

Tippett, Michael. 1959. "The Birth of an Opera." In *Moving into Aquarius,* 50–66. London.

Traubner, Richard. 1984. *Operetta: A Theatrical History.* London.

Tunick, Jonathan. Conversations with the author, 1988–91.

Tunick, Jonathan. 1991. "Introduction." In *A Little Night Music,* 1–11. New York.

Updike, John. 1991. "Top of the Pops." *ISAM Newsletter* 20, no. 2: 1–2, 15.

van der Merwe, Peter. 1989. *Origins of the Popular Style: The Antecedents of Twentieth-Century Popular Music.* Oxford.

van Leer, David. 1987. "Putting It Together: Sondheim and the Broadway Musical." *Raritan* 7:113–28.

Verdino-Süllwold, Carla Maria. 1990. "Opera, Operetta, or Musical? Vanishing Distinctions in 20th Century Music Drama." *Opera Journal* 23, no. 4: 31–43.

Wardle, Irving. 1992. *Theatre Criticism.* London and New York.

Wilson, John S. 1960. "Musicals: The Old College Try." *Theatre Arts,* August, 51–52.

Wilson, Stephen B. 1983. "Motivic, Rhythmic, and Harmonic Procedures of Unification in Stephen Sondheim's *Company* and *A Little Night Music*." D.A. diss., Ball State University.

Winer, Laurie. 1989. "Why Sondheim's Women Are Different." *New York Times*, 26 November.

Wittke, Paul. 1980. Review of *Sweeney Todd*. *Musical Quarterly* 66:309–14.

Zadan, Craig. 1990. *Sondheim & Co.* New York.

Index of Songs and Musical Numbers

This is not a comprehensive catalog of Sondheim's works, still less a comprehensive discography. Apart from its function as an index to this book, it is intended merely as a basic guide to where the songs may be found in print with their music (printings of the lyrics alone are ignored) and where they may be heard. Details are not given of Sondheim's own manuscript sources of his work; all of them are in his possession in the form of the originals or copies. The originals of most of the early works are in the State Historical Society of Wisconsin, University of Wisconsin, Madison.

Key

x   Cutout, incomplete or otherwise uncanonical (see further details in index or in main text). Incomplete songs are generally included only when a more-or-less complete draft of lyrics or music exists.

*   Original cast recording available

hr   For hire only (*The Frogs, Marry Me a Little, You're Gonna Love Tomorrow*)

(S)   Vocal selections

sep   Separate song

(st)   Original soundtrack album

unp   Unpublished

unr   Unrecorded

As *Assassins* (1991)*; As92 *Assassins,* London production (1992); ASI *All Sondheim I* (1980); ASII *All Sondheim II* (1987); ASIII *All Sondheim III* (1990)

Be *I Believe in You* (1956); Ber Leonard Bernstein Seventieth Birthday Concert, Tanglewood (1987); Bl *A Pray by Blecht* (1968); BM *Sondheim: Book-of-the-Month Club Records* (1985); Br *Madonna: I'm Breathless* (album 1989, sheet music 1990); By *By George* (1946)

Ca *Candide* (1974) (music by Leonard Bernstein)*; Car *Sondheim: A Celebration at Carnegie Hall* (1992); CH *Climb High* (1950–52); Co *Company* (1970)*

DC *Dress Casual,* Mandy Patinkin album (1990); DT *Dick Tracy* (1990)

EP *Evening Primrose* (1966); Eve *A Stephen Sondheim Evening* (1983) (material later published for hire as *You're Gonna Love Tomorrow*)*

F *Follies* (1971)*; F85 *Follies in Concert* (1985)*; F87 *Follies* 1987*; FF *The Fabulous*

Fifties (1960); For *A Funny Thing Happened on the Way to the Forum* (1962)*; Fr *The Frogs* (1974)

Gi *Girls of Summer* (1956); Gl *All That Glitters* (1949); GM *George's Moon* (from JF); GR Ginger Rogers's nightclub act (1959); Gy *Gypsy* (1959) (music by Jule Styne)*; Gy73 *Gypsy*, London production (1973)*

Hansen *The Hansen Treasury of Stephen Sondheim Songs* (1977); Hap *Happily Ever After* (1959); HS *Hot Spot* (1963) (music by Mary Rodgers); HT *High Tor* (1949)

Il *Ilya Darling* (1967) (music by Manos Hadjidakis); Inv *Invitation to a March* (1960)

Jet *The Jet-Propelled Couch* (1958); JF *The World of Jules Feiffer* (1962)

KFO *Kukla, Fran, and Ollie* (1952); Kn *I Know My Love* (1951)

LA *A Little Sondheim Music*, Los Angeles Vocal Arts Ensemble (1984); La *The Lady or the Tiger?* (1954) (written with Mary Rodgers); LLO *Love Lives On*, New York City Gay Men's Chorus (1991); LNM *A Little Night Music* (1973)*; LNM78 *A Little Night Music*, film (1978)

Mad *The Mad Show* (1966) (music by Mary Rodgers); Mar *Marry Me a Little* (1981)*; Me *Merrily We Roll Along* (1981)*; Miz [*The Legendary*] *Mizners* (untitled); MM *A Mighty Man Is He* (1955); MP *Mary Poppins* (1950)

Pa *Passionella* (from JF); Ph *Phinney's Rainbow* (1948); PO *Pacific Overtures* (1976)*; PO87 *Pacific Overtures*, English National Opera recording (complete version) (1987)*

Red *Reds* (1981); Res *The Last Resorts* (1956)

S7 *The Seven Percent Solution* (1976); Sa *Saturday Night* (1954); Si *Singing Out Loud* (forthcoming); SS *Symphonic Sondheim*, arr. Don Sebesky (1990); SSS *Side by Side by Sondheim* (1977)*; ST *Sweeney Todd* (1979)*; Sta *Stavisky* (1973); Su *Sunday in the Park with George* (1984)*

Th *The Thing of It Is*; Tr *Sondheim: A Musical Tribute* (1973)*; Tw *Twigs* (1971)

Wh *Anyone Can Whistle* (1964)*; Wo *Into the Woods* (1987)*; Wo91 *Into the Woods*, London cast recording (1991)*; WSS *West Side Story* (1957) (music by Leonard Bernstein)*; WT *Where To From Here* (1950); Wz *Do I Hear a Waltz?* (1965) (music by Richard Rodgers)*

Yes *Yesterday I Heard the Rain*, Tony Bennett album (1968)

In accordance with the preceding key, the following list provides the provenance of a song or musical number, indicated in parentheses before the song titles. The parentheses after the titles contain, first, an indication of the sheet music publication (vocal score unless otherwise stated), second, details of its primary sound recording or recordings. Page references to the text of the book follow.

General Index